Douglas Frantz and Catherine Collins

Celebration, U. S. A.

Living in Disney's Brave New Town

A Marian Wood Book

HENRY HOLT AND COMPANY / NEW YORK

Henry Holt and Company, LLC
Publishers since 1866
115 West 18th Street
New York, New York 10011

Henry Holt® is a registered
trademark of Henry Holt and Company, LLC

Library of Congress Cataloging-in-Publication Data

Frantz, Douglas.
Celebration, U.S.A.: living in Disney's brave new town
Douglas Frantz and Catherine Collins.—1st ed.
p.   cm.
"A Marian Wood book."
Includes bibliographical references and index.
ISBN 0-8050-5560-6 (alk. paper)
1. City and town life—Florida—Celebration. 2. City planning—
Florida—Celebration. 3. Celebration (Fla.)—Social conditions.
4. Walt Disney Enterprises. 5. Celebration (Fla.) I. Collins,
Catherine.   II. Title.
HT165.C45F73   1999   99-10392
307.76′09759′25—dc21   CIP

Henry Holt books are available for special promotions
and premiums. For details contact: Director, Special Markets.

First Edition 1999

Designed by Kate Nichols

Except where noted, all photographs are by Catherine Collins.

Printed in the United States of America
All first editions are printed on acid-free paper. ∞

1   3   5   7   9   10   8   6   4   2

For Nick and Becky,

whose partnership made this adventure richer,

and life, too

We shall not cease from exploration
And the end of all our exploring
Will be to arrive where we started
And know the place for the first time.

T. S. ELIOT
"Little Gidding"

CONTENTS

Prologue   5

1. The Cult of the Mouse   13
2. Back to the Future   37
3. Citizen Disney   69
4. Town & Country Marriages   82
5. Great Expectations   102
6. School Daze   124
7. The Zeus Box   147
8. Scorpions and Other Neighbors   170
9. Looking for Mayberry   193
10. Visitation Rites   208
11. Swamp Song   226
12. Bowling Together   245
13. An Epiphany   271
14. Civil Wars   287
15. Truman Didn't Sleep Here   307

Bibliography   329
Acknowledgments   332
Index   333

Celebration, U.S.A.

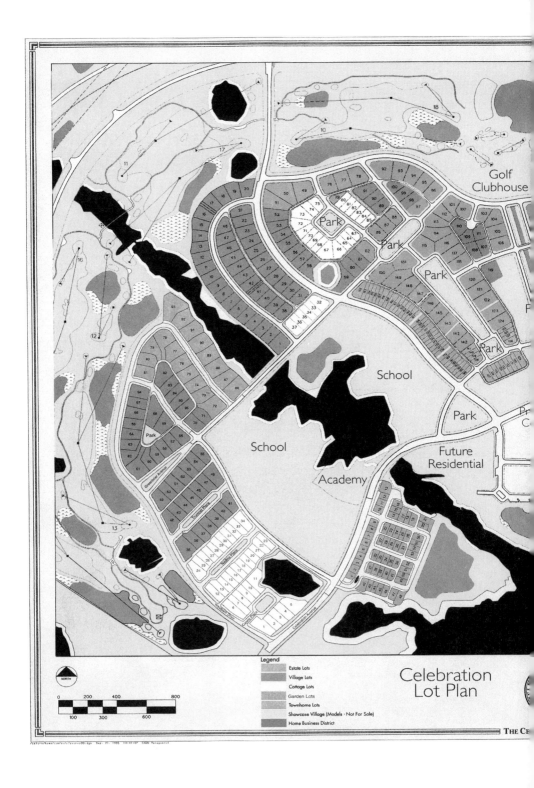

Golf
Clubhouse

Park

Park

Park

Park

Park

School

Park

School

Future
Residential

Academy

Celebration
Lot Plan

NORTH

0   200   400   800
100   300   600

THE CE

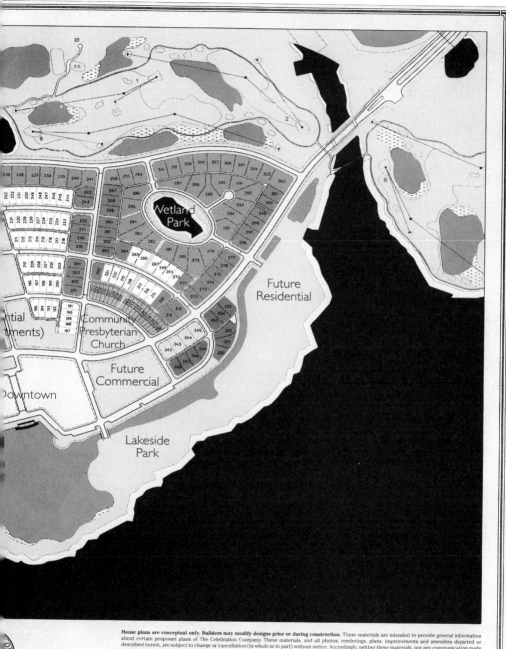

Wetland Park

Future Residential

Community Presbyterian Church

Future Commercial

Downtown

Lakeside Park

ntial (tments)

PROLOGUE

Our introduction to Celebration, the spanking-new town rising in the middle of a swamp just minutes from Disney World, was a little weird and a little sweet. From the start, it was clear that this would be like no place we had ever lived. But then, that was part of what had drawn us to the town.

We had made the decision to move quickly, almost on impulse. Cathy read an article about the town in late 1996, a few months after the first residents moved in, and thought it sounded like a great adventure. The basics were appealing. There would be a progressive community school and access to the latest technology. There were to be commodious parks and civic spaces and closely set houses with inviting front porches to foster neighborliness, a sharp contrast to the isolation in most cities and suburbs these days. Everything would be within walking distance of the town center as an antidote to the creeping horrors of car-dominated suburbs. Celebration was pulling its new residents from across the United States, and, in fact, from around the world. And finally, the developer standing behind it all, with its vast resources and reputation for quality and control, was the Walt Disney Company. It seemed like the biggest experiment in social engineering since Levittown, and we wanted to watch it unfold.

As journalists, we had lived many different places in the past decade—Chicago, Washington, D.C., Los Angeles, Washington again, and most recently, in our first venture to the suburbs, Westport, Connecticut. In each place, we had found attractive qualities and some drawbacks. Although Doug had grown up in a small town in Indiana, we had never lived in one as a family, never in a new town, and surely never in a town conceived and built by the folks whose primary business is make-believe and who brought the world Mickey Mouse and Main Street, U.S.A.

Our two younger children, eleven-year-old Nick and nine-year-old Becky, were eager to trade the gray skies and cold winters of the Northeast for perpetual sun. The proximity of Disney World was icing on the cake. Our oldest child, Elizabeth, was midway through her freshman year at the University of California, and she was horrified at the prospect of living in any place associated with Disney. Since her focus was decidedly elsewhere, we voided her vote.

Cathy made two scouting trips, and as her enthusiasm grew so did the pressure to make a decision. The waiting list for an apartment was eighteen months long. And as quickly as she could explore houses, they seemed to be sold. By the first Saturday in February of 1997, Cathy, Doug, Nick, and Becky were on a plane from New York to Orlando to choose from only a half dozen available building lots and pick a house plan. Twenty-four hours later, shortly after noon on Sunday, we signed the last of the contracts and addenda required for us to start building our house. The documents filled two large binders. We had signed promises not to leave a recreational vehicle parked on the street or complain about the mosquitoes ("mosquitoes are a fact of life") or harass the alligators (no problem with that one). We had agreed to hang tasteful curtains or blinds that showed only white on the street.

We wrote the deposit check on one of the eighteen models available in the price range we had chosen, $275,000 to $300,000. "Well, aren't you lucky," said the real estate agent in her chirpy voice. "You've finished just in time to meet your new neighbors. There's a block party out on Nadina Place."

We had driven out to Nadina Place just a couple hours earlier and selected lot 21 as the site for our house. So we knew that there was nothing there but sand, swamp, and lot stakes with little orange flags fluttering in a hot breeze. A block party seemed incomprehensible.

"Go on," insisted Gale Bagwell, the agent. "It'll be fun."

With some hesitation, we got into the rental car and headed past rows of newly completed houses, the half-done school, and idle construction equipment. There, under the blazing midday sun, about thirty sweating adults and children were milling around a half dozen card tables laden with macaroni salad and Vienna sausages in tiny buns.

As we walked across the sand, everyone turned and called out their welcomes. "It's our newest neighbors," said a sturdy redheaded woman. "They just signed up." Everyone broke into applause and shouted, "Hip, hip, hooray." Clearly, the small-town grapevine was already in high gear.

Cathy tried to push Becky out front and toward the people approaching us. Usually the most outgoing member of the family, with an ability to make a best friend quickly and under the most adverse conditions, Becky slipped back behind her mother, muttering, "You got yourself into this."

Within minutes, we had shaken every hand and were equipped with name tags and plastic glasses of champagne and soda pop. Everyone pointed to the orange-flagged surveyor's stakes and talked excitedly about where their houses would stand and exactly what model they had chosen. Their imaginations sketched in sunshine-filled windows and expansive kitchens where family would gather, and outside, billowing pink azaleas and neighbors sitting together on shady porches to watch the sun set as children raced bicycles up and down the street. Everyone was gracious and brimming with expectation. In fact, the intensity of those dreams was something we had not anticipated.

Donna McGrath, an ebullient woman from Massachusetts with long, hot-pink fingernails, described her house in great detail, right down to the plans for a seventy-two-inch television in the family room and a pool table in the living room. She and her husband, Mike, loved to entertain. They would be our next-door neighbors.

No one had higher hopes for Celebration than the effusive redhead who had greeted us first. Her name was Cheryl Scherer, and she had been an elementary school teacher in Buffalo, New York. She and her husband, Rick, a blue-collar worker, were moving to Celebration with their four young children. They were so eager to get there that they had rented a house in a nearby town until their place was finished.

"We think this will be the happiest place on earth," she told us earnestly. "We're all going to be best friends." And with that, Cheryl passed a clipboard onto which we all recorded our current addresses and phone numbers so that we could stay in touch during the upcoming months and jump-start those friendships.

These people had dreamed so hard about Celebration that this single stretch of sand seemed real to them long before ground was broken for the first house. There was a pioneering spirit that bubbled up in almost every conversation. In the shimmering heat, these people from Buffalo and Massachusetts and Indiana and elsewhere in Florida had molded an oasis of opportunity.

Certainly the dreams had been fed by the hype surrounding the town, a publicity tidal wave orchestrated by the image makers at Disney. That Sunday in February, Celebration was barely six months old. There were fewer than a thousand residents, and the overriding impression, both visual and physical, was of a frenetic work in progress. With each scouting visit, Cathy had been astonished at the change. It was truly an instant town, a just-add-water-and-stir kind of place. A time-lapse camera had been installed atop a pole across the lake from downtown to record its rapid progress. We imagined the old science footage, the time-lapse version of a flower blooming or a butterfly emerging from its cocoon.

Even as critics weighed in from around the world, the tiny town had been anointed the next great place to live in America, with more than seven hundred newspaper and magazine articles already written about it. Vincent Scully, Yale's esteemed professor emeritus of architecture, had decreed: "Celebration is the most important thing happening in architecture. It marks a return of community." *Professional Builder* magazine described it as "the biggest experiment in real estate development." Michael Eisner, the chairman and chief executive of Disney, boasted: "It will set up a system of how to develop communities. I hope in fifty years they say, 'Thank God for Celebration.' "

For some, the infectious camaraderie spawned by these outsized expectations proved too much. Standing off to the side of the main group at that initial block party was a slim woman in her early forties. Holly

Wade Conover was better dressed than the other women, in a pretty cream-colored ensemble to their shorts and blue jeans. She couldn't quite come to grips with the enthusiasm. She explained that she and her husband, Jim, a onetime University of Georgia football star, had thought Celebration sounded like a new version of the affluent, gated community on the other side of Orlando where they lived with their two children. So they had put down a deposit on a house and come to the block party to meet their new neighbors. But Holly was shell-shocked. "I'm not sure how much of this neighborliness I can take," she confided, with a shake of her head.

About that time, Ginny Wallace, a woman in her seventies with a beautifully smile-lined face, offered us some cake. "I baked it especially for the occasion," she said proudly. "But watch out, I baked a baby in there."

"A baby?" Cathy asked weakly, momentarily envisioning some peculiar Southern custom. She took a very slim piece.

Nick wandered over to where we were standing. In his hand he held a tiny plastic baby. "It was in the cake," he said, bewildered. "I almost broke a tooth."

Ginny laughed at Nick's surprise and explained that she had put the baby inside as part of a Mardi Gras tradition. "Whoever gets the baby bakes the cake next year," she said.

A few weeks later, we heard that Holly and Jim Conover had backed out of their contract. They would not be moving to Celebration after all. But we were.

E ven after putting down a deposit on the house, there were details to arrange. Doug had to persuade his editors at *The New York Times* that he could do his job as a national correspondent as well from Florida as from New York, at least during the year or so that we planned to engage in the experiment of living in Celebration. We had to rent the house in Connecticut for the time we planned to stay in Celebration, and take care of a hundred other details large and small, including regular trips to Celebration to monitor the progress of the house and make various decisions—from floor coverings to paint colors to the placement of phone jacks.

For us, part of the appeal of Celebration was the idea of writing a book about the place. The fact that a cultural icon as beloved and abhorred as Disney was building a town from scratch was too intriguing to pass up. It wouldn't be *A Year in Provence* or *Under the Tuscan Sun.* But here was an opportunity to learn something about America today, and perhaps about ourselves, too.

We had written nonfiction books before, separately and jointly. The topics had ranged from education and biography to architecture and financial skullduggery. We knew we worked well together. In fact, we had just completed an article for *The New York Times Magazine* about a terrorist in the Middle East and had collaborated more smoothly than ever during two trips to Israel and Europe.

Unlike in previous books and articles, however, we would be players in this story, not just its custodians. Our children would be guinea pigs at the new school. In writing the unauthorized biography of Celebration we would have to find our places in the community's life while searching for the middle ground between observer and participant.

For about five minutes we considered keeping the book a secret from the rest of the town. It would probably promote candor and ensure that no one said whatever they imagined we wanted to hear. But a little bit of thought told us that was not a good idea. The kids would have to lie to friends about what their parents were doing, definitely a bad precedent. And we would wind up betraying the trusts and friendships that were bound to develop over the course of our time in Celebration.

We made the right decision. Our project would not be concealed, even though, once they knew about the book, people might wonder what we would write. Some might fear an exposé and avoid us. But we figured that most people in Celebration would be eager to talk with us, openly and honestly, about why they had come there and what they found. Looking back, we think that is what happened. Only twice in the year this project took would anyone decline to talk.

In the course of researching and writing this book, we wanted to answer the question of what the changing nature of urban planning and design said about the changing nature of America—its values, its culture, its reemerging sense of community. The United States today is a predominantly suburban nation. But those suburbs are plagued by a sense of isolation and by a dependence on the automobile, both of which have created widespread dissatisfaction. Did Celebration represent an alternative or simply an escape? We wanted to explore the answer through the lives of the people who had chosen to live there, including our own.

Distinctive as the town's architecture and post-neotraditional planning were, and provocative as Disney's involvement was, we sensed from the start that the real story of Celebration would not be about the corporation or even the place. It would be about the people who had come there in search of something elusive in American life today, something that is as old as the nation itself—a better place to live. After all, the making of a new town, the search for a new utopia, is a great American tradition. And, as we approach the next century, what better time to find out if the pioneer spirit still lives.

We knew only one thing for sure: Nick would be making the cake for the next block party on Nadina Place.

1

The Cult of the Mouse

Our big yellow Ryder truck rumbled and squeaked down the ramp off Interstate 4 twenty miles southwest of Orlando and onto U.S. Highway 192, perhaps the ugliest and most garish stretch of blacktop in America. Less than ten miles from Walt Disney World, the once-quiet road is clogged every day of the year with tourists in rented minivans. In excess of sixty thousand cars daily, according to county traffic counters. If you were to hold out your hand and stop traffic for the day, that's 47.52 miles of vehicles, fender to fender, almost enough to reach to Florida's east coast.

The bad-tempered congestion on the four-lane road passes multiple outlets of every fast-food chain known to mankind, countless T-shirt shops and tattoo parlors, an American Gladiators dinner theater, endless cheap motels, discount outlets, and a three-hundred-foot-tall contraption called the Skycoaster that somehow induces people to pay $35 to be strapped into a harness similar to a swing and hurled toward the ground at speeds up to seventy miles an hour.

The right turn onto Celebration Avenue, past the shiny white fence and old-fashioned water tower proclaiming "Disney's Town of Celebration," provided a welcome relief from the tedious traffic and unrelenting orgy of shopping. Celebration seemed like a sanctuary. People turning off the interstate just a few miles farther along experienced the same sensation when they found themselves on the broad six-lane road leading to Walt Disney World. Of course, the similarity of the experiences owed everything to the fact that the same company that operates the most-visited tourist attraction on earth had conceived and built Celebration.

But if Disney World was meant to entertain and excite, everything within the town's confines was intended to be soothing to the eye and comforting to the soul. The street patterns and architecture alluded to another era. Unlike houses separated by the broad lawns of a typical suburb, homes were grouped close together and set close to the street, the way they were built a century ago in places like Savannah and Charleston. The architectural guidelines created a distinct sense of consistency that, to our eyes at least, was pleasing. The one- and two-story houses were variations on a limited number of designs, so they seemed to fit together like pieces of an architect's puzzle. Garages were tucked discreetly behind the houses along alleys that ran parallel to every street. Lawns were clipped, and there was no sign of litter anywhere. The streets themselves were laid out on a modified grid plan, attesting in that singularly American way to order, virtue, and rectitude. With their shade trees and wide sidewalks, the streets were also attractive and inviting to pedestrians. It was a town of pretty buildings, neat streets, and smiling people, with an overall effect quite similar to the one we would have found had we made that other turn and wound up in the Magic Kingdom.

But Celebration was a real town, and it was an ambitious attempt by one of biggest and best-known corporations in the country to advance town planning and community building in America. In designing Celebration, the Walt Disney Company had brought together some of the finest minds and biggest names in the architecture and urban-planning professions and come up with a concept that could serve as a model for other developers and, possibly, as an antidote to the isolation and sterility of the modern suburb. The company's team had examined the full range of town development over the last century, from Frederick Law Olmsted's groundbreaking 1868 design for Riverside, Illinois, to the hottest new trend in urban design, neotraditionalism, which relies on scaled-down, pedestrian-friendly planning. Disney's idea was to sift through the best practices of the last 130 years to build a new town that would resurrect the vitality and neighborliness of America before the postwar rush to the suburbs.

Several elements made the town Disney planned different from anything else in the country. The concept was far different from the vast tracts of homes in Levittown, New York, the prototypical American suburb. Celebration's scale was small, and its plan revolved around a town center that would serve as a physical and psychological anchor for the community. In addition, where Levittown had provided modest housing for veterans of World War II, Celebration aimed higher on the income scale, offering interesting architecture to the middle and upper classes. Celebration also was a sharp contrast to the suburbs that had followed Levittown. It was oriented toward pedestrians and endeavored to engineer away some of the reliance on the automobile that is the hallmark of the modern suburb. And it was different from other well-regarded new towns of more recent vintage, like Reston, Virginia, and Columbia, Maryland, in that its residential housing was denser and its individual lots less parklike. Celebration even attempted to improve on neotraditional design by incorporating broader streets and more commercial space. Whether or not you liked the results, the effort was worthy of serious examination.

Had the grand scale of the planning experiment itself not been enough to warrant our moving to Celebration, the involvement of Disney put it over the top. The entertainment giant is one of the most admired and reviled corporations in the world. To millions of people, its name is synonymous with fun and high-quality entertainment; thirty-six million people a year go to Disney World alone. But to others, Disney's products, from its theme parks and films to this new town of Celebration, have all the flavor and appeal of boxed mashed potatoes. Whichever side you are on, there is agreement that anything Disney does on the scale of town-building merits attention.

The town that Disney built is a lovely place physically. Eventually it will spread over a full five thousand acres, but the initial development occurred in an area shaped like a fat wedge of pie, American apple pie. At the tip is a small man-made lake, which was created to anchor the town center and provide the fill dirt that added three to four feet of elevation to the surrounding swampland, keeping the town high and dry.

The small town center nestles around one side of the lake, and three main arteries extend outward from it, defining the shape of the wedge. The two avenues on the edges, Celebration Avenue and Campus Street, are sweeping and embrace the residential neighborhoods. The third, Water Street, flows straight through downtown and follows a tree-lined canal up a slight incline to its end at the golf course clubhouse, which forms the lush green crust that encloses the top of the pie shape.

The town center is the place where most people get their first impression of Celebration, and therefore its most prominent corner lots were reserved for public buildings—the Town Hall designed by Philip Johnson, the bank designed by Robert Venturi and Denise Scott Brown, the preview center by the late Charles Moore. The intention was both to signal that this was a real town, with civic institutions, and to highlight the most architecturally interesting buildings. Less-distinctive three-story commercial buildings line Market Street, the town's version of Main Street, and extend in a semicircle around the small lake. There is a wonderful relationship among those structures, which planners call background buildings. They set the tone for downtown. In a salute to another era, they are clad in stucco in various shades of pastel, no two quite alike but all of them blending into a pleasing and seemingly timeless street scene reminiscent of small-town architecture found across the country. Fitting in with the tropical climate, the buildings feature deep overhangs, arcades, and the occasional fountain courtyard. The buildings sidle up to the sidewalk, reaching out to engage a street shaded by trees. As befits its stature, Market Street is lined with towering poodle-headed Washington palms. Above the shops are apartments, with broad balconies overlooking the street and lake. Those with a good view from the balconies can catch a glimpse of what once was—a stretch of undeveloped, protected wetlands—now flush against Disney's man-made lake.

Across a small green on the edge of downtown, along Campus Street, construction of the new school was proceeding at a furious pace the day we arrived. One of the great appeals of Celebration, to us as well as to a majority of other people moving in, was the school. It was billed as a true community school, serving students from kindergarten through twelfth grade. And it was billed as a model of education's "best practices." The latter point was particularly important. Given a choice, no right-thinking person would move to Florida for the schools, which are perennially at or near the bottom of national rankings. But Celebration School promised something special.

Osceola County would operate the school, but education experts from places like Harvard, Johns Hopkins, Auburn, and Stetson universities had designed its program. The school would be so good, the marketing line promised, that an affiliated teaching academy would share its techniques with educators from across the country. Indicative of its central role in the community was its placement, smack dab in the middle of town, unlike in other developments where the school is shunted aside on the cheapest land possible, usually next to a highway.

The town would also have a sixty-acre health campus, and this, too, was key to Celebration's appeal. Not just a plain hospital, the facility would combine medical care with a fitness center. The focus in Celebration's facility was not to be on fixing illness but on maintaining wellness. The health campus was at one far end of the wedge, and within the wedge were the homes of Celebration, though they spilled out over the edges and eventually would encompass a far larger area.

But the health campus was barely begun and the school was far from finished the day we arrived in town with our truck and pulled into one of the downtown parking lots, which are screened from view behind the buildings. We took up half a dozen spaces with the truck and its trailer, which bore Doug's midlife crisis, a taxicab-yellow Ford Mustang convertible.

Five days earlier, we had packed up the twelve-ton, twenty-four-foot-long Ryder with most of our belongings and driven south gingerly, wincing at every pothole from New York through the Carolinas. At the time, moving ourselves had seemed like a romantic way to start our journey. We shipped Nick and Becky off to stay with Cathy's parents in Nova Scotia. Elizabeth was staying behind at her summer job in New York City. So the two of us planned a leisurely trip to our new home.

We had discovered our error by the time we had traversed the Cross Bronx Expressway and arrived on the George Washington Bridge. The huge truck bucked at every bump, forcing Doug to wrestle the wheels back onto the pavement. The edge of the bridge seemed perilously close, particularly from Cathy's perspective in the passenger's seat. The slightest incline seemed to strain the diesel engine to capacity as big rigs and grandmas in compacts whizzed around us, often with horns blaring. By the time we passed out of New Jersey, three hours later, we had managed a compromise with the truck—we didn't drive too fast, it didn't throw us off Interstate 95. As a result, we made it to Florida two and a half days later, safe and sound and without breaking a single piece of furniture or china. But there was precious little romance, as we learned that our truck-driving skills required huge amounts of turnaround space, available only at restaurants where the best house wine was a cold Bud.

For the first three days, we stayed in Doug's parents' condominium east of Orlando while the last-minute work was done on the house, driving back and forth each day to watch. The pace of construction throughout Celebration was frantic. Four houses on our block alone were scheduled for completion in the same week. Inside ours, a two-man crew was painting the woodwork, electricians were hooking up outlets, and the guy installing the air-conditioning units was trying to make them work. Some items clearly would not be finished by the time we closed, but we wanted to be certain the air-conditioning was not one of the things left for later.

Three days after our arrival, at four o'clock on the afternoon of June 26, we met at the house with Todd Hudson and Jason Meyers, two builders with David Weekley Homes, the Houston company building our house. The purpose was to do a walk-through, noting anything that was not finished properly. The items would be written on a "punch list," and the builder would make them right in the days after the closing. Hudson and Meyers were surprised to find that we had brought along a building inspector, Bob Bidwell. Cathy explained that we had never bought a new house before, but we figured it was a good idea to get another set of eyes on the place before we signed off on it.

We spotted most of the aesthetic problems—a chair molding cut at the wrong angle, a bow in one of the bathroom walls, scratches on the porcelain sink in the kitchen, the absence of frosted glass in the window beside the Jacuzzi in the master bathroom, that sort of thing. Bidwell picked up a few bigger items—electrical wires that ran too close to the attic opening in the granny flat above the garage, the absence of a mandatory shut-off valve on the water heater. Bidwell said the house was sound structurally, and while he thought Celebration prices were very high, he seemed content with the overall quality of construction.

This was the sixth house we had bought in fourteen years of marriage, but it would be the first closing we had attended without our own lawyer. Gene Kane, the mortgage officer at the local branch of SunTrust Bank, where we got our loan, had told us a lawyer would be a waste of money. "Disney won't change anything in the contract anyway," he said. "It's their way or the highway." A quick check with other new residents bore him out. Buying a house in Celebration was sort of like buying a Saturn—no negotiating, everyone pays sticker price.

On June 27, 1997, we were ready to sign the final papers for the mortgage. As we walked toward the preview center, where Celebration Realty had its offices and where the house closing would occur, we were as nervous as might be expected. We were about to sign a mortgage on a new home when we already owned another, also mortgaged. Waiting for us were Kane, the mortgage officer, and Cheryl Marlin, a paralegal with the title company, who would actually conduct the closing procedure. She confirmed what Kane had told us: No changes were allowed to the contract.

"We've had attorneys from all over the country call up when they see this contract and say, 'What's going on here? I've never seen anything like this,' " Marlin explained. "We tell them that it's all legal and that's the way it is. The questions usually have to do with the buyer having to pay the entire cost of title insurance and all of the transfer taxes. Usually those costs are shared with the sellers. Not in Disney's case."

As we read through the closing statement, we could see clearly how much Disney's rules cost us. We were paying $1,589.50 for title insurance and $3,608.05 in state and county transfer taxes. In a normal closing, the seller would have picked up half of that total, or $2,598.77. We also paid the first installment of $213.36 in debt-service fees that would be used to pay off the municipal bonds that Disney used to develop the town, $360 for the annual homeowner association dues, and $113.28 in maintenance fees to cover garbage pickup for six months. None of these costs was a big-ticket item, but they added up to nearly $3,330 in extras for the privilege of living in Celebration.

Though it was no solace, we saw that the builder was playing by Disney's rules, too. Weekley Homes was paying $18,171.12 as a 6 percent real estate commission to Celebration Realty, part of Disney's development arm. Plus, Weekley paid an additional 1 percent "marketing fee" of $3,028.52 to the real estate company. Of course, these were costs that the builder had already passed on to us when we bought our home. (A year later, some of the builders would take over their own marketing and sales from Disney.)

In the end, we paid $302,852 for a two-story, three-bedroom house. There were two and a half baths in the house, a dining room, a living room, a kitchen with a large eat-in area, and a family room. Part of the price included a huge fourth bedroom and full bath above the garage, which was known as the granny flat. Overall, the house had about three thousand square feet of space.

The base price of the house, a Savannah model with a Colonial facade, was $243,990. We paid a $6,000 premium for the lot because it backed up on a small swamp and no one would be building behind us. The granny flat was an extra $30,000, and the remainder of the purchase price came from upgrades in the house, such as $13,000 for tile instead of carpet on the entire first floor and a better grade of countertops throughout. Adding it all up, we paid $100 a square foot for the house, compared with an average in the Orlando area of $75 a square foot for new construction.

The high cost of Celebration was not the only thing that nagged at us during those first days in the community, as we walked the neighborhoods and got to know the town better. At times there seemed to be a make-believe quality, an artificiality to the whole enterprise. Some houses that appeared to have second-floor dormers were actually only single-story buildings; the dormers, complete with windowpanes painted black to simulate a darkened space, were fake, assembled on the ground and hoisted into place by cranes. In the same way, the builders tried to create the illusion of space beneath the porches, like that where many of us as children hid while playing hide-and-seek, by tacking pieces of plastic simulating wooden latticework onto solid foundations. Upon closer inspection, we also saw that the long white fence that marked the entry to the town was plastic and the water tower functioned only in the sense that it bore the words "Disney's Town of Celebration." The studied nostalgia, right down to the picket fences bordering every corner house and the profusion of night-blooming jasmine, disturbed.

Also, there was the matter of the tourists. We had spent five years in a two-hundred-year-old house in the historic district of Alexandria, Virginia, so we were used to the smell of exhaust from idling chartered buses and the sight of tourists who thought nothing of pressing their faces to your windowpanes. But here there was a sense that Celebration was an unticketed gate at Disney World, even though there was no entrance gate or guard house, and anyone could drive in and take a look around.

Small matters, but symbolic. At times, the garish eyesores along Highway 192 seemed more real than the pretty neighborhoods and spotless streets of Celebration. Perhaps it is unfair to criticize a town for being too nostalgic or too clean or even too well planned. Still, the question in those early days was whether Celebration's developers had learned from the past or just gone back to some glorified version of it. Was Celebration selling nostalgia or peddling amnesia?

Certainly no corporation in the world is better at make-believe than the Walt Disney Company, which had built this town of Celebration in large part as a way to sell off nearly five thousand acres deemed unsuitable for yet another addition to its nearby theme parks. The company's major attractions, Disneyland and Walt Disney World, are marvels of escapism. For many children and adults alike, a trip to Disney World represents the perfect vacation—clean, controlled, filled with predictable magic and regulated fantasy. To critics, and there are plenty, Disney's theme parks, combined with its movies and animated films, are illustrations of the defilement of American culture. The parks are, as writer James Howard Kunstler described them in his book *The Geography of Nowhere,* capitals of unreality dedicated to temporary escape from modern life.

From its earliest days, Celebration was attacked along similar lines. Some of the criticism was inevitable, given the town's association with a target as juicy as Disney. The architectural uniformity, down to plantings and the color of curtains seen from the street, was ridiculed. Jokes were made about residents being required to wear Mickey Mouse ears and practice the aggressive friendliness that is the hallmark of the theme parks. At one point in the town's early days, the *Orlando Sentinel* ran a spoof about Disney extras being paid to walk dogs in Celebration to create a homey feeling. It was perhaps an early indication of the town's growing sensitivity that not many living there were amused.

During one of her scouting trips before we made the final decision to move to Celebration, Cathy was stopped on Market Street by a tourist who asked, pointing to the houses in the distance, "Are those real houses?"

"Of course," Cathy answered, slightly puzzled by her first run-in with an incredulous tourist.

"Well then, where are the real people?" he continued.

Looking at her watch, which read ten-thirty A.M., on a Tuesday, Cathy said, "They're at their real jobs, paying for their real mortgages, for their real houses."

On a more substantive level, there were questions about the escapist nature of Celebration, as there had been for years about other planned communities. Concerns were raised also about the impact of these increasingly privatized enclaves on urban social relations. Would there be room for poor people and minorities in Celebration, so outwardly and solidly a middle-class paradise? People seemed less willing to repair their cities and communities than to invest money in escaping to the latest version of Disney's Main Street, U.S.A. The model of a civil community, in the minds of some critics, had been replaced by something akin to a movie set. "Celebration is overcontrolled and lacks social conscience," fumed John Henry, an Orlando architect, in a trade journal. "It is elitist: gingerbread glosses over social inequity."

Some criticism had little to do with Celebration itself. The Walt Disney Company was a favorite target for people with legitimate concerns about the growing dominance of corporations in American cultural life and the sanitized version of history on display in Disney's parks. Not far away, Walt Disney World existed like a sovereign state. Disney's studios churned out animated and live-action films. Disney owned a book publisher, and the year before had bought a television network, Capital Cities/ABC. And it had even worked some of its magic on revitalizing Times Square in New York City, a change not universally admired by New Yorkers. Disney was even getting ready to launch its own cruise line.

Now the company that wanted to dictate the leisure-time habits of the nation was creating a whole town, and the price of admission was a mortgage. Celebration could be seen as the final step in Disney's drive to create a vertical megabusiness with products for every stage in a consumer's life, from the child who visits a theme park or buys a stuffed

Mickey Mouse to the adult looking for a Broadway play or shopping for the next best place to live. It was a disconcerting thought.

Celebration Company, the business unit set up by Disney Development Company to oversee the $2.5 billion town, invited criticism, too. As if the Disney name were not banner enough, the company orchestrated a media onslaught for the town's inauguration. It touted its panoply of big-name architects, bragged that it was doing something unprecedented in urban design, and appealed shamelessly to family values, sentimental longings for bygone days, and a barely suppressed fear of the present.

The town seal, a cameo of a little girl with a ponytail riding her bike past a picket fence, trailed by her dog, was emblazoned on everything from manhole covers and light poles to coffee mugs and golf towels. Russ Rymer in *Harper's Magazine* compared the sales pitch to a fable, and indeed the script itself had a mythic ring: "There was once a place where neighbors greeted neighbors in the quiet of summer twilight. Where children chased fireflies. And porch swings provided easy refuge from the cares of the day. The movie house showed cartoons on Saturday. The grocery story delivered. And there was one teacher who always knew you had that special something. Remember that place? Perhaps from your childhood? Or maybe just from stories. It held a magic all its own. The special magic of an American home town."

Celebration was crafted to deliver its biggest appeal to baby boomers, the generation that grew up watching the *Wonderful World of Disney* on television every Sunday night and was now trekking to Disneyland and Disney World for vacations with their own kids. For them, the Disney name connoted cleanliness, quality, and dependability, the promise of civility in an uncivil world—in a fragmented world where schools were no longer havens, where churches were empty, where parks were lifeless and neighbors were strangers, Disney offered the promise of order and community.

Like all good marketers, the people at Disney knew that the spiritual and cultural focal point for American society as a whole was the boomer generation. As boomers metamorphosed from Beaver Cleaver to hippie to yuppie, society had followed in their wake. With boomers in their forties contemplating the dread fiftieth birthday, market research showed they were spending more time with their families and were more concerned than ever about finding the right place to raise their children and settle down for the rest of their lives. Boomers were not the only people with those concerns, but they were driving the market.

We are both boomers—Doug was born in 1949, Cathy in 1956. Like many in our generation, we were always on the lookout for the next great place to live. Like many people our age, we read the lists of top places published in *Money* and other magazines. For years, Doug kept a copy of a *Newsweek* article on the best middle-sized cities, consulting it whenever he felt constrained, or angered at work, wondering what jobs and houses were available in Albuquerque or Charlottesville. We were restless and, for the most part, rootless. On vacations from Santa Fe to Nova Scotia, we kept one eye on where we would build our dream house and how we would fit in with neighbors and nature.

The locations that beckoned were places where we could walk, where a sense of history infused the community, where there was a neighborhood tavern or coffee shop, a theater, a decent diner, and neighbors on whom you could count. It wasn't surprising, then, that many elements of Celebration appealed to us—the school, the chance to participate in the start of a new community, forsaking our dependence on cars, Florida's interesting history, and the dramatic backdrop provided by its natural environment, not to mention the absence of snow. But Disney World had never made it onto our list of pluses in evaluating a place to live. In fact, we had visited only once, when our children were young, right after Doug's return from covering the Gulf War, when it seemed like an apt antidote for too much troubling reality.

For many people, however, Disney World was at the top of the wish list, and the strategy for selling Celebration relied heavily on exploiting the Disney name. Given the town's proximity to Disney World, it was obvious that the initial pool of buyers would come from the millions of people who visited the theme park every year. The planners couldn't very well use Mickey Mouse as the pitchman and be taken seriously, so they picked the next-best figure, the late Walt Disney himself. What better person to peddle a return to old-fashioned values than the man who created Main Street, U.S.A., as an idyllic replica of the Missouri town where he had spent his troubled childhood?

Though Disney had built Walt Disney Productions into a successful film and animation studio, he had nurtured the idea of an amusement park for at least twenty years before he finally broached the project with his brother in 1952. Roy thought the idea was crazy and refused to commit more than $10,000 of the company's money to it. Walt borrowed the rest from his life insurance policy and opened Disneyland, in Anaheim, California, in 1955. The next year, the park's revenues were $10 million, a third of the total gross of Walt Disney Productions. Success, however, brought unforeseen consequences. His biographers report that Disney was angered by the proliferation of cheap motels and souvenir shops outside the park's gates. They were both an eyesore and competition as they siphoned off profits from Disneyland. When he set out to build a second park, in Florida, he was determined to control as much of the surrounding land as possible.

The story is part of Florida and Disney lore. Walt flew into the state by private jet many times in the early 1960s. The trips to scout land were kept secret to avoid the inevitable escalation in land prices were the overall plan to become known. A clandestine operation, using phony company names, moved to acquire the land. But Orlando was not the first choice. At one point, Disney found a huge tract of gorgeous land in Florida's panhandle, along the Gulf coast. The St. Joe Paper Company, a large timber and paper-milling company founded in the 1930s by a du Pont heir, owned it. When Disney himself approached the company's patrician chairman, Edward Ball, about buying the land, Ball sniffed, "We don't deal with carnival people."

In the end, the Walt Disney Company picked a rural area straddling Orange and Osceola counties, about fifteen miles southwest of the city of Orlando. In a series of quiet transactions over many months, it accumulated thirty thousand acres. The amount of land, roughly forty-five square miles, was far more than necessary for the new theme park. The excess would allow Disney not only to control the buildings that would be constructed around the park, avoiding eyesores in the immediate neighborhood, but to build hotels and other facilities and thereby control the competition, too. Today, the small jet that transported Disney in and out of Orlando on his buying trips is part of the back-lot tour at the Disney–MGM Studios, one of the four theme parks that compose Walt Disney World.

Control was also the operative word for Walt's next move in creating his kingdom. Disney did not want just land. He wanted a private government that would control his land. Local politicians saw Disney World as an engine for enormous development, so they were more than happy to carry water for the company in the Florida legislature. In 1966, not long after the public disclosure that Disney planned to construct its huge theme park, legislation was introduced in Tallahassee to create a new government entity known as the Reedy Creek Improvement District.

Although innocuously named, the district was in fact a private government that gave Disney autonomy within its domain. As proposed in the bill, the district would have the authority to provide essential public services, from police and fire protection to drainage and flood control. It vested in Disney control over land use within the district, and the creation and enforcement of building codes. Finally, the unprecedented legislation would grant Disney the right to raise money through fees and taxes within the district and to finance its roads, sewers, and other services by issuing tax-free municipal bonds, an inexpensive means of raising the huge sums required to build and later expand Disney World and its environs. Virtually every element of land use within the vast acreage would fall under the purview of the company.

While most politicians in the area directly affected by the planned park were eager for an economic boom, others in the legislature and across the state had to pause at such a bold request. In order to win the legislative support and ease the fears of Florida residents, Disney studios created a film in which Walt offered his rationale for having his own government. The film was not shown to the legislature until February 1967, three months after Disney's death from cancer.

"We must have the flexibility in Disney World to keep pace with tomorrow's world," Disney said. "We must have the freedom to work in cooperation with American industry and to make decisions based on standards of performance. If we have this kind of freedom, I'm confident we can create a world showcase for American free enterprise that will bring new industry to the state of Florida from all over the country."

Another justification, Disney said in the film, was to govern the people who would come to live in the futuristic community that he planned to create as part of the park. He called it Experimental Prototype Community of Tomorrow, or Epcot, and it was to be an actual town. Its twenty thousand inhabitants would live beneath a giant dome and be zipped from skyscraper to skyscraper on a high-speed monorail.

The town, he explained, would be "starting from scratch on virgin land and building a special kind of new community that more people will talk about and come to look at than any other area in the world." There would be no slums, and no unemployment, because people without jobs would not be allowed to live in Epcot. There also would be no home ownership, because everyone would rent from Disney's company.

Faced with the promise of Disney's golden touch, the politicians rolled over. In May 1967, the legislature approved the creation of the Reedy Creek Improvement District, a sovereign government to manage a theme park. The Florida Senate approved the measure unanimously, and there was only a single dissenting vote in the House. The following year, the state's Supreme Court confirmed Reedy Creek's authority to issue tax-free bonds for internal improvements. Doing so, the court acknowledged, would "greatly aid Disney interests" but would also carry benefits to the "numerous inhabitants of the district."

But there were no inhabitants and there never would be, save forty or so Disney employees who lived in company housing. Some critics suspected that there was never any intention of building Epcot and that it was a smoke screen to secure approval of Reedy Creek. Even if Disney had intended to build a futuristic city, the intent had died with him. Epcot the utopian city of the future was transformed into Epcot the theme park, which opened its doors in 1982.

The utopian vision, and the venerated leader's words preserved on celluloid, were resurrected for the selling of Celebration. When we sat through the slick presentation video at the Celebration Preview Center on our family's initial trip, in February 1997, we watched Walt talking about his dream of building from scratch a community that people would talk about and visit. Although we knew he was talking about his dead dream for a city of the future, it appeared for all the world that Disney was describing Celebration. A man sitting next to us whispered to his companion, "He hasn't aged at all."

Selective editing had transformed Disney's speech about Epcot, a vision of stark skyscrapers and airborne transportation reminiscent of the movie *Blade Runner*, into a homily for Celebration, the antithesis of Epcot. Only the overall sterility stayed the same. There were some parallels, of course. Celebration would have twenty thousand inhabitants, the same number planned for Epcot. And the town's designers claimed it would provide the latest state-of-the-art technology, with a fiber-optic grapevine connecting every house and apartment to the model school, hospital, and even grocery store.

But where Epcot looked to the future, Celebration turned to the past. Where Epcot was a vision of the direction in which the American city might be headed, Celebration represented the country's disenchantment with the metropolis and its new embracing of the town of decades past. The emphasis of the marketing campaign for Celebration was always on old-fashioned values and resurrecting the small town where many Americans either grew up or wished they had grown up or, through the power of revisionist history, thought they had grown up. In its way, the promise of Celebration was to create a world so distinct from the contemporary suburb—let alone from contemporary urban areas— that it was a fantasy itself.

Celebration was not the only attempt to capitalize on rising disenchantment with urban and suburban life. Developers across the country were offering alternatives, though they tended to be exclusive, gated communities that heightened the divisions between the haves and have-nots. But other new towns were popping up, from Kentlands, a small community in Maryland, to DC Ranch, a town planned for twenty thousand residents on the edge of the McDowell Mountains, near Scottsdale, Arizona. Like Celebration, many of these places adhered to the tenets of the neotraditional movement, the revolt against modern suburbs that emphasizes the return to small-town planning, with sidewalks, town centers, small yards, and expansive public areas. But none of them could boast the one thing that made Celebration stand out—the involvement of the Walt Disney Company, with its long relationship with the American public. Disney's role as the progenitor of Celebration set the place apart from all the similar towns under construction across the country, putting it both in the spotlight and under the microscope, drawing residents who would never have thought of themselves as pioneers and attracting the scrutiny reserved for major corporations, celebrities, and wayward politicians. To be sure, Celebration boasted a bigger array of brand-name architects than the other new towns. And it represented the biggest and most closely watched test to date of the principles of neotraditionalism. But make no mistake, it was Disney's name that set it apart from all the rest.

The result was nothing less than remarkable. On November 18, 1995, a Saturday, nearly five thousand people arrived at an open field along Highway 192 for a lottery to determine who got the chance to move into one of the first 474 houses and apartments in Celebration. Unlike most planned communities and upscale suburbs, Celebration would offer $1 million homes next to rented apartments and $300,000 houses. The result was intended to be an economically integrated rubbing of elbows similar to that of small towns of the past. The difference was apparent in the crowd. There were singles and couples, families with children in tow and senior citizens. There were a few Asian faces and one man in a turban. But there was a noticeable absence of blacks, even though Disney executives had advertised the event in the local black press.

There wasn't much on display in the way of actual product. Bulldozers were at work sculpting neighborhoods out of cow pasture and sullen swamp, and the downtown buildings were still under construction. No ground had been broken for a house. Nor were there model homes to entice buyers or paved roads to delineate the neighborhoods. People would be buying on trust.

The sales office was a squat, prefabricated building with a two-story gabled facade tacked onto its front. It literally looked like a set piece from old Hollywood. The first of the eight thousand houses would not be ready until the summer of 1996, and it would take several years to reach the full population of twenty thousand. Prices for the houses were 20 to 25 percent higher than those for equivalent houses in the traditional subdivisions springing up across the Orlando region.

The turnout at the lottery surprised the people who had planned the event, despite the fact that interest in the community had been high from the time plans were announced, in 1991. Thousands of people had written to Disney seeking information, and thousands more had visited the preview center as work progressed. Already there had been dozens of stories in newspapers and magazines around the country. Indeed, interest seemed high enough that Disney executives were worried they would be overwhelmed if they simply opened sales that day. So Peter Rummell, the president of Disney Development Company, the subsidiary with overall responsibility for Celebration, told the community's general manager, Don Killoren, to come up with a fair and manageable means of selling the first homes.

"Don, we're going to open up for sales and the whole world is going to judge us and we won't get a second try," Killoren later told us Rummell had said to him. "I want good customer service and a big event. I want a press happening."

The result was the lottery, and the Disney touch was everywhere. Huge tents were erected as protection from the heat. Familiar Disney songs, like "When You Wish upon a Star" and "M-I-C-K-E-Y M-O-U-S-E," were piped over the loudspeakers. Magicians and clowns on stilts strolled among the crowd. There were a brass quintet and a hot-air balloon. Clean-cut young men and women, wearing matching shirts with the Celebration seal, sat at rows of tables inside the five tents to take the $1,000 deposit required to enter your name in the lottery for the chance to buy one of the houses or rent an apartment.

Actually, there was a series of lotteries. The five tents represented the five levels of housing available in the first phase of construction. They were Estate, Village, Cottage, Townhomes, and Apartments. The apartments, which were located over the shops and in areas adjacent to the town center, were available only for rent, starting at $737 a month for the smallest one-bedroom units. The least expensive of the homes for sale were the two-story and three-story town houses, which had eight to ten rooms and would sit on lots that were 28 feet wide and 100 to 130 feet deep. The town houses would line one of the town's main avenues and part of an adjacent park. Their prices started at $120,000 and went as high as $180,000. The Cottage homes were next, with prices starting around $220,000 for houses of about 2,500 square feet on lots that were generally 45 feet wide and 130 feet deep, about half the size of the traditional suburban lot. Next came the Village homes, which were larger and on lots that measured 70 feet by 130 feet. They started around $300,000. Finally there were the Estate homes, custom-built houses on premium lots that were 90 feet wide, 130 feet deep, and generally across from an open public space, like the golf course or one of the parks. The prices were expected to start around $600,000 and go up to $1 million.

Residential developers have long understood the market appeal of offering different models within the same community. Builders of rowhouses in the nineteenth century offered buyers choices in trim and other decorations, although the underlying houses remained the same. In Celebration, the builders offered multiple models and up to three different facades for each of them. The opportunity to choose a model and facade was an act of empowerment in a development where there were few opportunities for exercising choices.

What was not subject to choice were the prices, which were non-negotiable and well above the median for the rest of Osceola County, which in 1995 was only $80,000. Nonetheless, twelve hundred people put down deposits of up to $1,000 for a chance at one of the initial houses and apartments.

As the hoppers spun and names were drawn and read out, there were cheers for the lucky winners. Those who got low numbers got first crack at signing contracts with the Disney-approved builders and choosing among the six house styles—Coastal, Classical, Colonial Revival, French Normandy, Mediterranean, or Victorian.

Later, as we got to know our neighbors, we discovered that attending the lottery was a badge of honor, akin to having been at Woodstock in your late teens or early twenties. Some people had gone to extraordinary lengths to be there, and many entered more than one lottery to improve their chances of winning. The deposits were refundable for people who did not get a low enough number to buy a house and for those who decided to back out before signing their contract. Those who entered multiple lotteries had the option of consolidating their deposits on the house of their choice or getting the additional deposits back.

"I paid with three one-thousand-dollar checks at the entrance to each tent," recalled Dan Rudgers, a music teacher in his mid-fifties from Long Island, New York. "I entered lotteries for a town house, a Cottage home, and a Village home. What I really wanted was a town house. I remember my lottery number for the town house, like a kid who remembers his number in the military draft in the seventies. It was four hundred fifty-seven, and I wasn't sure I'd get one. But eventually enough people dropped out of the Townhomes that it looked like I'd make it. So I consolidated my checks into a single deposit on the town house. That day was euphoric. It was just like everybody was so into this community and you just knew it was going to work."

Like many people in the first wave of residents, Rudgers was drawn by the Disney name. As a child in upstate New York, he had been a Mouseketeer, watching Disney's afternoon television show with his mouse ears on and, like Doug, he had had a big crush on Annette Funnicello. As he grew up, he switched to watching the *Wonderful World of Disney* and eventually moved on to Disney World itself.

"Every Sunday night this image of this beautiful, happy place in California would be on the television screen, and I just fell in love with it," said Rudgers. "Then, in 1971, while I was a graduate student at the University of Michigan, I heard that they were opening Disney World down here. There was nothing that could keep me from coming. On spring break, a buddy of mine and I grabbed two women, and we drove twenty-four hours straight from Ann Arbor. Of course, they went to the beach, and I went to Disney World."

Since he finished graduate school and started teaching, in 1972, Rudgers estimated that he had come to Disney World an average of three times a year. Some years he wasn't able to make it at all, but the next year he would make up for the loss by visiting five or six times. "I'm a dyed-in-the-wool Disney freak," he said proudly one day as he sat in the kitchen of his town house.

Rudgers first heard of Celebration in the early nineties. During a Christmas parade he was watching on television, there was a brief announcement that Disney was going to build a town in Florida. For three years, he peppered Disney executives with phone calls and letters, desperate for solid information about their plans. He got on a mailing list and began to receive tantalizing information about the plans, still in their infancy.

As the time neared for sales to begin, Rudgers's dream was almost derailed. Disney, now in the form of Celebration Company, went into public registration for the development. Securities laws meant people in most states, including New York, could not be solicited by mail. Rudgers was undeterred. On one of his vacations at Disney World, he used the address of some family friends to get a Florida driver's license. He also registered to vote and opened a bank account in the state. "It was what I call my grand deception," he confessed later. "But otherwise I was afraid I wouldn't be able to buy in the first phase."

Tony Rizzo gave up his career in the air force to live in Celebration. A physician and now a colonel in the air force reserves, he and his wife, Jacci, had lived with their children all over the world. But in early 1994, he had come across a brief mention of Celebration in a Disney magazine. The family had always loved their vacations at Disney World. "Tony is never happier than when he is in an air force uniform or walking on Disney property," said Jacci.

So he began a correspondence with Charles Adams, one of the town planners. Eventually he and Jacci flew to Orlando to meet with Adams and learn more about the town. The description of Celebration's common purpose, like that of a military base, appealed to the Rizzos. The idea of raising their three young children in a safe environment and sending them to the state-of-the-art public school that Celebration Company was promising to build was so strong that they decided to turn their life on its head and move to the new town.

But the Rizzos faced the same problem that Dan Rudgers had. Rudgers had surmounted the problem by fudging his address. But the Rizzos, coming from a strict military background, were not about to create a phony address. They moved to Florida more than a year before Celebration was set to open, and Rizzo started working for Florida Hospital.

"My husband was up for full colonel, and he gave it up," said Jacci Rizzo. "I remember, after we moved to Florida, he was talking to Charles Adams a few weeks before the start of sales at Celebration and Adams said that it might be a lottery or it might be a line, sort of first-come, first-served. Tony became concerned. He gave up so much to get here that he wasn't going to take any chances. He was planning to take ten days off work and pitch a tent on the site, if that was what it took."

But there was no first-come, first-served. And the Rizzos got a low number for an Estate home in the lottery. The house would be a little bigger and more expensive than they had anticipated, but Rizzo's profession was going well, and it was a chance they felt they could not pass up.

Professional interest first brought Ray Chiaramonte to Celebration. He was assistant director of the Hillsborough County Planning Commission in Tampa, Florida, and for a number of years he had watched the rise of the neotraditional movement. He also was a fan of Disney World and had first visited the preview center at Celebration during one of the family's frequent trips to the theme park.

"I came over a number of times and brought my staff, too," he said. "I was more interested in the physical architecture, but as I learned about the health center and the school, my interest increased."

Chiaramonte still had not decided how deep his interest was when lottery day rolled around. He was supposed to attend a play in Tampa that evening. Instead he drove over to Celebration and put his name in for an apartment. He got number twenty-three, assuring him of success.

He remembered the next moments vividly. "I called my wife, Debby, and said, 'We're going to live in Disney World.' I was afraid. We had been in the same house for eighteen years. I have a very stable job. Everything was so set in a certain direction. But we decided to change directions. We decided, let's just go. It will be an adventure. I can find out if the planning really works. And if we don't like it we can come back."

Along with four other government employees who live in the nearby town of Kissimmee, Chiaramonte commutes an hour or so each way to his job in Tampa. He hasn't decided whether neotraditional planning works, but he is happy living in Celebration and wants to stay to see it evolve further. After living in the apartment for a year, the family bought a house in the fall of 1997. "I'm intrigued," Chiaramonte said one evening as he sat on his front porch.

The town's first phase, 351 homes in what is called Celebration Village, essentially sold out through the lottery. A few winners changed their minds and some did not qualify for mortgages. But the leftover houses were snapped up quickly by other people. The 123 apartments in the town center were filled immediately through the lottery, leaving a six-month waiting list.

The success allowed the company to speed up the schedule for the second phase, to be known as the West Village, which is where we bought our home. Of course, the success also permitted the builders to bump up the prices about 10 percent for the next batch of dream seekers.

Celebration was expected to cost about $2.5 billion over ten years. Disney itself was risking about $100 million, barely a blip on the company's financial radar screen. (The previous year the parent company had earned $1.4 billion on $12 billion in revenue.) Most of that $2.5 billion would be the money paid for homes by individual purchasers, though a significant chunk of the development costs also were going to be passed on to the residents through assessments over the life of the community.

Disney had more at stake than money. Michael Eisner, the chairman and chief executive of the company, had encouraged the creation of the town with the understanding that it would be someplace special, which would reflect well on the company and its brand name. He did not want simply to build a town, he had said repeatedly. If Disney was going to build it, he wanted it to be the best new town. Disney's devoted fans expected nothing less.

"People speak in almost religious terms about how wonderful it will be," an Orlando planning consultant, James Sellen, said a short time after the lottery. Within those high expectations lurked serious danger. The people attracted to Celebration were relying on Disney's presence to ensure nothing less than the quality of their lives. Many of them expected Celebration to repeat the ideal of Disney World, but for fifty-two weeks of the year, not just a week or two of holiday time. If everything did not run as promised and if problems were not hidden away behind the scenes, the fingers would be pointed right back at Disney. The vaunted brand name could be tarnished. And Disney couldn't walk away from Celebration anytime in the foreseeable future, because the community always would be associated with its illustrious parent and the town would be just a few miles away from Disney World.

Those concerns seemed to be heightened by the preponderance of Disneyphiles in the first wave of Celebration residents, a fact that caused consternation among the small circle of men who had brought the town to life. These developers and planners feared early on that the new residents would expect life in Celebration to be as smoothly predictable and consistently happy as a visit to the Magic Kingdom at Disney World.

"The ones we worried about were the people who believe Disney can do no wrong," Peter Rummell, the chief visionary behind Celebration, told us in recalling some of the planning for Celebration within the parent company. "Those are the people who go to Disney World eight times a year and think that because Main Street is clean they could extrapolate that to a community and think that it was going to be perfect. Those are the people who think their kids will never get a B in school and there is never going to be a weed in their lawn when they move to Celebration."

Not long after the first residents moved into Celebration, Rummell left Disney to become chairman and chief executive of the St. Joe Corporation, the company that had rejected Walt Disney's overture three decades before. But Rummell's initial fears were prophetic. The Disney brand name was a powerful lure, an implied promise of a cocooned town free of crime, drugs, and other excesses of a debased culture. Managing the rose-tinted expectations of a town full of people drawn to the Disney mystique would turn out to be far tougher than creating a day of fantasy at the Magic Kingdom.

2

Back to the Future

One evening in late 1985, Charles Fraser sat in the Café Europa in Harbour Town on Hilton Head Island, South Carolina, and listened intently to his onetime protégé. The younger man was a newly minted executive with the Walt Disney Company named Peter Rummell. He was in his late thirties, with a shock of prematurely white hair and a modest, soft-spoken demeanor.

Fraser had recruited Rummell after he earned a master's degree in business administration at the Wharton School of the University of Pennsylvania. At the time, Fraser was creating a real estate empire through his Sea Pines Company. By the early 1970s, he had six major developments under way, including Hilton Head Island, where he would eventually build 3,400 homes, and he was one of the first developers to hire M.B.A.s to manage his projects.

Fraser inculcated his young charges with his belief that developers needed to concern themselves with more than physical design. They needed to understand the importance of establishing a social infrastructure within the communities they built. That, he preached, was what separated real estate developers from a higher order of businessmen, community developers.

With those marching orders, Rummell and a handful of other young managers, known collectively as Charlie's Angels, were given extraordinary responsibilities for planning and running the big projects that Sea Pines Company was building. Rummell, for instance, was placed in charge of marketing for Amelia Island Plantation, north of Jacksonville, Florida.

Those heady days came to a crashing halt in the late 1970s with the twin shocks of the Arab oil embargo and soaring interest rates. Big-time community development came to a standstill. So Rummell left in 1977 for the Arvida Corporation, a big Florida residential developer. Six years later, he joined the management team at Rockefeller Center, in New York City. But Rummell was not happy in New York or with the stodgy ways of Rockefeller Center, and by the fall of 1985 he had returned to Florida as president of Disney Development Company, the real estate arm of the Walt Disney Company.

Rummell's first responsibility at Disney was evaluating the undeveloped portion of the thirty thousand acres the company owned southwest of Orlando. If he was going to develop the vacant land in the future, he had to know what was there and what might be done to extract the highest value from it.

Since the original Disney World theme park, the Magic Kingdom, opened near Orlando, in 1971, the company had added one additional park, Epcot. A third, Disney–MGM Studios, was under construction and slated to open in 1989. Thirty million or more visitors a year streamed into the parks, generating revenue that helped propel the company's stock to new heights. Even after the completion of Disney–MGM Studios, all three sprawling parks and the giant hotels on the property, with twenty thousand rooms, would occupy less than a third of the company's land. The question was how to get the highest value out of what remained.

Rummell commissioned an internal review. Over the course of several weeks, he and his associates in the development division evaluated the land, ordered marketing tests, and analyzed the potential impact of more theme parks. Some of the areas were environmentally sensitive wetlands, which would be politically touchy, not to mention expensive, to develop. There also was a question of how much traffic the surrounding infrastructure could handle. Interstate 4, the main road to Disney World, was already backed up for much of the day with cars coming and going to the parks and the nearby spin-off attractions that had sprung up in the last fourteen years. Finally, there was the question of whether the supply of customers for theme parks was inexhaustible, or whether Disney might create too many parks to sustain its profits. Too many parks would be like Disney eating its young.

"We took the whole thirty thousand acres, and after this complicated analysis, we decided that the reality was that it was not practical to think of more than five theme parks at Walt Disney World and about twice the number of hotel rooms already built," Rummell recalled years later. "So we cranked two more parks through the numbers and analysis, and we still had land leftover."

Flying over the property in a helicopter in 1985, it was easy to see where the least desirable land for the two remaining theme parks lay. It was on the southern half of the vast Disney World property, across Interstate 4 from the existing parks and the area where the future parks would most likely be built. This leftover land, more than ten thousand acres, was low-lying, mosquito-breeding, alligator-infested swamp and cow pasture. It was where Disney employees relocated alligators once they grew too big in the ponds dotting its golf courses and theme parks. Cattle still grazed in its large open areas, and it was home to deer, wild boar, panthers, the occasional bear, and numerous migratory birds as well as indigenous fowl, including the bald eagle.

Developing the property would mean draining the swamps and shallow ponds, adding thousands of tons of fill dirt to raise the overall level of the land so it would be dry enough for building. There also was the inevitable headache of dealing with the environmental issues raised by developing the wetlands, a habitat for so many species. All in all, Rummell knew it was an expensive, complicated proposition.

Still, the company owned the land and, Rummell theorized, if it sat fallow for too long, the state of Florida might come along and take it through condemnation proceedings because of its environmental value. Selling the property and letting someone else develop it was a possibility, but Rummell preferred to find a use for it on his own. It was a case of build it or lose it.

The question, of course, was what to build. The land was too far from Orlando to be considered a traditional suburb. One possibility, however, was to build an affluent, perhaps gated, subdivision around one or more championship golf courses. The arrival of Disney World had already spurred plenty of those developments in the general area. Indeed, many Disney executives lived in them. But Rummell wanted to do something different. He wanted to build an entire town, one that would stand out and bring credit to the Disney name and make a pile of money, too.

Rummell and his team of developers faced two primary obstacles in getting approval to build their town. First, they would have to convince Michael Eisner, who had taken over as Disney chairman in 1984, that it was the highest use of the land and that development could fall within the company's purview. Eisner rightly saw Disney as an entertainment company. The profits were generated by the company's core business, which was theme parks and movies. They knew parks and they knew movies, but despite his well-known affinity for architecture, neither Eisner nor his top deputies had been real estate developers. More than once in those early days at Disney, Rummell would unveil a new development idea for Eisner, only to hear: "Disney is not a real estate company, Peter. It is an entertainment company."

Finally, Rummell hit on a strategy to add appeal to his idea. To Eisner and other executives back at Disney headquarters in Los Angeles, he described the town in terms that resurrected Walt Disney's old dream of creating a real-life community as part of Disney World. Although Rummell had no intention of building anything like Epcot, he cast the concept of a town on Disney property as a logical adaptation of the founder's original vision. It was a storyline that anyone at Disney could admire, and it provided Rummell with enough intellectual cover to help overcome resistance to a residential development.

But what convinced Eisner to give a tentative green light to Rummell's plan was his concern over how the land might otherwise be used. "It really came down to the idea of use an asset or lose it," Eisner told us later. "Just to sit on the land didn't seem smart, and frankly I was loath to sell it off for development when it was pretty clear what kind of development would occur on the land. You remember, we had had some experience in the past when the company could not protect the land around Disneyland. I certainly did not want a repeat of that."

The preliminary okay raised a second hurdle. As a public company, Disney relied on annual earnings to keep its stock high and investors happy. More directly, the income of Eisner and other top executives was tied to stock performance. Building a town was not an earnings business. There can be good cash flow in the early years and tax benefits, but the real payoffs in land development are delayed until a project's final years. Simply put, Rummell's plan would bring nothing substantial to Disney's bottom line for many years, which meant it was an investment of dubious value to the number crunchers.

This posed a particular problem at Disney. Frank Wells, the company's president, had put in place a system that pitted the company's division managers against a strategic planning unit that acted as a check on their power. The strategic planners were drilled on the necessity of financial controls, and any project that could not be expected to churn out double-digit earnings fast was doomed. About one in ten proposals got a green light. Even then, a project would have to be justified continually to the finance and accounting division.

Disney's acquisition of the vacant land two decades earlier at bargain-basement prices was a plus. An internal memo by Gary Wilson, the chief financial officer, estimated the cost at less than $200 an acre. But the expense of making the site suitable for building a town necessitated selling the lots at premium prices if Disney was to turn a profit even down the road. Otherwise, the people in strategic planning would rather spend the $100 million or so on a safe bet—say, making another animated film. In fact, throughout the conceptual meetings on the new town, Charles Adams, as one of the town's developers, would remind his colleagues of the budget sword dangling above their heads. "Disney will make more money from one *Lion King* video than from all of this development," he would say.

The single way to cut through all the budget bluster was Eisner. If he got excited about the project, if he could be lured on board, it would be enough to keep the financial concerns at bay.

Rummell had never lost touch with Charles Fraser. Knowing that he needed a brilliant concept for his new town if he were to ensure Eisner's continued backing, he had flown to Hilton Head Island in late 1985 to talk with his old mentor. More than ever, Rummell needed to be a community developer, not just a real estate developer, as Fraser had advocated years earlier. A great community would appeal to Eisner and carry the added value required to make the project a financial success. And

Rummell knew that there was no better place to seek advice than from the old master himself—Fraser.

The solution did not come out of that single meeting. The real world rarely works in such dramatic fashion. In fact, the initial concept dreamed up by the mentor and his protégé would bear little resemblance to the final product. But the seeds for what would become one of the most talked-about planned communities in the world were planted that night at Café Europa.

In transforming Hilton Head Island into one of the country's premier resorts and permanent-resident communities, Fraser had had enormous natural advantages. The island has twelve miles of wide, hard-packed beaches, a temperate climate, and a charming history that he had packaged to enhance its appeal. The dilemma confronting the two friends that evening was how to generate similar allure and value in an area without the beaches or the history, on land that was nothing more than swamp and pasture. Even its brief history of cattle drives and citrus farming, though interesting, seemed insufficiently appealing.

"Both intellectually and from a sheer competitive point of view, we decided early on that the way to make some place special is not just to build a tougher Jack Nicklaus golf course or a bigger clubhouse or any of those things," Rummell said later. "We didn't have a beach, which was a stereotypical way to think about Florida. So how could we do something really interesting and carve out an important place that would be worth coming to and be something you couldn't find someplace else?"

Fraser suggested that they analyze the reasons, aside from location, that Hilton Head Island was so successful. One of them was its schools. When he opened the first residential portion of the community, he had started a private school. Over the years, it had been a major draw for residents. Also, Fraser's wife had started a Montessori school to satisfy the needs of families with younger children. Rummell believed that Florida's future growth meant augmenting the retiree population with younger people and families. Education went on the list as a cornerstone of the new community.

In addition, the residents of Hilton Head Island were especially active. There were miles of trails for walking, running, or biking, more than a dozen public golf courses, and better than a hundred tennis courts. The brainstorming on this subject ended not with a plan for a sports-oriented community but with an emphasis on wellness that would be attractive across generations. "Out of that first conversation, I figured out that learning and wellness were fundamental cornerstones for the place I had in mind," said Rummell.

The most talked-about location in residential development in the country at the time was a tiny new town in the Florida panhandle called Seaside. It had begun in 1981, when Robert S. Davis, who had belonged to the Socialist Workers Party during his undergraduate years at Antioch College and later worked for Miami developers active in federally subsidized housing, wanted to create an ideal community on eighty acres of land he had inherited on the Gulf of Mexico. He hired a husband-and-wife architecture team, Andres Duany and Elizabeth Plater-Zyberk, to come up with a master plan. Although Seaside was only a small resort on what was known as Florida's "Redneck Riviera," by the middle 1980s it was becoming an icon of the neotraditionalist movement in planning and architecture.

Neotraditionalism, which is sometimes called New Urbanism, was then still in its infancy, but its appeal was strong among planners and architects dissatisfied with the traditional suburbs sprawling shapelessly across the country. They felt those suburbs were out of sync with the quality of life sought by an increasing number of Americans, particularly the baby boomers.

Neotraditionalism represents the revival and reinterpretation of traditional town planning. It stresses building new towns in accordance with the planning and architectural schemes of old towns. Some of the towns that are its models are genuinely old, places of ageless grace like Savannah, Georgia, Charleston, South Carolina, and the Old Town section of Alexandria, Virginia. Others, like Scarsdale, New York, and Mariemont, Ohio, were built in the early part of the twentieth century. What they all have in common is a pedestrian-friendly design, architectural beauty, and something more difficult to define or quantify—a sense of place, which stood in sharp contrast to the bland interchangeability of most suburbs built after World War II.

While there are many variations on and interpretations of neotraditionalism, the principles are designed to foster a sense of community and an opportunity for social engagement. At the same time, these communities are intended to be environmentally sensitive, preserving green areas and decreasing dependence on automobiles. Without too much oversimplification, the concept can be boiled down to three key ideas.

First, density is good. Where a typical modern suburb will have one to two houses per acre and is laid out entirely for the convenience of cars, neotraditionalism strives for a density of five or six dwellings per acre. And they are not all detached homes; there is a mixture of housing styles—single-family homes, town houses, apartments, and "granny flats" above garages.

Second, public space is better than private space. In a typical suburb, the wide sweeping streets are just about the only public space. The rest is devoted to private lawns, deep setbacks from the street, and spacious backyards. Neotraditionalists believe that people should get out of their backyards and onto their front porches, where they will have a better chance of interacting with neighbors. So those planners shrink the size of the lots and use the extra space to create parks, village greens, and other outdoor public spaces where people can gather and socialize. This reduction has another salutary effect—almost everyone lives within walking distance of the prerequisite town center.

Finally, controls breed cohesiveness. In most suburbs and subdivisions, people are free to indulge their personal tastes in building a house or planting a yard. Some controls may exist in some communities, but by and large the emphasis is on freedom of choice. Even in a planned community like Reston, Virginia, homeowners have considerable freedom when it comes to the style of their homes. The neotraditionalists strive to create harmonious streetscapes by imposing strict design controls that regulate everything from the basic house design to the types of plants in the yards. Gables, dormers, and porches on every structure may seem excessive, but the planners believe that these elaborate devices foster a sense of community and establish the clear sense of place missing in most suburbs.

The cohesiveness of a neotraditional community should not be confused with the uniformity of a Levittown, the prototypical postwar suburb built on New York's Long Island and replicated in degree outside Philadelphia. In that first suburb, only one house type was offered in each neighborhood, and so there were bleak rows of the same three-bedroom "rancher" in one section and rows of two-story "colonials" in another. Half a century later, developers had learned to offer variety, even within the controls mandated by neotraditionalism. Nowhere is that variety more evident than in Seaside.

Visitors to the small community of Seaside in western Florida discover a network of narrow streets laid out in a strict grid pattern and surfaced with reddish concrete paving blocks, the contemporary equivalent of cobblestones. Most of the community's streets are only eighteen feet wide, which means that motorists must drive slowly over the bumpy surface, and that makes them all the more enticing for pedestrians and bicyclists. Lots for homes are small, with a density level of about five units per acre after public buildings are counted. Public buildings cluster around small squares, and everyone can walk easily to the town center. Property owners are free to select their own architectural style, though it must meet certain basic criteria and be approved by a community board.

Duany and Plater-Zyberk took a minimalist approach to architectural control, providing a simple aesthetic and construction code governing specific building forms, architectural guidelines, and materials. The document regulates roof pitch, window types, roof overhangs, setbacks, porches, and fences. Its basic requirement is that buildings reflect the character of the region, which means wood construction, porches, and picket fences. The strategy allows for wide variations in design within a cohesive framework that knits the houses into a unified whole. As a result, many of the 240 or so homes there today are fetchingly whimsical and idiosyncratic—so much so that when *The Truman Show* was released in the summer of 1998 against the backdrop of Seaside, many people thought the town was a movie set, not real.

Fraser had pioneered some of the same ideas in Harbour Town, relying on vernacular architecture and tight controls. But while he liked elements of Seaside, he was dismissive of it as a model for new urban development for Americans who have to go to work every day. It was a niche market, a place where affluent people built second homes and where the necessities of a real town, like a hardware store or a supermarket, were absent.

"The scale of Seaside was nothing like what Peter was planning," Fraser said later. "Seaside is a wonderfully successful horizontal community, with the homes serving as hotel rooms. Even today, only about twenty families live there year-round. It's a beachfront resort catering to one-week visitors from Atlanta and Birmingham and other places."

Nonetheless, Fraser and Rummell talked through Seaside's basic elements that night in 1985, and Fraser occasionally referred to its principles in later memos that he prepared for Rummell and his team at Disney Development. The neotraditionalist's sense of small-town design was added to the list that already included learning and wellness to create cornerstones number three and four: place and community. Where Walt Disney's dream of Epcot had looked toward the future for salvation, the plan for this new town was looking back to the future for its success. The heirs to Disney's empire were designing the place where Walt had wished he'd grown up.

As Rummell and Fraser kicked around the ideas that night and in later conversations, they decided the best model for their new community was a university town. The educational institution would be front and center in the new community, with the sense of place and intellectual livelihood flowing out from it. The models that they talked about in the earliest days were places like Chapel Hill, North Carolina, where Rummell had been an undergraduate at the University of North Carolina; State College, Pennsylvania; and Williamstown, Massachusetts, the home of Williams College.

In the months after the meeting with Fraser, Rummell's staff organized a series of informal focus groups to generate ideas about what potential residents would like to see in a new town. Rummell also solicited reports from a handful of consultants on various aspects of the project, from determining the mixture of commercial and residential space to ways to use architecture and employ quality builders to overcome their concerns about the generally low building standards in central Florida.

Fraser analyzed the results for Rummell, producing a twenty-six-page confidential report that would prove both useful and prescient. In it, he stressed several important, concrete elements: the need for a town center, uniform architectural standards to build a sense of place and unique identity for the town, and even a volunteer center to engage residents in the community. Promoting the volunteer center and active community involvement, Fraser wrote, would have the added benefit of "stopping at the door the self-indulgent who would otherwise expect Disney to pamper them at Disney's expense until they die at age 99, 35 years after a home purchase." But the developer took the social-engineering promise of the town a step further, describing it as a means of promoting Disney's image as "the Grand Design Creator." He added, "Disney should openly state its goal of creating a community where residents care about their neighbors, to create the matrix of a superior Disney American Home Town, an urban area that does not disappoint its residents."

A few months later, Rummell emphasized the benefits for the Disney Company when he wrote a memo to Eisner in which he summarized his vision for the new town. Indeed, he went so far as to compare the community to another theme park, writing: "Our fourth park will be a living laboratory for the American Town. It will be a laboratory in the sense that it will be experimental in many aspects, from the way residents are provided public services to the infrastructure that serves it. We will probably try some things that don't work. But I promise we will also develop some ideas that will be copied in many other places in years to come. And it will be developed carefully enough that it will become a model for new town development everywhere. And, along the way, further enhance the Walt Disney Company reputation for inspiration and innovation."

The memo makes clear that many of the physical concepts that would be embodied in the town were already in Rummell's mind. He wrote about walking paths and distinct neighborhoods. Though he described fiber optics and computerized "smart houses," Rummell said he wanted to build a place that was closer to Main Street than Future World. "Nothing here [will be] different just for the sake of being different, but designed to be enduring and comfortable," he wrote. "Ralph Lauren has become a symbol of American elegance for this very reason. So, too, we will focus on that which is wonderful and livable and will stand the test of time."

A hallmark of the new town, Rummell continued, would be an adult educational institution, the equivalent of a university located within the confines of the community. The idea of the educational institution caught Eisner's fancy, and he and Rummell began to discuss the nature of the institution. From those conversations the concept emerged eventually for the Disney Institute. Unlike the theme parks, the institute would be geared strictly to adults. It would offer social activities and cultural and intellectual programs. Along with classes in things like gourmet cooking and television production, there would be lectures by famous authors and mini-courses taught by big-name academics. Given Disney's financial resources and occasional intellectual aspirations, the company might have considered creating a truly important cultural or educational institution, something like the Rockefeller family's financing of the University of Chicago and Rockefeller University or Eastman Kodak's creation of a serious music conservatory. Instead, the company opted for something more directly related to its entertainment mission, something that would appeal to middle-class Americans and keep adults coming to Disney after their children had grown too old for Disney World. Eisner was most excited about the prospect for keeping these adults within the company's orbit. Rummell saw the institute, with its collegelike campus, as a way to solidify his new town's place among the strategic planners and give the community itself a focus. Along with attracting outsiders, the institute could be used to offer continuing education to the adults in the community, an attraction expected to appeal to the persistent need of baby boomers to reinvent themselves.

With a small preliminary budget, Rummell had solicited master plans from three architectural firms. The three were very different from one another. An obvious choice was Duany and Plater-Zyberk, who had their headquarters in Miami. The second was Robert A. M. Stern, a respected New York architect known for the strong American vernacular designs of his Shingle-style cottages and his profound attention to detail. As a plus, Stern also was friends with Eisner. The final choice in that early going was Charles Gwathmey, a principal in the New York firm of Gwathmey Siegel and Associates. In contrast to Duany, Plater-Zyberk, and Stern, Gwathmey was an unreconstructed International Style architect who had made his reputation by designing what *The New York Times* described as "sumptuous, meticulously wrought modernist grandeur for the rich and famous," though he had also received a recent commission for an addition to the Solomon R. Guggenheim Museum in New York City.

Within the company, the project was known simply as "Disney's New Town." Although the overall concept was still under discussion, the planners were given some basic building blocks to shuffle around the drawing board. There needed to be a campus for the Disney Institute and a place for a large hospital. Residential lots would be small, and in keeping with neotraditional doctrine, there would be a mix of houses and apartments for a population of twenty thousand or so, a business district in the town center, and an office park and shopping mall away from the center. The parcel south of Interstate 4 was roughly ten thousand acres and could have accommodated a bigger town, but using all of the land was deemed too expensive because of the costs of reclaiming wetlands and mitigating the environmental impact.

The plans were presented to Rummell and other Disney executives in New York in late December 1987. Predictably, the Duany–Plater-Zyberk plan was a pumped-up version of Seaside, with the familiar narrow streets laid out on a tight grid that spread out from the small town center. The concept struck some involved in the process as too doctrinaire. Rummell wanted to draw on the principles of neotraditionalism, but he wanted to make some exceptions. For instance, there would have to be enough broad, sweeping streets to carry the substantial amount of traffic expected to be drawn to the town center and the Disney Institute, and Rummell wanted to incorporate a large shopping center somewhere within the community; both elements fell outside the strict definition of neotraditional. In addition, the Duany–Plater-Zyberk plan covered an area three times the size of the town site. "Duany made some assumptions about what we should be doing with the other land that were uninformed and confusing," Rummell said later. Stern's schematic plan was far less rigid than that of Duany and Plater-Zyberk, but it didn't have enough commercial space to satisfy Rummell. As for Gwathmey and his partner, Robert Siegel, their concept did not reflect the vernacular American architecture that Rummell and his executives envisioned. "They followed the rules of the competition (unlike Duany), but were very true to their architectural philosophy, even in land planning, and produced something more angular and contemporary than we were comfortable with," said Rummell.

The result was that the Disney team was left without a single master plan. Stern, who was already designing two projects for the company at Disney World—the casting center and a hotel called the Yacht and Beach Club Resorts—recalled what happened after the presentations: "In the Disney way, they said, 'We like everything you've all done. Can't you work together?' They all went back to Florida and we all spent the time between Christmas and New Year's, when all architects are supposed to be relaxing, working in Charles Gwathmey's office melding all this stuff together to create a new plan. We came up with something and submitted it to them and then the thing stopped."

In early 1988, the project stalled. Rummell's development team was finishing up plans for Disney–MGM Studios, the third theme park at Disney World, which was scheduled to open in 1989. They were also working on plans for a new theme park outside Paris, which would be called Euro Disney. Not until 1990, with these two projects moving ahead, did Rummell return to the town idea. But he still wasn't happy with the architectural plans for it, so he added three more firms to the stew. One was Charles Moore, a leading figure in architecture and architectural education for thirty years, whose postmodern designs for buildings like the festive Piazza d'Italia in New Orleans reflected his penchant for whimsy and eclecticism. Moore's Sea Ranch, clusters of redwood-clad houses at a vacation resort on the coast of California, had served as a prototype for many new towns across the country. Also on the second list was Jacquelin Robertson, a former dean of the University of Virginia's architecture school and onetime New York City planning commissioner. He was known as a planner who emphasized individual neighborhoods, small-scale buildings, and open space. And the third new entrant was Skidmore, Owings & Merrill, the nation's largest architectural company. SOM, as the firm was known, had the resources to execute a plan, but there were questions in some minds about whether it was too staid to come up with a compelling new vision. Along the way, Duany and Plater-Zyberk dropped out of the running.

For a time after the new plans came in, Rummell was leaning toward a design produced by SOM, which provided a hefty amount of commercial space, including a two-million-square-foot shopping mall. The chances are that Eisner would have rejected the plan anyway, but it did not get that far because of the presence of two experienced community developers on Rummell's staff.

Earlier in 1990, as Rummell started to gear up again for the new town, he had hired two community developers, Charles Adams and Don Killoren, to beef up his staff. Killoren, a developer and homebuilder from Palm Beach, was especially strong about his feelings that the SOM plan was too urban, that the extensive commercial and office buildings would overwhelm the small-town atmosphere. He and Adams fought hard to convince Rummell to jettison SOM and work with some of the other designs. Rummell finally agreed, and he asked Stern, Robertson, and Gwathmey to collaborate on a master plan for the new town. When Gwathmey dropped out, Stern and Robertson were left as the new team for the new town. Both were graduates of Yale's architecture school and friends who ran in similar social circles in New York City, including having summer homes in East Hampton. They also were traditionalists when it came to architecture, and had once joined with Moore to write essays that took issue with the modernist stance of five fellow architects, a group that included Gwathmey.

In early 1991, although the Stern-Robertson plan was far from finalized, the decision was made to announce the new-town project to the public. Before that could happen, the new town needed a name. The development team had been kicking around dozens of names, but nothing seemed to click. Some people liked Oak Tree. Others favored Green Meadows. But nobody liked any of them much.

One day Eisner and his wife, Jane, dropped by the team's offices in a nondescript building off the Disney property, near International Drive in Orlando. Eisner asked whether a name had been selected and was told it had not. However, "Celebration Gardens" had been listed as a potential name for the shopping mall.

"I think it's a better name for the town," replied Eisner, with his wife nodding her agreement. It was just a passing remark, but it came from the company's chief executive and was endorsed by his wife. That was enough for the development team.

"We were so happy to find a name that he actually liked that we latched on to it," said Killoren, although the decision was later made to chop off the final word and just call the town Celebration.

The Disney planning team had looked at some of the thriving old cities in the South and seen that each had a rich history that provided a strong sense of community. Being Disney, their first instinct was to make up one for Celebration, too. In a way, this was predictable. One of the most prized divisions of the company is Walt Disney Imagineering, the creative end of the corporate structure. "Imagineering" is the company's practice of combining technological know-how with creative ideas to develop new rides, services, and even places. As a nod to their creative side, Imagineering is the only staff exempted from the company's appearance and dress-code rules—those prohibiting facial hair on men, flashy jewelry, and blue jeans. And a key part of the Imagineering process is developing what is called a "backstory" for the product, the mythological history that provides a focus as the development proceeds.

Concocting a backstory for a town did not seem too different from concocting one for a new ride. But some of the ideas were ripe. At one point, the Imagineers suggested the tale of a city rising from the ashes of General Sherman's march across the South, though the fact that he never set foot in Florida did not seem to matter. In the end, the more pragmatic development people recognized that the town would not be a ride or a movie, but a real place. "We decided that it might not look good down the road," recalled Rummell.

Probably a smart move, because when the developers of Riverside, Georgia, did just that—concoct a colorful past, complete with fictitious tintypes and quotations from early residents—it was cause for great fun in the press.

On April 29, 1991, Disney Development Company unveiled plans for Celebration, which it described as a futuristic city that would ultimately have twenty thousand inhabitants in four villages. There would be twenty miles of walkways and bike trails, a variety of architectural styles and prices among the houses, and a fiber-optic computer network through which homeowners could do neat things, like select a movie without physically going to the video store. There would be a town center—its stores to open the day the first resident moved in—and eventually a two-million-square-foot shopping mall, the largest open-air mall in central Florida and an attraction expected to draw ten million people a year. The centerpiece of the town would be the Disney Institute, which would house academies teaching classes on a wide range of subjects in a campuslike setting. The campus would include a performing arts center, fitness spa, hotels, and time-share units. "We're aiming at a learning resort and community of tomorrow that will focus on entertainment, innovation, and enrichment," Todd Mansfield, the development company vice president, told the press that day.

Despite the announcement, there was still a considerable amount of planning to be done. The company had just started its negotiations over the necessary approvals with the Osceola County planning officials, a touchy situation that would take two years to finalize. Indeed, the company seemed to be making a commitment to spending a large sum without a fully realized plan. And some aspects of the original plan, like the huge shopping center, contradicted the notion of creating the small-town atmosphere critical to any neotraditional community. The planned shopping mall represented Disney's inability to overcome its commercial instincts and raised questions about whether the nostalgic vision of small-town America might someday be overwhelmed by the less appealing image of mall-town America.

By early 1992, Stern and Robertson had refined the community's master plan. The basic elements of the community remained unchanged. The emphasis would be on education and health, and the town retained a neotraditional feel. But the plan violated some of that movement's principles, too. For instance, the shopping center remained, though it was delayed until the later phases of development. There were also some curvilinear streets and a couple of cul de sacs, both prohibited in strict neotraditional communities, where streets are on a grid. Charles Fraser, who had remained involved as a consultant, liked the plan because it marked a smart evolution of neotraditional thought. He dubbed it "post-neotraditional."

New towns are not news. Every place in the United States was new at some point in the not-too-distant past, and there is a long and healthy tradition of creating new towns and cities in this country. Celebration needs to be viewed on the evolutionary scale of planned communities that really began in 1947, when ground was broken for the first of the 17,447 houses that became Levittown on New York's Long Island. Other planned communities followed through the 1960s and early 1970s, and many of them, such as Irvine, California, Reston, Virginia, and Columbia, Maryland, were new cities and towns. They offered parklike settings and central business districts. Columbia, built on fourteen thousand acres of farmland by developer James Rouse, was the most successful of those new towns. It had nine village centers, seventy-eight miles of foot and bike paths, three lakes, and 84,000 residents by the mid-nineties. Still, Columbia, Reston, and the other new towns developed in that period remain oriented to the automobile because of their parklike settings. And in fact, most of the country's postwar growth occurred in traditional suburbs, not new towns.

Levittown was built to answer basic housing needs for thousands of people who could not find space in an America that had built little housing since the stock market crash of 1929. But the suburban developments that followed were fueled largely by white flight from crowded conditions in the nation's cities, a pattern that continued unabated for four decades. The 1990 census showed that 46.2 percent of the United States' population lived in suburbs, but by then the dream had soured for many people.

In many cases, the suburbs had turned out to be isolating and devoid of any sense of community. Neighborhoods were purposely shut off from each other and sequestered from commercial and office districts in a conscious effort to sell privacy and security. The result was the creation of separate "pods" that forced the construction of sweeping, fast-moving streets because residents depended on cars for the simplest trips to shop, work, or visit friends. The distance between houses and the streets themselves became barriers to real community and fostered the sense of isolation and disconnection that has infected American suburbs. Also, with more dual-income families, both husband and wife found themselves far from home and children while they were at work. In direct response to this parental absence, those children spent more time in front of the television, prowling the local mall, or getting into trouble with the law. Sociologists and urban planners blamed the suburbs for all manner of social ills, from the dysfunctional family to bad architecture.

We had seen some of this firsthand in Westport. Even while our two younger children were still of an age to be entertained by turning over rocks and examining the treasures to be found in the dirt, we became worried about joining the brigade of parent chauffeurs: Children in the suburbs, at least in our suburb, with its narrow roads and absence of sidewalks, were totally dependent on adults for all their activities away from home.

These concerns are not new. Thirty years earlier, Lewis Mumford lamented that the end product of postwar development "is an encapsulated life, spent more and more either in a motor car or within the cabin of darkness before a television set." He saw the suburbs as a symptom of the disintegration of civil life itself.

By the early 1990s, however, the reaction of Americans was new. Just as their middle-class parents had fled the nation's cities a generation earlier, Americans were beginning a new kind of migration, away from the old suburb. Some of these refugees from ranch homes on an acre of grass were returning to the cities, bringing gentrification to the decaying old neighborhoods their own parents had fled. Others were locking themselves behind the gates of new suburbs, a retreat that promised no relief from the anonymity of suburban life. Indeed, as this concept of fortress America spread across the country, it seemed destined to increase the polarization of society.

In addition, a growing number of people were seeking to trade their suburbs for small towns and even rural counties, where they might discover a sense of community and an alternative to the social fragmentation suburbs had seemed to encourage. The migration, fueled by a deep dissatisfaction with those traditional suburbs, was abetted by advances in technology that allowed more and more people to work out of their homes or shift businesses far from population centers. Suddenly the suburbs were no longer the address of choice for middle-class Americans.

The neotraditional movement in architecture and planning sprang up in response to this search for an alternative to traditional suburbs. These planners, who might better be called "traditionalists," turned back to look at what made America's small towns thrive and tried to adapt those concepts to new towns that were quite unlike Irvine or Columbia. The key to this new movement was the recognition that neighborhoods are the central building blocks of a strong community. Rather than separate "pods," as in traditional suburbs, or parklike neighborhoods, as in Reston and Columbia, these building blocks must be arranged in a fashion that allows the community to flow, with grace, charm, utility, and elegance, the traditionalists argued. Neighborhoods need to be close enough to the commercial district that residents can walk to the shops, and they need to be linked by pedestrian-friendly sidewalks. This means higher density, which translates into houses that are built on smaller lots and a mixture of housing types, such as apartments next door to single-family homes. In turn, the increased density promotes social interaction. The density also means streets can be narrower, straighter, and shaded by trees, which slows down traffic and creates an environment that is conducive to walking and bicycling.

These concepts were well known and had been implemented in Seaside and other communities by the time Disney developed the final outlines for Celebration in 1992. While the design owed a good deal to Seaside and its brethren, Stern is a connoisseur of architectural history who reached much deeper into America's past for many of the ideas incorporated in the plan for Celebration. And, in the end, the company's master plan was a hybrid that recognized the marketing appeal of small towns and neotraditional motifs yet refused to reject commercial development.

"As residents of a new country, Americans pioneered the design of towns," Stern explained to us. "Whereas European or Asian towns evolved naturally, what America had to do was lay out and fill in towns very quickly. But we also had to design our environments differently from Europeans, because we have no aristocratic hierarchy and no rigid code of social mores. As a result, we had to develop new rules for organizing our public space, and this tradition really began in the nineteenth century with places like Llewellyn Park, in New Jersey, and Riverside, in Illinois."

Indeed, in the 1850s and 1860s, curving roads tucked into picturesque landscapes emerged as central components of suburban planning in the United States and in contrast to the democratic grids of the cities. In 1853, architect Alexander Davis laid out Llewellyn Park in the Watchung Mountains of West Orange, New Jersey, creating a planned town highlighted by sweeping streets and a pastoral setting. In 1868, Frederick Law Olmsted, the founding father of American landscape architecture and the cocreator of New York City's Central Park, designed Riverside, which some people describe as the first modern planned community in America, but which is more accurately seen as the first large planned American suburb.

Olmsted was hired by a group of businessmen, who formed the Riverside Improvement Company, to build the new town on a swath of prairie about ten miles southwest of the bustling city of Chicago. On the banks of the Des Plaines River, Olmsted created a village that blended urban and rural settings and included a mixture of curved roads, public squares, geometrically designed parks in every neighborhood, and spacious front yards with a profusion of flowers and shrubs. In rejecting straight streets, Olmsted argued that they suggested an "eagerness to press forward, without looking to the right hand or to the left." Curved streets, he suggested, translated into "leisure, contemplativeness, and happy tranquillity." Olmsted also imposed certain rules on Riverside's inhabitants, dictating the amount of setback from the street for each house in an era long before zoning regulations, establishing a minimum house size, and requiring everyone to plant and maintain a front yard. Even before the first residents moved in, the Riverside company was at work building a town center made up of shops, small businesses, and a hotel.

The seeds of the contemporary suburb can be seen in both the designs of Llewellyn Park and Riverside and the motivation for their creation. The city's grid plan was replaced by sweeping roads in pastoral settings to create havens for those lucky enough to escape the bustling cities. In his own writings on Riverside, Olmsted described it as a reaction to the desire of city dwellers to find residential settings of more natural beauty and quiet. Olmsted noted that the migration out of the cities to the new towns was spurred primarily by the "more intelligent and more fortunate classes."

In the century between the creation of Riverside and the planning for Celebration, the suburb had changed considerably from Olmsted's original conception. Public spaces and parks had given way to ever-bigger private yards, and the town center was replaced by strip malls and shopping centers. Celebration represented an attempt to resurrect the best qualities of Riverside and adapt them to contemporary times.

"Olmsted employed the highest levels of civil engineering, real estate savvy, and architectural controls to create something that everyone recognizes to this day is very special and lasting," explained Stern. "The Disney company is not doing anything very different in Celebration."

Indeed, there were many parallels between Riverside and Celebration, though Stern, who by 1992 had joined the board of directors of the Disney company, hoped that the developer would not suffer the same fate—the Riverside Improvement Company eventually went bankrupt. In its final plan, downtown Celebration was situated in a semicircle to embrace the lake, which was created as part of the water-management system, in much the same way Olmsted had controlled the flooding of the Des Plaines River to build Riverside. But the water-management system in Celebration would be far more sophisticated than anything Olmsted could have imagined—it would use an elaborate system of underground pipes to return runoff water from the lake to the higher end of the property so that it could filter through the ground water a second time before going into wetlands. The Disney Institute would be placed directly adjacent to the town center. Houses would be close together and clustered in four villages, three of which would wrap around championship golf courses. Parks, squares, and wide grassy medians were designed into every neighborhood, and controls were planned for such key design elements as house color, setback from the sidewalks, and plantings. But where Olmsted insisted on large front yards, Stern and Robertson pushed the houses to the front of small lots.

There were other differences from Riverside. The invention of the automobile had transformed those hallmark curvilinear streets in Riverside from the leisurely byways of the nineteenth century into mini-autobahns. So most of Celebration was laid out in a modified grid, with narrow streets and frequent intersections to slow traffic and accommodate pedestrians. However, Stern and Robertson defied the neotraditional doctrine by including a handful of sweeping, curving main arteries, created to carry traffic to and from downtown. The plan also diverged from neotraditionalism by including a huge shopping mall, though it was situated well away from the town center. The design was truly a hybrid, with one foot in the nineteenth century and one foot in contemporary neotraditionalism.

Once the master plan was in place, the next step was commissioning architects to design the houses, public buildings, and background buildings for downtown. In the end, some of the biggest names in architecture were chosen for the high-profile public buildings. Philip Johnson was commissioned to design Town Hall, and Michael Graves was hired to design the post office. The bank was placed in the hands of Robert Venturi and Denise Scott Brown, and the movie house, obviously a key component of any Disney project, went to Cesar Pelli. The sales office, to be known as the preview center, was designed by Charles Moore, who died in December 1993, before it was built. Helmut Jahn defeated Stern in the competition to design the shopping mall, and Stern got the nod for the health center.

Each of the architects was told that he would have to adhere to the design controls developed by Stern, Robertson, and the rest of the Disney team, which led to some funny exchanges. When Stern invited Johnson to design Town Hall, the aging architect objected to the requirements for a classical building. "I haven't done classical since the 1960s," he protested, to which Stern replied, "Philip, have you forgotten how?" Likewise, Pelli said he wanted to create a modern movie theater, and Stern said that was fine, as long as the architect understood that modern ended with the 1930s as far as Celebration's design was concerned.

Eisner liked the roster of architects. Just as he had wanted buildings at Disney parks to contribute to the dialogue on architecture, he saw the new town as a way for the company to leave its mark on planning. "This is a design contribution to American architecture that the Disney Company is making," he told the executives and consultants after viewing the Stern-Robertson plan. "We've got to do it in a fashion that brings honor to the company. Don't just make it a real estate subdivision. Anybody can do a subdivision. The Disney Company will not do real estate subdivisions." Eisner sounded a similar theme later in an interview with us when he said, "Once you decide to do something, you want to do it in an excellent way. The least expensive part of building a building is what the architects draw on a piece of paper. It's the bricks and mortar that are the most expensive. Why not go to the best talent in the world to create something beautiful? It was simply trying to do it well."

The compelling vision behind building the new town, according to Eisner, Stern, and others who were involved in the process, was to demonstrate on a large scale, and under the bright lights of public scrutiny, that American urbanism was alive. They felt that the time was right—there was an architectural movement afoot, people were searching for a better place to live—to orchestrate a project that demonstrated how a company with Disney's resources and access to top-drawer architects and planners could execute a contemporary Riverside. "This is a great company, with a great sense of public obligation," said Stern. "Everybody knew the world would look at this and debate it. Every effort was made to make it rock solid."

Hence, another important reason for choosing top-quality architects was that the town's public buildings, which included normally private ones like the bank and movie house, would give a focus to the entire project. "Every city in America is judged by its downtown," said Stern, who was appointed dean of Yale's architecture school in 1998. "If you have a crappy downtown, an empty downtown, no matter how much activity you have in your neighborhoods and suburbs, you are perceived as a crappy place. Nobody understands that better than the Disney Company."

One of the company's riskiest innovations had been the decision that the Celebration town center would be ready for business the day the first residents moved into town. Normally a developer waits until there is a critical mass of residents to begin work on the commercial buildings to serve them. Yet Rummell and his Disney counterparts felt the vitality of a town center would help put the place on the map and attract visitors and potential residents. The danger was not only that there would not be enough residents to support the businesses but also that the scarcity of residents would make it hard to attract the high-end, non-chain stores that Disney wanted to make the downtown as special as the architecture of its public buildings.

"We knew it would take years to have enough homes to support the retail businesses, but we felt it was necessary as an amenity for the residents right from the start," Killoren explained. Yet the initial mix of stores was aimed not at creating a rock upon which to build community life but at attracting enough tourists to keep the stores open until Celebration grew up enough to support a real downtown, one for the residents.

Downtown was where Disney was spending most of its money. The roads, sewers, and other infrastructure would be financed with bonds and paid off over time by people who bought the land. Likewise, individuals would be putting up the money to build the houses every time they signed a mortgage. But the up-front money for the eighteen-acre downtown was coming directly out of Disney's corporate pocket, and the developers were determined to make it work.

The company found plenty of eager tenants for its commercial space. The golden touch of Disney was well known in central Florida, and numerous business owners wanted to cash in on Disney's new town. As a result of the demand, Disney was able to sift through applications from tenants and select the medley of businesses that they felt would turn downtown into a tourist draw and still provide some essentials for residents. Also as a result of that demand, tenants received none of the deep rent discounts normally associated with new developments. Nonetheless, several shop owners told us that they felt compelled to open a store in Celebration to have a foot in the door when the town grew.

Not only did they not get any discounts, but the new business owners had to agree to the sorts of restrictions that would be imposed on home-owners. For instance, businesses were forbidden to display any goods on the sidewalk in front of their stores without filing a written plan with the company and receiving permission. "My last three leases had been a handshake and two pages long," explained Thomas Dunn, the owner of a high-end furniture and interior design shop in Celebration. "This is my lease for Celebration," he added, holding up a thick document of eighty-plus pages. "The table of contents is six pages long. My lawyer said, 'Well, I have never seen such a one-sided lease in my life, but we didn't expect anything else, did we?' But I didn't have a problem with it. There was nothing surprising."

As with everything else, Disney approached the downtown develop-ment—from the combination of retail goods to lease restrictions cover-ing everything from window displays to hours—with great care and deliberation. Disney prohibited chain stores, in part to lend the town center a unique feel and in part to avoid repetition down the road when the shopping mall opened. In addition to Dunn's home-furnishings store, there was to be an antiques-and-reproductions shop, a corner gro-cery store, a bakery, three clothing stores, a fancy perfume shop, an up-scale kitchen store, a clothing-and-fly-fishing store, and a combination bookstore–gift shop. Residents would later complain about the absence of some basic stores, like a hardware store, a hair salon, a larger super-market, and a video store. But Disney's officials would counter that they had brought in the best mix possible until the town got bigger.

While the design and tenant mix for the town center was being de-cided, work on determining what the houses would look like was also under way. Houses and apartments in successful communities across the country have their own distinctive character, and everyone involved real-ized that Celebration would need to have its own architectural style, too.

"We wanted a variety of housing types, but we didn't want the selec-tion to be completely random," Rummell explained later. "There was a philosophical decision that we wanted to mix neighborhoods as much as we could in terms of densities and price point. Unlike [planners of] more sterile developments, we were pretty aggressive about wanting to put apartments next to single-family homes. It is more characteristic of the way organic towns tended to grow up. But it was kind of a risk from a development standpoint, because you couldn't be sure about the value of the single-family homes next to apartments."

Walt Disney modeled Main Street, U.S.A., in the Magic Kingdom after a Missouri town that never existed. In much the same vein, Celebration's planners created a mythical town in New Jersey and set it in the early 1940s as part of the intellectual exercise of coming up with the housing types for the new community. Stern and Robertson believed that American small towns lost their vitality after World War II, so modernism was forbidden. Because the two lead planners both had weekend homes in East Hampton, the Long Island resort town, and admired its design, Stern and Robertson also examined that enclave of privilege. "East Hampton seemed to Robert and me to have almost all of the touchstones of early American urbanism in its earliest phases, and yet every practical issue was addressed in the plan," Robertson told an architectural publication. The idea was not to re-create an existing town but to examine the manner in which a town grows organically, the types of buildings and houses that emerge, and their relationships to one another and to the people in the town. The architecture of Celebration would not be drawn from this mythical town, or from East Hampton, but the developers used both as a model for examining the manner in which a town evolves over the decades.

As the discussion progressed, the focus sharpened. Planners would restrict the architectural styles to the pre-1940s. Then they narrowed it further, to types of houses built in the Southeast before the 1940s. While he had no quarrel with the direction of the discussion, the artifice was too abstract for Charles Fraser. "You can't deal with styles as words," he insisted at one meeting in late 1991. "You must deal with them as pictures and visual references."

So Fraser and Charles Adams went to the headquarters of that arbiter of Southern taste for generations, *Southern Living* magazine. They scoured its voluminous files for photographs of quintessential Southern homes and came away with nearly three hundred examples, from simple coastal homes in Florida to antebellum plantations in Louisiana. Fraser got the photos blown up and plastered them across all four walls of a meeting room in Orlando where the development division had its offices at the time. When Stern, Robertson, Rummell, and the others in-volved in the project came into the room, the photo spread had a stun-ning impact. "Suddenly everybody had a much better idea of what we had been talking about for weeks," Fraser said.

Charles Fraser would receive little public credit for his role in help-ing to plan Celebration, but the touches that he brought to the project were invaluable. Likewise, Fraser found sustenance in his consulting jobs with Disney Development at a time when he needed it most. In the midst of the conceptual work on Celebration, Fraser was diagnosed with lymphoma cancer. Some of the alumni of his company had begun to raise money to put a bronze statue of Fraser in his beloved Harbour Town. Rummell had another idea.

"Peter simply increased the volume of requests for my participation in Celebration," said Fraser, whose cancer has been in remission for sev-eral years. "Peter understood that my mind was working at full throttle and that this would be a wonderful project for me to work on."

Fraser's idea of drawing on real towns and cities was so appealing that in the summer of 1992 a young architect who had been hired as an intern was given the pleasant task of taking more photographs. Joseph Barnes had master's degrees in architecture from Princeton University and the University of Virginia. For that entire summer, his sole job was to drive across the southeastern United States and take photographs of what worked best and had withstood the test of time, not only in hous-ing but in retail, too. He even went so far occasionally as to pull out his tape measure and measure things like the distance from a porch to the sidewalk in a search for the optimum relationship between passersby and porch sitters.

"I'd just get in a car and drive and go for three or four days at a time to do research," said Barnes. "I went to Savannah, and Charleston and Mount Pleasant, South Carolina; Tampa, Key West, Coral Gables; and Alexandria, Virginia. I spent a lot of time in Natchez, Mississippi, and in the Garden District of New Orleans. I went to Princeton, New Jersey, to see how they did their retail. We looked at Williamsburg, Virginia, for how they did Merchant Square and how they dealt with the dual-sided parking on Duke of Gloucester Street. In Winter Park, which is next to Orlando, there are great neighborhoods that were developed in the 1920s and 1930s.

"It was funny. There I was with my camera and rental car, and no one was suspicious. They would act as if, 'Of course you want to photograph our street and my house.' They had a sense of pride about their neighborhoods. They had a sense of belonging to the place. And it was in these places that people would invite me in. They'd show me their backyards. They'd tell me the history of their house, who had lived there in the past."

Indeed, some of the very town centers that were emptied in the rush to the suburbs, like Savannah and Charleston, were now popular models for developers like Disney who sought to create the next great place to live. What Barnes and his colleagues were trying to do, with photographs and models and tape measures, was map the genetic code of old neighborhoods that worked. If Disney was looking back to the future in Celebration, so was much of the rest of the country.

Nowhere was that backward vision more evident than in the *Celebration Pattern Book,* which was assembled to serve as the design bible for the town. In the past, pattern books contained the design principles that represented the consensus among builders, architects, planners, and homebuyers about the style and form of good neighborhoods and houses. The details for designing houses were set out clearly, with illustrations for elements like porches and windows. By the turn of the century, widely dispersed builders used some of the books, such as Asher Benjamin's *The American Builder's Companion,* as handbooks for sophisticated details, like staircases and cornices. Pattern books disappeared gradually after World War II, and so did the consensus about what constituted a good house and a good neighborhood.

Using the photographs and measurements that Barnes had assembled from thirty Southern towns and cities, the Celebration developers created a contemporary pattern book to provide the town's builders with strict interpretations of the design and planning principles required to create a cohesive community. One of the principal authors, Raymond Gindroz, a Pittsburgh architect, described the details contained in the book as "absolutely critical in creating the quality of the public space." But the *Celebration Pattern Book* was fun to read, too, with its pages and pages of line drawings and details. In fact, Barnes received hundreds of requests for copies of a book that had come into being to serve as just a simple manual.

The first step was to select the styles for the town's houses. Barnes had collected photographs and data on about twenty different architectural styles, which was too many for a single town. The debate involved in winnowing the list to a manageable number took several weeks. Stern and Robertson argued strongly for six styles, while Fraser wanted only three or four. In the end, the master planners won.

The easiest choice was the Classical style, inspired by the gracious houses found throughout the South. Many elements, like the symmetrical front, porches with columns, and vertically composed windows, were drawn from Greek Revival architecture. Also popular was the Victorian, with wraparound verandahs and elaborate ornamentation. There also was a Colonial Revival, based on houses built between 1900 and 1940 in neighborhoods of Orlando, Tampa, and other Florida cities. Although similar to the Classical style, the proportions were broader and details were simplified to create a less formal appearance.

Environmental conditions of the low country and coast regions of the South produced a unique house form known as Coastal style. Its large verandahs, second-story porches, and windows that sometimes reached the floor all were designed to provide a breezy escape from the heat. In a nod to Florida's Spanish architectural legacy, the developers also chose a Mediterranean style. These houses would have stucco exteriors, asymmetrically placed windows and doors, arches, and tile roofs.

Last and most controversial to the developers was the French Normandy style. Many veterans who served in World War I had been intrigued by French architecture and built homes based on French country styles when they returned. The style called for stucco walls, tall windows, and a mansard roof. Fraser objected particularly to the French Normandy style, arguing unsuccessfully that it was incompatible with the others.

Within these six styles were elements intended to retain consistency and respect tradition. Celebration would have no picture windows from the fifties or walls of glass from the sixties. There would be delicate mullioned bay windows and real windows, albeit inexpensive metal-framed ones, except in the Estate homes, which would use wooden frames, and lots and lots of columns, albeit termite-resistant plastic ones.

The pattern book governed more than the architectural style of the houses. It dictated their relationships to the street and neighboring houses in a wide variety of ways. For instance, driveways that entered a lot from the front were prohibited, and garages and drives were placed at the rear of the house. Exterior colors were restricted according to house style. Hence, the preferred color for a Classical house was white, but some pale pastel shades of blue, yellow, pink, and buff were permitted. Victorian houses could be pastels in a range of yellows, beige, grays, blues, and greens, although again white was the preferred color. The repetition of colors was also regulated; a color could not be repeated on the same side of a street within three houses unless the color was white. In the same vein, a variation in house styles was mandated; for instance, a Classical-style house could not be built within two doors of another Classical-style house.

No detail was left to chance or whimsy, right down to types and locations of the trees and shrubs to be planted in the yards of Celebration. Front-yard hedges and fences could be no higher than three and a half feet, and a minimum of 25 percent of the front and side yards had to be planted in something other than grass. "The landscape design of these areas," read the final version of the pattern book, "should include no more than 2 different species of canopy tree, 2 different species of ornamental tree, 5 different species of shrub or hedge, and 4 different species of ground cover."

Cathy, our gardener, was disappointed by the landscape plan's total disregard for native plantings and its insistence on lots of grass. The grass is St. Augustine variety, which grows by putting out runners across the top of the sand, not by sinking roots. "It is," she said disdainfully, "a weed." The fact was confirmed one day when a neighbor used a combination fertilizer-herbicide on his grass and killed the entire lawn.

The one area left untouched by the book was the interior of the house. Interiors were the domain of the contractors, and they reflected the popular style of contemporary living. Most front doors would open into a small foyer, with a dining room on one side and a living room on the other. A wide center hall would lead to the heart of the house—a modern kitchen opening onto a large family room lined with windows overlooking the backyard. The master bathrooms would be huge; the kitchens would have too much counter space. In many of the plans, the natural flow of the kitchen, from stove to sink to refrigerator, is interrupted by a mammoth island: This is not a cook's kitchen.

As the pattern book was being assembled and architectural styles were being refined, changes also were taking place in the overall master plan. The most significant among them was necessitated by the loss of the Disney Institute.

A tug-of-war had developed within the Disney Company over the location of the Disney Institute, which had grown dramatically from the early concept of Rummell and Eisner. It was clear that it would have to draw thousands of people to support the programming being planned. Many people believed that it had outgrown Celebration, and they were pushing to build it closer to Disney World and the hotels on the property. Rummell and his contingent argued that it was essential to the town. In late 1992, during a meeting of senior Disney staff and some of its architects, Eisner agreed that the institute would be better off nearer the parks. "The decision was made that the institute would just swallow the town," said Stern, who attended the meeting as both an architect and a Disney board member.

This decision sent the planning team scrambling. Education was one of Celebration's cornerstones, but the original planning had been for the Disney Institute and providing opportunities for adults. The planners had toyed with the concept of a small innovative school for some of the town's children, but they had not made it a priority. Over several weeks of discussion and brainstorming, the emphasis shifted 180 degrees from adult learning to teaching the children of the community. Instead of attending Osceola County's public schools, outside the town, Celebration's children would become the focus of the educational cornerstone. The education campus envisioned for the Disney Institute was reduced in size and reconfigured for a school to serve the needs of the community.

The plan to create a school sparked a debate among the planners over whether it should be private or public. There were good arguments for a private school, not least that it would allow Disney more control and keep Celebration's children out of the beleaguered Florida public school system. But Eisner and others insisted on building a public school, which they saw as more in keeping with their vision of the town. "One of our goals was to have a community that could be replicated elsewhere and benefit other places," said Killoren. "We thought it would be an opportunity to blend Disney's education division with an august group of education institutions and come up with a vision for a public school that would be a lighthouse for new ideas."

The loss of the Disney Institute and the substitution of a local school was a golden opportunity for Celebration's planners. They did not recognize it at the time, but the presence of a neighborhood school would be a huge selling point for the town, particularly with young baby boomers. But the decision to create a model of academic excellence within the mediocre Florida public school system would prove difficult and controversial. Those same parents who moved to the town in search of the educational excellence promised by Celebration got a hard dose of reality, and so did Disney. Before that happened, however, the company had some difficult negotiations of its own to complete with government officials in Osceola County, where the new town was to be built.

3

Citizen Disney

From the outset, the Walt Disney Company had insulated its huge Florida holdings from most outside governmental interference through the Reedy Creek Improvement District, which provided Disney World with the autonomy and centralized control of a private government. "The Vatican with mouse ears" was the way Rick Fogelsong, a politics professor at Rollins College and an inveterate Disney watcher, referred to Reedy Creek.

If the company wanted to build a new ride, it did not need to seek approval from the Orange County planning department. If the parks needed new sewers, the company did not need to seek approval through a voter referendum. When Disney put up a new building, the only construction codes it met were its own. Those codes and standards were high, and the quality of construction was generally good. All you have to do to see the benefits is compare the careful and controlled development of Disney's property to International Drive, the tacky commercial strip that connects Orlando to Disney World.

With the creation of Celebration, Disney was giving up that autonomy and, for the first time, agreeing to submit its development plans to outside government agencies for review and approval. Its buildings and houses would have to meet county codes. Its development plans for each parcel also would be subject to government approval, including an assessment of impact on wetlands. There would be public hearings and public accountability. Disney would be assessed a host of development fees to help pay for roads, schools, fire and police services, and other infrastructure improvements. Disney would have to play by the same rules as everyone else. As painful as it was, it was also inevitable.

The inevitability stemmed from this simple fact: If Celebration had remained part of Reedy Creek, its residents would have been entitled to vote on matters within the district. For nearly a quarter of a century, the only votes in the district had been cast by the forty or so Disney employees who lived in company housing within the borders of Disney World, which meant the company had complete control. But adding twenty thousand residents would have cost the company that cherished control. "They didn't want eight thousand dwelling units full of people voting on how to paint the Magic Kingdom," said Michael Kloehn, the planning director for Osceola County.

The solution was to de-annex Celebration, transferring the land from the jurisdiction of Reedy Creek to that of Osceola County and the various state agencies that would be involved in approving the creation of the new town. As with so much involving Celebration, this was not a simple proposition. The company executives did not want to give up control over the property unless it was certain the development would be completed. They did not want to relinquish control, then get six months into the planning process and come up with some deal-breaking demand from the county that would scotch the whole town, because they feared that once they gave up control they would never get it back.

"So before the owners were willing to de-annex—the technical word is 'contraction'—the Celebration project from what we refer to as the warm bosom of Reedy Creek and go out into the cold world and face the same requirements as everybody else, there had to be some assurance that the end product would be something that everyone could live with," explained Gloria Lockridge, one of the army of outside lawyers hired by Disney on the project.

But de-annexation wasn't a simple matter. Exercising planning and zoning control over the development of Celebration was a huge undertaking for Osceola County and its four-member planning staff. There were only two incorporated towns in the county, Kissimmee, with thirty thousand people and St. Cloud, with fewer than twenty thousand. Before negotiations with Disney could begin, the county commission would have to pass an ordinance giving its planning staff authority to develop new guidelines and regulations specifically to deal with a project as large and complex as Celebration. The problem was that the commission could not pass an ordinance covering land that was not yet within its jurisdiction.

Disney's lawyers went to work. They researched state law and found that it was possible to make an ordinance contingent upon the occurrence of a certain event. So they drafted language for the county specifying that the amendment to the comprehensive plan for Celebration would go into effect only upon the de-annexation of the land from Reedy Creek. In turn, the de-annexation was contingent upon the company's reaching an agreement on the general development of Celebration with Osceola County and the state and federal agencies that would be involved in the negotiations.

"The critical thing here was timing," said Lockridge. "We all agreed that, if everything went as everybody planned, the property would be de-annexed from the boundaries of Reedy Creek, would become part of Osceola County, and the development order and the comprehensive-plan amendment would all be final at the same time. Everything would take place simultaneously."

To simplify the planning process, Disney's lawyers also came up with an interpretation of state law that allowed various agencies to waive their authority and give the final say on planning decisions to Osceola County. A total of sixteen state and federal agencies would be involved in the negotiations with Disney, but the last word would come from the leaders of the small, rural county where the project was to be located.

The resulting burden on the county planning staff was enormous, far beyond anything they had experienced in the past. Arrayed across the negotiating table from them would be the best consultants and lawyers available to a company with Disney's resources.

"Compared with the limited number of administrative staff of the county, Disney had what appeared to be an army of consultants and staff members ready, willing, and able to work night and day to resolve issues and address the concerns of the county," said Kloehn. "Disney appeared to be willing to go to any expense to keep the negotiations in motion. It was a common perception that for each agreement there was a new consultant on their payroll."

The first step was development of the amendment to the comprehensive plan. This document would be the basic map of land use in Celebration. It would designate by law where Disney would be allowed to locate its commercial buildings, retail stores, hospital, apartments, and houses. The amendment was necessary because of the density and complexity of Celebration. For example, the county did not even have a zoning designation that permitted apartments above shops, a central feature of downtown Celebration.

Every developer wants the right to obtain the maximum value from his land, and that often means retaining the flexibility to alter the master plan in response to changes in the market. So Disney fought for as much flexibility as possible. In turn, the county wanted to make sure that the density of the development did not outstrip the availability of services, like fire and police protection, and the planning staff fought to impose reasonable restraints.

Kloehn found that Disney had a tough time adjusting to the county's demands. "In particular," he said, "they objected to having to show the geographic distribution of the uses within Celebration. If they changed their minds down the road, another public hearing would be necessary. This format ran counter to their usual close-to-the-vest way of doing things. But they finally understood that all developers are required to provide the same level of detail and that we couldn't make an exception."

Because it was Disney, the negotiations took place in a highly charged atmosphere. Some county residents had bemoaned the steady loss of the area's rural character in recent years. Every time they had the misfortune to drive on U.S. Highway 192, they encountered reminders of the changes wrought by the arrival of Disney and its tackiest acolytes. This vocal minority wanted to make sure Disney did not get special treatment in the planning process.

At the same time, there were strong forces pushing for rapid approval of the new town. They saw an opportunity to put the county on the map and extract some of the Disney-related tax revenue that for more than twenty-five years had flowed to adjoining Orange County, where Disney World and most of the hotels that served its customers were located.

Years before, Osceola County had tried to increase revenue by taxing Disney's unused land in the county at a higher rate, based on its development potential. Faced down by Disney's lawyers, they had backed off, and it had remained taxed as agricultural land, the lowest rate on the books. The proposal to develop a new town on the land meant that the tax rate could finally be pushed higher, and it also meant the creation of new jobs, homes, and businesses, all of which would generate revenue, too. Responding to both grassroots pressure to increase the tax revenue and the urgings of Disney executives, the county commissioners pushed the planning staff to reach an agreement with Disney on a planning package that the commissioners could approve to get the ball rolling as soon as possible on building the new town.

"The sense was that Disney does things right, that they are very concerned about aesthetics, so let's get rolling," said Mary Jane Arrington, a professional planner and populist Democrat who was elected to the county commission after Celebration's approval.

To speed the process, Kloehn had asked Disney's lawyers and planners to use their greater resources to write their own first draft of the amendment to the comprehensive code. The intention was not to allow Disney to dictate the planning restrictions but to come up with a starting point for the negotiations. The talks and negotiations would last nearly a year. In the end, Disney got a fair amount of flexibility.

In a speech given three years later to the American Planning Association, Joel Ivy, one of Disney's outside land planners, said the agreement with the county allowed the company to transfer land uses from one category to another, say from commercial to retail, without seeking county approval. The company also got the right to shift the roads and land parcels within the 4,900 acres pretty much at will.

A related document allowed the county planning staff to approve certain modifications in the land-use plan for Celebration without a public hearing. "Without this allowance, every time we changed our minds, which believe me [has been] frequent, we would have to go through the trilogy of hearings, being the technical review committee, the planning and zoning, and the board of county commissioners," Ivy explained. "That process was too slow and unwieldy, given that we were trying to construct under the speed that we were assigned."

The amendment, which covered hundreds of pages, was approved by unanimous vote of the commission on May 17, 1993. Kloehn and the other members of the planning staff felt that they had given the amendment a thorough and fair review, but others would find later that they had overlooked some key matters. For instance, it would be discovered that the new town had been exempted from the county's tree ordinance, which required developers to protect existing trees and plant new ones.

Other major issues remained, and it would be another ten months before the final touches were put on the approval for Celebration. Among those issues was affordable housing. Florida state law required developments that were large enough to have a regional impact to provide low-cost housing or set aside money to pay for housing for lower-income families and individuals within a certain distance of the development. While advocates for affordable housing prefer it to be located within a particular development in order to integrate low-income families into the community, most developers are reluctant to do so and negotiate to move it off site.

When it came time to fulfill its obligation, Celebration found itself between two conflicting demands. The state officials wanted Disney to include houses that cost less than $100,000 in the development. But the officials in Osceola County had a different strategy: They wanted Celebration to contain upscale housing, because those properties would pay more in taxes to the county. Indeed, by means of a complex formula, county officials had determined that a house needed to be appraised at least at $150,000 in order to be assessed enough in property taxes to pay for schools, sewer, police and fire protection, and other services provided by the county.

Tom Lewis, a vice president of Celebration Company and former Florida state official, conducted the negotiations with the state and county and said the company had been caught between the conflicting demands. "We had the state telling us we have to do affordable housing," he recalled. "We had the county telling us they didn't want any of that affordable stuff."

Because the county had the final say, Osceola officials offered Disney an enormous gift: They said the company could contribute money to an existing affordable housing program run by the county and build more-expensive houses in Celebration. The county program provided subsidies to low- and moderate-income people for down payments on houses and assistance on apartment rents. Participants who used the money as part of a down payment could buy a house anywhere in the county so long as its cost did not exceed $80,000 for new construction, or $75,000 for an existing home, roughly the median prices of such houses in the county. Using a formula based on the number of jobs to be created in the new town, Disney's contribution was estimated at $100,000 a year. "We basically said, 'Let's skip it. Why don't you give us some money, and we'll use it in our programs for these people,' " Kloehn told us. "They said okay, and the state said okay."

"We asked Disney for this and to our surprise they agreed and we were to be given the funds," said Anna M. Pinellas, the administrator of the county program. "The allocation was $300,000, at a rate of $100,000 a year, starting in 1993."

The county's proposal was a godsend for Disney on several counts. First and most obvious, the company was getting off cheaply. Celebration was a $2.5 billion project being assembled by one of the country's richest corporations, and it was being asked to provide a mere pittance for affordable housing. At least as important to Disney from a financial perspective, the deal would allow the construction of more-expensive houses in Celebration, which meant more revenue for Disney. And money would be going to a program that would have no impact on Celebration. In addition, home prices in Celebration, though not then determined, would certainly be well above the $80,000 level set by the subsidy program, so there would be no subsidized housing in Celebration. Finally, the county's willingness to sweep the issue off the table for so little money indicated that the officials involved were more concerned with generating tax revenue than with providing places for low- and moderate-income families to live.

While the county made things easy, Disney was not an innocent bystander. In its proposal to Osceola County to build Celebration, Disney had argued that it was not necessary to provide affordable housing within the town because there was already enough elsewhere in the region. Once Disney's affordable housing money started to role into the county, however, Pinellas found that many of the moderate-income applicants applying for assistance were Disney employees. But they would not be using the money in Celebration, because even the lowest-priced units were 50 percent higher than the maximum cost of a house that qualified for the subsidy.

"I am a black female, looking to retirement at the end of next year, and I would love to live in Celebration," Pinellas said in the summer of 1998. "I belong to the Celebration fitness center. I'd love to live there, but I cannot afford it. To provide town houses or condos or apartments in the affordable range would have been very positive for local residents, but the town is kind of out of the local, everyday Osceola County person's economic reach. Housing, like going to school or going shopping, needs to have a variety. I can go to Saks Fifth Avenue and find something in all price ranges. I can't go to Celebration and find something in all price ranges. Disney made it possible for us to help a lot of folks, but it did not help them move into Celebration."

The county's capitulation had occurred without so much as a ripple in public, allowing Disney to avoid the type of controversy that had occurred in 1991, when the company had incensed government leaders of Orange County by grabbing the right to issue $50 million worth of tax-exempt revenue bonds. Because federal law restricts the amount of municipal bonds that can be issued free of federal taxes, the state of Florida had set aside specific amounts of bonds for each region of the state. The 1989 amount for Orange County was $50 million, and they were available on a first-come, first-served basis. Orange County had intended to use the money raised from the bonds to build more affordable housing, but when the county government filed its application for the bonds, officials discovered that the Reedy Creek Improvement District had gotten in line ahead of them and been given the right to issue the bonds to improve the sewers on its property. So the county lost the chance to increase its stock of affordable housing, creating a public uproar and lasting anger among local officials.

Another key element of the planning was the agreement to build a toll road, eventually called Highway 417. With Interstate 4 already over its capacity for traffic, the new road would provide an alternate means of getting to Celebration and the surrounding area of Osceola County. This was one area of planning where the state retained control, and Lewis, the Disney official whose state jobs had included running the Department of Transportation, assembled the plan that persuaded them to approve the new road. Disney and three other owners of undeveloped land in the area agreed to provide free right-of-ways for the highway, sharply reducing the cost of the road and helping to win approval of the project in the Florida legislature. In exchange, the new access greatly increased the value of the land owned by Disney and the others.

The road provided essential access to Celebration and the rest of the area, including a new "doorway" into Disney World itself. However, a four-lane highway slicing through the town presented Celebration's planners with a tricky problem. In the end, they mitigated its impact by planting fast-growing slash pines along the road's path even before highway construction began and by avoiding new lighting regulations just implemented by the state. Instead of the higher, brighter lights called for by the regulations, Celebration came in under a grandfather provision that allowed for less obtrusive lights.

On December 13, 1993, the county commission approved the final package of planning documents for Celebration. Along with the amendment to the comprehensive plan and the de-annexation of Celebration, the stack of documents set up the affordable housing program and required Disney to contribute to the costs of improving roads outside the town. The approval left only one last piece to the Celebration puzzle, but it was an important one.

The land on which the new town would rise was primarily low-lying pasture and wetlands. Developing it with roads, streets, sewers, and other routine infrastructure elements was projected to cost more than $300 million over the ten to fifteen years anticipated to build out Celebration. In most new developments, these costs would come out of the pocket of the developer and be recouped over the years as the land was sold for houses. Disney had another idea. It planned to keep its up-front costs to a minimum by taking advantage of a Florida law that would allow it to pass the development costs on to home buyers in Celebration.

Florida has always been hospitable to land developers, some would say too hospitable for its own good. State law allows developers of large-scale communities and subdivisions to establish a community-development district. The mechanism permits the developer to issue tax-free revenue bonds to raise money to pay for virtually all of the infrastructure, including water management and supply, sewer, wastewater management, bridges, roads, streets, alleys, and public parks. Because the bonds are backed by a government agency, they are tax exempt, and the developer can therefore sell them to investors at a lower interest rate. This permits the developer to raise the necessary money to pay for a project's infrastructure less expensively than if the company had to use its own cash reserves or borrow from a lender at commercial rates.

The developer saves money a second way by passing on the cost of paying off those bonds to the people and businesses that buy property within the development district. In such a district, tax assessments are levied on individual homeowners and other property owners, and those taxes are used to pay off the bondholders over the life of the bonds. So not only does the developer get cheap money to pay for the infrastructure but the ultimate purchasers of the property are handed the bill.

To take advantage of this largesse, Disney needed the approval of the county commission to establish two separate districts in Celebration, one for the residential development and another for the commercial. Four months after the commission quietly okayed the overall development plan for Celebration, it voted to allow the creation of the two development districts, which would be capable of issuing more than $300 million worth of bonds. The vote was not on the public agenda for the March 1994 meeting. It was raised at the end of the session and voted on without public comment. After all, no one yet lived in Celebration to register any objections.

Not everyone likes these development districts. Critics see them as a semiconcealed way to pass on to home buyers costs that should rightly be paid by the developers themselves. And those costs are not minimal for homeowners. In the case of Celebration, as houses are sold, property owners are assessed a tax that is dedicated to paying off the bonds over twenty years. The tax is included on the regular property tax bill sent out by Osceola County. Even though it is a separate item on the bill, many homeowners are unaware of where the money is going. For 1997, the payment added about 25 percent to the average property tax bill in Celebration and ranged from $650 a year for a town house to $2,000 a year for the most expensive Estate homes. The company expected the amount to remain roughly the same over the course of the bonds, since more houses would be sold as more bonds were issued.

"I think that you, as a homeowner or purchaser of property, shouldn't have to pay for development costs," said Mary Jane Arrington. "I will never vote for one." She said that the county commissioners elected after the approval of Celebration agreed that they would not approve any development districts without putting the issue on the agenda for public discussion. But in the spring of 1994, approval of the development districts was an important green light for the Disney development team. The master plan had been refined. The pattern book was being compiled. Still to be resolved, however, was who would build the houses in the new town.

Todd Mansfield argued strenuously that the development division should create its own company to handle the construction. He saw two advantages. First, it would allow Disney to capture more of the profits from Celebration. It would take several years for Disney to recoup its expenses in developing the land, even given the benefits of the development districts. But a builder receives his money, and profits, immediately upon the sale of a house. Adding the builder's profits to the revenue stream would provide more money for Disney and a faster cash flow to satisfy the accountants at Disney headquarters in Los Angeles.

Second, he argued that creating a construction company would give Disney complete control over the quality of the work. The reasoning was straightforward: Disney was going to get blamed if the quality was poor, whether its company built the houses or not, so why not set the standard and bank the profit. "Latent liability" is the way that Joe Barnes would later refer ruefully to Disney's role as the ultimate guarantor of construction quality.

"Todd felt very strongly that it was another way to get another incremental value per acre out of the property," recalled Rummell. "He also knew that one of the best ways to dictate what happens in a community is to have your own home-building capability. You can set the pace and govern the quality. He put a proposal together, and the company was uncomfortable with it. The company was not ready to take on the additional level of commitment and risk. I was never passionate about it."

Disney is, in fact, a risk-averse company in many ways. When the company developed Disney's West Side, a retail area of movies, restaurants, and stores near Disney World, it leased the store space to outside businesses, despite the fact that Disney has a massive merchandising operation of its own within the nearby theme parks. Disney's West Side proved to be wildly popular, and one company executive estimated that Disney lost $40 million a year in revenue because the merchandise was sold by outside retailers.

Charles Fraser saw another factor at play in the decision not to create a construction company for Celebration. "They could have managed the construction well, and it was the only way for them to reap the full profits," he explained. "But it was understood in those discussions that, if Disney builders did the work, Michael Eisner would want to approve every kitchen design and bathroom before they did it, as he typically does with each hotel and other building. Eisner is passionate about the details of design, and he is very good at it. But two things would have happened. First, his insistence on top quality would probably have driven prices out of the range of most customers. And second, he doesn't have the time for it. There would have been endless delays while everyone waited for California to make a decision."

Whatever the reason, for a company as insistent on quality and control as Disney and with a project destined to have such a high public profile, the decision was shortsighted. Celebration Company, the development arm set up for the new town, would be a land developer only. It would build the infrastructure and sell lots to builders. The builders would in turn sell the lots to customers and build the houses.

If all of the homes had been custom built, the problem would not have been so serious, but Celebration would have houses in all price ranges, and given the economics of home building, most of them would be production houses. That means they would be built from uniform plans in a fashion akin to a factory assembly line.

Production homes are common across the country. As a rule, buyers understand that a production house lacks the top-quality craftsmanship and special touches of a custom-built home. At the same time, the buyer expects to pay less. In Celebration, however, because of the market demand and the architectural elements imposed by Disney, buyers would be paying something closer to custom-built prices for production-built homes. And because of Disney, they expected first-rate quality.

For its part, Disney conducted a nationwide search to find first-rate production builders. They settled early on David Weekley Homes. The company was based in Houston and built about 2,400 houses a year.

While most of those houses were in Texas, Weekley also had done work in Denver, Raleigh, North Carolina, and Orlando. The second and final production builder chosen was Town & Country Homes, from Oak Brook, Illinois. The company had a strong reputation, but it had done little work outside its home state. William J. Ryan Jr., who had taken over the family operation from his father, was eager to grow the business, and he had pursued the Celebration project aggressively as a high-profile means of expanding the company.

As we discovered to our annoyance and occasional amusement upon moving into our new home, any greater risks to the company's bottom line or delays imposed by Eisner's high standards would have been worth the investment for Disney. To satisfy demand, the pace of construction was furious, outstripping the ability of the builders to provide quality homes within the promised time period. The results would mean headaches for everyone, from residents and builders to senior Disney executives.

4

Town & Country Marriages

No one has ever called Donna McGrath sheepish. Her fingernails are too long and brightly painted and her smile too high-powered. But our nearest neighbor was pretty close to meek as she sat in our living room, explaining how her side porch ended up being built on our property.

It was mid-July, and we had been in the new house on Nadina Place about two weeks. We were discovering new construction problems every day, dutifully passing them on to the representatives from David Weekley Homes, which had built our house. The list was approaching four pages, but most items were niggling—outlets with no electricity, a bow in the kitchen ceiling, no weatherstripping around the front door, strange lumps in the newly sodded lawn, a shower door in the master bathroom that kept popping open and spewing water all over the floor midshower, hot and cold water lines reversed upstairs. This last problem was intriguing. At first we thought it was only with the sinks, showers, and tubs. Then one day Doug asked, "Why do you think the toilet steams?" We checked the tank. Sure enough, hot water in the toilet, too. We checked the kids' bathroom. Same thing. It turned out that the plumber had crossed the lines at the point on the first floor where the water was sent upstairs, and the repair entailed chopping a hole in a wall and switching the pipes. Every day, a different workman came into the house, adjusted, replaced, or added something, created little piles of dust, and left. We came to know them by name and tried to trade cups of coffee and cans of diet Coke for better-quality work.

The business with the porch got our attention in a serious way. We had not noticed the lot lines on the survey map when we signed the papers to buy our house. The woman from the title company had not mentioned them. Nor had Gene Kane, the mortgage guy from the bank. But Donna, who had sold real estate on Cape Cod before she moved to Florida and switched to selling time-shares, spotted the mistake when the McGraths were closing on their house.

"On the survey I could see that your lot line came up within inches of our house, and it was obvious that our porch stairs are your property," she explained, sipping a Coke and wanting a cigarette. "They said we should go ahead and sign the papers and work it out later. I called David Weekley's office this morning and told them what happened. They said the four of us should work it out. They thought maybe you'd just grant us an easement to the steps." She paused and offered a pained smile. "So," she said finally, "Mike and I thought maybe you'd just want to give us the easement."

As you might expect, we were taken aback by the builder's mistake. We told Donna that we would have to think about it and promised to let her know. We looked at each other with something close to panic. It was not enough that the builder had made this stupid error. Worse was the fact that they had tossed it like a live hand grenade into our laps.

Celebration was supposed to be a happy place. It was almost a town ordinance that neighbors get along. Yet we faced what appeared to be a no-win situation—sacrifice a fair chunk of our tiny ten-foot-wide side lot, probably clouding the title or lowering the value of our house when it came time to sell, or risk irritating our brand-new next-door neighbors by making them rip out the porch, seal off a door, move it all to the other side of their house—a process that would probably take our slow-moving builder weeks.

We understood the perils of proximity. In Alexandria, Virginia, our house was two feet from one neighbor and separated from the other by a small courtyard. Soon after we arrived, the neighbors on the courtyard side, Robert and Nancy Pollard, had presented us with a curious housewarming gift—a charcoal starter that used newspaper. They explained that the odor from the starter fluid we used drifted up to their second-story deck and bothered them. So we understood the necessity of getting along in tight quarters.

In Celebration, not everyone was accustomed to living so close together, as we discovered one morning soon after we moved in. Doug was sitting at the desk in our first-floor office, working on the computer. Cathy appeared in the doorway and was about to say something when her gaze drifted out the window. A look of horror crossed her face.

"What is it?" asked Doug in some alarm as he started to turn toward the window.

"No, no," Cathy shouted. "Don't look."

"What are you talking about?" he asked.

"The grandmother," she said as she dissolved into laughter. "She's naked in the window."

Our office faced the bedroom of Mike McGrath's mother, Mary. The McGraths had not put up blinds yet, and Mary, who was in her eighties, had obviously forgotten how exposed she was, literally.

So, given our desire for good relations with the McGraths and the near-mandatory neighborliness of Celebration, Doug said maybe we should just give them the easement. It was the least confrontational solution. The McGraths would be grateful, not angry. But it would leave us with the loss of part of our yard and a problem down the road when we tried to sell the house.

As always, Cathy proposed the practical approach. Granting an easement was a bad idea, but somebody else had to say that for us if we were to keep the peace. We needed to find the bad cop for our good cop.

"I'll call Gene Kane at the bank and that woman from the title company," she said. "Let's see how serious this really is."

The woman from the title company was surprised. "Whoa," she exclaimed. "This is a major problem."

Kane had about the same reaction. He thought an easement might jeopardize the value of the house, possibly creating questions about the mortgage he and his bank had just written on our property. He said he would talk to his legal department and get back to us.

Cathy also called Charles Dennis, a construction supervisor with

David Weekley Homes. He wasn't in, so Cathy left a message explaining the situation and registering our objection to granting an easement.

Dennis stopped by the next morning. He appeared tense and edgy as he apologized for the mistake. He said that just before construction started, the McGraths had decided to flip the floor plan for their house. In doing so, no one had taken account of where the side porch would wind up. Contrary to what Donna had been told, Dennis insisted that Weekley intended to tear out the porch and rebuild it on the other side of the house, where they had more room. Kane called soon afterward, emphatically seconding the decision.

This was good news for us. We spoke to Donna and Mike that evening, explaining what Dennis and Kane had said. The McGraths said they had no problem with moving the porch. Everyone was happy again in Celebration, though it did take six weeks before the work was completed.

The dilemma explained, finally, how our garage had ended up on the wrong side of our property, lined up with our house, blocking our view of the swamp for which we had paid a premium, rather than set off to the side. By not thinking ahead, or to the side, the builder working on the McGraths' house made it impossible to put our garage where it was supposed to be when he flipped their floor plan. To our frustration, there was no compensation from the builder when we complained about the placement of the garage and the loss of our view.

Many more months would pass before the niggling items with our house were repaired, and even then new problems kept popping up. For instance, one day we noticed that several sides of the house and garage were covered with mildew. A guy from Weekley came out to look at it, scratched his head, and left. The next day he returned with a guy from the paint company and a guy from the company that made the clapboard siding, a synthetic concrete called Hardiboard. The builders say Hardiboard is termiteproof and therefore a good thing in Florida. They couldn't figure out what was causing the mildew, and a noticeable growth covered much of the exterior of our house and a handful of other houses in town.

In July, we had a real scare. The air-conditioning unit for the second floor went out, and when Doug peered into the mechanism, he saw that the piping was frozen. The repairman came out, took a look, and, as re-pairmen are wont to do, blamed us.

"You Yankees run the damn thing too cold," he said with disdain. "Set it below seventy degrees, and the unit will freeze up, just like this."

We were suitably cowed until we checked the thermostat—seventy-five degrees. We called the repairman over and showed him, but he was not convinced. He seemed to think that we had pushed it up to cover ourselves. He thawed the lines and did some other stuff and got it running. For a day and a half. Then it froze up again.

Another repairman came. This one was friendlier but more alarming. After examining the unit for several minutes, he determined that there might be a leak in the piping that was spewing coolant.

"Boy," he said, wiping his forehead with the sleeve of his shirt. "This is our worst nightmare. The lines are buried in the walls and in the concrete floor. I can see us taking apart this whole house."

We had seen houses under construction around Celebration and marveled at the way the contractors handled the plumbing. Once the concrete blocks were in place for the foundation, they filled the area under where the floor would be built with fine sand. Then the plumbers came and buried white plastic piping in the sand. The riser pipes for the bathrooms and kitchen would be sticking out of the sand like ghostly white arms when the builders poured the cement floor in place. Getting to those pipes in case of a leak would mean using a jackhammer to take out chunks of concrete until they found the right spot.

Back when we first arrived, one of the plumbers had explained to us that there was no need to worry about ever getting access to the pipes. Since it doesn't freeze in Florida, the reasoning went, the pipes would never burst. We had remained dubious and had asked Doug's father, a retired homebuilder from Indiana, about it. Yes, he said with a grimace and a shake of his head, that was how they did things in Florida. Now this repairman was suggesting that our concerns had been legitimate. What we wouldn't have given at that point for a basement or even a crawl space.

Before summoning the wrecking crew, the repairman wanted to try something. He went to his truck, poked around for a long time, and came back with some sort of widget. He installed it in the air conditioner and said earnestly, "Let's give this a try. Cross your fingers." We did, and the widget worked. We never had another problem with the air conditioner—and we scrupulously kept the thermostat set well above seventy.

In all honesty, the difficulties with our house were mild, and most were resolved. The problems seemed to be with work that was not finished properly, something attributable in part to the race to build houses as fast as possible throughout Celebration. Fortunately we had learned the hard way long ago not to get emotionally involved with a piece of real estate. For many of our neighbors, however, these houses were not just a piece of real estate. They were the embodiment of dreams and aspirations, the everyday symbols of what their owners had taken implicitly as Disney's promise that life would be better in Celebration. And some of them were pretty angry.

Porter Metcalf looked like the marine corps captain he used to be. He was solidly built, with close-cropped blond hair and a complexion that turned beet red when he was provoked. We discovered that latter fact not long after meeting him at the Celebration Golf Course. He had won a marine golf tournament shortly before retiring, so when he got out he had gone to golf school and become a club professional.

This was his first civilian job, and he had taken it at less pay than he might have received elsewhere in order to live in Celebration. He'd bought a three-story town house overlooking Savannah Square, a short walk from the school and the golf course. But for the past six months, Metcalf, his wife, Sonia, and their two children had been living in a cramped apartment twenty minutes away, waiting for the house to be finished.

"You can't believe the way we're getting jerked around on our town house," he said, his voice rising and face reddening. "I had my own inspector in yesterday for a walk-through. We have a wall that is bowed out and so many other problems. That big rainstorm last week, it leaked through the roof. Second leak so far. They put in the wrong carpet on the stairs and the wrong cabinets in the kitchen. They're going to have to tear out the carpet and the cabinets before we move in."

The hardest part of not being in the house, he said, was the effect on Sean, his nine-year-old son. Instead of watching him ride off to school each morning on his bike, Metcalf woke Sean at six every morning and brought him to the golf course, where Metcalf started work at seven.

Sean would sleep in the backseat of his father's Ford Explorer until his dad woke him to go to school.

The first week in December was the worst for the Metcalfs. On his way home from work, Metcalf stopped by a neighbor's town house. The family was putting lights on the Christmas tree, laughing and talking about their first Christmas in their new house. Metcalf got caught up in the spirit and described the scene to Sonia and Sean when he got home to the apartment, where unpacked boxes stood where the tree should have been.

"I want to be in our new house and have a real tree," sobbed the nine-year-old.

Metcalf told his wife that he knew what he was going to do. He would drive back to Celebration with his sobbing son in the car and go to the offices of Town & Country Homes, his builder, and confront the construction supervisor.

"Let him look my son in the face and explain why we won't be in our house by Christmas, even though it was supposed to be done last July at the latest," he told her. "I can handle this, but Sean is having a lot of trouble with it."

Sonia convinced him to stay home, but his anger returned as he told us the story.

Beth McCarthy could scarcely be more different from Porter Metcalf. She is petite and attractive, soft spoken and even tempered. She sings in the church choir and is raising three daughters. She confessed that she hates change. She married her seventh-grade sweetheart, and they had moved from Miami to Tampa because of crime. Beth felt safe and content in Tampa, but she and her husband, Tim, became so enamored with the concept of Celebration when they heard about it that they decided to take the plunge.

"It put me very much outside of my comfort zone, but I was determined," she said one morning over coffee at Barnie's, the downtown coffee shop where Cathy conducted many interviews beneath the live oak in the courtyard. "I like things planned out. I like to see what I'm getting into. I'm a merry-go-round sort of person. Unlike Tim, who likes roller coasters. Just give him an hour to pack his bags, and he'd be game."

Beth moved to Celebration anyway, persuaded in part by the chance to build a house just up the street from the new school, where her and Tim's two younger daughters would attend classes while their oldest daughter went to college nearby.

"We liked the whole Disney outlook," she said. "The whole idea of family, community, education. Everything was close. We wouldn't be driving."

But she started out with a lot of driving. In the late summer of 1996, two months after the McCarthys signed the contract to build their house here, Celebration School opened in temporary quarters. Beth and Tim wanted their younger girls, Jaclyn and Ashley, to be part of that first class, and they expected to move into the new house within three or four months. So each school day, Beth or Tim drove the girls to Celebration, an hour and twenty minutes from Tampa, and picked them up at the end of the day. Some days they carpooled with another Tampa family waiting for their home in Celebration, but the other family decided to buy a completed Estate home and moved in quickly, leaving Beth and Tim to handle the driving alone.

"It was nice at first," Beth said of the drives. "Good quality time. We talked. It was great. We could really bond with these kids. Then it changed. It started to get on our nerves. And it lasted the whole first year of school."

By the summer of 1997, they were still without the new house. Beth's mother had been on a waiting list for an apartment, and when one opened up in downtown Celebration, the McCarthys took it instead. They thought it would be for just a couple of months. The builder kept promising that their house was almost finished. Their stay in the apartment lasted six months.

One of the things that upset the family the most was when their oldest daughter, Jennifer, had to come home from college to live with them because of health problems. She brought the number of people in the apartment up to five, one over the limit imposed by Celebration Company. "They said we couldn't stay there because we had too many people in the apartment," Beth recalled, still incredulous months later. "We said, 'We have to stay because we don't have anywhere to go. We don't have a house to live in.' "

They talked about giving up. "We were frustrated, but we didn't want to walk away," said Beth. "We still loved the community. We wanted to stay and make it work. That was the interesting thing. There were so many people who were so stressed and yet they weren't walking away. In any other community, they would have.

"I think we all expected Disney to fix it," she continued. "Just like if you have a problem at the park. People there say, 'What can we do to help you out?' But we all became frustrated and didn't know where to go when Disney told us their hands were tied."

The final insult came when Jennifer was scheduled to have heart surgery in Birmingham, Alabama, at the end of September 1997. There were questions about her chances of survival. Her parents had begged Town & Country to get the house done in time for them to bring her there to recuperate. "We said to them up front that we didn't want to play the health card, but we were going to play it because we didn't want to bring her back to a place where three girls shared one room," said Beth.

The company managed to finish the house the same week that Jennifer was taken to the hospital. But though they were months behind the promised delivery time, Town & Country now insisted that the McCarthys close on the house the day after Jennifer's surgery.

"They actually wanted Tim to come back from the hospital and close," Beth recalled. "We said, 'We have waited this long, and you're telling us you can't wait another day or two.' It wasn't like we were leaving the state for minor surgery. We weren't even sure that Jennifer was coming back with us. At that point, we turned the tables and said that we weren't closing until we were ready."

While rarely entwined with such life-or-death matters, the construction delays caused strains in other families, too. Things became so serious that the minister of the local Presbyterian church felt compelled to weigh in.

There were four religious organizations in Celebration but no church. A nondenominational group, which included Baptists and other Protestants, held their services in the school cafeteria, which probably violated the separation of church and state, but no one seemed to care. A Jewish congregation met at the restaurant at the golf course, and the Catholics conducted education programs for children but no formal services in town. The Presbyterians held services at the AMC movie theater downtown.

Though we were raised as churchgoers, as a family we had never attended services regularly. Coming to Celebration offered us a chance to give it a try. We started attending the Presbyterian service because, of the two Protestant services, it was closer to the churches of our upbringing and because the seats were comfortable. It must have been the only church in the county with plush stadium seating. The whole atmosphere was, in fact, very casual. People would come in shorts and shirts; anyone in a suit was pegged immediately as a tourist or first-time visitor. You could even bring your morning coffee to services, resting it in the cupholder where the previous night someone had placed his Coca-Cola while watching *Scream* or *Good Will Hunting*.

One Sunday in the middle of August, Reverend Patrick Wrisley was going through his opening ritual of asking the congregation to pray for sick members and others in need. Without a pause, he added an odd request. "Pray for those Town & Country marriages," he asked. There were titters in the congregation, and Wrisley paused to explain.

"I know it may seem humorous," he said earnestly. "But some of our friends have been waiting a long time to get into their Town & Country homes. They go from apartment to house to apartment. People are living in a state of flux. This is stress. I've counseled more than one family since I arrived here last November. So put these Town & Country marriages in your prayers this week, please."

A few days later, the two of us sat down with Reverend Wrisley over lunch at Max's Café, the retro diner in the center of town. He is a self-described Georgia cracker who came to Celebration with his family to start the Presbyterian church. We asked about his reference to Town & Country marriages and how deep the problems really ran.

"One of the teachers at the school had a good word for what's going on," he said. "She said it was swirly time. This is a stressful time for many people. All of us are creating traditions as we go, and it's scary. Town & Country has not made it easy for people. Their inability to move into their homes has created additional stresses for many of these people, and I've counseled them about it."

Town & Country had been building homes in the Chicago suburbs since 1958. They had been chosen in part because the Celebration Company's head of residential real estate, David Pace, had heard Bill Ryan Jr.—who was running the company with his brother, Mike—give several talks on architectural design. Pace had examined Town & Country's financial strength and interviewed several of its customers before picking them as one of the town's two production builders.

Despite the background check and Town & Country's good record, by the middle of 1997, the company was months behind schedule on dozens of houses and encountering angry homeowners and concerned Disney executives. The worst delays were with the town houses that curved gracefully along Campus Street and lined two ends of Savannah Square. Porter Metcalf was not the only person who was angry. One frustrated owner waiting for his town house had tracked down a painting crew at another building site and screamed and cursed at them. He then marched off to find the company foreman and repeated the outburst. Feelings were running so high that Town & Country had hired a night watchman to prevent possible vandalism, and some town-house owners were contemplating a lawsuit.

Part of the blame rested with Disney and Celebration Company. Eager to capitalize on the rush of attention, the company had pushed builders to put up houses as fast as they could. The problem was that the two production builders had more work than workers. In the case of Town & Country, the house designs were barely completed in time for the opening of the town, so they were not ready for the wave of customers that crashed down on them. The general labor market exacerbated the problem. The Orlando region was in the midst of a building boom. With subdivisions popping up almost overnight, there was a shortage of experienced workers, and there was no effective union to provide the assurance of qualified workers. On top of that, both Weekley and Town & Country had come into the area from out of state, which meant that they did not have long-term relationships with dependable subcontractors who could be counted on not only to show up on the job but to do it right.

Weekley fared better than Town & Country, in part because the company had started building in the Orlando market earlier, hoping to be chosen by Disney for the Celebration project. As a result, Weekley was able to send supervisors and crews into the area two years before Celebration began to build houses. "We wanted to establish a good pool of subs before we started at Celebration," one of the Weekley supervisors explained. "It made all the difference."

Mike Ryan refused to criticize Disney, but he told us later that the lack of time for advance planning had put his company in a hole from the outset. "Looking back, we should have said that we were not ready," he said. "Instead, we tried to honor the opening date. So not only were we in an unknown market with an unfamiliar base of subcontractors, but houses were selling out before we were ready. You end up with everyone really scrambling, trying to put things together."

In addition, the architectural demands of the Celebration homes put a strain on the production builders. Adhering to the standards of the pattern book and adding the design bells and whistles was expensive and time-consuming.

Town & Country might have dealt with the obstacles better if it had been making money in Celebration. There would have been a financial cushion to hire more workers and take additional time to get things right. The former president of Town & Country's Florida division, Timothy Edmond, said the company had estimated it could build the houses for $62 a square foot, but the actual figure came in at $82 a square foot. When combined with the price the company paid Disney for the land, Town & Country was losing money on every house it built, said Edmond, who added, "Town & Country never understood Florida, and they never invested in the people to make it work down here." Mike Ryan declined to say how much the company lost. "Celebration has not been profitable for us," was as far as he would go.

Weekley did not experience the same delays. It was only a few days or at most a couple of weeks behind on some of its houses. But there were some complaints about the quality of the work. One customer became so disgruntled over the condition of her marble floor that she parked her white Volvo sedan in the middle of downtown one night, covered it with lemons, and put up a sign that read "David Weekley Built My House." The sign said the floors of the $400,000 house were so rough that it was painful to walk on them, and invited anyone to come take a look for themselves. Tourists, who are as much a fixture of downtown as the shops, gawked and laughed at the display.

Some of the woman's neighbors were not so pleased when she plastered her house, which overlooked the golf course, with big posters of lemons and more signs berating the builder. "We're thinking of starting a campaign with signs that say 'David Weekley Built Our Houses and We Love Them,' " one of the neighbors, Bob Carson, said, only half in jest.

Few people had higher—or more detailed—expectations than Michael McDonough and Marty Treu, who had moved to Celebration from Sarasota in their continuing quest to find the perfect town. Both are architects, and over the years they had developed a five-point program for evaluating the livability of a town or a small city. The points were deceptively simple, but McDonough and Treu had refined them through years of observation and believed they represented the overt evidence of a healthy, interesting community. There had to be a movie theater, a hardware store, good civic buildings, quality housing stock, and not too many antiques stores, lest the town be too cute and overrun with tourists.

Only a handful of places met all the criteria. Beaufort, South Carolina, made the list, and so did Charlottesville, Virginia, where they had studied architecture at the University of Virginia. Celebration did not meet all five criteria. It lacked a hardware store and there were lots of tourists, though they were not attracted by an overabundance of antiques stores. What the architects did not discover until too late was that the quality of the housing, or at least theirs, was suspect.

McDonough and Treu had initially planned to build an expensive custom home in Celebration, but in the summer of 1997 they were drawn to what was then the town's newest neighborhood, Lake Evalyn. The scale attracted them and so did the feel of the Garden-home district set on the man-made water feature called Lake Evalyn.

The Garden homes were the smallest and least-expensive single-family homes in Celebration. They were really an afterthought and had not been included in the original plans or pattern book. Celebration Company introduced them as a way to keep prices below $200,000 as the cost of the Cottage homes skyrocketed in response to demand. The Garden homes were small, less than two thousand square feet, and to keep costs down, the builder, David Weekley Homes, had limited the number of options available. It was basically take it or leave it when it came to exterior colors and interior materials.

In many ways, Lake Evalyn was the closest thing to a purely neo-traditional neighborhood in Celebration. The architecture was the most vernacular in town, creating a setting similar to a mini–Key West. Streets were laid out on a strict grid and the houses were no more than five feet apart. Downtown was only a five-minute stroll away around the edge of the small lake and across a picturesque boardwalk through the swamp.

The concept was an instant success. When we moved, in late June, the Lake Evalyn building site was an open field. Two months later, in August 1997, the company held a lottery for the fifty-six available lots, and they sold out immediately. McDonough got the second number in the lottery, and when the family that got number one backed out, he had first choice among the lots and styles. He and Treu chose a two-story house overlooking Lake Evalyn.

"We wanted to take a production house and make it wonderful," said McDonough. "We wanted to learn how to deal with production houses because we want to do some of this, though with more authenticity and better-quality materials."

What he and Treu discovered was that some of the Garden homes were built with little attention to key elements. For instance, many of the homes facing Lake Evalyn, including theirs, had second-story porches that were installed using incorrect material. Plastic support columns designed to bear 1,300 pounds and for use only on single-story porches were supporting the weight of the second-story porch and the roof, which one subcontractor estimated was nearly twice the maximum weight. It was clear from the sidewalk that some of the columns had twisted and bowed. The columns on McDonough and Treu's porch had to be replaced.

There were other problems. Their house had to be repainted several times to get the thickness and uniformity of coverage that McDonough demanded. Parts of the framing had to be reconstructed to make the house plumb. The punch list was so long that McDonough questioned whether the houses would still be standing in twenty years. "A place like this should really be about excellence of the environment, and that includes the houses," he said.

Despite their complaints about the construction, McDonough and Treu loved living in Celebration. They especially loved sitting on the porch, just four feet back from the sidewalk. "Our porches are so close to the street that it makes them like little theater seats," McDonough explained. "Our movie screen is our front porch. We have such a wonderful framed view of the activity, particularly with the lake as a backdrop. It's a wonderful parade. It is thoroughly entertaining."

Almost everyone we talked to in Celebration felt much the same way: The construction difficulties were troubling and annoying, but the end result was worth the woe. And there was an unforeseen upside to all the consternation. The delays and the nagging problems people found once they moved in became a shared experience. While certainly not the backstory that the Disney Imagineers would have envisioned, these common problems resulted in a common vocabulary. There was a vitality and even humor to the conversations. Like residents of new towns and subdivisions everywhere, people in Celebration were eager to share the latest tale of woe and then offer one to top it. "People actually bonded together in this foxhole mentality," observed Beth McCarthy. "We were all in the same boat. We'd laugh hysterically some days. We'd be laughing one minute and in tears the next."

One morning Cathy bumped into Gene Kane outside the SunTrust Bank. An outgoing man who smiles easily, Kane knew almost everyone in town. After all, he wrote the mortgages for many of them. As a result, he was always a good source of stories about the building problems, and he had seen some common themes. The themes would have been familiar to new residents of most production-home developments, but the difference was that no one moving to Celebration had expected these sorts of problems. After all, this was not just another development; this was Disney's town and there was no margin for error or omission.

"Because everyone is coming in and they are new to Celebration, the one common experience is the fact that they are building their houses," Kane said, standing in some shade near the entrance to the bank. "That gives them something to start talking about. 'How's your house? You know those guys, they put my sewer lines in wrong.' These things happen in production housing." In an odd way, Kane said, the problems were creating a bond.

"Some of these stories must be more urban folklore than truth," said Cathy. "Like the story about the crane that fell on the house. Or the house that was built without a connection to the sewer. Those can't be true. They must just grow up from rumor."

"No, no," insisted Kane. "They're true. The family that moved into a house and found out several days later, in the worst way you can imagine, that their sewer lines had not been hooked up. True. And a crane did fall on a house, it was a town house, and the owners still aren't in.

True. And don't forget the house they had to knock down and start over. True."

This last one brought Cathy up short. It sounded like the mother of all construction fiascoes, and somehow she had not heard of it.

"Whose house was that?" she asked.

"You're the reporter," he said wryly. "Go find out. And while you're at it, what about the house where the owners woke up one morning to find the neighbor's porch in their yard?"

"That was ours," Cathy responded quickly, before remembering that Kane knew exactly whose house had had the porch problem.

The importance of these gaffes and delays, it seemed to us, was not only what they said about the quality of construction in Celebration but how the community's way of dealing with them reflected the genuine desire to make the town work. As Beth said, people could have sold their houses and walked away from the town, but many people recognized that the promise of living in Celebration embodied more than the quality of construction. That was precisely the spirit we discovered after tracking down the people whose house had been leveled. It took a couple of days, but Cathy's sources at Barnie's coffee shop came up with the answer.

In the weeks after we moved in, Cathy had begun stopping by Barnie's most mornings for a cup of coffee. The shaded courtyard, with its wrought-iron tables and chairs, offered a pleasant vantage point for watching the town and, when necessary, a good place for interviews. On the steamiest days, she took refuge at one of the small tables inside.

Every day brought a steady stream of regulars. Sometimes she spoke to them, sometimes not. Often ad hoc groups would form at one of the tables, trading stories about goings-on in town and offering sometimes acerbic observations. That was the thing about Barnie's. It was a clearinghouse of information and gossip, and the natural place to find out, by quizzing a couple of the regulars, that it was Ken and Patty Liles whose house had been bulldozed.

Not long after, we met the Lileses for lunch at Max's Café. As is usual with these stories, their tale was so unlikely that we knew it had to be true. The Lileses were living in San Antonio with their three teenage children when they first heard about Celebration, in 1994. They were members of the Disney Vacation Club, a time-share operation with locations at Disney

World, Hilton Head Island, and similar resort areas, and the sales representative mentioned the new town that Disney was building. When they returned for their vacation-club stay the following year, they picked up more information about the town and the upcoming lottery.

Ken and Patty both were restless. They had moved to San Antonio from Minneapolis, but they never really liked the Texas town. Ken was the vice president of a small technology company back in Minneapolis, and his job was portable. Patty had finished paralegal school. In November of 1995, they were talking about moving, to either Seattle or somewhere in Florida.

"Christopher, our oldest, said one day, 'If we have to move, can we stay in the warm weather?' " Patty recalled. "It was two days before the lottery at Celebration, so I flew down and entered it. We didn't really know much about Celebration, but we decided to try it anyway. We figured if it didn't work out, we could always move again. It was a gamble. We'd see how it worked out."

In the Saturday morning drawing, Patty's name was chosen as number twenty-two in the Village home drawing. But her lucky streak had a little further to run. Before leaving the lottery, she struck up a conversation with a lawyer who worked for Disney. He encouraged her to apply for a job with the company, and he gave her a telephone number to call on Monday. "Don't get discouraged," he said as they parted. "Disney takes a while. Maybe six months."

Perfect, thought Patty. By that time, the kids will be almost out of school, and we can all move here together.

On Monday she called the number, which was for the Disney Development Company, the division that created Celebration. She was told to drop by that day and she did, with her résumé in hand. Two weeks later, the company called and offered her a job. By the way, the caller asked, how soon could she start? Everything had gone so smoothly that it seemed like fate.

Patty moved into an apartment near Disney World in February 1996. The family had chosen a Village model by Town & Country on a lot near the golf course, and construction on the house started in April. The Lileses expected to be among Celebration's first residents by the coming summer. Ken and the kids moved into the apartment at the beginning of summer, but the house still looked a long way from completion.

A June or July move-in was pushed back to late fall, but the builder seemed to be making progress. By the end of July, the cinder-block walls that Town & Country used to build the first floor of its houses were up, and the prefabricated roof rafters were dropped into place by a crane. Then the unbelievable happened.

"We came by the house one Friday afternoon to check on it," recalled Ken, with a grimace. "The whole thing was jacked up. Windows were torn out, and they were using jackhammers on the foundation. We couldn't figure out what in the world was going on."

"Dad," said the Lileses' youngest son, Ryan, "they're flipping the house."

Ken looked closer. His son was right. The workers were raising the house off its foundations and preparing to move it, without ever having mentioned the matter to the Lileses. They immediately called the Town & Country offices and demanded a meeting at the site on Saturday morning.

The construction supervisor tried to explain what had happened. The draftsman who drew up the plan to locate the house on the lot had put the attached garage on the right side of the house. The Lileses wanted it on the left side, to open up a better view out the back of the house. They had told the builder, and the plans had been redrawn with the garage on the left.

Unfortunately, the location of the house on the lot had not been adjusted to compensate for the new position of the garage. When workers started to pour footings for the garage, they discovered that the location on the left meant the garage extended three feet onto the neighboring lot. The solution, explained the supervisor, was to jack up what they had built so far and rotate it 180 degrees. It would result in the garage's being on the right side, but the house would fit on the lot.

The Lileses objected strenuously. What would moving the house at this stage do to its structural integrity? How could the builders do this without telling them? And anyway, they didn't want the garage on the right. Another supervisor was brought in, and the builders and the prospective homeowners stood in a small knot, arguing. Patty tried to call Disney Development for help, but no one was answering the phone on a Saturday. They told the builders to stop everything.

Working for Disney paid off. Over the weekend, Patty sent e-mails to senior executives with the Disney Development and Celebration companies. Disney executives—Patty doesn't want to say exactly who—told Town & Country to make it right: Knock down the house and start over.

In July 1996, there were not many people living at the end of Sycamore Street, where the Lileses were trying to build their house. But the town was attracting lots of tourists, and they liked to walk over to the golf course after visiting the model homes at the other end of Sycamore. The prospect of a bulldozer and jackhammers tearing apart a house was a public-relations nightmare. So Town & Country got special permission from Celebration Company to work at night, under spotlights, so as few neighbors and tourists as possible would see what was happening. "When we came the next morning, the bulldozer was kind of topping off the lot," Patty remembered. "Nobody was around. Nobody seemed to have noticed."

The Lileses finally moved into their house on May 5, 1997, nearly a year late. But they didn't hold any grudges. "When you think about how many things have to work right to start a new life, the house is really a small part, and everything else really went well," said Patty, as she finished her lunch. "You get over the hump, and you deal with it. It was a frustrating thing, and a lot of people have gone through it. But when you think about everything, it's amazing to see how it all kind of fell into place. Worst thing I thought would happen was that the kids would move back to Texas or hate the school. But they're still here, and they like the school."

After lunch, as we rode our bicycles back home, we talked about the healthy attitude of the Lileses toward the house problems and life in general here. They had not expected perfection. To them, Celebration was a town with some cool ideas and infinite possibilities, not some version of the Magic Kingdom. They were willing to work to make the community a better place; both of them were active in town affairs, from their church and the school to the barbershop quartet, of which Ken was a founder.

We were getting to know more and more people in town. They were candid in responding to our questions. Those who seemed to be most disappointed that everything was not perfect, the ones most distraught by the roof that leaked or the house that didn't get completed on time, were the ones who had believed most strongly in Disney.

As Peter Rummell had feared, many people had moved to Celebration expecting Disney to make things perfect. Their surprise and disappointment were inevitable. The question in our minds was whether these people would roll up their sleeves and work to make Celebration the place they wanted, or whether they would be content to carp from the sidelines. Good architecture couldn't make the town work, and Disney couldn't ride to the rescue every time. The people who lived there had the power to determine the future of Celebration. As Le Corbusier had said, "Life always has the last word."

5

Great Expectations

The early afternoon had been hot enough to strike fear in any Northerner venturing outside. One step, and your breath seemed to be sucked out of your lungs in the sweltering furnace. In deep summer, the afternoons are curiously unreal in central Florida. The combination of heat and humidity imposes an emptiness on the streets and a curious sense of detachment from the real world. Any sudden or industrious activity out of doors is impossible. Then come the daily afternoon storms. And with them come the lightning strikes, sometimes numbering in the thousands in a single storm.

Impressive storms are a constant threat in what meteorologists call "lightning alley." Kids are warned of the danger in school, but nobody really expects to be struck. One day, two golfers were killed on a course a few miles away. In 1996 alone, 105 Floridians and visitors were hit by lightning; 96 survived. The state has an active chapter of a group with the self-explanatory name Lightning Strike and Electrical Shock Survivors International. We had new respect for nature and new rules to follow to stay out of harm's way.

As evening approached on this particular late-August day, the storms had given us a pass, and the temperature and humidity both were dropping. Outside our front bay window on Nadina Place, card tables and chairs were being set up in the street and two barbecue grills were being lit. On the tables were two dishes with marshmallows and one seven-layer bean dip, two dishes of baked beans and three tossed salads, a wonderfully colorful antipasto plate, some platters of brownies, and a bowl of pretzels covered with white chocolate. On the grill, sausages, hot dogs, and hamburgers were crackling. There were coolers of soda pop and juice, but no alcoholic beverages in sight. It was the Sunday of Labor Day weekend, and the block was throwing a party.

Unlike the day of the first block party, this time the street was lined with finished houses, the sidewalks were in, and grass and trees graced the strip that ran down the middle of the street. In all, twelve families were living on Nadina Place. Eight houses, four at each end, were still to be constructed. Two houses on the block stood empty because of absentee owners, a violation of Celebration rules that no one seemed inclined to complain about but which we felt subtracted from the neighborhood.

While Celebration mixes apartments and single-family houses in the same general part of town, and prices range from about $160,000 to $1 million, most streets are segregated by price. For instance, every house on Nadina is a Cottage home. They cost anywhere from $225,000 to $325,000, depending on model and options. And among the twelve houses occupied that day were six different models; the most popular model was the Savannah, which we had chosen, and there were four of them. Each model was offered with three or four different facades. Our Savannah had what was called a Colonial facade, with yellow-painted Hardiboard siding. The other three Savannahs on Nadina also had Colonial facades, but with stucco; two were pale beige and one was white. Despite the variety of models, the houses were similar in size and price, and the same held true for every other street in town.

On Nadina that afternoon, kids raced back and forth, firing giant squirt guns and throwing water balloons at each other and the occasional adult who wandered into the line of fire. Two small children pulled a red wagon containing a smaller child. Neighbors chatted amiably with neighbors, and nobody minded that outsiders from elsewhere in Celebration had crashed the party. It was a budding tradition that had given rise to the name "Block Busters." Even the mosquitoes seemed to have taken a night off. The scene had all the hallmarks of the postcard of old-fashioned America that Disney was trying to re-create.

Shailesh Adhav, who lived in the beige Savannah model with a Colonial stucco facade at the other end of the street, sat on the curb, cooling off from grill duty. He watched his five-year-old daughter, Devon, dash down the street in pursuit of an older kid and shook his head at his good luck. "This is what I remember from growing up," he said. "It was a small town in Canada, between Ottawa and Toronto, called Lindsey. We rented a huge brick Victorian house, with a big porch. There were bats in the attic. I think it was two hundred dollars a month. Instead of this grassy median, we had a train track down the street. It was wonderful, and so is this."

Shailesh was a certified public accountant, working for one of Disney's divisions in an office building near the entrance to Celebration. He and his wife, Leigh, had two young daughters, and Leigh stayed home to care for them. Most days, he scooted home in his Honda Civic to have lunch with his wife and younger daughter, Lauren, who was too young for school.

"We've been married eleven years," he said. "Yesterday was our anniversary. We sold every liquid asset we had to move here. This is where we wanted to live. We've been in Florida since we got married. We lived over in Lake Mary, which was a nice neighborhood with lots of kids, and we knew people. But you'd never have anything like this. You'd never see people out talking and having fun at a party like this."

In the two months since we had moved in, we had come to know everyone on our street. There had been a couple of impromptu potluck suppers and numerous casual chats as we walked our new dog, a rescued greyhound named Walt. Apart from simple proximity, our neighbors shared a sense of commitment to the town. Some of them had sacrificed comfortable lives and good incomes to move to Celebration. For these solidly middle-class, socially and economically conservative people, this was the adventure of their lives. It was an attempt to start over, with a clean slate, in a town paved with promises and expectations.

To a person, they loved watching their kids fly off on their Rollerblades or bikes, headed for a friend's house on the other side of town or to one of the shops downtown. The atmosphere was carefree, almost wanton, when it came to freedom for kids in Celebration. We had marveled—and shuddered—when Nick or Becky brought home a friend for dinner and the youngster, a complete stranger to us, stayed until long after dark without ever calling home. At times we thought some Celebration parents had left their common sense out on Highway 192. They seemed oblivious to the potential harm from the tourists visiting the town. Not everyone was a nice person, even in Disneyville.

Still, we allotted our children a measure of freedom that they had never experienced. In Westport, we had lived on three acres at the end of a private road. Play dates, with one of us driving them to and from a friend's house at specified times, were the norm. Traffic at the street end of our small lane in Westport was thick and fast, making it too dangerous for the children to venture out on their own. By contrast, Celebration traffic was slow and sparse, with the only serious vehicular danger arising from rubbernecking tourists who weren't paying attention to where they were driving.

The ability to strap on their Rollerblades and scoot down the street at will was brand-new and exhilarating for Becky and Nick. The adventure made them impervious to the heat. Midafternoon would find Nick deep into a street-hockey game in the parking lot of the school gym, red-faced, drenched with sweat, and smiling sweetly. Becky was on the go constantly, racing from a friend's house to home to the community swimming pool, a tireless redheaded social dervish. The kids didn't even seem to mind the few rules we imposed, like calling home every two hours and never going into a stranger's home, Celebration or not.

At one of the tables that evening of the block party, Jere and Earlene Batten (blue Ashland Coastal model) were deep in conversation with Alice and Dick Joossens (white Savannah Colonial stucco). The Battens and their son Alex had moved to Celebration from Pottstown, Pennsylvania. They felt that life was going downhill in that former steel town. The schools were deteriorating. Jobs were disappearing. The spirit seemed to have been sucked out of the town. At the same time, demands on them were increasing. They spent long hours at their jobs, Jere as a software designer and Earlene as a computer programmer. They devoted several evenings a week to church work. And they had raised four Vietnamese foster children, along with Alex and his older brother, Steve. They wanted to find a simpler life and a better place for Alex to grow up. They had chosen Celebration for the same reason as many of the town's first residents—Disney.

"We had taken every vacation for years at Disney World, and we were members of the Disney Vacation Club," said Jere when we joined them at the table that evening. "We weren't blind believers, but when we heard about Celebration we knew that Disney would do it the right way. So, yes, Disney played a pretty significant role in our coming here. When you vacation here, both in the way Disney runs their parks and the Disney hotels, there is a tremendous sense of quality. Most of the people who vacation with Disney end up very pleased. So there was that sense of quality that goes with Disney. Our assumption was that that quality would translate over into the new town. I think if it had been any other community in central Florida, our motivation wouldn't have been that strong. We wouldn't have come."

The Battens participated in the lottery but put off moving until their last foster child left for college. Their eventual landing in Celebration, the same day we moved in across the street, had been a little rough. They both had been offered jobs at an Orlando software company, but when Jere decided to work out of his new house as a consultant for his former employer, the offer to Earlene was withdrawn. Earlene did not have a college degree, and after searching in vain for several weeks for something related to computers, she wound up working for little more than minimum wage behind the front desk at Port Orleans, one of the Disney resort hotels.

"It's been a humbling experience," she had confided a few nights earlier when the four of us had dinner downtown at our favorite restaurant, Café D'Antonio. "I'd always thought that smart people made the money. But these people I work with are smart, and we're not making any money. It's hard work, and I can feel it at the end of the day."

Earlene had also gotten a taste of how outsiders perceived Celebration, even people within the Disney family, as they liked to call it. "Everyone thinks that you're rich when you say you live in Celebration," she said. "When I tell another worker where I live, their whole attitude changes. One of the women said to me the other day, 'Why are you working here for minimum wage when you live in Celebration?' I told her that I wasn't rich and wasn't getting rich on Disney wages. They ask about the rules, too. 'Is it true you have to paint your house a certain color?' That sort of thing."

Despite the bumps, neither Jere nor Earlene had a bad thing to say about Celebration. They loved it, and they trusted in God and Disney that everything would work out for the best.

Many people had made enormous sacrifices to move to Celebration. Lance and Karin Boyer had lived in fourteen places in the seven years before they moved to Disney's new town. As far back as 1990 they had decided that they would find the perfect place to live by the time the oldest of their three children was ten. They still carried in Lance's calendar organizer a list of the qualities of that perfect town, which they had written years earlier. There were twenty-three items, ranging from a rural setting and strong schools to safe drivers and no nuclear plants.

Lance was a systems manager for Domino's Pizza in Michigan, and he was visiting a store near Disney World in July of 1996 when he saw a map on the wall that mentioned Celebration. He asked the manager about the name and was told that it was Disney's town. Boyer immediately called the Celebration sales office to see how late it was open. It was nearly five-thirty in the afternoon and he was told the office closed at six.

"I'll be there in twenty minutes," he said. "That leaves you ten to convince me that it's the most wonderful place in the world."

In truth, Boyer said later, he was convinced before he set foot on the property. Everything Disney does, they do right, he said.

When he got to the sales office, Boyer discovered that it was the last day for prospective purchasers from the lottery to exercise their options and sign contracts to buy town houses, the least expensive homes in Celebration. The sales agent said they expected that some of the town houses would come back on the market the next day, when people decided not to proceed. But the agents said they had appointments booked for the whole day, starting at 10 A.M., and could not fit Boyer in.

"No problem," said Boyer. "I'll be here at nine A.M. Eventually somebody will be a no-show and I'll take their time slot."

That night, he called his wife in Michigan, described Celebration, and said he was going back in the morning to see about buying a house. Accustomed to his impulsiveness, Karin said he should do what he thought best.

The following day, Boyer waited patiently until one in the afternoon. There were no no-shows. As he sat there, he wondered about the impact of what he was doing. Things were tight financially for the family, and he would be giving up his job to move. Finally he wandered back to the sales agents' offices and ran into Ellen Sullivan, one of the sales people, who asked what she could do for him.

"I want the least expensive house you have," he said.

"Okay," replied Sullivan. "We have a $150,000 town house that just became available, and it's yours."

He waited while she went to get the paperwork. Ten minutes later, she returned with a frown. The house had been taken. The same thing happened with a second town house. Finally, she said, she had lined up the last available one, but the price was $180,000 because of its location and the addition of a granny flat over the garage.

Boyer could not afford the $150,000 model, let alone one for $180,000, but he persuaded Sullivan to hold the property long enough for him to make some phone calls, and he rushed out to a pay phone. His parents agreed to help with the down payment by taking some of the equity out of their own home. He called Karin, and she figured they could come up with the rest of the money if she got a part-time job while raising their small kids.

So Boyer returned and filled out the papers. He ran into another potential hitch when Sullivan explained that he had to pay a $5,000 deposit on the spot to secure the house.

"I don't have it," he said.

"We do accept checks," she laughed, misunderstanding him.

"Well," he replied. "I don't have any checks with me. Even if I did, I don't have five thousand dollars sitting in my account. But give me an hour. I'll be right back."

Boyer had three credit cards in his wallet, all of which had a zero balance. He took them to three different banks and withdrew enough money on the cards to come up with the deposit. He walked back into Sullivan's office and handed the surprised sales agent $5,000 in cash.

Then the struggle began to come up with the money to make the move from Michigan, where they rented a house, to Celebration. In addition to his eight-to-five management job with Domino's, Boyer had started driving a limousine from six in the evening to one in the morning every day. Karin took a job delivering newspapers in the early morning, while her husband was still home with the kids, and she had begun teaching art at the children's Montessori school.

"I thought we really wouldn't be able to pull it together," Boyer said one evening after they moved to Celebration. "Remember, not only were we trying to buy this house we couldn't afford, but I wasn't going to have a job either. The pressure was enormous. Then one day, I don't know how to describe it, but I heard a voice, and it said, 'Everything is going to work out.' From then on, I was as calm as could be."

Even before moving to Celebration, Lance was offered a job with Domino's in Orlando. After the Boyers arrived he began moonlighting by booking vacation-home rentals over the Internet at night. Still, it was a struggle to make ends meet month after month. Gesturing around the family's bare-bones living room, he said: "We're sitting on a house of cards. We paid twelve hundred dollars for all this furniture and these plants. It's the only thing we've bought."

Celebration met only fifteen of the twenty-three items on the Boyers' list, and Lance and Karin both said it was not exactly what they had expected. But they also were filled with hope that the town would turn into the kind of place they had envisioned when they put together that wish list in 1990.

This search for a new and better life, the desire to start fresh, is as old as America itself. Right from the start, the American way of life fulfilled the demands of generations for freedom and expansion, the longing of men and women whose ancestors had lived constrained by strict social and religious codes. Through two centuries, the country has remained at heart a frontier society, though the geography of its frontiers has changed dramatically.

In a sense, the people who moved to Celebration had much in common with the immigrants who came to America in the nineteenth and early twentieth centuries. They had pooled their resources, pulled up stakes, and moved to a new place, and this place was about as different for some of them as America had been for the European immigrants. "The fact that they would, in many cases, take great risk to come to a place like Celebration indicates that they were looking for something that they didn't have," said Ronald Clifton, a retired foreign service cultural attaché who had come to Celebration as the liaison between the town's school and Stetson University, one of the institutions involved with the school's development.

Of course, there is a word for what so many of these people seek. It is utopia. But it's a word that has gone out of fashion. For many today, utopianism connotes a naïve and impractical approach to life. Certainly few of our Celebration neighbors would be pleased to hear themselves described as utopians. Yet what they were doing there was nothing less than trying to remake their environment and its institutions in the belief that life could reach a higher level. They were trying to build the city on a hill, the very definition of utopia. And, like most other utopian experiments, this one was created in response to dissatisfaction with contemporary life.

There is ample precedent for using town planning to shape a utopian alternative. Indeed, the word, which means "no place" in Greek, was first used to designate a perfect society in 1516 when Sir Thomas More published his famous book *Utopia*. More created his vision of a worldly utopia to criticize contemporary economic and social conditions in Europe and England, especially war, oppression of the poor, extravagances of the wealthy, taxation, and unjust laws. The overcrowded cities, the poverty, and the near-nonchalance with which vagrants and petty thieves were tried, sentenced, and hanged in the markets appalled More, who twenty years later was himself beheaded after refusing to acknowledge Henry VIII as supreme head of the Church of England.

As a humanist antidote to the conditions of his day, More depicted the way of life and the social institutions of an imaginary two-hundred-mile-long island whose chief city, Amaurot, was situated in the center. Poking fun at the gaudy clothes and precious metals of the rich, he imagined chamber pots made of gold and placed people who loved fine clothes in a lower caste. There were no idle rich on the island of Utopia. Instead, every man, woman, and child knew how to cultivate the soil and also had a special trade, such as carpentry or masonry. There were fifty-four cities on the island, each ruled by a magistrate who divided labor and goods fairly among the populace. The country's economic base was agricultural, and its citizens rotated regularly between living in the cities and on the farms. Rather than striving for riches and material goods, the chief pleasure of Utopians was cultivation of the mind, with leisure hours spent in lecture halls and reading and studying. More's Utopia gained a wide audience, and the term he coined eventually became part of the language of social thinkers and visionaries.

Two centuries later, the New World became the testing ground for utopian ideas, most of which were grounded in religious beliefs and practices. One of the earliest sects was the United Society of Believers in Christ's Second Appearing, also known as the Shakers, who sought to develop simple, self-sufficient communities. The Shakers did not aim to change society. They sought only to build their own community in accordance with the rules and religion they imposed upon themselves. By the nineteenth century, an estimated 100,000 utopian communities existed in the United States, the vast majority based on religious beliefs. Although we remember some of them, like Robert Owen's famous cooperative town in New Harmony, Indiana, and the Oneida community in New York State, most are forgotten. Interestingly, one of the few utopian communities that survived, Chautauqua, was modeled after the small towns that many Americans were leaving in the late nineteenth century, though its initial purpose was to serve as a summer school for Sunday school teachers. Today, the small community in southwestern New York, with its pastel-colored Victorian cottages that are similar to some in Celebration, remains a thriving haven for about 7,500 summer residents interested in the arts and spiritual pursuits.

By the late nineteenth and early twentieth century, utopianism had shed the robes of religion. The three great utopian dreamers of this period were urban planners and architects who rose up against what they saw as the squalor and overcrowding of cities: the British planner and philosopher Ebenezer Howard, the American architect Frank Lloyd Wright, and the French-speaking Swiss Le Corbusier. These men did not just dream of utopias. They designed in great detail the ideal cities that were intended to have an impact on economics and environment as well as on architecture.

Their visions of utopia were starkly different. Howard devised the concept of the garden city, where shops and cottages were clustered in a town center that was surrounded by farmland. Wright's Broadacre City was the ultimate suburb, where the automobile was king and the best way to get around was really a personal helicopter, fancifully designed by Wright himself. Le Corbusier worshipped technology and conceived of a utopian city comprised of cruciform skyscrapers set down in open parkland.

These cities were the most ambitious plans yet for using architecture and planning to transform society. Despite the radical differences in concept, as Robert Fishman wrote in *Urban Utopias in the Twentieth Century*, all three men shared the belief that old cities could not be repaired and the only solution was a wholly transformed urban environment. Celebration was the next logical step in that continuum, a rejection of old suburbs and an attempt to turn the page and start fresh.

Is it outlandish to argue that the evolution of utopian thought should find one of the world's most powerful and wealthy corporations championing the notion that careful planning and architecture can lead to a better society? Some of the most ambitious planning projects were the work of autocrats. Only a Caesar could have built the great Roman highways, and only a Robert Moses could have rammed through the vast parks and rampant developments of New York City. Maybe only a corporation could pull off the millennial utopia.

Today's autocrats are the megacorporations, and none exerts more influence over our culture than Disney. But few people envision a utopia in which adults wear Mickey Mouse T-shirts. Beloved as it may be by the masses (except for Southern Baptists, who object to its tolerance of gays), the Walt Disney Company is widely distrusted and even despised among the intelligentsia, the very people who could be expected to embrace a new utopian concept. To them, Disney is low-brow and omnivorous. Carl Hiaasen, the popular chronicler of Florida public sociopathic behavior, is representative. In 1998, in a scathing pamphlet on Disney called *Team Rodent,* he wrote: "Disney stands as by far the most powerful private entity in Florida. It goes where it wants, does what it wants, gets what it wants. It's our exalted mother teat, and you can hear the sucking from Tallahassee all the way to Key West." But Hiaasen was not content to scold Disney's performance in Florida. His broadside condemned the company for everything from making Times Square in New York City too clean to its unsuccessful attempt to develop a Civil War theme park outside Washington, D.C. The point was not subtle: Disney was threatening to devour the whole world.

Clearly Disney is a cultural force to be reckoned with, whether it is transforming 42nd Street, deciding what Americans will see on television and at the movies, or building a new town. The company generates more than $20 billion in revenue a year from a staggering array of sources— theme parks in the United States, France, and Japan; Walt Disney Pictures as well as Touchstone, Miramax, Caravan, and Hollywood Pictures; the

ABC television network, ESPN, the Disney Channel, and Lifetime; nine television stations and twenty-one radio stations; home videos, music and book publishing, cyberspace, and newspapers; baseball and hockey teams; hotels, shopping centers, retail stores; and even Broadway plays.

Disney tells us what to watch, what to read, where to go on vacation, and, in the case of its planned town of Celebration, where to live and what color to paint our houses. So vast and complex is Disney's cultural reach that its every action is—and should be—scrutinized for broader implications. Small wonder that the company's creation of an entire town raised skepticism about its motives. Small wonder, too, that an attempt to understand that town in any context other than as a profit-making venture contradicted conventional wisdom. It is easy and trendy to dismiss Celebration as another Disney product—an off-the-shelf town designed to appeal to the same predominantly white, lower- and middle-class people who flock to its theme parks and jam Disney stores from Times Square to every major airport in the country.

And indeed, Michael Eisner is not Sir Thomas More any more than Robert Stern, with his Mickey Mouse ties, is Frank Lloyd Wright. Celebration is first and foremost about making money, not bettering society. In creating Celebration, the company was motivated by the desire to turn idle swampland into profits. But accomplishing that goal required a cohesive vision and what now sits on that former swampland is strikingly similar in its physical environment to the garden city conceived a hundred years ago by Ebenezer Howard. As the father of British planning, who described large cities as "ulcers on the very face of our island," Howard proposed a community that offered housing in a broad range of incomes, a town center, well-defined civic and public spaces, and a walking scale that made it all accessible. Basically, Howard strove to overcome social problems by wedding the best of the city to the best of the country. The basic concept would be familiar to anyone who has visited Celebration or any number of other American towns, from Riverside, Illinois, to Columbia, Maryland.

Yet Celebration stands out from those earlier endeavors as well as more recent ones like Seaside, Florida. Disney's town represents an effort to balance the urban and rural in a way that is missing from Riverside and Columbia, which are too parklike. Yet it is also different from Seaside and its neotraditional cousins, which are too claustrophobic to function smoothly as sizable communities. With its blend of curvilinear arterial avenues and straight, narrow neighborhood streets, coupled with its mixture of income ranges in housing and its civic institutions, Celebration is a unique attempt to marry what worked in the past with the imperatives of modern conditions.

That is not to say that it succeeds on every count, or that the vision behind Celebration should be adopted as a solution to the ills of urban and suburban America. This refinement of the American dream is too constrained, too middle-class, and too white to represent a true solution. In Celebration, there is no public transit, no room for the working poor, and little racial diversity. But Celebration is a place that enhances rather than frustrates everyday life, a hybrid town that demonstrates a new and workable alternative to suburban sprawl and isolated neighborhoods. People who move to Celebration also have the chance to indulge in a time-honored American tradition—they can reinvent themselves and their lives.

There is ample evidence that Americans, particularly those with the money and jobs to be mobile, are searching for an alternative. Pollsters and social scientists tell us that, for many, the search focuses on qualities of life outside their homes. Unlike residents of traditional suburbs, where the private yard and spacious house seemed all the castle any man needed, Americans today are more concerned with the quality of their neighborhoods than the houses in which they live. Merely being able to buy a nice house in the right suburb is no longer enough. There are several reasons behind this trend. One is that people seem to be selecting neighborhoods in which they feel safe and comfortable, and therefore are more likely to develop a sense of community. Another reason is that, with an estimated thirty million Americans now doing some part of their work at home, home is becoming more central to a person's lifestyle. No longer is home simply where a working person ends up at the end of a long day at the office or factory. More and more of us are spending the workday in our homes, which means we want more amenities within walking distance, from restaurants and shops to post offices and Kinko's.

Rummell and others within the Disney Development Company recognized this trend early and sought to develop a community that would capitalize on it. At the same time, they did see the town as a planning exercise that could contribute to the overall betterment of society. Driven by Eisner's lofty aspirations, they wanted to come up with a concept that could, with alterations, be replicated elsewhere. The thinking went beyond design to the very philosophy behind the town.

"It's funny," Rummell said one day as he pondered the attention devoted to Celebration. "Most of the writing about Celebration has focused on the architecture. It was about seventh or eighth on the list of what we thought was important." More important, both to the quality of life and to the marketability of the town, were the five cornerstones on which Celebration was founded. The Disney executives believed those cornerstones were meant to reflect the values and the aims of the town. Granted, they were developed as marketing devices, but that does not make the ideas any less valid as a blueprint for a civil society akin to the imagined prescriptions of Thomas More. The cornerstones represent a new way of living as much as a new development. Like the backstory that keeps Disney Imagineers focused, the cornerstones generated a clear understanding of what the developers wanted to build. And like earlier utopias, they set out a vision that attracted followers. These cornerstones are education, wellness, technology, place, and community.

Education was embodied in the school and its affiliated teaching academy as well as in the promise of adult education facilities. Disney recognized that education was an important factor in marketing the town, and it proved to be the primary motivating factor for most people who bought houses or rented apartments in the first phase of Celebration. But the definition of education was intended to be broader than the local school. Disney wanted to ingrain education in the community as a whole by offering adults classes from languages to law.

Wellness was defined as the simple idea that better health makes better living. The philosophy was reflected in the sixty-acre combination hospital–fitness center built and run by Florida Hospital, the state's largest nonprofit hospital corporation. In this era of for-profit health care, Disney gave special weight to the nonprofit status of Florida Hospital, which is affiliated with the Seventh-Day Adventist church. Experts in health care around the country, including former U.S. Surgeon General C. Everett Koop and futurist Leland Kaiser, were consulted to develop a system that would actively promote health in addition to providing quality care for illness and disease.

Technology was supposed to bring the latest fiber-optic cables into every house in Celebration. It promised a computerized community network that would let any resident call up his or her medical records at the hospital, monitor his or her child's work at school and communicate with teachers and administrators, or simply chat with neighbors or order carryout from one of the restaurants.

A sense of place was reflected in the post-neotraditional planning and the attempt to create a pleasant, workable physical environment: the public parks, the easy walk to shops, the distinctive architecture, and its hoped-for front-porch culture. The intention was to provide the safe neighborhoods and opportunities for social interaction that surveys showed most people wanted.

Most nebulous among the cornerstones was the fifth, a sense of community. The word itself is overused and ill defined. To us, a community should be a place that encourages a sense of belonging and inclusiveness, meaningful personal relationships, and a degree of shared responsibilities and goals. In the case of Celebration, the sense of community is best seen as the opposite of the way most people felt about the subdivisions and suburbs where they were living before they moved to paradise. Disney's long-range market research showed that a community's quality of life was going to be a strong marketing factor as more people were able to choose where they work and live in the evolving information era. The other four cornerstones contributed to the quality of life—good schools, access to health-care and fitness facilities, availability of a telecommunications network, place. But quality of life also included participation in a community, the availability of volunteer activities, the presence of events, activities, and festivities that draw people together. This social infrastructure made up the sense of community.

To promote this infrastructure, the company took the unusual step of creating the Celebration Foundation. The nonprofit organization was set up as a clearinghouse for clubs and organizations and a coordinator for volunteer activities in the community and within the larger area surrounding the town. The foundation also was seen as a means of sharing the innovative community practices with other organizations and developments.

Part of what makes Celebration unique, and worth examining, is the people who were drawn by this vision of an ideal town and its five cornerstones. By the end of its first full year, about fifteen hundred people were living in Celebration. The majority had come from other cities and towns in Florida. But people had moved there from thirty other states. One family had sold a farm in Washington State, another a garbage-hauling business in Minnesota, and a third a transient hotel in the Midwest. There were bankers, accountants, engineers, and investment planners. Lots of teachers, computer programmers, and people in the building trades. Three retired New York City firemen and a few retired policemen were living here. There were even two other families from Westport, Connecticut, our last home. Of course, there also was a fair number of Disney employees, from executives in charge of big divisions to minimum-wage employees struggling to pay for apartments. Some people had come with new jobs, some had portable jobs, and others came without jobs.

We discovered that the most common trait among them was trust in Disney. Paul Kraft, a patient, cheerful man who took the job as the director of the media center at Celebration School, had spent twenty years in public education in Pennsylvania as an English teacher, department chairman, and media specialist, all the while also teaching English and media studies at the college level. When Cathy asked why he had taken a $30,000-a-year job and moved to Celebration, he said simply: "It is the Disney thing for me. I am not a fanatic, like some people. But I am a Disney fan and have faith in Disney."

Many of the people in this group had, like the Battens, spent every vacation for a decade or more at Disney World. Their expectations were the highest. Some of them believed the pixie dust would work its magic in Celebration.

A woman who approached Don Killoren demonstrated the strength with which she connected Disney and Celebration. She had a complaint about her apartment. She said that she had not been allowed to use the small area outside her front door as she wanted because, she was told, it was common space.

"That's right," Killoren told her. "It's common area. It's not yours. I'm sorry, but there's nothing I can do about it."

The woman paused and then said, "Well, do you think you could get me some free passes to the parks and some Disney dollars?"

The degree of dependence on Disney in some quarters of the community was evident when the company name disappeared overnight from the water tower at the entrance to the town. The sign on the tower had always said "Disney's Town of Celebration." But in the fall of 1997 a company employee had scaled the tower and painted out Disney's name, leaving only "Town of Celebration." For several days, we had watched people wring their hands and express anxiety that Disney was abandoning the town.

"I heard that they were sick and tired of dealing with the construction complaints," one resident told us.

"I have it on good authority that Michael Eisner himself is upset about the school," offered another.

Rumors are a fact of life in a small town, and in this case they spread so fast that Brent Herrington, the town manager for the company, was forced to reassure the residents in his November newsletter. Disney, he explained, was not pulling out of Celebration. The company was simply "eager for the public to begin recognizing Celebration as a real, thriving community with its own unique identity."

Alongside those who believed in pixie dust was another, larger segment of the population that, though also drawn to Celebration because of Disney's involvement, tempered its views with a strong dose of realism. This group did not expect perfection. They expected good quality. They liked the concept behind the school, or the small-town atmosphere, or some combination of those and other attributes. When it came to Disney, they simply trusted the company to ensure that all of it would be well executed.

Lise Juneman fell into the realist category. She moved to Celebration from Naperville, Illinois, when her husband, Ron, got a new job nearby. "We had never heard of Celebration," she said. "Some friends said, 'Oh, you have to see the Disney town.' So we drove out to the preview center. We loved the architecture. We had always tried to live in older houses and renovate them. The idea of living in a home that looks older, but with everything new inside, was so nice. And I liked the idea that the kids would go to a K-through-twelve school and never have to leave their school."

Juneman wanted to illustrate one of her other reasons. She had come to Barnie's to meet Cathy for a cup of coffee and brought along a handful of black-and-white photographs taken in 1949 or 1950. That was when her husband's family had moved into a new community at the rural edge of Chicago. The houses were identical. They all were concrete block and painted white. His parents had bought one of the model homes, complete with furnishings from Marshall Field's, the grand Chicago department store.

"Ron remembered this community with such great fondness," explained Juneman. "All the families worked together. Among them they probably had six cars, so when somebody needed to go somewhere, they shared. They helped each other start schools and churches. We thought maybe this could happen here.

"Even though we weren't Disneyphiles, knowing their name was on the town, I knew the quality would be here," she said. "The Disney influence on our choice was pretty strong. When you go in the preview center and they tell you about the cornerstones, the wonderful hospital, and the school with Harvard and Johns Hopkins involved, it makes a difference."

Garry Stephens echoed Juneman. He had moved to town from a nearby subdivision because of the school. "People trusted Disney," he said. "They trusted that Disney standards would ensure that the community they were going to live in would be better than most, if not superbly better than most. I think that is the only reason most people came here."

The expectations of both of these groups, the outright Disneyphiles and those who trusted that Disney's involvement guaranteed a high level of quality, were based on their belief that the controlled reality of Disney World could be transferred to a real town where they could escape the vicissitudes of urban and suburban life. We met virtually no one in Celebration who had not gone to Disney World in the years before they decided to move to the town. This is not to say that everyone believed in pixie dust or that Disney was their principle reason for moving there. Many of the people we came to know had their own strong ideals and were well centered. They were searching for an alternative place to live, with the real hope that it would mean a new way to live. But, whether on a conscious level, like the Disneyphiles, or on a subconscious level, most of the town's residents expected the exercise in fantasy executed so flawlessly at the Magic Kingdom would translate seamlessly into a new community just outside the gates.

Not everyone had outsized expectations, and we encountered few people who were more realistic than our neighbor Donna McGrath. She and her husband, Mike, who had retired from Conrail with a medical disability, had come to Celebration with their thirteen-year-old daughter, Kayla, and Mike's mother, Mary. Within days of moving in, Donna and Mike had turned their house into party central. It always seemed to be filled with neighbors dropping in for a potluck dinner or Donna's pals from the Hilton corporation, where she sold time-shares, who had come by to gab and play cards. Donna was the ever-bubbling master of ceremonies, with a smile and an open door.

"We didn't move here for any other reason but the fun," she said one evening as we sat on their front porch. "We thought that here we could kick back and relax. We read about it and thought we'd like to be part of it, for a short time anyway. When our daughter graduates, we'll leave Celebration. This isn't our ultimate dream. That's living on a boat in the Caribbean. Five years from now that's where you'll find us.

"The problem that some people have is that they come here expecting Disney to fix their problems. I got news for you. You had a bad marriage back home? There's nothing here that can fix that. Or your kids. They're having problems in school? Getting in trouble? Well, it's up to the parents to instill those values. And that has to be done anywhere. Disney can't solve your kids' problems. Even our terrific, cutting-edge little school is no more equipped to solve those kinds of problems than anyplace else."

Her gut response was echoed one day when we stopped in the alley behind our house to chat with some new neighbors, Al and Judy Ziffer. They had moved to Celebration in 1996 in the first wave of residents and had recently moved into a larger house near ours. Judy, a psychologist, had been observing the town and its residents with a professional eye for many months. What troubled her, she explained, was the families that had moved to Celebration expecting all their problems to vanish. "Those people don't need Celebration," she said. "They need counseling. Those sorts of problems—rocky marriages, troubled children—must be solved from within the four walls of the home, not from without."

Indeed, some people had landed in Celebration in full retreat from chaos, hoping to find instant order and convinced that a new environment would heal their troubled marriages or straighten out their wayward kids. Such people are found in every town and city. What made them more apparent in Celebration was the physical proximity and the almost mandatory neighborliness of the place. You could ignore a disruptive person in Manhattan or even one whose house was across the street in your subdivision. It was a lot harder to do in Celebration.

No one we had met had higher expectations for their life here than the husband and wife who were standing beside one of the barbecue grills at our block party that last Sunday in August, and therein lies the story of how the peace of Nadina Place was broken, at least for our two families.

In the two months since we had moved into our house, we had learned a good deal about Cheryl and Rick Scherer and their four children. They had moved to Maitland, on the other side of Orlando, from Buffalo, New York, but all along they intended to move to Celebration. Cheryl had fifteen years of experience as a schoolteacher, but she had taken a big pay cut when they came to Florida. Rick worked as a repairman for a division of Honeywell.

One afternoon in July, Cheryl had dropped in for a drink of water and some relief from the heat. They had been doing a final inspection before closing on their house, and for some reason the electricity was off. As she sat at the kitchen table, she talked about her two youngest children, Abby and John, who were seven years old.

Abby was born early and spent several weeks in the hospital. Spending her days in the pediatric intensive-care ward with her newborn, Cheryl had noticed another premature baby. She learned that the baby, whose name was John, had been born to an unmarried teenager who still lived at home. Over the weeks, Cheryl came to admire John's indomitable spirit. Of all the babies in intensive care, he had seemed the least likely to make it, yet somehow he had clung to life.

When it came time to take Abby home, John was staying behind to await a foster family. But one of the nurses said to Cheryl, "Too bad you can't take John home, too, because he's almost ready."

Cheryl called Rick at work and said, "Do you want to have another baby?"

"When?" he asked.

"Right now," she replied.

So the Scherers wound up with two babies, both of whom required heart monitors and almost full-time care, and they eventually adopted John. "Imagine the journey John has made," Cheryl said proudly. "Now he lives in Disney World."

Over the course of several other conversations and casual encounters in the neighborhood, we found that the Scherers were very strict with their children. We were thus a little uneasy when one night Rick said to us, "What I like about this street is that we can all be the parents of every kid on the block."

The oldest Scherer child, a boy named Nick, was a year older than our son. There were four boys on the block approximately the same age, and the Scherers had envisioned them becoming the best of friends. But the boys had different interests and different personalities, so they had never clicked as a group and rarely played together. On occasion, Rick and Cheryl Scherer had suggested that the neighborhood boys needed to sit down and "talk things out" and "establish a dialogue," but the boys had seemed to go their separate ways most of the time.

So it was unusual that we watched the neighborhood kids playing together as dusk fell over the block party that Labor Day weekend. Everything seemed to be going smoothly as the kids raced between the houses with water balloons and Rollerbladed along the closed-off street.

About seven o'clock, Doug walked back to our house to grab something from the refrigerator and found Becky and Nick on the back porch. Becky's face was ashen and Nick was near tears. Donna McGrath was standing nearby and so was Nick Scherer. A handful of other children stood silent in the alley.

As our children told the story, the kids had been playing in the alley when Becky had grabbed Nick Scherer's hat and tried to run off with it. He had caught Becky—who is a wisp of a child—and hurled her to the cement. His own brother, John, had run next door to get Donna, who came over and stopped the mayhem.

Doug sent our kids into the house and told Nick Scherer to go home. In hindsight, he may have overreacted, but he was angered by the bigger boy's attack on his youngest. A few minutes later, Rick Scherer arrived, with his son in tow. He said that his Nick blamed the episode on Becky and that our children had been making life miserable for his son by avoiding him.

"Now, Doug," he said, "we have to sit down and talk about this. We have to put the kids in a room and have them work it out."

"Rick, I'm not talking about anything right now," said Doug, trying to control his anger. "My kids are upset, and whoever is at fault, we're not going to discuss the thing now." With that, he walked inside and closed the door.

Cathy came in from the block party a few minutes later. The kids and Doug were still upset by the encounter. Earlier in the day, the McGraths had invited us to spend the evening watching a movie on their giant television screen. Under the circumstances, we didn't feel like going, and Cathy went over to make our excuses.

As Cathy was leaving the McGraths, Cheryl Scherer walked onto the porch and said sharply, "Cathy, you and I have something to settle." Right behind Cheryl came Rick, blocking Cathy's way down the steps. For the next half hour, the Scherers complained about what had happened earlier in the evening, with Rick especially angry that Doug had refused to talk things out. Then Rick shifted his criticism to our kids, blaming them for the encounter. "That Becky," he said, "she deserves to be smacked."

Stunned and chilled, but trying to stay calm, Cathy said, "Rick, I'm sure you didn't mean that. Please don't talk about hitting my daughter."

"Yes, I did mean it," he countered. "With a mouth like that, she deserves it. I'd like to smack her myself."

As Cathy moved to leave, Rick tried to switch gears, saying that he hoped this episode wouldn't ruin the friendship. Cathy nodded, extricated herself, and returned home.

Over the next few weeks, we maintained a polite distance from the Scherers. We nodded and said hello. Nick Scherer dropped by occasionally to invite our son to Rollerblade or play catch, and sometimes Nick went with him. Cheryl never again sat at our kitchen table telling stories, and Rick didn't come back and suggest that we patch things up with a conversation. Had all of us lived in Celebration longer, we might have drawn on years of watching our kids grow up and sharing good times as well as rough spots to work things out. But this was a new situation, and those bonds had not developed yet.

6

School Daze

In the central courtyard of Celebration School, behind the twin towers with their green metal roofs, volunteers were passing out green and white pompoms. A thousand or more people had gathered, and the mood was festive and anticipatory. Dot Davis, the new principal of the school, watched in silence from the edge of a temporary stage erected at the rear of the courtyard. For a moment she turned away, as if to leave; then she faced the crowd again with a hesitant smile.

August 8, 1997, was an important date in the short history of Celebration. It was the first opportunity for the residents to tour their new $20 million school. Classes did not start until Monday, but, taking a page from the movie business, Celebration Company had organized a "sneak preview" for this Friday night, and much of the town had turned out. They couldn't wait to see the school. And they couldn't wait to meet the new principal, the woman who had come to rescue their children.

No one in the crowd that night could have known how much that woman hated the limelight. Although she had been the principal of a nationally recognized performing-arts school in Huntsville, Alabama, before coming here and had made countless speeches and public appearances, she remained uncomfortable at center stage.

But Davis's anxieties that night ran deeper. She had left the security of her old job almost on an impulse. "It was the hastiest decision I ever made," she explained to Cathy months later.

In the end, she had come at least partly as a means to allow her husband, Jim, to retire early from his backbreaking job as director of juvenile services for the State of Alabama. As for herself, Davis didn't really have any desire to start from scratch at a new school after twenty-seven years in education. Had she understood the full challenge of what she had taken on, and that the coming year would be the most difficult of her distinguished career, Davis might have never come near the stage at Celebration School that night.

From the days when Celebration was just a notion Peter Rummell and Charles Fraser were kicking around, education had been the centerpiece of the town. When the decision was made to build the Disney Institute elsewhere, the town planners had scrambled to find an alternative anchor. They thought that they had hit on exactly the right one—a unique combination of public and private efforts to create a model for education into the next century that would, like the town itself, combine the best of the old and new.

The school became integral to the company's desire to share the concepts behind Celebration with the larger world. Public funds were used to build the school; outside money was needed to fund an accompanying teaching academy. The original idea was to bring together experts from around the country to create for Celebration School a program that would have the best teaching practices and curriculum possible. The program would be shared with the rest of the education community through the Celebration Teaching Academy, which would train teachers and administrators from the larger world. The sales brochure handed to visitors at the preview center described the school as "a unique public/private collaboration" and boasted that it would be "an outstanding example of progressive learning."

"By bringing in experts from places like Harvard and other places and blending their theories with real-world practices, we began to think that there would be a vision of a public school that would be a lighthouse for new ideas," said Don Killoren, the general manager of Celebration in the early years. "So many of the places we had visited in gathering ideas for Celebration were working on the same issues. Everyone was starting from scratch. Nobody learned from the mistakes of other people. The teaching academy would be a way to bring in people from around the country to preach about the best ideas, teaching methods, and curricula."

In the best Disney tradition, the first step in creating the school and academy had been to organize a number of sophisticated brainstorming sessions. These began in late 1992 and continued through 1993. The sessions were organized and directed by Larry Rosen, an associate vice president of Stetson University, not far away in Deland. Disney had formed an alliance with Stetson to help design the new school. For its part, Stetson viewed the project as a way to enhance its reputation and perhaps move onto the national stage as a university for educators. "The question we posed," Rosen said later, "was 'What sort of school do we create to showcase the best ideas and practices in public education?' "

To get the answer, Rosen and his colleagues leveraged the Disney name to draw people like Howard Gardner of Harvard University, the author of *Multiple Intelligence;* one of his Harvard colleagues, Lois Hetland; David Johnson and Roger Johnson, professors at the University of Minnesota and advocates of cooperative learning in which students work together to solve problems; and William Glasser, who wrote *Schools Without Failure.* Alongside the academic heavyweights were teachers and principals who came from both Osceola County and across the country.

Rosen remembered those first days as a period of tremendous excitement. "I believed and said from the very beginning that Disney was one of the few companies in the world that, if it chose to, could make a serious difference in the world of education," he said. "Disney owns a little chunk of so many people's hearts that it hits them on an emotional level. At the same time the company has a great capacity to make learning fun and interesting."

A key decision made early on was to build a school that would house kindergarten through twelfth grade. No other school in the county has this range of students, and few public schools anywhere in the country do either. Indeed, at one point, the planners considered building only an elementary and middle school, and perhaps creating a satellite of one of the nearby high schools within the town. According to Rosen, they went for the K–12 idea for two primary reasons. First, a lot of educational research has found advantages in keeping siblings together in school. There is continuity for students, teachers, and families. Plus, parents can devote more time to volunteering at a single school. Second, there was a feeling that resources could be shared among the grades. For instance, if the high school had an excellent physics teacher, from time to time that teacher could also work with children in the lower grades.

Once the decision was made to build a K–12 school, the planners focused on the learning practices and theories that would be used within the school. What emerged from those meetings and reams of memos was a school designed to enable students to discover the individual learning style that suited them best. The school would have large classrooms, with up to one hundred students and four teachers in each classroom. The students would often work collaboratively, mostly in teams of three or four. And the teachers were expected to work with one another in leading the classes.

To an outsider, or anyone who has spent much time in a room of one hundred kids, it seemed like a recipe for chaos. But in reaching this approach the planners relied heavily on Howard Gardner's theory of multiple intelligences, which holds that children learn at different rates and in different ways. To allow for the varied learning rates of the children, the classes were combined into what were called "neighborhoods," where children of different ages would progress at their own rates. The early plans envisioned classrooms broken down into fairly narrow age ranges: kindergarten to second grade in one neighborhood, third through fifth in another, sixth and seventh together, eighth and ninth in another, and tenth to twelfth grades together.

The idea of learning freedom affected the design of the physical structure of the classrooms. They would be three to five times larger than normal classrooms, with as much as five thousand square feet of space. Instead of rows of desks, there would be learning centers throughout each room, with small groupings of chairs, tables, and even sofas. The rooms were of a size such that while a large group in one section listened to a teacher give a math lesson, three or four children might be gathered in another spot to work on a science project, and a lone student might read undisturbed in a window seat.

Within the classroom, the daily schedule would not follow the traditional approach of one subject per time period. Instead, the plan called for a flexible approach that would encourage students to take the time they needed to get assignments done, which was intended to develop self-discipline. There would be no fixed time for math or science. Rather, students would be expected to pursue learning projects that incorporated an array of disciplines into a single project. For instance, a child might decide to spend several weeks learning about the swampland surrounding Celebration. He or she would be expected to incorporate biology and geology along with history and literature and to use mathematics to quantify the findings. Students also might tap outside resources through the computers or use nearby libraries or research facilities or contact experts directly.

An integral part of the multi-age approach was the personalized learning plan, the PLP, and to ensure that every child was working to full potential, the teachers were to sit down with the student and his or her parents to devise such a learning plan. The PLP was supposed to take into account the student's strengths and weaknesses and map a journey toward knowledge that would help make sense of the bewildering freedom offered to these youngsters.

Monitoring the progress of students along that journey would be even more radical. Rather than using traditional written tests and letter or number grades to measure a student's progress, the planners developed what they called "authentic assessment." Under this rubric, teachers would evaluate the student's ability to use many different learning tools, such as computers, videos, and texts, to explore an idea or complete a project. For each quarter, the student would create a portfolio that laid out not only what he or she had learned, but how. Integral to the portfolio would be the student's critique of his or her own work. Teachers would then write a detailed assessment of each portfolio. In addition to assessing the quality of work, teachers had to decide if the work actually represented a student's best effort. At the conclusion of each quarter, there would be report cards that, instead of grades, would contain evaluations like "not yet" or "achieving."

We saw the implementation of these concepts firsthand with our children. Nick's first assessment covered four areas: communication, reasoning and problem solving, personal development, and social responsibility. In a further fine-tuning, he was assessed as "extending," "proficient," and "in progress" in subcategories such as "approaches new situations with an open mind, healthy skepticism and persistence," "makes healthy choices," "learns by serving others," and "knows the re-wards of giving one's energies for a larger good." You really had to dig to find fundamental academics in there. We were confused. And worse, Nick was confused.

In case anyone missed that this was to be no ordinary school, the planners came up with their own cumbersome jargon, much like the special vocabulary developed at Disney World where customers are "guests" and employees are "cast members." Celebration would not have just a school, it would have the Celebration Learning Center. The students were to be called "learners" and the teachers were "learning leaders." As noted earlier, the places where they all gathered each day were "neighborhoods," not classrooms. The language reinforced the unique-ness of the school, but in ways that Rosen and the others could not fore-see, it also would come to symbolize an orthodoxy that separated believers from nonbelievers. (In the end, the "Celebration Learning Center" proved too much for county officials, and the name was simpli-fied to Celebration School.)

The new school would place high demands on students and teachers alike. The children would have to exercise unaccustomed discipline over themselves and authority over their peers. The older students and more advanced learners would be expected to bring along those behind them and to do it in an acceptable manner. The belief among the school designers, Rosen explained, was that even very young children, given the chance, are capable of self-discipline and helping their peers to control themselves.

As for the teachers, they would require special training to work as a team and integrate diverse subjects into broad, interdisciplinary themes. It would not be a simple matter. Later in the year, we heard an award-winning high school chemistry teacher exclaim, "I'm not qualified to teach in a school like this; I just know chemistry."

In addition, teachers would have to learn to deal with students who no longer sat in rows, eyes ahead and pencils at the ready. They would have to be up on the latest uses of technology and computers, because their students would not be using textbooks. Classrooms would be brim-ming with computers, and the teachers would have to know how to use them.

The nature of the school meant that teachers, students, and parents would face a steep learning curve together. At one of the planning sessions, Robert Peterkin, an education expert from Harvard University, advised Disney to expect problems in the early stages. "Having worked with other companies," he said, "I understand how discouraging it can be when the public arena seems not to acknowledge or appreciate your efforts. In the glare of the public light, it is sometimes very difficult to be a partner with a public entity that is undergoing the kind of scrutiny that public education is today. I would just urge Disney to realize that there will be ups and downs, that this is a long haul."

It was a logical and wise recommendation. Though none of the concepts was necessarily radical on its own, combining all of them in a single new school represented a radical break with normal practices that would require adjustments on all sides, from parents and students as well as from teachers and administrators. What Peterkin and the Disney officials failed to anticipate was that many parents would be unwilling to ride out the bumps for the long haul because the people experiencing the bumps firsthand were their children. Countless times over the year, we would hear parents say, "My child gets only one shot at second grade," or variations on that theme. Sometimes we were the ones saying it.

The basics for the school were in place by the end of 1993. Concerns remained, however, over whether the county school board would approve it and finance its construction. Funds for the school were not part of the bonds issued by the community development district; those funds were strictly for town infrastructure. Further, while Disney was willing to kick in money for some of the extras, and ultimately would contribute a substantial amount, there was no way the company was going to be the deep pocket for building an entire school. But recently the school district had built Poinciana High School not far away, and the board had been criticized sharply by residents in other parts of the county because Poinciana was not at maximum enrollment. Board members had responded by promising never again to authorize construction of a school where there was not a commensurate need. And here was Disney asking for a school in a town where nobody yet lived.

Celebration Teaching Academy was the carrot dangled before the board. A sort of teaching hospital associated with the school, the academy would offer training in the best educational practices to teachers from around the country. While others would pay to attend, Osceola County schools would be given 1,500 free training days a year as part of Disney's contribution to the county. The Florida Department of Education was so taken by the concept that it included $4 million in its budget to build and operate the academy.

On January 18, 1994, the Osceola County School Board voted to proceed with plans for the progressive school. Although nonbinding, the vote was seen by Celebration Company as a key commitment to the concept and an important political victory. Unlike most places in the country, Osceola's school district superintendent was an elected official, as were the paid school board members, of course, and the district was dominated by the county's political establishment.

Osceola County had long felt neglected by Disney. The development of the theme park and surrounding area had occurred in adjoining Orange County, and that was where the tax revenues stayed. What Osceola County got was the leavings—heavy traffic on its roads and exactly the type of tacky development along Highway 192 that Walt Disney had purchased thirty thousand acres to avoid on his own property.

"There was a lot of animosity toward Disney," said Mary Jane Arrington. "When I go places, people say, 'Where is Osceola County?' I say, 'Well, we share Disney World with Orange County. They got the tax base and we got the traffic.'"

Disney executives expected Celebration to ameliorate those resentments. It would create jobs and provide a major boost to the county's tax base. But to some people, using their tax dollars to build a new school in a town of wealthy outsiders smacked of Disney cheating them one more time. In fact, Celebration's gain would be a loss for the students at Kissimmee Middle School, which had enough students to qualify it for a new wing. Instead, Kissimmee Middle School got portable classrooms, while Celebration's students got the school. It was, and remains today, a bitter pill for many parents in the county.

The new school was expected to cost about $20 million. The county was providing $15 million, approximately what it would cost to build a normal school. But the county would be diverting that $15 million from building and renovation projects in other parts of Osceola. Disney was providing the remaining $5 million to pay for the bells and whistles that would make the school a standout. The $5 million did not include the thirty-six acres the company donated for the school, which it valued at $6.9 million. In exchange for the money, however, Disney wanted a waiver of the $4.5 million in impact fees it would owe the county to finance costs associated with Celebration, such as extra police and fire protection. The Disney money was essential if the school were to excel in a state where per-pupil spending on education ranked forty-ninth in the nation.

Eventually sentiment came over to Disney's side, in part because a large number of students who lived in the county would be allowed to attend the school until Celebration had enough of its own children to fill the one thousand openings in kindergarten through twelfth grade and in part because of the teaching academy's potential contribution to the rest of the county. Eighty percent of the first-year enrollment came from the county because the town was still small, but even when Celebration reached its maximum population, the agreement called for county students to retain 20 percent of the slots. Indeed, the prospect of sending their children to Disney's school, as it was commonly known in the county, was so appealing to local parents that the school district had to conduct a lottery to determine who from outside the town was allowed to fill the spots. Along with building support within the county for the school, the inclusion of children from outside Celebration would provide diversity in the student body that would otherwise have been missing. The non-Celebration students included blacks and Hispanics as well as kids from poor rural families, with a fair number of them qualifying for free breakfasts and lunches under federal school-aid programs. One of Becky's closest friends would come from a family that couldn't afford to live in Celebration but was intent on seeing that their daughter get the best education possible.

Despite the progress, there would be other town-county spats. Some were petty. In early 1995, several school board members complained about the construction of a 380-foot boardwalk to provide a dry path over the swamp that lay between the main school and the gymnasium. The board members argued that Disney should cover the $256,000 tab because it had chosen the swampy site. Disney countered that the cost was part of the original $20 million budget and refused to pay. The county went ahead and paid the tab. "The bottom line is, had we been picking a site out there at Celebration, we would not have picked a site that required a boardwalk," said Martha Anderson, one of the board members.

A potentially more serious hurdle arose in May 1995. At the last minute, the Florida legislature had transferred the $4 million for the teaching academy to another part of the state budget. Instead of going for an innovative facility to train teachers, the money was earmarked for new juvenile prisons. The loss of the academy's financing threatened to upset the delicate support for the school on the board. So Disney stepped up and promised to build the teaching academy and provide some of the money necessary to run it.

Just as Disney's role in financing the academy and various extras at the school was unusual, so was the company's involvement in selecting the first principal. The company and the school district cooperated in a nationwide search. It was to be a hunt for the most qualified administrator in the country, and in the end there were one hundred and sixty-two applicants from across the country. The selection, however, was the principal of an elementary school in nearby Kissimmee, Bobbi Vogel. A respected educator, Vogel had spearheaded a number of innovative programs at her school. She was also a veteran of the county's political-education wars and married to the county's assistant school superintendent for personnel. While Vogel may have been the most qualified applicant, her selection also helped to smooth the way for the school with the hierarchy that ran the Osceola County schools, because, after all, she was one of theirs.

With a principal chosen and the financing in place, the board gave final approval to the school in early 1995, a year after the tentative okay. The school was to occupy a prominent location in the town, and Disney agreed to pay the design fees for the architectural work in order to get a building that fit with the theme of the town. The commission went to William Rawn Associates, a Boston firm whose principal architect, William Rawn, was best known for exploring the line between modernism and premodern traditions in buildings like the Seiji Ozawa Hall at Tanglewood, in Massachusetts. Rawn's firm had started work on the plans before the final approval from the school board, but completing that process and starting construction was still several months away.

As a result, in the fall of 1996, only weeks after the first residents moved into Celebration, the new building was not close to being ready, and would not be for another year. Instead, the two hundred students from the town and county went to classes at Celebration Teaching Academy, a single building where they were squeezed into classrooms and often spilled out onto the sidewalk.

More than half the families moving to Celebration in the first year had school-age children, according to Disney's demographic information. And the school was listed as the number-one reason for moving to the town. Indeed, the school was a major selling point, and information about it was provided to every prospective resident. The concepts were explained in brochures and by salespeople. Terry Wick, an education expert who worked for Celebration Company, was quite candid in explaining the importance of the school to the success of the town from a marketing viewpoint. "Frankly, the major reason for the school, and one that we as a company have been very up-front about from the beginning, is that not only would we attract families by having a school, but by having a school here first it sold homes." Larry Rosen from Stetson and other experts talked with countless prospective home buyers and parents. As part of marketing the school to prospective buyers, Disney even hired a professional film production company to make a video. Called "A Day in the Life," the video followed a fictional student named Eddie through what was described as a typical day at Celebration School. It showed how he had developed a personalized learning plan, or PLP, that was monitored by a committee of teachers. His day began with an internship with a physical therapist at Celebration Health Center. At the school, he joined a study group in a multi-age "neighborhood" to interview young children about their injuries for a health-and-safety booklet the class was preparing to publish for parents. Then he spent time in "distance interactive learning," receiving instruction from France in French, via satellite. At the conclusion, the narrator said, "Wherever he is, we can all be assured that Eddie is applying the kind of critical thinking essential for success."

The technology-based, individualized learning plans depicted in the video were a long way off when Celebration School opened in 1996. As parents discovered the gap between the video and the reality, they dubbed the film "Eddie Does Disney."

But the progressive program, which eschewed textbooks and the usual tests and grades, was in place, and it quickly became clear that a fair number of home buyers had not understood the nature of the school. Perhaps the old-fashioned architecture and marketing rhetoric about old-fashioned values lulled them into believing their kids would be going to a school just like the one they had attended. Although still a far cry from the experience described in the film, Celebration School was clearly nothing like the school most of the parents had attended.

Nine weeks into the school year, Richard Adams, a retired fire chief from Pennsylvania, packed up his two children and returned home. In a scathing letter to Disney, he wrote: "We came here as a family with a dream, and all we received was an educational nightmare. My children not only did not progress in this school—they regressed. Not only in their academics but also their discipline."

He was not alone. Roger Burton sold his house and moved his family back to Illinois because he and his wife were disenchanted with the school. "They told us the school was going to be up and running, that they had been planning this for years," he complained to newspaper reporters. Michael and Luba Bilentschuk felt the same way and took their two children out of the school and sold their home in December, just four months after moving in.

Problems are inevitable with any start-up operation. School administrators and Disney's education manager for Celebration, Terry Wick, tried to put the best face on the situation. They acknowledged that there was room for improvement and asked the parents and students for time to make things better. There was nothing wrong with that. The mistake came when they tried to silence the critics.

Several families were approached by Celebration Company officials and offered help selling their houses in return for a promise not to disclose their reasons for leaving. This was not an idle offer, because Celebration has some of the strictest regulations in the country governing resale of houses. Intended to discourage speculators, the covenants signed by every homeowner require them to live in the house nine months before selling, except in the event of a hardship like a divorce or job transfer. Disappointment with the school was scarcely considered a hardship.

Luba Bilentschuk refused the offer and blew the whistle in the local press, transforming a bad but understandable situation into a public relations nightmare. On February 14, 1997, under the headline "Ex-

Celebration Owners Asked to Keep Quiet," the *Orlando Sentinel* ran a story about the ham-fisted attempt by a Celebration Company lawyer to trade permission to evade the resale restriction for silence. The lawyer, Larry Pitt, had drawn up a release in which the sellers agreed not to disclose "to any third party . . . the facts and circumstances which motivated you to sell your home."

"It was a gag order," Bilentschuk complained, adding that they had gone ahead and sold their house on their own and left town without repercussions from the company. A spokeswoman for the company was forced to acknowledge that offers were made to several families, and that it had probably been a mistake.

On its own, the community did not seem to do much better in handling the tough situation. Often, particularly in small towns, schools are the rallying point for the community. Sports teams evoke community pride; academic achievements reflect well on everyone. In Celebration, the school was clearly a central vehicle for the effort to develop a sense of community and pride of place in the new town. As a result, when criticism of the school became public, its supporters reacted emotionally; it was as if the town itself had been attacked. They lashed out at the disgruntled parents at public meetings, and soon anyone with a critical word about Celebration School risked being branded a traitor. The tensions threatened to split the town. Meetings of the Dream Team, the local forerunner of the Parent Teacher Student Association, whose members were elected from among the parents of children in the school, sometimes erupted into shouting matches. Some neighbors stopped talking to each other. Teacher morale sank. Kids found themselves defending the school in interviews with reporters.

As the situation spiraled out of control, Celebration Company executives recognized the potential for harm to the town. In response, Jackson and Sara Mumey, residents whose small firm had been hired earlier by Celebration Company as public relations consultants for the school, emerged as articulate defenders of the school. When out-of-town reporters or prospective residents called the school or Celebration Company with questions, they were referred routinely to the Mumeys as representative parents with children at the school. Though Jackson Mumey told us they disclosed their consulting arrangement, some callers did not realize that the company was paying the Mumeys. In fact, when Cathy first called the school to ask for information in early 1997, as we were considering moving to Celebration, she was given the phone number for the Mumeys and told they were parents who would be happy to answer her questions. There was no hint that they also were paid consultants to the company.

Brent Herrington also was enlisted in the campaign. From Town Hall, he organized a series of pep rallies and picnics for the beleaguered teachers in February and March of 1997. Herrington also used his normally folksy monthly newsletter to solicit contributions to a fund to keep the support going, with the money paid to an ad hoc group to which he gave the unfortunate name "Positive Parents." The message was clear: You were either a positive parent in support of the school or a negative parent engaged in destructive criticism. "If they were the 'positive' parents, what did that make us?" asked one parent. "Think about it."

Paying for a public-relations spokesman and Herrington's boosterism were not the only ways in which the Celebration Company involved itself in the school. There was a suspicion among some parents that the first slate of parents elected to the Dream Team had been put together by company officials. And the company employed a full-time liaison with the school. Her responsibilities included overseeing the extra money that Disney provided to the school and consulting with the principal on personnel and financial matters. In the second year, when the Dream Team became the PTSA, the president of the school's PTSA met every two weeks with representatives of the company to discuss various issues.

By the end of the first school year, more than twenty families had pulled their children out of the school. Frank Stone, the town doctor, and his wife, Janette, fretted throughout the school year before withdrawing their older child and enrolling her in a Catholic school half an hour away. Eventually they put their younger child in the private school also. "My gosh, we live on Campus Street," said Stone, a gentle and sincere man who was building a new practice in Celebration. "We expected to be able to watch our kids walk to the school down the street. But it was not working at all. Our fourth-grader did nothing the last nine weeks of school, and no one took responsibility. We stuck it out for the first year, anticipating growing pains, but then we realized that a child only has one chance to do second grade, or third or fourth. We didn't feel we could waste that time any longer."

Six of the nineteen teachers left at the end of the first school year, and Bobbi Vogel, the principal, notified the school superintendent early in 1997 that she would not be returning. She suggested that the school was so unwieldy that it needed two principals, one for the lower grades and one for the upper.

We were oblivious to the feud and underlying problems when we signed the contract to buy our house in early February 1997, midway through the inaugural school year. By the time we moved in at the end of June, however, we were well aware of the splits. Earlier that month, they had gained national attention in an article in *The Wall Street Journal*, which ran under the catchy headline "Disney's Model School: No Cause to Celebrate."

But Dot Davis never got the news.

"I felt really bad for her, I was worried," said Robin Delaney, who had worked hard at the school since the beginning as a parent volunteer. "I just thought that someone should have sat down with her and given her a realistic picture of the ongoing challenges here."

In 1984, Davis had become principal of the Academy for Academics and Arts in Huntsville, Alabama, a new magnet school for kindergarten through eighth grade. Over the next thirteen years, she had helped transform it into a huge success that drew students from the city's wealthiest neighborhoods as well as from its poorest. Test scores were consistently well above the national average; the U.S. Department of Education had selected it as an outstanding school. By the time Davis left, seven hundred students were on the waiting list to get in.

Davis and her husband, an Alabama native, were respected and comfortable members of the community. Jim had doctorates in criminal justice and theology, and he was not only head of the state's juvenile justice system, but also a Baptist preacher. The only problem that Davis saw was her husband's demanding work schedule. The phone seemed to ring twenty-four hours a day. The hours and the emotional involvement of working with juvenile offenders were taking a toll on him. The Davises had not taken a vacation in six years.

One day in February, Jim dragged in from the office at about ten-

thirty at night. "Look at this," his wife said, holding out an advertise-
ment from an education publication. "They are advertising for two principals at a new school in Florida. One for the elementary grades and
one for high school. Do you think I should look into it?" To his wife's
amazement, he said, "Why don't you call right away and see if you can
be certified in Florida?"

After twenty-seven years in the justice system, Jim Davis had been
searching for a way to reduce his workload with an eye toward retiring
in a couple of years. And he felt that his wife had done everything she
could in her present job. Maybe a new challenge would be good for her.

There were only five days until the application deadline. Davis assembled a quick résumé and mailed it off, not really expecting to hear
back. For two months, there was no word, and that suited her fine. The
ad had started her thinking about the best way to change their lives, and
she was contemplating retirement, not a new job.

"I had pretty much forgotten about it," she said later. "I was very, very
happy with my job. Really. The only reason I was thinking about retirement was because I had been there thirteen years and the faculty was so
well established. Jim was under so much pressure. My parents were not
well. I had a lot of leave time that I could take off and go home to help
my mother. Plus, I really like being at home. I've always said that I am
basically a very lazy person."

The silence was broken in April. Davis learned she was a candidate.
She was interviewed by telephone, asked to respond to a set of standard-
ized questions that had nothing to do with education but were designed
to screen out people whose personality might not fit the job. She was
asked things like: Can you tell us one time when you were the life of the
party? What was your most embarrassing moment?

She was so flummoxed by the questions that she couldn't remember
any of her answers, but they provided grist for the mill in her daily
e-mail exchanges with her family, in which they, too, all answered the
offbeat queries. There was a second, similar but longer, interview a few
weeks later. At the end of May, someone on the search committee called
to say that they were submitting her name as a finalist. But the caller
said there had been one change. The school could not afford two principals. Would she still be interested in the job as the single principal?

"That was my mistake," said Davis, who had no high school administrative experience. "I said yes. I probably should have said no, because it is a tough job with a huge responsibility."

A week later, she was in Celebration taking questions from the search committee, which included Brent Herrington; Cynthia Hancock, the president of the Dream Team; two people from the school staff; and a couple of other parents. She and Jim had come down primarily to check out the town and the job situation. Because there had been no face-to-face interviews so far, she assumed the selection was still a long way off.

While Dot was being grilled, Jim was inspecting the town. He stopped at the preview center and looked at house prices. He knew that his wife felt strongly that a school principal needed to live where she worked as a visible reminder of her commitment to the town as well as to the school. When he met up with his wife later in the afternoon, the first thing he said was: "No way. We cannot live in this town. We can't afford it, and there's nothing available for months."

The next morning, Davis had an interview with Larry Rosen from Stetson University, Terry Wick from Celebration Company, Blaine Muse, an assistant school superintendent, and Thomas McCraley, superintendent. The first thing they told her was that she was one of three finalists. Then they asked a set list of questions, which took about fifteen minutes. Then they stood up to leave.

"Wait a minute," said Davis. "I have my own questions for you."

"You may ask one question as we walk out," she was told.

Miffed, both Dot and Jim went to the school and talked with Vogel, who was packing her desk on her final day. They also talked with Donna Leinsing, the school administrative employee who had helped develop the curriculum. As they were about to leave the school to go to the airport and fly home, the county school superintendent, McCraley, called the office. The teacher who picked up the phone—Davis doesn't remember who it was—emerged and announced to the Davises and several teachers in the hall that Dot had been selected as the new principal. The staff cheered and applauded. Dot and Jim looked at each other in disbelief. The superintendent had already hung up.

Davis called McCraley back and discovered that he was preparing a press release to announce her hiring. She protested that she had not decided whether to take the job and had not informed her own superintendent, a man with whom she had worked for twenty-seven years and whose son was a student at her school.

"Are you having second thoughts?" McCraley asked.

"I just need time," she said.

"Okay," he replied. "Call me tomorrow morning. I've already called your superintendent anyway and told him myself."

"No, this is Friday and I won't be home till after midnight tonight. I'll let you know by Monday, or Tuesday at the latest," she said.

On the way home and the next day, the Davises thought hard about the decision. The cons outweighed the pros. Neither wanted to leave their aging parents. They would be giving up established positions. Dot would be taking on huge new responsibilities. And then there was the attention. Dot now knew enough about Celebration to know that the school principal was going to get some serious press attention.

"Do you really want to do this, Dot, because you know you don't like the limelight?" Jim asked.

"Well," she said, "I've always done it."

And so there she stood on that early August evening, watching the hoopla, ducking as Larry Rosen placed a Stetson hat on her head, holding aloft a three-foot key to the school presented to her by McCraley and wondering just what she had gotten herself into.

Davis, who would be our next-door neighbor when her house was finished, was not the only person watching the proceedings with some amazement. The sneak preview had all the earmarks of a Disney extravaganza. As the new principal, the superintendent, and other distinguished guests stood by, the teachers were introduced. The voice over the public address system was deep and professional and it sounded suspiciously like the guy who announces the character parade at the Magic Kingdom. Actually it belonged to a Celebration resident who summoned each teacher by name, identifying those who were here the year before as "returning players" and the new teachers as "first draft choices." Each of them rushed onto the stage and was handed a green-and-white football jersey. The most enthusiastic pulled them on over their clothes, but some didn't seem to know quite how to respond.

For Nick and Becky, the festivities were a brief respite before the dreaded Monday, when school would start. After the confetti and balloons and refreshments, they didn't want to see the new classrooms, or "neighborhoods" as we were struggling to call them, that were open for tours that night, but we dragged them along. Their reluctance was due not only to being uprooted and transplanted to a new town. They would have felt much the same way back in Westport. They both were bright kids. They did their homework without much complaint. Usually well. They rarely faked illness to stay home. Becky especially loved the social action at school. But they had the natural reaction of almost any normal kid—they didn't want to go back to school after a long, lazy summer.

As we toured the school that Friday before classes began, Becky's anxieties were given substance. Her new classroom, Lower Neighborhood 1, was on the first floor of the building. It was shiny, bright, and big, at least five thousand square feet, three times the size of her last classroom, at Long Lots Elementary School in Westport. The reason it was so big was that it would house eighty children, not third through fifth grade as planned originally, but kindergarten through fifth grade. It was the tiny desks and chairs for the kindergartners that set Becky off.

"I don't want to be with little kids," she said with a shake of her red hair and a glare. "I was supposed to be with big kids this year, and now I'm gonna be in here with a bunch of kindergartners. This is unpaid baby-sitting."

In Westport, students moved to the middle school for fifth grade. Becky had been looking forward to the new freedoms and challenges of her "graduation" from elementary school to middle school. Now, she was going to be trapped in a room in which a majority of the children would be younger. We tried to explain that it would be a good opportunity for her to learn from helping the little kids and that most of her class work would be done with boys and girls her own age. But she wasn't buying. Becky was still glowering later that night when she went to bed.

Nick was more sanguine. His neighborhood, Upper 2, was for sixth and seventh graders, a manageable age range. And he liked all the computers stacked along the walls of the classroom. "This is cool," he said, running one hand across the top of a new MacIntosh. But even the computers could not motivate Nick to say he was looking forward to school. Still, at least he wasn't overtly angry when he went to sleep that night.

The computers looked enticing to us, too. Both kids spend a lot of time on our computers at home, doing school research, playing games, and participating in children's chat rooms. We knew that they could be powerful tools for young minds. But we were a little surprised that another powerful tool was in short supply in both classrooms. There were very few books, and the teachers told us, with some pride, that there would be no textbooks. Students would use newspapers, magazines, and computer-generated research as their texts for the year. Further, the single library designed to serve all twelve grades seemed quite limited, and, the librarian informed us grimly, there was neither room nor money to expand it. "What you basically have," she said, "is a facility that is big enough for a middle school but is supposed to serve an entire school." You can imagine the twin chills that this discovery brought to two people who make their living writing and have worked hard to instill a love of books, even textbooks, in their children.

Only recently had we learned that there would not be a public library in town, at least in the near future. Though land was set aside for one across from the school, the county political leaders had refused to authorize a library for Celebration. The feeling was, we had been told, that Disney's town was already getting a school and therefore the next library would be built someplace else. Indeed, not until early 1998 could the county library be persuaded to open a small satellite branch four hours a day at Celebration School.

After we returned home from the school tour and the kids had gone to bed, we sat in the living room and quietly reviewed our reactions. Certainly there were positives. The school was beautiful, computers plentiful. The teachers were enthusiastic, exuding the sort of pioneering spirit that we had seen in many of our neighbors. We weren't hung up on grades, so we thought we could live with detailed and personalized assessments, particularly in the lower grades. The lack of books in the classrooms and the library was deeply troubling, as was the absence of a public library. But we would make sure that our kids read plenty at home. We just hoped the absence of books at school didn't signal some larger problem with the academic standards.

Becky's predicament was our biggest worry. We had met her three teachers and they seemed bright and friendly. But how in the world could they handle eighty students across such a vast age range? The demands of five-year-olds, many of whom still need naps, are far different from those of ten-year-olds, at least most of the time. We just did not see a way for these three teachers to find the time to provide personalized instruction to everyone in the classroom.

The big classes and wide age differences had been a leading complaint from parents the previous year. Most parents simply did not realize what they were getting into when they moved to Celebration and put their kids in the local school. They expected the world-class school promised by Disney and a new educational philosophy but not one that was still evolving. Perhaps it was only the rationale of hindsight, but in his 1998 autobiography, *Work in Progress,* Michael Eisner claimed that the company had expected a certain amount of difficulty with the school. "We knew that an experimental approach would be controversial," he wrote. "My children attended a similar school, the Center for Early Education in Los Angeles. When Breck was eight years old, my parents asked what grade he was in. 'Continuum purple,' Breck blithely replied. A simple 'second grade' would have been far easier to explain to my mother. Jane and I were relieved when the school adopted a more standard language."

If Eisner expected controversy, the parents certainly did not. They complained that their children tended to get lost in the chaos and din of a single classroom with eighty children between the ages of five and ten, leaving students without adequate supervision or instruction. And some questioned the educational theory behind putting such a wide range of students in a single classroom. "I know there's been research on combining grades, but has there been any on an age range like the one we have here?" asked Joseph Palacios, a parent, at a meeting for parents and administrators. "A six-year spread? None that I've been able to find. The classes here have been configured solely for the convenience of the school, without taking into account what works for the children."

From our tour of the school, we had seen that the design of the building had locked Celebration School into grouping children in large classrooms. Unlike most school buildings, where classrooms are designed to hold twenty to thirty children, this one was comprised of a series of very large rooms to accommodate the big multi-age classes. This was not unintentional; the architects had responded to the requirements of their clients, the educators who had developed the philosophy behind the school. If that philosophy changed one day, or even if the school wanted to modify it and reduce the size of the classrooms, it would be difficult without major renovations.

We had seen more schools than most parents. A few years earlier, we had collaborated on a book about teachers and interviewed more than 150 of them around the country, asking what problems they faced and how they would solve them. They spoke in many voices from many perspectives, but the common thread in almost every conversation was that nothing would work without a good ratio of teachers to students. Opinions varied on the optimum ratio. Some teachers said they could manage with fifteen students per teacher; others thought the ratio could go as high as twenty to one, under the right circumstances. But none of those teachers, or any other expert we had ever talked to or read about, advocated anything as high as the ratio of twenty-six students per teacher that was the norm at Celebration School. And even more important, we felt, the huge numbers of children in a single space would change the usual classroom dynamics significantly, rendering the usual ratio debate moot and requiring even more teachers per students.

One of the consultants that Disney brought in to comment on its model school in the late planning stages was the headmaster of one of the country's most elite private schools. He asked that we not use his name because he did not want to anger Disney. But one night as we talked about his reaction to the Celebration plan, he shook his head sadly and said he did not see how the innovative curriculum and multi-age groupings could work in a public-school setting. "You have to have a ratio of one teacher for every six to nine students to make something like that work."

The academics and urban planners who developed Celebration School viewed the world through a different lens. The teachers were supposed to act more as catalysts than instructors, hence the term "learning leaders." The kids were expected to help each other, and their primary motivation was supposed to be their own thirst for knowledge. The overriding principle on which the school was founded, in a nut-shell, was the idealized vision of every student being a lover of learning.

It was the view taught by the nation's education professors. A survey that would be released just two months later by a nonpartisan research group, Public Agenda, found that the professors put their priorities on "teaching kids to be active learners," not on discipline and basics like math, punctuation, and grammar that parents ranked at the top.

Some parents are blessed with children who have to be ordered to put their homework away late at night and who wake up every morning eager for more learning. We've known a few, though we tend to discount the claims of some parents as braggadocio. There may be more than we think. But it's not the norm. Many kids are comfortable doing just enough to get by. They need genuine inspiration, firm guidance, and a clear sense of what is expected of them. And those expectations need to be high. Our question was whether Celebration School, with its new orthodoxy, would prove flexible enough to deal with the learners who would occupy most of the space in those neighborhoods, and whether the teachers could maintain control of Becky's classroom and teach her something at the same time.

The problems of Celebration School, we would discover, would continue to plague the town because of a basic flaw—the overly ambitious attempt to do too much. All of the innovative techniques, from multi-age classes and the absence of grades to individualized learning projects and cooperative learning, have been employed successfully in schools across the country. Nowhere, however, had there been an attempt to combine all of these concepts in a single school, let alone in a single school designed to serve kindergarten through twelfth grade. It may well be that the school will turn out to be a world-class institution, but that will not happen for several years. And the parents who moved to Celebration, many of them expressly because of the promises embodied in the school, did not feel that they and their children had the time to wait.

7

The Zeus Box

The school was not the only place infused with technological fervor. The night before the sneak preview at Celebration School, we attended our first meeting of the AT&T Advanced Technology Panel in one of the downtown offices. About forty other residents were seated around small tables, and the atmosphere was one of controlled eagerness as Heather Meister from AT&T described the panel's role.

AT&T was one of several corporations that had formed alliances with the Walt Disney Company in Celebration. Disney is big on corporate alliances. These partnerships are a way for Disney to shift some of its costs to outside corporations eager to tap in to the millions of visitors to Disney's theme parks and, in this case, to Celebration. Many rides and attractions at Epcot, for example, are sponsored by corporations like General Motors and Coca-Cola, which help pay for their construction and operation. The rides in turn plug the corporations in ways both obvious and subtle.

More than economics is at play. The partnerships with other big corporations reflect an underlying belief within Disney that corporations improve our lives and are working on our behalf for the future. The rides and other displays at the theme parks are a way to instill this positive image of corporations in the minds of visitors.

In the case of Celebration, General Electric, Honeywell, AT&T, and others had helped pay for the construction of three expensive model homes, called the Showcase Village, in exchange for touting their products to new residents and visitors alike. But the partnership with AT&T went further. The communications giant already sponsored interactive exhibits at Epcot. In Celebration, AT&T donated the hardware and installation components to create the Celebration Community Network, an intranet that provides town residents with e-mail, chat rooms, a bulletin-board service, and access to the Internet, all free of charge.

What had drawn the forty or so of us together that August night was the second aspect of AT&T's alliance with Disney. In exchange for financing the intranet, the communications company was permitted to use the town as a testing laboratory for new communications technology and services.

Celebration was attractive as a lab for several reasons. Its residents were expected to be pretty computer savvy or at least willing to learn, since technology was one of the cornerstones of the town. The population also was a good representation of middle-class America, tucked into one accessible place. And, unspoken but significant, the folks in Celebration were people who would be expected to trust a corporation. After all, they had moved to the ultimate company town: Clearly these were people who trusted in the corporation and its intentions to improve life. As a result, the town was used as a testing ground for a variety of products, from new laser surgery to remove varicose veins to the latest innovation in the move toward a cashless society, the so-called smart cards. So it was that we went to listen to the telecommunications giant's pitch.

"AT&T wants to understand how people use existing technology and, more important, how you adapt to new and emerging technology products and services," Meister explained as she passed out folders to all of us. "Our researchers will evaluate and analyze what you use and how you use it over the next year, and your participation will be very valuable in helping us create a model of development for the future."

At Epcot, AT&T gives people scrip to spend in the park if they agree to take a quick survey on technology and communications. "We incent them with Disney dollars," she said. In Celebration, the "incenting" was a good deal cooler. The first 350 families that agreed to participate on the panel would each receive a Tandy personal computer, with 133 MHz Intel Pentium processor; a Hewlett-Packard combination printer, fax, and copier; the most advanced Nokia cellular phone; and an AT&T telephone that was not yet on the market and that offered so many features the company called it a "personal information center." In addition to performing the usual tasks of making and receiving calls, this telephone had a built-in directory that held two hundred phone numbers, a caller-ID screen that let you see the name and number of the person calling before you answered, a programmable reminder calendar, and a clock, among other goodies. We would not have been surprised if it had had an optional expresso machine. In addition, for a full year, AT&T would pay for all basic services related to the computer and phones, like monthly telephone and cellular service and frills such as the caller ID, call waiting, and three-way calling.

Meister told us the value of these items was $3,500, but we could have everything for nothing, or almost nothing. "All you have to do is agree to use everything we give you as your primary household device for a year and participate in a survey every few months," she said. "Then it will be yours to keep."

Meister's presentation was smooth and professional. Only after this grand "incenting" did she mention the catch. "Of course," she said casually, "we will be monitoring your usage of these devices through the Zeus Box."

We already knew this hook was hidden in the high-tech bait. A week earlier we had run into Jere Batten as he was walking home from his technology panel meeting. As a software designer and programmer, Jere knows a lot about computers and technology, and he is a serious and thoughtful fellow. He and his son Alex had built a personal computer for Alex, and Jere's entire working day was spent in front of a computer terminal. He even composed music for the church choir on a computer. This particular night, however, he was no fan of technology.

"It's not for me," he said firmly. "They are offering a bunch of stuff, and the computer's not that good anyway, and if you take it they are going to monitor everything you do on the computer and the telephone. They are going to install this Zeus Box in the house to keep track of the phones, and the computer will automatically download a report to AT&T every few days. It will tell them every Web site you visit.

They won't know what you do there, but they'll know every place you've been on your computer. I told them I'd have to think about it. I don't think so though. I don't like the idea of a Zeus Box."

We thought Batten's reaction was sensible. We are as alarmed as the next person about the disappearance of privacy in America, the way in which, bit by bit, our right to be left alone seems to be vanishing. Any time you use an automated teller, the bank records the time, date, and location of the transaction. You buy something with a credit card and it goes into a database that is accessible to the police and, potentially, to other people and organizations. Browse the Internet and the Web sites you visit record what you are looking at and when you are looking at it, with something innocuously called a cookie. Polls have shown that we are not alone; lots of Americans are concerned about our disappearing privacy.

So we sat in the office on August 7 listening to Meister's pitch and waiting to hear the wails of objections to the Zeus Box as she explained that the box and software on the computer would combine to record our use of the phones and fax machine, every application and keystroke on our computer, how often we sent and received e-mail, and every Internet site we visited and how long we stayed. The room was silent. Two men at our table had already signed their contracts and were so busy filling out other papers to get the free incentives that they didn't even raise their heads. The only question anybody asked was how soon we could get our equipment.

Cathy tried to start something, raising her hand and asking Meister, "And what exactly will you be tracking and recording?"

"Basically everything," replied the woman from AT&T. Still silence from the rest of the room. Didn't anybody see the Big Brother aspect to this? Well, apparently they did not.

Perhaps we should not have been surprised. This was a crowd that had already agreed to accept some pretty stringent rules for the opportunity to live in Celebration. And frankly, the reaction might not have been much different anywhere. We want to guard our privacy in the abstract sense, yet every day we trade away a bit of it for things that make life easier and more efficient.

Over the weekend, we were talking to Batten, and he asked about our reaction to the technology panel. Sure, we said, we had signed up.

We had nothing to hide. And, to tell the truth, it would provide yet another window onto the community, and we liked the idea of getting all the freebies.

Batten grimaced and confessed. "Earlene liked that computer and phone, too," he said. "She filled out the paperwork last night. She's signing up. I told her I wasn't going to have anything to do with it. I told her she'd have to do all the surveys, and I was going to use the other phone line."

A few weeks after we signed up and got our new computer and other items, the first AT&T on-line survey flashed onto the computer. A little icon popped up at the bottom of the screen, and it would not go away until someone clicked on it to open the survey and answer the questions. They were standard questions about time management and computer usage. In later months, however, the surveys took another tack. Rather than asking about reactions to technology, it was a psychological survey with some weird twists.

"Given the opportunity," asked one question, "would you watch an execution live on the Internet?" "If you could lie and cheat on the Internet without getting caught, would you?" asked another, followed by, "Have you ever been embarrassed by anything you have done on the Internet?"

Cathy answered the questions, even the weird ones. She tried to print out the survey for a record of its strangeness, but it would not print. She called AT&T's technology-panel office in Celebration, but no one would say anything about what the survey was trying to elicit. We were left wondering what AT&T could possibly be doing with this information. The answer, we found out later, was nothing.

Over the months, the only complaints we heard came from people who had not arrived in time to sign up and from one of the AT&T people involved with the technology panel. The AT&T employee was a senior official who said termination was certain for talking about the fiasco, so we agreed not to use a name.

The official said the technology panel had been a $12 million blunder for the company. Not long after signing its alliance contract with Disney, the two divisions of AT&T that planned to use the research data were sold off, leaving the company with no real need for the research. But it had to fulfill its contract by providing the free computers and other technology and services to the Celebration residents, so AT&T had essentially gone through the motions of collecting data, too.

About eight months into the first year of the experiment, the company stopped downloading data from the computers and Zeus Boxes. Then it terminated almost everybody in the Celebration office. A few weeks after that, some workers were sent around to remove the Zeus Boxes and delete the downloading software from everyone's computer.

The willingness to swap some privacy for a free computer and phone was related to the willingness of people to move to a place where rules and regulations restricted personal freedom, too. The belief was that these restrictions would make life better. All in all, it probably was not a bad trade for most people: Home buyers agreed to be governed by a homeowners association and a set of restrictive covenants in their deeds whose goal was to balance individual freedom with communal responsibility.

A growing number of Americans, particularly affluent white ones, are willing to swap certain freedoms in order to live in what they think are safer, better communities. The evidence of this is the sharp growth in planned communities springing up across the country. The latest count by the Community Associations Institute estimates there are 225,000 planned communities nationwide compared with 84,000 units of government. These communities often privatize the normal functions of government, like sewer installation, garbage pickup, street cleaning, and general maintenance of public areas. Some of them have gone so far as to control police and fire protection, too.

The most extreme version is the gated community, where residents have retreated from any unplanned contact with the outside world. Extreme, but far from rare. In their book *Fortress America,* Edward J. Blakely and Mary Gail Snyder estimated that eight million Americans were living behind gates in 1997. The gates, they pointed out, represented more than physical barriers. They were a political act. Gated communities are a clear manifestation of the widening divide between the haves and have-nots, a sad example of the triumph of tribalism over democracy.

Celebration is not a gated community, and some of its services, like police and fire protection, are provided by Osceola County and paid for through property taxes. More than once, however, we heard neighbors bemoan the lack of gates.

One night over dinner in the spacious Estate home of an electrical contractor and his wife, our hosts told the story of a tourist couple who showed up on their back step at midday.

"I went to the door and saw these strangers standing there, a middle-aged couple," our hostess, Susan Sheppard, remembered. "I opened the door and asked what they wanted. They said they'd like to come in and see the house. I said, with some heat, that it was a private home, and they most certainly could not. The wife was embarrassed, and she said to her husband, 'See, I told you this was a bad idea.' As they left, I could hear him muttering that he didn't see what was wrong with asking."

There were frequent complaints, too, about tourists creeping through town in their rented minivans or Buicks with Indiana plates, slowing to marvel at the architecture or stopping in an alley for a closer look over the back fence. Because a backyard is private, this scrutiny was regarded as an invasion of privacy, an intrusion on a private realm.

"Tourists are driving five miles an hour all over town, and I've seen them stopped in the alley behind my house, standing on the hood of the car to look into my backyard," a woman complained at a meeting for new residents not long after we arrived. "Couldn't we block off the alleys to keep them out?"

Chuck Murphy, a Celebration Company official attending the meeting, explained that there would never be gates. "Celebration was never envisioned to be a gated community," he said. "It was envisioned to be a town, just like Kissimmee and St. Cloud. We want to invite people in. It's the right way to develop real estate." And, he added, the alleys and streets were public byways, not private property. In fact, the roads and alleys had been financed through municipal bonds issued by the Celebration Community Development District. The bonds are considered public funds, so the roads cannot be closed to the public.

But Celebration is not like Kissimmee or St. Cloud, the only other towns in the 1,300 square miles of Osceola County. It has rules and regulations that do not exist in those old communities, although similar restrictions are common in other planned communities in Florida and elsewhere.

The rules are an endless source of curiosity for outsiders. Anyone who had heard of Celebration, it seemed, had heard of the rules. Sometimes the notions were outlandish. One woman asked us if everyone had to wear certain clothes, and another was certain she had read that there were restrictions on the number of children per household.

One day Doug was golfing at Celebration Golf Club with Mark and Virginia Tolfo, a couple from Barry, a town north of Toronto. The Tolfos were visiting the area on holiday. They had heard about Celebration and were particularly curious about the rules.

"Is it true that you have to paint your house a certain color?" asked Virginia.

"The color has to be within a certain palette," explained Doug.

"What about washing? Can you hang your clothes on a line outdoors?"

"No, that is prohibited in the rules."

"And the yards, can you put what you want in the yards?"

"Not exactly," replied Doug. "Not exactly."

The Tolfos had driven around Celebration and had gotten a good view of it from the golf course, too. They said they thought it was pretty and liked the architecture. But they could not abide the rules.

"I want to do what I want with my own house," said Virginia.

Doug explained that the rules were intended to insure a uniformity and consistency within the community. Celebration residents, he said, are required to maintain their yards and keep their houses painted. The color of the exterior paint must be reviewed and approved by the architectural review committee if it differs from the original color. Those original colors were chosen from a fairly narrow palette of pastels, and they could not be repeated in next-door houses, unless the color was white. The side of all window coverings visible from the street must be white or off-white.

"We also signed promises not to complain about the mosquitoes or harass the alligators," Doug said.

Fences and new shrubs, he continued, have to meet committee standards, in writing, thank you. You cannot park a junk car or a recreational vehicle in front of the house, or even behind it for that matter. Indeed, no one is allowed to park more than two vehicles per housing unit on the street or alley. Exterior television antennas and satellite dishes are prohibited unless they are affixed discreetly to the house.

"Our neighbor down the street, Jim Williams, he put up one of those little dishes for Direct TV on a post near his back door, and he got a letter saying he would have to take it down and put it on the house," said Doug.

You may hold only one garage sale a year, he continued, and post only one political sign, measuring no more than eighteen by twenty-four inches, in your yard for forty-five days before the election.

Then there was the matter of those other popular neighborhood signs, the ones that read "For Sale." Residents who wanted to get out of paradise had to sell their houses without posting any sign on the property. In the sixties and seventies, some inner-city neighborhoods adopted regulations prohibiting "For Sale" signs to slow the block busters who were taking advantage of white flight. In Celebration, the reasons seemed to be more self-serving and anticompetitive. With the community far from built out, the no-sign rule meant that residents were handicapped in their efforts to compete with the builders, who were allowed to post discreet "Home Available" signs.

The rules are enforced by the Celebration Residential Owners Association, which will be controlled by Celebration Company until the town is three-quarters completed, early in the next century. The association can write strong letters, hire attorneys, and, in the case of serious infractions, place liens on property. But few incidents in our first year rose above the level of a friendly letter or telephone call. Not even the aging and rusting Dodge Dart that sat for months on end along Celebration Avenue, the main artery into town, had provoked a call from the lawyers.

"A couple of neighbors called me and they were very nice, but they asked if I would mind contacting the guy about moving the car, because he hadn't responded to them," said Brent Herrington, who bears the title Community Services Manager for Celebration Company but is really the pseudomayor. "I called him, and he was not at all interested in moving the car. He was angry that his neighbors had mentioned it, and then he was angry at me."

Herrington raised the matter with the association board. Technically the board could require the removal of the car, since it sat immobile for more than the allowed two days at a time. On the other hand, the board was reluctant to make an issue of something so slight.

"Look, it's a town," Herrington explained to us later. "There are going to be jalopies. There's going to be the eccentric widow with all kinds of stuff on her porch. You don't want the definition of 'citizenship' to come down to such sterile matters as pristine maintenance of your lawn or strict compliance with all the rules."

The car stayed, and the owner bought a green-and-white Celebration license plate to hang from the rear bumper.

The rules were explained to everyone before they bought their houses, and everyone signed numerous pages acknowledging that they understood them. Most people found them another reassuring sign of uniformity and consistency.

"I love democracy," said Stu Devlin, a retired lieutenant in the New York City fire department and a marine corps veteran. "I fought for democracy, but I don't mind giving up certain freedoms to be in this town. Gee, I'm glad my next-door neighbor can't pull a tractor-trailer in behind the house or paint his house some weird color. People are willing to give up that stuff. Celebration can't be for everyone. Some people don't want it. There's gotta be another town for them."

Doug tended to agree with Stu, especially since the rules were well understood before you bought your house. But the whole regime never sat well with Cathy. She argued that if a rule was stupid, it should be ignored. And she had flouted community standards before.

For several years, we lived in the Old Town section of Alexandria, Virginia, a beautiful neighborhood with quaint cobblestone streets and elegant Federal-era houses and town houses. The house we owned was two hundred years old and the plot had been surveyed by George Washington.

One year the house was in need of paint and we hired a local painter, Patrick Schurman. His crew began to scrape off the old paint, and it attracted the attention of some neighbors.

"What color are you going to paint it?" asked the midlevel bureaucrat at the Commerce Department who lived across the street.

"Be sure to keep it close to the original," advised another resident of our block.

Nothing could have irritated Cathy more. She discussed her annoyance with Schurman, and he agreed to participate in her retaliation. The next morning our neighbors awoke to a huge purple paint test patch across the front of the house. They were shocked into silence, at least to our faces. One person slipped under our door an unsigned note, which read, "In two centuries, nothing so horrible has happened to this house or this neighborhood." Sometimes we heard passersby whispering. One said, "They're from California, you know." It wasn't true, although that was the last place we had lived before Alexandria. For the painter, the consequences were potentially serious. A customer called and warned that he would not get any more business if he painted the house on Royal Street purple.

After two or three weeks, a lawyer arrived on our doorstep. He said he represented the town and the historical society. "The Hysterical Society," Cathy called it. We invited him in and discussed the nuances of regulating the color of houses in historical districts. After a few minutes, we took him into the courtyard at the side of the house and showed him what the painters were doing. The side of the house was painted a mellow and creamy yellow. He didn't know whether to laugh or be angry, so he just left. That night Cathy painted two words in yellow across the purple patch—"Just Kidding." So she was immediately drawn to the plight of Jacci Rizzo and the red curtains.

A couple days before we moved into our house, we met with a decorator to measure for blinds in the bedrooms. She said it would take about a month. We said we'd just hang sheets until they came.

"No way," she warned. "The porch police will be down on you. They won't let you put up anything but curtains, and they have to be white to the street. I was getting blinds for a guy over on Mulberry and he had put moving boxes in front of his windows for privacy. The porch police made him remove them." She gave us temporary paper shades in the appropriate white.

When the Rizzos moved into their new house, Jacci didn't have time to buy or make new curtains. She put up the red ones from their old place. The result was the first verified sighting of the Disney porch police.

"They were never meant to be a statement," she explained of her curtains. "We just didn't have time to think about it or change them. We had better things to do. All along, Celebration Company said they would never put garages in front of houses, but they did. They would never let people rent out their houses, but they did. They promised a worship center, where all the congregations could come together, but they didn't come through. If they could change the rules, I didn't have time to change the curtains."

Then came the call from Brent Herrington. He was polite and low-key, as always. But this was no mere jalopy. It was a real threat. "You are interfering with the development of the town," Rizzo recalled Herrington telling her. "If we can't control you, then how can we control others who don't follow the rules? What is to stop someone from painting his house bright orange?"

It was not the prospect of a bright orange house that carried the day. Rizzo just figured it was not worth the hassle. She replaced the red curtains with some white ones and called Herrington at Town Hall. "You'll be pleased to know that the big red menace is gone," she informed him.

Our own run-in with the rules in Celebration might be dubbed "the yellow peril," with apologies to the politically correct crowd. Celebration Company regulated the exterior colors of houses to avoid too much uniformity. The guidelines specified that adjacent houses and houses directly across the street from each other could not have the same exterior color unless the color were white. The interpretation of what was the same color was not in the eye of the beholder, but in the eye of the holder of power.

We had chosen a soft yellow for the exterior of our house, and we were surprised to discover that the houses two doors away and three doors away were about the same shade of yellow. In fact, when we moved in there was a total of four houses in a row in the yellow family. Then the Davises built their house right next to ours and painted it what sure looked to us like an identical shade of yellow. Finally, the house on the other side of the Davises' was painted yet another very similar shade of yellow. It was a small matter, but after a while the sameness of Celebration got on our nerves. Having so many houses—a total of six—the same basic yellow became an irritant to us.

Cathy wrote to Joe Barnes, who oversaw such weighty matters for Celebration Company. She complained that there were six houses in a row, all in the yellow family, some nearly the same shade. She even sent along some snapshots. After several weeks, Joe wrote back and said he and others from the company had examined the houses and determined that the colors were within the Celebration guidelines.

"While the exterior colors for the lots you have concerns about are similar and close to the same shade of yellow, they are different colors and are consistent with the exterior color guidelines that have been developed for Celebration," wrote Barnes. And he listed the colors, so that we would know they were different—Antler, Sunny White, Egg Nog, and Ricetone.

A few days later, Cathy visited the paint store and asked a clerk about the differences in the colors of the Davises' house and ours. He said they were virtually identical formulas. Even our builder's painter agreed. "Maybe a shade of difference," he offered as he compared our house to the Davises' house. "Hard to see it though."

Cathy fired off another letter to Joe, writing, "You guys at Disney are so clever, coming up with so many original names for the same color—yellow."

Like Jacci Rizzo with her curtains, we were not willing to go to war over the color of our house. But there was a frustration. You couldn't beat City Hall, or, in this case, Town Hall.

All power is relative, of course, as illustrated by the case of the musical mushrooms. From Thanksgiving through Christmas, downtown Celebration was filled with the kind of canned, generic holiday music that is so seasonally dispiriting. It driveled out of small round-topped speakers scattered around town like so many singing mushrooms. There were Christmas carols and the most saccharine Disney tunes and even the occasional Hanukkah song. It was hard to carry on a conversation in the rocking chairs along the lakefront. The music was not so much loud as it was cloying and irritating. We expected it to end with the holidays, but we were wrong. The music kept on playing. Not even the merchants liked it anymore. "I don't understand why they persist with this racket," complained Thomas Dunn, who ran an eponymous and elegant furniture shop on Market Street.

One night we were having dinner with Pat Schroeder, the former Colorado congresswoman, and her husband, Jim, an undersecretary at the Department of Agriculture. At the urging of their grown children, they had bought a house down the street. While they still spent most of their time in Washington, they were in Celebration a weekend or two a month, and Pat's parents lived full-time in the granny flat behind their house.

In our dining room, Pat listened with her wry grin as Cathy described the growing frustration over the canned music. Pat had an immediate solution: mount a guerrilla campaign; eliminate the speakers under cover of darkness.

"Let's form the Celebration Liberation Army and take out the mushrooms," she joked, obviously having spent too long on the House Armed Services Committee.

Complaints were lodged at Town Hall. The list ran to seventy names, then one hundred. Even Robert Stern, the master planner and Disney board member, complained about the speakers one day when he was visiting town and had to hold a hand over one ear as he shouted into the telephone. Citizens buttonholed Joe Barnes, the taste-master of Celebration, on the street. All to no avail. "It's in the original plans," countered Barnes when asked why there was no peace downtown. "It's in the original plans."

Then, miraculously, there was silence. No one seemed to know why. Town officials were mum. The gossipmongers had no explanation. It was not until several weeks later that we learned what had happened. A senior Disney executive, with the promise that we would keep his name secret, told the story to us.

Jane Eisner, the wife of Disney's omnipotent chairman, had been visiting Celebration. She heard the music and was appalled. She called Robert Stern, and complained that Celebration wasn't a theme park and shouldn't sound like one. After all, Stern had been in Celebration only a few weeks earlier and had himself been annoyed by the music, so he agreed that it should be turned off. But the final decision had to come from Michael Eisner. After his wife and Stern each raised the matter with him, the music stopped. "Michael was appalled," explained the Disney insider who told us the story. "We don't want Celebration to be a theme park."

But you did not have to be named Eisner to stand up to Town Hall. The Ziffers showed us that when they ran afoul of the Celebration architectural guidelines. Judy and Al Ziffer moved into a home around the corner from us, and a friend gave them a set of unusual doors for the front of the Victorian-style model as a housewarming present. Etched onto the glass of each was the figure of a golfer, a man on one and a woman on the other.

The Ziffers don't play golf, but they loved the doors for their style and for the thoughtfulness of their friend. So they were defiant when a letter came from Barnes, in the name of the architectural review committee, saying that the doors did not meet Celebration standards. Over several weeks, there was an escalating exchange of tough talk about suits and countersuits. Finally, Al Ziffer ended the matter with a one-sentence declaration. "It will take a brick to get rid of our doors," he wrote. The doors still stand.

Ron Dickson also took on Town Hall, though with his tongue planted firmly in his cheek. Dickson and other residents of the town houses along Campus Street, across from the school, often went days without getting mail delivered because their mailboxes were blocked by parked cars. The problem occurred because, despite the density of the town, Celebration was considered a rural route and postal carriers refused to get out of the mail trucks to deliver mail.

To dramatize the dilemma, Dickson, the author of a baker's dozen books, with titles like *How to Buy a House Without Losing Your Assets*, mounted his mailbox on an arm that extended eight feet out toward the street. He went a step further and printed up an order form to share his invention with neighbors. "Get Your Mail Delivered Daily," it blared. "Avoid the Hassle of Cars Parked in Front of Your Mail Box. Enjoy Your Constitutional Right to Equal Treatment & Service."

The first day he deployed the new mailbox, he was the only person on the street to receive his mail. He also received a visit from a sheriff's deputy, who explained that he was responding to a complaint from Herrington at Town Hall. After a brief talk with Dickson, the deputy recognized that the device was nothing more than a prank, and he decided to play along. Carrying a copy of the order form, the deputy went to Town Hall and told Herrington that Dickson had orders for eleven more devices and that his phone was ringing off the hook.

Herrington telephoned Dickson in a fury and left a sharply worded message on his machine. The next morning the inventor went to Town Hall and confronted Herrington. The first thing he told him was that it was a joke and he had no intention of selling the mailbox extender. The problem of mail delivery, however, was not a laughing matter, particularly for Dickson and people like him who operated small businesses out of their homes.

"This cannot go on any longer," he told Herrington. "So go downtown and tell those turkeys at the post office that you have to put up with people like Ron Dickson and they've got to solve this problem."

It took several weeks, but eventually Celebration Company moved the mailboxes on Campus Street to the alley behind the homes, where they were accessible.

By and large, however, in the early days of living in Celebration, we heard few complaints about the rules or about the larger fact that a corporation controlled the town. Indeed, the contrary seemed to be true. People tended to speak of politicians with distrust or downright derision, but few complained about the corporate blanket in which Disney had enfolded us. Paul Kraft is an intelligent man who taught school in Pennsylvania before moving to Celebration and going to work at the school's media center, so Cathy was a bit disconcerted by his response when she asked for his views on Disney's control of the town. "I haven't given it a thought," he said. "I know a lot of people do think about it. I knew what I was moving into. I was okay with it. I suspect that, as we grow, there will be pushes for independence. Right now, we are just too small. Everything is fine now, I think. I am satisfied. I have a little problem, I call Brent Herrington. He's not an elected official, but better. I want to plant something, I go to Joe Barnes and ask, 'May I put this here?' I accept this. I'm happy with it. I personally am opposed to elected officials. People who want to go into elected positions, I am suspicious of their motivations."

Each of us carries a mental map of the perfect small town. Whether or not we are of religious temperament, this exercise in mental cartography invariably includes churches. When Robert and Helen Lynd conducted their classic study of Middletown—in reality, Muncie, Indiana—in the early 1920s, they counted forty-two church buildings serving a community of 36,000 people—a church building for every 857 residents.

When Charles Fraser was consulting on the planning of Celebration, he advocated scattering numerous sites for churches throughout the community to provide focal points for neighborhoods and convey a sense of inclusiveness. But Disney had never before allowed a worship site on company property, and the company executives had a different vision. They insisted on a single church in a prominent downtown location, in keeping with Walt Disney's plans for a single ecumenical worship site at Epcot. The spot the company selected was a prime two-acre

parcel across from the bank. The church would be the first civic building to welcome visitors when they drove along Celebration Avenue into
town.

Initially, the site was to be for joint worship, but the different religious groups could not come to an agreement. The bishop from the
Catholic diocese in Orlando toured the site set aside for the church
when there was nothing but sand and swamp there, but he balked at the
price, which was nearly $300,000. But plenty of religious groups were in-
terested, and there was a competition among a dozen denominations
for the right to build a church on the site. After all, Celebration was the
most highly promoted new town in America, and any church built there
would be bound to attract enormous attention. Indeed, the anticipated
publicity surrounding Celebration and the parentage of the Disney
company made it a magnet for many businesses and people who wanted
to capitalize on the glow. In the end, the Presbyterian Church USA won
the right to build the church by stressing its ecumenical heritage and
its thesis of inclusion. The Presbyterians bought the land at roughly
market price, with a donation from Walt Disney's niece, Dorothy Puder,
a daughter of the eldest Disney brother, Herbert, and her husband,
Glenn Puder, a retired Presbyterian minister, who sold some of their
Disney stock to make the contribution.

"It is our way of remembering Walt and Roy, and is a great fit as far
as we are concerned," said Glenn Puder. "We remember conversations
when Walt said he was planning on creating much more than another
Disneyland-type theme park. He envisioned building a city so revolu-
tionary and innovative it would serve as a prototype for future urban development. That longtime dream seems to be coming to fruition with
this new community of Celebration. You could say that money represented in Disney stock which we inherited is coming full circle."

In keeping with its vision of a traditional small town, Celebration
Company insisted that the building resemble an old New England
church, complete with white clapboard and steeple. The sanctuary
would be small and intimate, with seating for two hundred or so wor-
shippers. The Presbyterians balked. For one thing, the sanctuary would
be too small for the only church in a community that would grow to
twenty thousand. Equally important, they insisted on the right to design
worship facilities that met their needs and style.

Instead of a traditional clapboard church, the Presbyterians wanted a contemporary, technologically advanced worship campus that would recast the church's appeal at a time when many leaders fear organized religion is dropping off the radar screen of most Americans. The result was an $11 million complex, with forty-four thousand square feet spread through a welcome center, an eight-hundred-seat sanctuary, a small chapel with room for ninety, and a meeting hall. There would be facilities for televising services, and satellite links with other churches and with seminaries to develop educational programs. It was an ambitious project, but the church expected Celebration to provide a national showcase for Presbyterians and for new evangelical techniques.

The Presbyterians won the right to build the church complex the church leaders felt they needed, with the proviso that the architectural plans would be submitted to the company for approval by Michael Eisner. Nobody wanted the boss to drive into town and find out that the church didn't look like the one from Vermont he imagined.

If it couldn't dictate the design for the church, the company argued, it should have a voice in selecting the minister who would build a new congregation. Company officials asked for a seat on the pastoral search team being assembled by the Presbyterian Church USA. Again, the church elders said no. Instead, they conducted their own nationwide search for a leader with the charisma and stamina to develop a new church in what would no doubt be a national spotlight. After months of interviews, church leaders selected Patrick Wrisley, a thirty-six-year-old associate pastor at Peachtree Presbyterian Church in Atlanta, one of the largest and richest congregations in the country.

The Georgia-born Wrisley brought a folksy informality to the town and the church, often lacing his sermons with homespun stories about hiking in the mountains or picking up bits of wisdom from the characters who lived in the hollows. Like most who came to Celebration, he had given up a comfortable position. Unlike most, however, his success or failure would be measured in the harsh glare of publicity.

One day over lunch downtown, Wrisley explained why he had taken the chance. "It was a big step out of the box," he said. "It was a risk on many levels. Professionally, it was a big gamble, because this has never been done. Usually a church has twelve months or more to build momentum. A pastor will come to town and get to know the community and work with the community and then start the church. My job was to go from zero to a full congregation almost instantly, sort of like the way Celebration itself went up."

Not all the risks were professional. Wrisley and his wife, Kelly, had two daughters, Lauren and Katie. "We took our kids out of a proven school system and put them in a system that is just beginning to find its way," he said. "We left behind our roots and our assurances. But I have no regrets. Everybody gave up something to come here. Everybody took some risk."

Wrisley's position and his level-headed nature qualified him to become part of a little-known ad hoc group that dubbed itself the "town fathers," though three of the six members were women. In addition to Wrisley, the members were Herrington; Charlie Rogers, manager of the local branch of SunTrust Bank; Terry Wick, Disney's liaison with the school; Kathy Johnson, executive director of the Celebration Foundation, an organization that was set up by the company to promote good works in the community; and Dot Davis, once she arrived in town as school principal. The group was self-selected, with Herrington leading the way, and it had been formed in response to the difficulties at the school in early 1997. It met on an irregular basis, when an emergency arose or the rumor mill began to work overtime about some simmering problem.

Few people outside the group knew that it existed. There was no newspaper or radio station in Celebration to publicize such matters. The town relied mostly on the Celebration Company and Herrington's monthly newsletter to supplement the normal gossip. And the town fathers had kept their existence low key enough to avoid detection by the gossip police. In fact, we discovered it only by accident. One Friday afternoon we were headed for the first tee at Celebration Golf Club when Cathy noticed Wrisley and the others huddled around a table outside the restaurant at the course. We waved and they waved back. Later she pried the existence of the town fathers out of a couple of people who had been at the table. Their purpose, as one of the members explained, was to work on ways to head off problems before they erupted. "Think of us as an early warning system," said this member. But whom were they warning?

Kathy Johnson was surprised when Cathy asked her about the town fathers, and she sputtered a bit before replying. "It's an informal group that gets together to support each other," she said. "For example, if Dot is at the end of her rope. We gather on occasion to deal with whatever needs arise. We ask, 'What is going on? What do you need? What can we do?' I wouldn't say it's a support group, but that's how I think of it."

Most often the discussions involved school-related flare-ups—how to calm angry parents, how to retain teachers, that sort of thing. Other times the subjects were construction delays, promoting community spirit, getting the long-promised technology links up and running, and satisfying the downtown merchants, who regularly complained that they were not getting the amount of business they had expected. The theme that ran through the conversations, according to people involved in them, was finding ways to deal with the expectations of the people who had come to live and work in Celebration.

Herrington had come up with the name "town fathers" and initiated the informal gatherings. As time passed, Johnson had advocated a more public and formal structure, something akin to a town leadership committee. The membership would include leaders from each of the five cornerstones—education, technology, health, community, and place.

The group may have been a good idea, given the absence of any real government in Celebration. In a town where form so thoroughly dominates function, where the water tower is dry and the houses have fake dormers with windows painted black, no structure is as disconcertingly false as Town Hall, at the head of Market Street. Philip Johnson designed the building, surrounding it with a forest of fifty-two white columns, the traditional symbol of democracy. The building looked silly, as if it were lost behind that forest of columns. Even the front door was small and hard to find. Perhaps the reason was that Johnson, who was in the twilight of his long and illustrious career, had not really wanted to build it at all, but had been cajoled into accepting the commission by Robert Stern. Or maybe it looked silly because there was no democracy in Celebration.

Town Hall, like every other building in downtown, was owned by Disney. And Disney ran the town itself, through its control over the boards of the homeowners association and the two community development districts that raise money for municipal services. The landowners of Celebration elect all three boards, but Disney remained the largest landowner because most of the land had not yet been developed. As the build-out continued, the company would gradually relinquish its control over the boards.

Hundreds of thousands of similar privatized communities dot the country. In virtually all of them, control rests with a homeowners association, whose members are elected by the property owners. Most developers view the associations as a nuisance even when they control them, because they must hold public meetings and provide a small measure of accountability to the homeowners themselves, so the developers are more than happy to bow out when the time comes. But the prospect of turning over the keys to Celebration to its residents troubled Disney executives. Unlike most developers, who are content to finish a project and move on to the next, Disney would remain a neighbor of Celebration forever. Indeed, World Drive, the main road into the Magic Kingdom, was eventually to be extended to connect the town to the theme park. Further, the company knew its name would be linked always to the town it had created.

So, in the midst of the thicket of legal phrases and regulations of the covenants, the company's lawyers had inserted an unusual section that gave Disney veto power over any substantive decision by the homeowners association. The veto power was good as long as Disney owned a single piece of property within Celebration, which meant it was good forever, since the company owned the entire downtown.

"It is one of the most undemocratic clauses I have ever seen in a covenant," said Evan McKenzie, a professor of political science at the University of Illinois at Chicago and a lawyer who often represents homeowners in suits against developers. "Frankly, I've never seen anything quite like it."

Herrington tried to cast this veto as the last resort of a benevolent despot. "There are two things that are true about the veto power," he said one morning as we sat in his conference room on the second floor of Town Hall. "One is that architecturally, as long as Disney owns a piece of land they have the ability to veto major changes. Imagine somewhere down the road the community decided it wanted to change Town Hall into some other kind of building. Or imagine they wanted to make some really radical change in the residential architecture that would let people tear the porches off the houses. The company preserved the right to protect this architecture. It was such a huge linchpin of this project to bring together this galaxy of the world's finest architects and they want that to be permanent. So they have preserved the right to step back in. The second piece is that they reserved for themselves the ability to veto any decision that substantially changes the structure of Celebration, such as trying to gate the community or dismantling the home-owners association."

Herrington maintained that none of the current Celebration Company executives even knew the veto power existed until it was mentioned in an article in *The New York Times Magazine* in December 1997. "It sounds crazy, but we didn't know it was there until the article pointed it out," said Herrington.

The article, which was written by Michael Pollan, created a stir in town. A few days before its publication, advance copies circulated like samizdat in the old Soviet Union. Although much of the ground covered in the article was old news, the piece was pretty evenhanded in assessing the pros and cons of Celebration, and the section on the problems of governance was especially good.

On the Friday morning before publication, however, the article was the talk of the Rotary Club at its weekly breakfast meeting at the golf course. The buzz was that it was another negative story on Celebration. Herrington complained to his fellow Rotarians that he considered the article "scathing," which it was from his personal perspective. He had come out looking like a wanna-be mayor. The portrayal was unfortunate, because he seemed to us to have done a pretty good job of balancing his roles as the Disney point man in Celebration and the people's advocate.

By Saturday morning, enough people had read the article or heard about it that Herrington got a standing ovation at a town meeting in the school gymnasium. The applause was genuine, but also at play was the siege mentality that gripped some community residents.

Much of the press attention given to Celebration had been glowing, but there had been a fair share of stinging articles, too, particularly when the first families had left the school in such a public manner. As a result, many residents were defensive. Like another kind of pioneer in the Old West, they circled the wagons and returned fire. We would learn how deep those feelings ran over the coming months when we found ourselves on the receiving end of some shots.

8

Scorpions and Other Neighbors

The scorpion was not very big, about the size of a silver dollar. As she reached down to pick it up, Cathy thought it was a plastic toy left by one of the children as a practical joke. When it flicked its tail at her hand, she screamed. Cathy is not girlish. She lifts weights and throws a ball hard enough to burn your hand through the glove. But her scream was instinctive and loud.

After a couple of minutes, she calmed down, set a drinking glass over the night visitor, slid a piece of paper beneath it, and flipped the glass upright. She and the kids watched the scorpion strut around its prison with jerky movements, thrusting its tail aggressively at the sides. If it had not frightened her so badly, Cathy would have laughed at its brave attempts to do battle. Instead, she replaced the piece of paper on top of the glass with a heavy book.

Though scorpions navigate by stars, it was a mystery how this one had arrived in our kitchen. Equally mysterious was whether it was dangerous. Cathy called next door to ask the McGraths if they knew anything about scorpions. About thirty seconds later, Tim McCarthy was ringing the doorbell, kitchen tongs in hand. Cathy could not decide whether he was ready to do battle with the intruder or toss it in a pot and boil it. Before he could be assured that all was well, the kitchen filled with more guests from the McGraths' house, where the usual Sunday night party had been in progress.

Everyone stayed for an hour, discussing Florida wildlife and trading tales of alligator sightings in ponds and lakes around town. Even Nick and Becky participated, describing how the 'gators at Lakeside slipped up and grabbed the small fish they caught with hooks and hot dogs. The conversation had the easy flow of banter among longtime friends, though these friendships were only weeks old.

Ever since arriving, we had noticed the extreme friendliness of our neighbors. It was a distinct and not unwelcome contrast to the largely disinterested reception we had experienced when we moved to Connecticut three years before.

One advantage of making a sudden departure from an old life is that it allows you to look back and understand what you left behind before its outlines are smeared by memory. We had formed a few strong friendships in every place we had lived, but these were the products of common interests and a shared outlook on life. They took time to develop. Cathy's rule of thumb was that making real friends took at least a year.

In Celebration, friendships, like the town itself, were instant, popping up as fast as the moving trucks unloaded new lives. The natural inclination was to resist these new relationships even as we went on forming them. On the surface, they sometimes seemed too easy.

Yet what was this community itself except common interests and a shared outlook on life? The same dreams brought most of us to Celebration, just as the earliest city dwellers sought safety and better lives through group living five thousand years ago at the dawn of recorded history. Little is known about how the social structure we call a city came into existence, but we know that the archaeologists do not hold all the answers.

"In seeking the origins of the city, one may too easily be tempted to look only for its physical remains," cautioned Lewis Mumford in his book *The City in History*. Look instead, he wrote, for the reasons the rudimentary city was born—the search for social stability and continuity, the communal urgings, and the yearning for permanence.

On the night of the scorpion, the conversation turned eventually to the reaction of the neighbors to the illness of Tim and Beth McCarthy's oldest daughter, Jennifer. When Tim and Beth took her to Alabama for risky heart surgery, Beth's mother, Pat Miller, had come to stay with the McCarthys' two younger girls. Pat was confined to a wheelchair, so she could rarely get out of the second-floor apartment where the McCarthys were stuck while their long-delayed house was being finished. Every night while Tim and Beth were with Jennifer at the hospital, a different family took in dinner for Mrs. Miller and the two girls, often staying to chat and hear the latest news about Jennifer's ordeal.

After the successful surgery and the completion of the house, Tim described how he had gone back to the apartment to clean up. Within minutes, Kathy and Len Gross were knocking on the door, cleaning items and a vacuum in hand. They stayed for nearly two hours, until the place was spotless.

"You know, with everything else that had been going on, we hadn't cleaned in months," Tim recalled that evening at our house. "It was so bad that I was embarrassed by having someone see this. But it also was a wonderful feeling."

A few days after the apartment cleaning, Beth, who had been so nervous about leaving the certainties of her life in Tampa for this new town, dropped notes in the mailboxes of the people who had been helpful.

"When people ask us what it's like living in Celebration, our thoughts immediately turn to people like you," she wrote. "It's really not about houses or the architecture or Disney. It's about neighbors that become friends, for a long time, I think."

Celebration is not the only place where neighbors help neighbors, or even where people go to the aid of strangers. But if Celebration were to turn into a real community where friendships lasted for a long time, it would require the sort of commitment Beth and Tim McCarthy described. Disney provided the physical setting, but there is no pattern book for putting a soul into a town. Building a real community depends on the people who have packed up their belongings and come to it.

No one had a more harrowing and ultimately inspirational journey to Celebration than Jan and Bob Parker and their four children. They owned and operated a hotel in Dearborn, Michigan. It was a demanding, time-consuming job. They had talked often about selling out and starting fresh somewhere new.

One day in early 1997, with several inches of snow coating the Detroit suburb, Bob turned to his wife and said: "I really need a break. We need to get away." The kids were in school, so Jan stayed behind and sent her husband to Florida by himself. Her last words as he walked out the door were "Don't buy anything." The following day, there was a message on Jan's answering machine from a real estate agent. Somehow the agent thought the Parkers were moving to Florida.

Jan had to wait until her husband called that night to find out what the message meant. Bob explained that he had seen a small hotel that was for sale. He protested that he had not said they were moving, and had not made an offer on the property. He was just looking and thinking.

A few days later, Jan picked Bob up at the Detroit airport. He was excited. "I visited Celebration," he said. "You've just got to see this place."

The Parkers had been hearing about Celebration for several years, but they had never talked about living there. A few weeks after Bob's trip south, they flew back with their twelve-year-old daughter, Lisa. Walking around the community, they fell in love with it. A man was standing by the lake in the center of town with his young son, who was dangling a fishing line in the water. "I can't picture myself living anywhere else," the man told them.

The Parkers felt the same way. They walked into the Celebration Preview Center, at the end of Market Street opposite the lake, and, in a matter of a few minutes, bought a nearly finished Estate house on Arbor Circle, one of the town's prettiest streets. They sat right in the real estate agent's office and chose the colors for the walls and floors to finish off the house.

"Back home, our other kids didn't react well," remembered Jan. "It was kind of upsetting. They thought we had gone down to visit, but that we wouldn't go through with it. Although Lisa had liked it and even looked forward to a new start, she didn't say so to her brothers and sister. She felt like it would be a betrayal of them. But I'll never forget what Lisa told us. 'Mom, this is going to be my second chance. I want to be more outgoing, more popular, to do things differently this time.' "

Jan and Cathy were sitting outdoors at Barnie's when Jan told the story. Remembering her youngest daughter's words, she could not help herself and she started to cry quietly. After a few minutes she said, "We had no idea how much of a new beginning she would be making."

By June, the Parkers had sold their hotel and put their house up for sale. They decided to pack themselves and move to Celebration in a rented truck. The money they saved would be used to install a pool at the new house.

One day while she was packing, Jan found a St. Anthony medal in one of the boys' rooms. She had never seen it before, and she thought it was odd. She looked up St. Anthony and found he was the patron saint of miracles. Without saying anything to her family, she attached the medal to a chain and hung it around her neck.

"I was so exhausted, between the packing and the good-byes," she said, remembering that last day in Dearborn. "For days people had been coming by and asking why we were doing this. Bob would just tell them that there was some force that said we had to go and that we thought it would be good for the kids."

In the early morning hours of June 28, not long after midnight and after more friends had trickled out the door, Bob announced that it was time to leave. "When it's light, there will just be more friends," he said. So he got behind the wheel of the big rented truck, and Jan drove the family van, and they headed south. About five in the morning, they stopped for a breather and a quick nap.

"How do you feel?" Bob asked Jan.

"I'm okay, but maybe we should stop to sleep at a hotel for a while," she answered.

They got back in the vehicles and drove on, planning to stop at the nearest hotel. The next thing Jan remembered was a scream. She thinks it was Suzanne, the oldest child. Then she heard Bob's voice. He was calling for Lisa, asking if she could hear him. There were sirens and helicopters. Later, Bob would tell Jan that he had glanced in the rearview mirror as the van slammed off the road. He watched as Lisa and one of the boys, Tim, were thrown from the van.

Jan had been trapped in the van, and rescue workers freed her with the "jaws of life." She was unconscious for a time and suffered serious injuries. Tim had suffered a broken leg. Suzanne had some scrapes. Lisa had sustained the most severe injuries. She was unconscious when she was rushed by helicopter to the University of Lexington Hospital in Lexington, Kentucky, not far from where the accident occurred.

While the Parkers were waiting for Jan to be cut free from the van, Suzanne had gathered some of their belongings scattered along the highway. She bent over and picked up the St. Anthony medal and handed it to her father, saying: "I don't know why, but this is important to Mom. Give it to her when she wakes up."

Tim and Jan were hospitalized for four days. Lisa would stay in the hospital much longer. While they were there, friends from Michigan drove down. Bob decided to go on to Celebration to close on the house. The builder was not insisting that he come, but Bob wanted to do it so he could start getting the new place ready for his family. Before he left, he offered his wife a choice. "Our house in Dearborn hasn't sold yet," he said to her. "We can turn around and go back home."

"We can't go back," she said firmly. "We can't undo what has happened to us, especially to Lisa, but we have to go forward."

The day he arrived in Celebration with the rented truck, a dozen people he had never seen before greeted Bob at the house. His new neighbors unloaded the truck. They arranged the furniture. They brought meals, night after night.

Pat Wrisley stopped by that first day, and later that night he called Jan in her hospital room in Lexington. "I want you to know that the whole community is praying for you and Lisa," he said. "The Presbyterians, Catholics, Jews, Baptists. Everyone."

Every Sunday for weeks, Wrisley never failed to ask his congregation to remember Lisa Parker in their prayers and to ask for her speedy and full recovery. The other members of the family often sat in the front row of the AMC theater in Celebration, where the church had its Sunday services while trying to raise money for its building. Near the end of July, Lisa was transferred from the Kentucky hospital to a facility in Orlando. A month later, she was released and came to her new home. Not long after that, Lisa joined her family in church. Even for those who had not yet met the brave young girl, it was a moving homecoming.

Jan wept briefly as she finished telling her story to Cathy. For her, she said, Celebration had become a healing place. She was going to physical therapy and was recovering from injuries to her left arm and leg. She had watched as her youngest child made slow and steady progress, too, in recovering from severe head injuries, though Lisa had not yet recovered all of her motor skills. At that moment, Wrisley came out of Barnie's. He walked over and gave Jan one of his patented hugs. She hugged him back, hard it seemed.

By the start of the new year, Barnie's had become a fixture on Cathy's daily calendar. She would ride her bicycle to town after the kids left for school. There were a number of groups that met at different hours of the day at the coffee shop. The group to which Cathy was granted membership fluctuated between four and six people. Outsiders were regarded with some suspicion, and it had taken Cathy a few weeks to overcome the wariness generated by her role as a writer about Celebration.

To thrive, any city, town, or village must have places where people can congregate away from home and work, where neighbors can get to know one another without the formalities of the office or the encumbrances of family. There must be places where people meet each other face to face, as in the Athenian agora of classical Greece. The English know this, and so their pubs thrive. In France and Spain, there are sidewalk cafés; piazzas in Rome and *Biergartens* in Germany serve the same function. Ray Oldenburg, a sociology professor at the University of West Florida, calls these "the great good place" in his book of the same name.

You will notice these places in any city or town where there is a thriving public life. People will be sitting on benches or gathered around a bar. The main activity is conversation. Arguably, you do not have a community unless there are places where you can go to see and spend time with people you know.

Several regulars were in their usual spots at one of the tables under the live oak in Barnie's courtyard when Cathy was first invited to join the group. She had noticed their lively conversations several times in past weeks. A few days earlier, she had been introduced to one of the women, Cath Conneely, a Brit who also had moved down from Westport, Connecticut, a few months before we arrived. Her husband worked for the Hard Rock Cafe chain, traveling often to scout new locations for restaurants. Though they had never met in Westport, it was Cath who invited Cathy for what she did not realize was an informal audition.

The conversation that day was about Celebration School. A woman named Wendy and her husband, Dennis, were angry about the so-called report cards that had just been issued for the first nine weeks of school.

Instead of the proscribed grades, each "learner" received marks in eighteen separate categories. The categories ranged from "listens actively for a variety of purposes" and "uses the tools of information technology to communicate" to "thinks abstractly and creatively" and "respects human diversity as part of our multicultural society and world."

On this morning, Wendy and Dennis both expressed concerns that without grades and the precise expectations that come with them children might not be driven to excel. They wanted a tracking program that would provide extra challenges for academically gifted children. One of the other people at the table, Marguerite Saker, defended the school, saying that the individual approach to education would render traditional gifted education a moot point.

Over the next few weeks, the group solidified into a form that would remain basically the same for months to come. Wendy's job kept her away from coffee most of the time, and Dennis, a lawyer who stayed at home with the children, gradually faded out of the scene. He had been openly skeptical about chatting with Cathy at the table and disgruntled in general with the "liberal media." His absence left Cath Conneely, who proved to have a sharp wit and equally sharp tongue; Marguerite Saker, the group's optimist and a transplanted Floridian who had moved thirty miles to Celebration because she and her husband wanted to participate in what they thought was a grand social experiment; Niki Bryan, a native of Orlando, who brought all the drama of a Southern belle with brains to the table; and Cathy. There were the occasional visitors, "guest speakers," Cath called them, but it would be months before the group changed again.

Oldenburg describes great good places as "stages," with their own unwritten rules. And certain informal and unspoken guidelines did evolve within the Barnie's group. You learned to stay silent and let everyone speak. You tried to avoid hurting the feelings of those in the circle but were not required to spare those on the outside. Gossip was to be avoided, unless it was of general interest. As with any group, there was the question of whom to invite to join.

At one point, Cath Conneely planned a trip out of town, but she was so concerned that her chair would be filled in her absence that the three other women provided her with a guarantee, which read: "Bum's the word. We, the undersigned, hereto promise to save a seat, henceforth known as the SEAT, at Barnie's for Cath Conneely, of Celebration, FL, for a period of, but not more than, seven days. And if the aforementioned Ms. Conneely returns in said time period, she may even take said SEAT at the same table as we, the undersigned. Otherwise, she must find a SEAT at another table, because the hurly-burly competition will be great for this SEAT from the hoi polloi, and there is only so much the undersigned can do to protect said SEAT. After April 1, 1998, the SEAT will go to the highest bidder. All proceeds will benefit the Musical Mushroom Society of Greater Celebration." Marguerite, Niki, and Cathy signed the document. Conneely left town reassured.

Several people were rejected in the early days. Too loud. Too domineering. Too whiny. Interlopers usually moved off, waving from another table in the coffee shop. One day in late January, Teresa and Dave Haeuszer sat down. They were an intriguing couple. Our daughter, Becky, was friends with their daughter, Amy. In the usual direct way of children, Becky said that Amy's parents were rich and didn't have to work.

They sure seemed young to be retired. They had also seemed standoffish in the past, but as they sipped their coffee and weighed in on the conversation that day, it was apparent that they were smart but shy. The next morning, they were back.

"Geez," said Teresa, "I was glad to find you guys here. I was afraid you'd start meeting in somebody's house to avoid us." They joined the group and stayed, turning into some of the many friends we made in Celebration.

What had started without plan evolved into an integral and joyous hour each day. Failure to show up almost required a medical excuse. Each weekday morning, for an hour, sometimes longer, the group traded observations, keeping the gossip to the essential minimum. They would talk with animation about the ups and downs of the school, Town & Country, books, even politics. Among them, the group's members knew everyone, and few were spared the skewer.

Brent Herrington's monthly newsletter always sparked a debate. While well written and informative, the newsletter's tone sometimes tilted toward preachy, and occasionally it sounded downright pedantic. For instance, one month Herrington devoted nearly a full page to the proper "Celebration style" for furniture, plants, and decorations on front porches. Nice-looking furniture was okay as long as you kept it clean. But, apparently fearing some invasion akin to Faulkner's Snopeses, he warned that indoor furniture, light fixtures, and appliances were "probably never appropriate on the front porch." Plants were okay as long as they were alive and in good condition. But silk or plastic plants were not a good idea, and macramé hangers "don't stay looking good for very long." Decorations should be used sparingly and cautiously, limited to items that would look good in a photo spread in *Architectural Digest* or *Southern Living*. And finally, he wrote: "Here's a tip I'm certain will never fail: Skip the animal statues, cutesy thermometers, windmills, ornamental house numbers, banners, wind chimes and other knickknacks. Live plants, an abundance of flowers, wooden or wicker patio furniture, traditional porch swings, and outdoor ceiling fans are the ultimate front-porch decorations."

In case anyone failed to heed the warning, there was a subtle reminder of the consequences. "One thing I'm certain we can agree on is that we don't want Celebration to be the kind of place where the 'porch police' perform inspections to ensure everyone's porch remains in compliance," he wrote. "On the other hand, it is hard to ignore this subject because these are such visible spaces and one of the community's most recognizable architectural features." It was great fodder for the crowd at Barnie's.

One morning, Cath Conneely was spitting nails over an item in the most recent installment of the newsletter. Herrington had gently chided residents for referring to the latest area under construction in Celebration as the "North Village." The designation seemed logical, since the area was in the northern part of the community and it was called North Village virtually everyplace, including on the big topographical display at the preview center. But Herrington did not like it.

"I am increasingly of the opinion that these types of labels, while appropriate in building a subdivision, may not be a fit for the Town of Celebration," he wrote. "When we refer to different areas of the community as discrete, separate districts, it tends to reinforce parochial thinking, stratification and division, words that do not currently come to mind when I think of Celebration."

Herrington was engaging in Disneyspeak. In developing its Herculean corporate culture, Disney had created its own language to sugarcoat and sanitize activities within its theme parks. Just as employees were "cast members" and customers were "guests," job interviews were "auditions," a crowd was an "audience," restricted areas were "back-stage," accidents were "incidents," and the ever-present lines were a "pre-entertainment area." Within this mindset, it was obvious that the new residential area under construction at the north end of Disney's Celebration could not be the "North Village," with its connotation of separateness and distance. It had to be "the area north of the center of town" or some such nonsense. As an employee of Disney's Celebration Company, Herrington was, after all, a "cast member."

Responding, Conneely was in full dudgeon. "Does anyone else in town have the right, or the ability, to write a monthly letter to everyone else, inflicting his unsolicited opinion on every bloody household?" she fumed, banging the table so hard that a couple of lattes lapped over the edge of their cups as Niki, Marguerite, and Cathy rescued them in unison. "Did I ask Brent Herrington for his thoughts? No. What we're talking about is a simple geographic designation. It's just a name, for goodness sake. He's really gone over the top this time."

Her theory was that Herrington was trying some Orwellian trick so that no one would realize that the North Village was going up very close to Highway 192 and next door to Old Town, a down-scale amusement park.

One could hardly miss the proximity to Old Town. Music and loud-speakers from the park could be heard almost anywhere in this newest section of Celebration. Further, you could not miss the horizon-piercing twin poles of the three-hundred-foot Skycoaster swing.

A house full of guests from Britain no doubt contributed to Conneely's dark mood that morning. But her agitation over the semantic issue was so extreme that she spent several hours over the next two days getting the e-mail function on her computer fixed so she could share her sentiments with Herrington himself.

"I am at a loss to think of an alternative way of referring to the different neighborhoods in town," she wrote. "Would you suggest that we all memorize the new street names and use them instead? It would be nice to have the mental capacity to do that but the other terms of reference are just easier. My suspicion is that what you really are uncomfortable with is when people talk about other parts of the development in slightly negative terms, like saying perhaps they would not like to live in the 'North Village' because it is two miles from downtown, it has attractive views of 192 and a huge fluorescent catapult and that you can smell the Old Town popcorn from the lots."

Herrington's reply was logical and serious. "If you lived in Savannah, Georgia, or Cambridge, Massachusetts, or any other 'normal' town, you would not refer to which 'phase' or 'village' you lived in," he wrote. "Instead, you would use all the normal descriptions people use. . . . 'I live on Maple Street' or 'I live on the north side of town.' The lexicon of subdivisions and phases and projects doesn't seem to complement the town model that Celebration is based on."

He did, however, acknowledge that some neighborhoods of Celebration may be perceived as better than others, a rather startling divergence from the company line. "At Celebration, neighborhoods near the town center will always have a special prestige," he wrote to Conneely. "I'm glad about that, since I own a house there, too. I can tell you, though, some of the future phases to the south will absolutely knock your socks off. There will be many high-prestige areas in Celebration."

In fact, we found the North Village less appealing than the neighborhoods closer to town, where the first residents lived. And the other phases planned for the future, such as the South Village and Island Village, also would suffer because they would not be within comfortable walking distance of the town center. It seemed clear that the character of life in those portions of Celebration would be different from what we experienced, whatever spin Herrington tried to put on things.

Despite providing some laughs for the coffee group, Herrington's comments on the issue and many others in the newsletter, while tending toward the saccharine, were almost always well meaning. He had crossed over from employee to true believer within weeks of buying a house for himself and his family on Celebration Avenue and moving to town in 1996.

"A lot of people in the community have come to view me as the community's biggest cheerleader," Herrington, who had managed planned communities in his native Texas and in Arizona before coming to Celebration, told us one day. "Well, I do love this town. I've made it no secret. When I came here I expected to be professionally challenged. I did not expect to fall in love with the town personally."

On rare occasions, outsiders were invited to join the conversation at Barnie's. One morning Cathy recognized a young German journalist who had been pointed out to her earlier in the week. She introduced herself and invited him to share his observations of the town with the others at the table—Cath Conneely, Marguerite Saker, and Joe Judge, a sometime member who ran the local bike shop.

"I came here with a clear idea of what Celebration would be," said the journalist, Nicholas Maak, who was working for a radio station and a small magazine in Germany. "I was quite surprised when I found that it is not at all artificial. What is amazing is that these structures downtown are European in origin, with the sense of a European marketplace." The use of public spaces, the coffee shop, and the idea that people came together in the city center particularly took him. It was not a Roman piazza or a Parisian café, but the town center worked its small spell on Maak and turned the cynic into a fan, though a cautious one. "I see a danger in the concept here," he explained. "It works now, but what about when there are twenty thousand people here? You must pay attention that you are not the happy few in the center. These small spaces, these windows on the community, must not be limited."

Groups like the Barnie's clique formed all over town, coalescing around common interests, like the garden club, a small book club, and the barbershop quartet, or simply out of a love of conversation and camaraderie. Once a month, Becky and Scott Biehler, refugees from the cold of New Hampshire, organized a potluck lunchtime gathering at the picnic tables in Lakeside Park. Along with assorted residents, the regulars included Joe, the local post office manager, some employees from Town Hall, and the Osceola County Sheriff's Department deputies who patrolled Celebration. Tuesdays were martini nights at Max's Grille, the most expensive restaurant in town, and people often wandered in to begin the week on a high note. On Sunday nights, a dozen or more people could be found in the big wooden rocking chairs beside the lake in the center of town. They rocked and chatted and swatted mosquitoes.

We really liked those chairs. They were almost constantly in use, by residents and tourists alike. People sometimes sat in solitary contemplation. More often, they pulled the chairs together into a semicircle and talked animatedly. The chairs exemplified the idea that, in designing public spaces, the small things can matter the most.

Celebration residents gather on the great lawn at Lakeside Park for the annual town photo on Founders Day Weekend. Right, small-town mythology embodied in a lamp design.

A panorama of the town center shows Market Street ending at the manmade lake and the twin towers of Cesar Pelli's Art Deco movie house on the far right.

A forest of fifty-two columns surrounds Philip Johnson's town hall. To its right are the post office, designed by Michael Graves, and shops along Market Street.

Celebration School (above) and Celebration Health (left) embody two of the town's five cornerstones.

Community Presbyterian Church, when it is built, will be the first religious building on Disney property (rendering courtesy of Moore/Andersson Architects).

Nadina Place was only sand and dreams for the first block party, but the street is livelier by the time Donna McGrath arrives with a cake for the second neighborhood gathering.

Conversation, camaraderie, and coffee made Barnie's a regular meeting place for (from left) Catherine Conneely, Niki Bryan, Catherine Collins, and Marguerite Saker.

Principal Dot Davis doesn't suspect the difficulties ahead as she accepts the symbolic key to the new school from Thomas McCraley, the school superintendent.

Our house (above left), on Nadina Place, is dressed for Christmas and finally green after long battles with the builder.

The Garden Homes, (above right), designed to evoke Key West, were added to the master plan to try to keep prices below $200,000.

Three-story town houses curve gently along Campus Street in an effort to re-create the feeling of Savannah or Charleston (photograph courtesy of the Celebration Company).

Apartments above the shops contribute to the old-fashioned feel and help keep downtown lively at night.

Estate Homes, the town's most expensive residences, are custom built but still must conform to architectural standards.

You can always find at least one child racing through the interactive fountain in the center of town.

In his landmark book *City*, William H. Whyte praised a wonderful invention, the movable chair. Along with being comfortable, the biggest asset of these chairs is their movability, he wrote. They enlarge choice: You can move a chair closer to someone or farther away, into the sun or into the cool of the shade. These choices are subtle but important. Unlike fixed seats or benches, movable chairs contribute to the varying social dynamics of public spaces.

No better example of the importance of movable chairs exists than Bryant Park, behind the New York Public Library, in the heart of Manhattan. The wildly successful rejuvenation of the park earlier in this decade hinged as much on the eight hundred simple green folding chairs spread throughout the park as it did on the removal of junkies and litter. People love them. They collect them into big groups. They move them into a solitary corner. You can watch the same orchestration of chairs along the Serpentine in London's Hyde Park.

The chairs of Celebration were the inspired contribution of Charles Fraser. The developer was familiar with Whyte's studies long before they were compiled into a book. In fact, he had first put out the rocking chairs in Harbour Town in 1969. By the early nineties, fifty chairs were scattered around the public areas near the harbor.

"As soon as we started planning downtown Celebration, I started preaching the doctrine of movable chairs instead of benches," Fraser said. "I thought I had a commitment to chairs. But without telling me, they had let the landscape firm specify twelve-hundred-dollar bolted-down benches. When I saw those long redwood benches on the plan, I made a pest of myself."

Herrington laughed when told of Fraser's recollection of his championing the chairs. "We were all proven wrong," he admitted. "Charles insisted on having movable furniture on the lakefront. He said people like to go down there, drag up chairs, and get their own little thing going. We predicted they would be gone in a week. Then we'd get our benches. A year later, two are missing. As a result, we just met yesterday to plan the common amenities and park spaces for the South Village, the next phase, and there will be movable furniture in all the parks there. It works."

What had not worked nearly as well were the front porches. Before World War II, even the most humble houses in America were built with porches. People spent time there, socializing with neighbors and family members. The neighborhood was an important network that provided stability, vitality, and information to a community. The postwar move to the suburbs brought a shift in outdoor life to private backyards, with decks and patios. Porches, and the sidewalks that served them, lost their social significance. Even in older houses in established neighborhoods, the trend for years was to close off the front door, maybe even enclose the porch. The side or back door, accessible from the family car, became the main entryway. People preferred the private spaces of their backyards or family rooms, where television came to rule. Neighborhood vitality withered.

Disney's planners wanted to resurrect the porch, not just as an architectural element but as a mechanism for creating vigorous neighborhood life. "Front porches allow people to come out of their houses so they have an engagement with their neighbors and the street," explained Joe Barnes. "We want them to reach out to the street, which is no longer just a place you drive on to get to and from your garage."

This laudable piece of social engineering through architecture ran into two problems. First, Florida is hot and buggy for much of the year. Even with big ceiling fans and large overhangs, Celebration's porches are often uncomfortable places. Screened porches could have solved the bug problem, but screens were deemed unsuitable from a design standpoint and were prohibited on primary porches. Second, and more intractable, people no longer depend on neighbors for information and entertainment. Most of us get both of those commodities from television. We tend to come home from work, eat dinner, and plop down in front of the television. Few of us have the time, inclination, or need to venture onto the porch.

This pattern is not unique to Celebration. We once owned a house in Chicago that had a beautiful, wide front porch. It was a Sears house, built in the early part of this century from plans ordered from the company's catalog. We loved that porch, and we sat on it almost every evening, weather permitting. It was so lovely that Frito-Lay once filmed a television commercial on it. Nick was born in that house and many evenings we rocked him to sleep on the porch. But even in that turn-of-the-century neighborhood on the city's northwest side, nobody else spent any time on his porch.

Walk or ride a bicycle around Celebration just after the sun goes down any evening of the week, as we did regularly. The porches are invariably empty. Beautiful wicker rockers sit idle. "Porch props," quipped Mike McDonough, a neighbor and architect. Someone would be sitting on a porch at maybe one house in twenty on a cool evening. Even on Verandah Place, the showcase square on which full-facade front porches were mandated on every house, the porches were empty most afternoons and evenings. But from almost every family room visible from the street or the alley came the glow of a television set.

A porch culture may develop over time in Celebration. A small group of neighbors in the Garden homes, the smallest and closest-together of the town's detached houses, gather occasionally on their porches to sip drinks and gossip. The visits are regular enough that Dick Rianhard took to bringing a pitcher of something cool out with him, just so he could be prepared. From their porches, this handful of people often call out to passersby, who sometimes stop for a chat. It is pleasant to pause for a few minutes, but it does not happen elsewhere in town with any regularity.

Far more successful at pulling people out of their cozy homes was the street life downtown. The first two phases of construction, known as Celebration Village and the West Village, provided houses and apartments for about fifteen hundred people. All of the homes were within an easy, ten-minute walk of the town center. For those on the outer edge, it was a little farther than the optimum walking distance, which social scientists tell us is about five minutes, after which people will resort to a car. But the sidewalks were wide enough for comfortable movement. The closeness of the houses to the street provided a sense of intimacy and safety. People could hear you yell for help. The parks along the way offered pleasing vistas, and a canopy of trees was forming slowly over many of the streets.

Most important, there was a reason to go for a walk. The town center was active most nights, bustling on some. Each of the four restaurants offered sidewalk seating. Vertical geysers of spray rose regularly from a fountain, beckoning squealing children and the occasional adult. Cesar Pelli's art deco movie house, with its twin neon-lit spires, was a beacon beside the lake. Sixteen stores, from the corner grocery and a bakery to a bicycle shop and perfumery, stayed open late three nights a week. One of the friendliest stores, Village Mercantile, allowed kids to use the phone free of charge so they could check in with their parents.

Granted, many of the visitors were Mickeys, the local nomenclature for tourists. Some residents griped that the mix of stores was geared toward the tourists. They complained about the lack of a hardware store or a place to get your hair cut. Disney executives said they had courted those sorts of stores, too, but could not land any of them. The plain fact was that Celebration would not be large enough to support a traditional downtown for several years. So the company brought in stores that would draw much of their business from tourists in the first years. But though many of the kids dashing through the fountain and the parents laughing at their antics were from somewhere else, they still contributed to the vitality at the center of Celebration. And their parents spent enough money to keep the restaurants and shops open for those of us who lived there.

Disney used the town center as its stage. The attempt to dream up a fake history for Celebration was thwarted by a reality check, but the development company tried to drum up a sense of community through regular events, often dubbed "new traditions." There were parades and sock hops at the head of Market Street, a Saturday farmers market, and an annual arts and crafts fair, a pumpkin carving contest at Halloween, and a fireworks display on the Fourth of July. In mid-1998, there was even an event billed as a "surprise party" at which the company and merchants gave the residents a trailer filled with barbecue grills, folding chairs and tables, and a sound system for block parties. The block-party trailer was free, reserved on a first-come, first-served basis.

As with many things in Celebration, our initial reaction was that these ersatz traditions smacked too much of Disney and too little of citizenry. There was a vague feeling that people who moved here expected things to be done for them. Disney would not only build the town but also would provide the entertainment. Over the months, our feelings were mitigated by the genuine fun inspired by these events (hey, we like to be entertained, too) and by our repeated observations that people were actually getting to know each other better as a result of them.

Halloween provided a good example of the way the community was starting to work together. Hundreds of people turned out for the pumpkin-carving contest at the end of Market Street the night before Halloween. A dozen long tables were arranged in the street, and at each, adults and children were carving like demons. Some of the entries were exquisite, and the winner reproduced the Celebration seal, with the little girl on her bicycle followed by the dog, in stunning detail on a huge pumpkin. But the real test came the following night, on Halloween itself.

Literally moments before the town's children were supposed to begin trick or treating, the heavens opened in the kind of torrential downpour we have seen only in Florida but which is probably also experienced in India during monsoon season. Halloween looked like a washout, and then phones began ringing all over town with a message of salvation: "Bring the kids and candy to the school cafeteria."

Within an hour, the cafeteria was bustling with hundreds of children in costume, racing from adult to adult for candy and other treats. The Grinch might have stolen Christmas, but Celebration had saved Halloween. By nine that night, everyone was back home, safe and dry, while a handful of parents remained behind to mop up the sticky floor.

By far the biggest event in town was Founder's Day, one of those new "traditions," held in November to commemorate the initial lottery that opened the doors to the first residents. For 1998, the festivities were spread across a long weekend, beginning with a "Taste of Celebration" on Friday night and ending with the Founder's Day 10K race on Sunday morning.

The main event was the massive group photo taken Saturday afternoon on the lawn at Lakeside Park. Everyone in town was asked to show up, and, by our estimate, nearly two-thirds of the fifteen hundred residents were there. Before the photo, several people made remarks about their wishes for the town's future, and five children from the school spoke. There was a consistency in their vision of the future. They wanted more special events, more entertainment downtown, a skateboard park.

When it came time for the prayers, Pat Wrisley, sweating in his long-sleeved white shirt and tie, tried to remind these founders that the good life here came with responsibilities. "Our dream, dear God," he said, "is that our legacy will not be the style of homes we live in, the manicured lawns. Nor that we be known as the town with pretty parks. Rather, when people hear and learn about Celebration, may they think and learn of a place where people care for others, where sleeves are rolled up, and where challenges are met with a can-do spirit." (Wrisley's original prayer had been a bit more pointed, as his Sunday sermons often are. When the Celebration Company officials had reviewed his remarks in advance, they had insisted that he delete one sentence. It read, "We pray we are not remembered as being a town living in Disney's Tomorrowland nor a town that's all facade and no depth.")

For the group photo, the photographer stood on a small crane, about forty feet above the throng on the lawn. We all had assembled between four orange traffic cones, but some adjustments were required to fit everyone into the photo. Just before snapping the first picture, the photographer pointed to someone among the thousand faces and yelled down, "You aren't smiling." The crowd broke into laughter and he started to click away.

In keeping with the nostalgia that was the central theme of Celebration, Saturday night's Founder's Day dance on Market Street was a fifties party. Dozens of people came in poodle skirts or with their hair slicked back into ducktails. The entire Sublette family, Tom and Lisa and their children, Kaci and Clint, had slicked-back hair and high school letter jackets. Disc jockeys spun platters from the golden days of rock, and there were hula-hoop and limbo contests. The street was filled with whirling, twisting dancers of all ages until nearly midnight.

Doug's parents, Don and Jody, were visiting for the weekend. They had come to the fifties party with us and showed that they could still cut a mean rug. Halfway through the evening, Jody turned and said: "This is amazing. I haven't seen a crowd so mixed in ages in years. There are people my age, yours, and the children's. Even teenagers."

Several weeks later, Jere Batten and Doug were having lunch at Columbia, one of the downtown restaurants. Doug asked Batten if he had a favorite memory of Celebration yet. Batten, whose only regret since moving here was the friends he and Earlene had left behind in Pennsylvania, stopped and thought for two or three minutes before he answered.

"Founder's Day weekend," he said finally. "We came downtown every night. Even when Earlene was working, Alex and I came down by ourselves. There was a sense of community. It was one of the first times since we moved in back in June that I had a sense that I was getting to know a number of people. I came into town for that, and a lot of people stopped to talk. After that weekend, I realized that I was starting to feel at home in this town."

There were other stirrings of community, not all orchestrated by Disney. Though the small lots and town restrictions on planting left little to do in the way of landscaping, a small garden club had formed. It was mostly women, though a couple of men attended, and it sponsored lectures and walks through interesting backyards around town. It also was the most unlikely source of the first known act of civil disobedience in Celebration. The Garden Club Rebellion was not the Boston Tea Party, but it was a step toward independence.

Every Saturday morning, Market Street was closed to cars and transformed into a farmers market. Some stands sold produce, others offered plants and flowers, and the crafts booths ran the gamut, from beautiful hand-woven reed baskets to tacky porcelain figurines. The variety and quality did not match that of the established farmers market that thrived half a block from our old house in Alexandria. But for many residents, us included, the market was part of our Saturday routine.

The Celebration Company decided unilaterally to disrupt that routine. After a year and a half of operation, the market was not drawing as many people to town as expected. Merchants, who had never liked the competition, were complaining that it was siphoning off customers. In addition, the town was paying for the booths and other upkeep, and the market was in the red. So the company decided changes were in order. Before anything official could be announced, the rumor mill got wind that something was up. As often happens, the facts were slightly askew by the time word reached the Celebration Garden Club at one of its regular meetings at Lakeside Park.

Someone told the thirty or so women at the meeting that the town planned to cancel the market. The women were angry. They often bought plants and flowers from the vendors, and they thought that the market added a nice touch to the town regardless. They also were angered that the step was taken unilaterally.

"No one had a voice in how this decision was made," said Lise Juneman, who was at the meeting. "We didn't know why it was being changed. Was it going to help the community? Or was it just to benefit the Celebration Company?"

At the end of regular business, the garden club marched en masse to Town Hall. All thirty of them jammed the small foyer and demanded to see Herrington. The flustered receptionist called upstairs.

"There's a huge group of women who have just shown up here," she said urgently into the phone. "We need someone to come down right now."

Herrington was out, but his assistant, Susan Galpin, met with the angry gardeners in the conference room. She tried to mollify them with coffee and soft drinks while she telephoned around the company to find the answers to their questions. Eventually she reported back. The market would not be canceled outright. To save money, it was going to be moved to a small area beneath the porticos at one end of Market Street. The craft stands would vanish, but the flower and produce vendors would remain. The women were satisfied, and the short-lived Garden Club Rebellion was over.

The episode was one of the early signs that not everyone was willing to have the Celebration Company dictate the way things ran. People wanted a voice in what affected them. Here were the stirrings of democracy, and we would see them again in the coming months as the town grew and its residents began to give voice to their frustrations.

We had noticed another culture forming in Celebration, the "potluck supper" culture, if that isn't an oxymoron. Growing up in small-town Indiana in the fifties, Doug had strong memories of the potluck suppers held by his parents and their neighbors. Everyone brought a favorite dish—meat loaf, scalloped potatoes, Vienna sausages. It was a tradition that Cathy, who had grown up in Montreal, had never experienced, and one that Doug hadn't seen in many years, or missed. But in Celebration, the town marketed on a theme of old-fashioned values, the old-fashioned potluck supper was alive and well.

Most often, the folks on our street gathered on Sunday nights at the McGraths' house. There would be twenty to thirty people, mostly neighbors but some from outside Celebration, too. Kids were encouraged to come, and most did. Cathy invariably brought chocolate-chip cookies fresh out of the oven, but some people contributed a bag of chips and container of dip. Food is a noncompetitive sport in Celebration. Those who do it, do it. Those who don't, clean up. People would start to arrive about six o'clock and find Donna putting the finishing touches on a roast and Mike stocking the cooler with beer and soda. The food was hearty and plentiful, and occasionally there would be a dish containing Vienna sausages. "It's not the food," Donna said one evening as we sat around their family room after cleaning up. "It's the people. We know where the kids are. I don't need to put out an elegant spread. Everyone brings something special to them. That's gourmet to me. It's better than a restaurant."

The potluck supper was elevated to a formal rite over on Honeysuckle Avenue, about a five-minute walk from our street. In a deliberate effort to create a friendly neighborhood, the thirty or so families on that street gathered for the "Honeysuckle potluck" one night a month. Usually the neighbors hosting the dinner would have it at their house, though some people preferred to set up tables along the sidewalk. Wherever it was held, everyone would show up with a special dish and the entire family in tow. The event was so popular that the months were booked until the year 2000. "The Honeysuckle potluck is a serious community-building effort," explained Lise Juneman, who lived on Honeysuckle with her husband, Ron, and their two children. "It isn't the food that counts. It's the people. Some people bring family favorites, some just go to Publix [supermarket]."

The purpose of these gatherings was simple and straightforward—they provided occasions for nurturing friendships, an essential ingredient if a community is going to develop a sense of place. They were better than block parties, which tended to be frenetic, and they were far more natural than the Disney-planned festivities. And they were far less trouble than the dinner parties that we had put on most other places we had lived, where food *was* something of a competition. Food wasn't as good in Celebration, but eating it was more fun.

We still held the occasional dinner party, and both of us would spend much of the day making the food. It was something we enjoyed doing together, but it was more difficult in Celebration because finding the ingredients was like going on a scavenger hunt. The small local market, Gooding's, could handle special orders for beef tenderloin or fresh fish. Though there was a good kitchen store in downtown Celebration, featuring wonderful cookware and dishes, shelves of cookbooks, and some specialty canned goods, the owner told us she would have gone out of business if not for the tourists who bought goods to be mailed home. Once a month or so, one of us would drive thirty minutes to Winter Park, an affluent suburb on the other side of Orlando, to stock up at the specialty shops there, but we objected to the specialty prices. Several times, the price of admission for visitors from New York would be a couple pounds of pancetta, which was difficult for us to find in central Florida. Luckily, we had stumbled across a small family-run deli, Paul's, about ten miles east on Highway 192, which got a weekly order of fresh mozzarella and stocked a good range of Italian sausages and salamis. But, like the architecture, the food culture in Celebration was a throwback to a simpler era, and the potluck supper didn't seem any more unusual than leaving your doors unlocked or knowing the name of every person on your street.

9

Looking for Mayberry

Everyone dreams occasionally of trading his or her life for a fresh start somewhere new. You promise yourself that one day you will live in that special place where now you can manage only two or three weeks a year. The desire comes as much from a yearning to enlarge your psychic space as it does from an urge to change your physical address. As the poet Rilke said, "You must change your life."

So few of us ever fulfill that dream that when someone comes along who has, we become eager voyeurs, soaking up every word of their story. How else can you explain the wild popularity of beautiful little books like *A Year in Provence* and *Under the Tuscan Sun?* How else can we explain our fascination with Dave and Teresa Haeuszer and their search for "Mayberry," the fictional hometown of Andy Griffith, Opie, and Aunt Bee in the early-sixties television series?

In the months before we got to know the Haeuszers, we had often seen them around town, holding hands as they walked, or riding their old-fashioned bicycles. We smiled and waved, a Celebration thing. But not until they joined the group at Barnie's and grew comfortable in that tight little circle did Cathy begin to pick up intriguing pieces of how they and their three children ended up in Celebration. They had owned a waste-hauling business. They had traveled extensively with their kids.

Now they owned a doughnut shop at Blizzard Beach, one of the attractions at Disney World, except they never seemed to be there.

One of the best things about Celebration was the drop-ins. The last two places we lived, Westport and Alexandria, were filled with busy, formal people who got together mostly by appointment and reservation. Even the kids had play dates. Nobody had time for spontaneity. In Celebration, people would be out for an evening stroll or bike ride, pause in the street or on the sidewalk, and decide to drop in.

The Haeuszers were great drop-ins. They would come by after dinner for a round or two of beers at the kitchen table. Sometimes we would run into them downtown and wind up throwing something on the barbecue at their house. Late one Saturday afternoon, we bumped into them downtown and they invited us to stop by for a beer. When we got to their house, we found six of their other friends, including one who was a chef and was bent over the barbecue, grilling lobsters. Over the course of many such impromptu sessions, as well as coffees and a couple more-formal conversations, their story emerged. And over the course of those conversations, we came to like and admire the Haeuszers enormously. They were smart and straightforward. We were awed by their uncanny business sense, and warmed by their story.

In Rochester, Minnesota, Dave was in the waste-hauling business with his father. In 1988, Waste Management, the industry giant, bought out the company. Dave thought he owned fifty percent of the company, but his father had never put it in writing. It turned out that Dave's share was only six percent, not enough for his family to get by on. Just as bad, his father had approved noncompete clauses for himself and Dave that prohibited either of them from working in the same business for ten years. It was okay for the father, who had walked away with almost all the money. Dave fought the clause in court, and a judge reduced it to three years, but Dave and Teresa never got over the bitterness toward his father, and relations remained strained.

For a while Dave received unemployment benefits. Then he washed dishes at the Radisson Hotel in Rochester. No one wanted to train him for a new job, because they knew he would return to the garbage business at the end of three years. The problem was how to feed the family in the meantime.

The load fell to Teresa. In October 1988, she started her own business hauling trash, with a single aging truck that she leased for $183 a month. Because of the noncompete clause and their paranoia about Waste Management, Dave was afraid even to offer her business advice, let alone repair the truck after each of its regular breakdowns.

Teresa remembers those first days clearly and with humor now, though their plight seemed desperate at the time. "I was like,'What do I do?' I didn't know nothing about garbage trucks. I knew how to get accounts," explained Teresa, who has a natural's gift for selling and had worked in the office at the company owned by Dave and his father. "I hired another girl. She probably weighed all of ninety pounds soaking wet. We'd put coveralls on over good clothes in the morning and go out on the route to pick up the garbage. Then we'd take 'em off in the afternoon, and we'd go out and try to get more customers."

Impressed with the David versus Goliath aspect of Teresa's struggle to compete with Waste Management, some customers signed up. Others were helpful in different ways. Teresa could not afford to buy the big Dumpsters required by commercial accounts. The man who owned the local Dumpster business delivered $25,000 worth of them to the new company's customers without charging Teresa. He said she could pay when she got things up and going. As the opportunities grew, she raised additional capital by selling half the firm to a small group of local investors.

After nearly two years, Dave's paranoia waned, and he began offering the occasional advice. When the three years expired, he was ready to join as a partner. But the investors objected, arguing at a partnership meeting that Dave should contribute "sweat equity" before he got a share of the company. Teresa's face reddened, and she sputtered her objections. In anger, one of the investors threw down the gauntlet. "We should just liquidate the company," he said, naming a value off the top of his head. Teresa agreed to the price, and a few days later she bought out the other investors.

"One of the investors' wives didn't like me because she was always angry about her garbage pickup," Teresa said with a hearty laugh in the courtyard at Barnie's one day. "We used to pick up their trash for free. They had two ninety-gallon carts, and she'd unlock her garage door on garbage day, and the driver would have to walk up and get them, empty them, and take them back into her garage. All the paying customers had to wheel their own carts to the edge of the drive. Not her. A lot of times she would complain that the trash wasn't picked up, but that was because she forgot to unlock her garage. Only she would call and say nobody came by. I was out doing the route one day, and the door wasn't unlocked. So I had to call and go back a second time, and that time her daughter came out, spouting off. I said, 'That's fine.' And I wheeled the carts down to the truck, threw 'em both in, and said, 'Have somebody else haul your trash for free.' "

Within weeks of the buyout, the company landed a contract to collect municipal trash in a Rochester suburb, doubling its revenue overnight. By early 1994, the hauling business had eleven trucks and thirteen employees. Tired of the long hours, often in subzero weather, the Haeuszers decided to sell the company and try something new.

They had dreamed for years about what they would do if they got rich by winning the lottery. While building up the garbage business, Dave and Teresa often relaxed in a hot tub behind their farmhouse outside Rochester. Even on the coldest nights, they would sit under the stars, drinking beer, throwing the bottles in the snow, and talking about where they would go if they had the money. Except for a handful of trips to visit relatives, neither one of them had ever spent any time outside Minnesota. "We never expected to get rich from the garbage business," said Dave. "That was just survival. Our dream was always to win the lottery."

But in February 1994, they sold the garbage business, and suddenly they were rich. Still in their mid-thirties, they had enough money to live comfortably without ever working again. The first plan was to build their dream house on a beautiful piece of land outside Rochester. They hired an architect, and Teresa worked with him for weeks, making sure every detail of the house was exactly right. Their child, Mitchell, was two years old, and Amy and Matt, Teresa's children from her first marriage, were not yet ten. The plan was that after they moved into the house, they'd spend time with their children and eventually come up with another business idea to keep them occupied.

Life took a sharp turn on Memorial Day weekend. Fittingly, the whole family was out for a drive that Sunday when the talk turned to motor homes. They had always liked the looks of the behemoths of the highways and envied the carefree possibilities of carrying your belongings with you in a vehicle.

"You wanna get one?" asked Teresa on impulse.

"I don't know," said Dave. "You wanna go look at them?"

"You betcha," she replied. "Let's go."

And go they did. They bought a Winnebago Chieftain that day. On Tuesday, Teresa went to the architect's office to tell him they had decided not to build the house and she was there to pay for the plans he had drawn. His jaw hit the ground at the news.

"You've done all this work and you're not going to build it," said the incredulous architect.

"I've already built it in my head," replied Teresa.

By June 28, Dave and Teresa had put their furniture in storage, packed the three kids into the Winnebago, and headed west to see the country. They stopped first in South Dakota to visit relatives, then kept on going, following the Oregon Trail, stopping on a whim anyplace that looked interesting, until they reached the end of the trail, in Seaside, Oregon.

The carefree life was lovely. The kids got along well, even in the tight quarters, and everyone turned out to have a fondness for adventure. But as that summer on the road rolled by, the Haeuszers were worried increasingly about educating the children.

"We talked between the two of us," recalled Dave. "We wondered if this was a selfish thing we were doing. Were the kids going to end up stupid? We weren't qualified to teach them. We're garbage people."

Fortune intervened. In early September, just days before Dave and Teresa planned to start home-schooling the children in the back of the Winnebago, they were parked in a campground in Oregon and an older couple pulled into the adjacent space. Campgrounds tend to be friendly places, and they struck up a conversation. It turned out that the woman was a retired schoolteacher. The Haeuszers described their dilemma with the children, and over the next two weeks, the woman worked with the children and Dave and Teresa to get everyone on the right track. She assessed the strengths and weaknesses of Matt and Amy, the two older children, and worked up lesson plans to carry them through the coming months. She even helped them buy schoolbooks at a nearby textbook warehouse.

As the books piled up in the back of the motor home, the Haeuszers saw they were going to need more room. They traded the Winnebago for a much larger, forty-foot Newmar Mountainaire. For months, they crisscrossed the western United States. They would stop for a few days or a couple of weeks and move on when they pleased. They hiked trails and wandered along rivers and streams. Teresa lost fifty pounds in the first six months just from the walking. They visited thirty-three national parks; as part of their schoolwork, the children earned junior ranger badges at each of them. Earning a badge did not mean following a guide through the woods or counting the minutes until Old Faithful blew. It was real work, involving an understanding of the different flora and fauna in each park, the geology of the surrounding region and where it fitted into the overall ecosystem. In each park, the children would spend two to three days earning their badges.

As a writing exercise, Matt and Amy were required to write a postcard from each place they visited, and the cards were then tucked into an album for each child. Matt spent three hours struggling to fill the back of his first postcard. He managed to write a few lines. By the end of the journey, he and Amy both were filling pages with information and anecdotes about the places they stopped and the people they met.

About a year into the adventure, Teresa turned to Dave while he was driving through Nevada and asked a question that had been on her mind for weeks. "When are we going to stop?" she asked.

"When we find Mayberry," he answered.

Nothing more was said. Dave fell in love with Olympia, Washington, and wanted to stay there. Amy and Matt were enchanted by the vineyards and rolling green hills of California's Napa Valley. Teresa thought they might have discovered Mayberry on the Nevada side of Lake Tahoe, and she went so far as to investigate the schools and look at a few houses. They wanted the kids to develop roots in a new community, meet other kids, go to school with peers. But no place seemed quite right, and they kept driving, eventually putting 28,000 miles on the two different motor homes over the course of two and a half years.

In the winter of 1995, about eighteen months into their odyssey, they left the snow out west and spent several weeks at a campground near Disney World. The kids loved the theme parks, especially the two water parks, Blizzard Beach and Typhoon Lagoon.

One day driving back from Disney World, Teresa said, "What are those ugly buildings?" She was looking at two office buildings designed by Aldo Rossi and built near the entrance to Celebration, the first structures in the new town. They pulled off Highway 192 and found the preview center.

The Haeuszers had seen the signs for weeks and were simply curious about this new town. They immediately liked the plans for the community, particularly the focus on the town school. They liked the idea of a place where kids could walk to school and parents were seen as part of the education team. The scale was pleasing. They could ride bikes and walk downtown. It seemed a little like Mayberry.

In the office, a sales agent asked them to fill out a questionnaire about why they were interested in Celebration. The choices included architecture, location, and school, among others. At the top of the list was Disney. Dave looked at the item and scratched his head.

"Look at this, hon," he said, pointing it out to Teresa. "That's nuts. Who would ever move here just because of Disney?"

The salespeople were discouraging. The lottery had been held a few weeks earlier, and there were lots of people ahead of them, waiting for a chance to live in Celebration. "They said we were out of luck and we said, well, whatever," remembered Dave.

A year later, the idyll ended abruptly and the Haeuszers drove back to Minnesota. Teresa's mother had died, and Teresa needed to care for her father, who was ill and in the hospital. At first the Haeuszers thought they would add him to the bus and keep on traveling, but he was clearly too sick for the rigors of the road.

"That's when it hit home," said Teresa. "We can't travel anymore. It was a whole new world we got thrown into. We didn't ask for it, but somebody had to do it. Somebody had to take care of Dad."

Dave was philosophical. "You know," he told Teresa, "we had a life anyone would envy, and now we have a life that nobody would take." They both laughed.

Celebration had never left the back of their minds. So when Teresa's father was well enough, they got back in the motor home and headed south to the Orlando area. They found the same campground and returned to the preview center. This time, their luck had improved.

Many prospective buyers who won lottery positions had backed out, and nearly a fourth of the homes scheduled for construction in the first phase were unsold at this time. Disney's early hype and get-in-line approach, while creating a buzz, had backfired, because many prospective purchasers had assumed it would be years before they would have a chance to get into Celebration and had gone elsewhere.

"We were there, we were ready, and we had financing," one person told a reporter after the lottery. But when that person drew a high number, he and his family bought a house elsewhere.

By the middle of 1996, the company had changed tactics and was actively wooing customers by sending out notices to people who had visited the preview center. Along with a recipe for oatmeal pancakes, the leaflets said: "Your site's ready now. Come and get it. Call us as soon as you can."

The unexpected surplus was good for the Haeuszers. They were able to buy a lot and begin building a house almost immediately. In the meantime, they rented one of the town houses and traded their motor home for a minivan.

Settling down brought an idleness that gnawed at both of them. Both had worked since graduating from high school. Traveling had been exciting and fulfilling. Now they needed something to hold their attention, a job or a small business. But they did not want to work for someone else. So they developed some guidelines for a new business: nothing that required a big investment of money or time, nothing that demanded they learn new skills, and something that they could do at Disney World. They both admired the quality and consistency of services at the Disney parks, and they recognized the profit potential from thirty-six million visitors each year.

Doing something at Disney meant the Haeuszers would have to come up with a unique idea, because the company does not permit duplicate businesses in the parks. After several weeks of careful study, eliminating ideas that were already taken or did not fit within their guidelines, they hit on something that would be novel. They would open a doughnut kiosk at Blizzard Beach, the larger of the two water parks within Disney World. Doughnuts were cheap and easy to make and offered a good profit margin even when sold at a low price. The location seemed perfect—there was a restaurant there and several snack shops, but no one was selling doughnuts.

As anyone who notices the doughnut shops on every corner in every city in America should know, these culinary delights are really cheap to make. The Haeuszers discovered that they could make a bag of a dozen minidoughnuts for twenty-five cents, including the cost of the bag. They sold them for $3 a bag at Blizzard Beach and, within weeks, sales were so brisk that they were on a track to net a sizable profit, even after Disney took its percentage off the top, as it does with every concession in the parks. They hired a person to run the kiosk, and the doughnuts seemed to go over the counter on their own. A few months later, they added a second kiosk at Typhoon Lagoon, the other water park, and put frozen drinks on the menu at both places. The new kiosk was as big a success as the first.

The business did not burden Dave and Teresa unduly. One of them usually stopped by once or twice a day to check on things and pick up the day's receipts for deposit. Occasionally Dave would grab a bunch of bags of doughnuts and hawk them to people lounging near Mount Gushmore at Blizzard Beach or waiting for a tube ride down at Castaway Creek at Typhoon Lagoon. On the annual take-your-daughter-to-work day, Teresa and Dave took their daughter, Amy, and our daughter, Becky. For a whole afternoon Becky delighted in learning the doughnut business.

Running a business at Disney World introduced the Haeuszers to backstage life at the parks. Behind the beautiful facades and smiling Disney employees they found the chaos and clutter of a normal business. From that perspective, they offered us a new way of examining Celebration.

"You go to any one of the parks, you'll see this beautiful, well-manicured, pristine place," explained Dave. "But yet if you go backstage, they're slobs. It's stuff all over. It's all hustle, hustle, hustle. It seems out of control. But in the park, there's nothing out of control. Everything is seamless and calm."

Disney World is obsessive about quality control. The goal is to limit the variability in a visitor's experiences at the parks and attractions. They want to make sure that each person has the same set of experiences as everyone else, and that these experiences are equally wonderful. Employees are drawn into this corporate culture during their mandatory training, where the central message is "The guest is king."

To enforce the high standards, undercover quality-control people patrol the parks pretending to be customers and checking up on the performance of the cast members. Is Mickey Mouse friendly enough? Are the counters clean at the Sunshine Season Food Fair? Is the person operating Space Mountain smiling and encouraging, practicing what is known as "aggressive friendliness"?

Cathy was introduced to the concept of undercover quality control during one of her early visits to Celebration, before we bought the house. She was watching a country band perform in the town center and writing her observations in her notebook. The band took a break, and its leader walked up to her.

"I know what you're doing, purty lady," he said in a friendly, pseudo-country tone. "You're with the Disney police, and you're checking up on us."

In fact, the Disney police are pretty much a myth in Celebration. From time to time, Brent Herrington would hop into his bright red Jeep Wrangler and patrol the town, watching for infractions—like the red curtains or someone who was piling too much trash behind their house. But a town cannot be run like a theme park, and in Dave Haeuszer's view, therein lies part of the problem with Celebration's failure to meet the expectations of a lot of people.

"There is no backstage, and you can't have quality-control people lurking around," he said. "You're building a city, and the city has real people in it, and that was an issue that Disney didn't quite take into account. The workers are right there every day, and so sometimes you see that it's out of control. And sometimes Disney can't get the quality that it demands." In other words, there are no tunnels in Celebration in which to hide life's nitty-gritty.

The Haeuszers were happy in Celebration. All three kids were thriving in school, in large part because their home-schooling had taught them to think independently and find out information for themselves. They planned to stay for four more years. By then Dave figured the traffic congestion from the expanding theme parks and other attractions, coupled with Celebration's growth and other residential construction, would make the place less appealing. They would take off, looking for Mayberry all over again.

In the early months of the year, the Florida sun lacks the conviction of summer, and the Barnie's group was able to gather in comfort at one of the large iron tables in the courtyard, beneath the shelter of the live oak. Everyone rode a bike or walked to the coffee shop after the kids had left for school. They usually wore shorts and polo shirts. The exception was Niki Bryan. Each morning she arrived in a flurry of outrageous magnificence. She drove up in her white Mercedes-Benz, dressed to the nines in silk, nails painted a dazzling red, and not a blond hair out of place. Her cellular phone was still pressed to her right ear as she sat down and nodded hello while giving instructions to one of her employees on the other end of the line in a gentle but firm drawl.

Niki was as Southern as a moss-hung oak tree, the only member of the coffee group born and bred in Florida. People say that Florida is not the South. For the most part, they are right. Miami isn't the South, and neither is Orlando. The tremendous population growth in the twentieth century transformed the entire state, supplanting its traditional agricultural base with tourism and high technology. The culture became bland and plastic, distinctive only in terms of beaches, heat, and humidity.

But there are grand families that have lived in Florida for generations, prospering from cattle ranching and citrus farming. They are genuine Southerners, the same as the gentry of Savannah and the blue bloods of New Orleans.

Niki's family arrived in Florida in the middle 1850s as farmers and ranchers. By the turn of the century, they had amassed holdings of seventy thousand acres northwest of Orlando, where they raised cattle and grew oranges and grapefruit. Niki had strong memories of Sunday dinners at her grandfather's home listening to the old man talk about the early days. She grew up on the ranch, a member of the landed class, part of elite society in the Orlando area. She picked oranges and punched cows alongside the workers and considered herself a cowgirl at heart, though she was always the owner's daughter, and she went away to college.

When Niki was twenty-three, she married Paul Bryan, a twenty-five-year-old lawyer and member of another wing of the local aristocracy, the professional class that had sprung up to provide for the ranchers and farmers. This was her introduction to Orlando society, and the newlyweds immediately assumed their place at the top of the city's social pyramid. The birth of their first child was duly recorded in the newspaper, as were the glittering parties they threw and their memberships on civic and charitable boards. Paul was a partner at a prestigious Orlando law firm, and Niki opened a series of salons and spas in the early 1980s.

The go-go years in the eighties drew Paul Bryan out of the law office and into the real estate development business. He joined forces with William du Pont III, one of the heirs to the chemical-company fortune. Together they built a vast real estate empire, buying residential construction companies and developing a huge mixed-use project in downtown Orlando, du Pont Centre. Bryan personally chose the art for the marbled lobby in the office tower.

In 1987, du Pont became a local hero by bringing the city its first big-league team, the Orlando Magic of the National Basketball Association. The Bryans shared the luster by acquiring a minority interest in the franchise. When the new Orlando Arena was under construction for the Magic and the whole town seemed to be clamoring for season tickets, Bryan looked at the seating chart in the architect's office and chose four prime seats in the fifth row, behind the Magic bench.

In November 1991, it all came crashing down. Like thousands of other high-flying investors at the time, Bryan watched helplessly as his real estate interests soured. His holdings with du Pont were lost to foreclosure, and German investors bought du Pont Centre, renaming it Barnett Bank Center. The Bryans filed for bankruptcy, and the *Orlando Sentinel* duly recorded the filing in its news pages. The Bryans kept the season tickets but were forced to sell their share of the team. They kept their house, protected by the state's homesteading law, but the pressure fell on Niki to expand her spa business and take up the financial slack until Paul landed something new.

It did not take long. He joined his brother at the family real estate brokerage, and three years later, the company was acquired by a large brokerage and management firm out of Columbus, Ohio. Then in 1997, LaSalle Partners of Chicago, one of the nation's premier real estate management companies, bought that company. After initially planning to start his own business, Bryan changed his mind and joined LaSalle as president of its real estate development subsidiary. He refused, however, to leave Orlando. Doing that would take the persuasive powers of his wife.

Niki had started reading about Celebration in the early nineties, when the family's finances were heading south. Disney was one of her best clients. Her company managed the health clubs at its hotels and owned the spa at the Grand Floridian, the most expensive resort in Disney World. Sometimes when she was in the parks on business, she would swing by Celebration to get the feel of the place. The Bryans' oldest daughter, Dowell, had gone off to college, but Niki liked the idea of sending the three younger children—Caroline, ten, Alex, nine, and Breece, eight—to a public school for the first time. She also liked the idea of being able to be home more with them, since Celebration was close to her Disney clients. Finally, the idea of escaping from the social strictures of Orlando held enormous appeal for Niki.

In the fall of 1997, after a campaign of many months, she convinced her husband to move to the new town. Part of his reluctance had involved the commute. He'd never been more than a five-minute drive from his office, but Celebration was half an hour from downtown Orlando under the best traffic conditions. Part of it was an unwillingness to give up the comfort and familiarity of their old neighborhood. They had rebounded financially. They loved their home in the city's elegant College Park section. The young children were doing well in private school. But Niki was a force that he could not resist. They rented a small town house in Celebration, put their grand Orlando house up for sale, and began to design a million-dollar Estate home on the golf course.

Within certain quarters in Orlando, Disney is not held in high esteem. The company's arrival transformed the city irrevocably, and not all for the better in the view of some. There are people who resent what they consider the taint Disney brought to town, who dislike the impression that Orlando is only some kind of adjunct to a theme park. And for those people, the thought of Celebration was awful. So the sudden departure of the Bryans caused a stir in their social circle at the Orlando Country Club. Since Niki was the outsider (from the farm area) and a bit of a rebel to boot, the blame fell on her.

A close friend confronted Niki at a party. "You know, we kind of expect this of you, but we don't know how you got Paul to go," said the woman.

Another longtime friend said, "Niki, you have been avante-garde from day one. You were the first woman I knew who owned her own business. I fully expected that if anyone from Orlando were to move *there*, it would be you."

On the other end, in Celebration, the arrival of the Bryans was a stamp of approval for the few people who knew anything about Orlando society. Even the people who didn't care a bit about Orlando—and that was the vast majority of residents—still liked the dashing figure that Niki and the rest of the Bryans cut, with their expensive cars, courtly manners, and the British nanny and chef who came with them. The glow seemed to rub off on those around them.

Niki dove right into the community, taking over the committee that had been set up to raise money for the school's sports teams, joining the church softball team with Cathy, and buying a table for ten at the town's biggest social event, the Red Rose Ball.

Held on Valentine's Day at Disney's Yacht and Beach Club, the Red Rose Ball was the main fund-raising event for the Celebration Foundation. Set up by Disney to provide a social conscience in its new town, the foundation's goal was to organize volunteer efforts to help Celebration and surrounding Osceola County and foster a sense of community involvement. Its efforts ran from arranging for volunteers to build a playground at the shelter for battered women in Kissimmee and collecting food for victims of the tornadoes that had swept through the county earlier in February to hosting quarterly orientation meetings for new residents of Celebration.

We were invited to the ball as guests of the Bryans, so we donned our formal gear and drove with them to the yacht club. It reminded both of us a bit of our senior proms. People we were accustomed to seeing in shorts and T-shirts looked vaguely uncomfortable and out of place in tuxedos and flowing gowns. A local surgeon had donated money so that each couple could have their picture taken, and we dutifully and stiffly lined up for our turn.

Part of the fund-raising effort was a silent auction before dinner. Some of the items were interesting, like a business Web page designed by Science Applications International Corporation and a spiffed-up version of a golf cart, called a Neighborhood Electronic Vehicle, which some people used to scoot around Celebration. Others were just plain weird, like fifteen minutes of electrolysis. Doug paid $80 for two rounds of golf at a course over in Poinciana, where he would eventually win some of the money back from Dan Wagner, the bartender at Café D'Antonio downtown and his regular golfing partner.

As we sat in the huge ballroom and listened to the obligatory speeches before dinner, Niki leaned over to Doug and began to talk about her reasons for coming to Celebration. "We were the golden couple of Orlando when we got married," she confided. "We didn't understand the pressure until we were in our early thirties. There was such a demand to maintain appearances at all times. What I like about Celebration, for myself and for Paul and especially for my children, is the chance to start anew. I look around this room and realize that all of these people came here for different reasons. But the point is that we all are starting from scratch."

"You mean with a clean slate," said Doug.

"Exactly," Niki replied. "There are no expectations for how you will behave. You have a chance to start life again, and that's a lucky thing.

"This is the first place I've lived in years where you can go to public places without your makeup," she said. "Or, more symbolically, without your public face. I would never have gone to a private school event without my face, but look at me at Dream Team meetings. Here, I get to look at someone and judge them by their actions. People are real. And my kids get to start out without baggage, too."

Not everyone was in the mood to provide accolades for Celebration, even on that festive night. Steve Saker, Marguerite's husband, and also a guest of the Bryans, overheard the conversation. He leaned across that table and, in his best British accent, complained that Celebration was not a community, chaps, and not very real. "It's a bunch of people who have lived in the same place for, at most, a year and a half," he said. "You cannot possibly judge it yet."

We understood Saker's point, but we disagreed. Surveying the ballroom that night, watching people who had paid $100 a seat to support the Celebration Foundation and enjoy an evening with their neighbors, we saw a sense of community. There were people with different dreams who had come from different backgrounds, even as different as the Haeuszers and the Bryans. But everyone was involved in a common effort to build a new town, and any social distinctions were slim. Steve Saker was right, however; it was too early for a final verdict, as we would see plainly in a few months with the Bryans.

10

Visitation Rites

In winter, the heat dissipates and the days are gloriously sunny and warm, often ending with magnificent evenings of red and orange mottled skies. Historically, the coming of cooler weather signals the start of the tourist season. In truth, there is no longer a time of year when the Orlando area is not inundated with tourists. Even on the most searing August day, people are lined up at Disney World and Universal Studios. Many of these foolish souls seem to be Brits who have turned the color of boiled ham, though plenty of South Americans, Middle Easterners, Europeans, and, of course, Americans also have braved the heat for their turn on Space Mountain. But January through April is when the weather is the most blissful and the roads are busiest, filled with minivans that roll out of Hertz and Avis like fat steaming loaves of bread from an oven.

Like most people who have moved to Florida from the North, we were prepared for the onslaught of snowbirds. The expectation of a steady flow of friends and relatives was the reason we had paid an extra $30,000 to put the granny flat above the garage, filling it with enough beds and futons to sleep six. In addition to providing a comfortable place for our guests, it meant they would not be constantly underfoot. Given that we had a continuous run of visitors, for stays ranging from one night to two weeks, from Christmas until late April, it was the best decision we made about the house.

In February, Tommy and Suzanne Zarilli arrived from Westport, with their two daughters in tow. We had spent countless evenings together in Connecticut, lounging by their pool or ours, drinking wine, and talking late into the night. We had always had fun, and we genuinely looked forward to their coming.

The week of the Zarillis' visit passed uneventfully. They made many trips to Disney World and Universal Studios, generously taking our kids along. Suzanne cooked a fabulous Italian dinner one night, and the Chianti and conversation lasted until late. Tommy was trained as an engineer but made his living as an investment banker specializing in real estate. He was intrigued by Celebration and shared with us a wealth of information about how developments like this one are financed. The kids all got along.

But something was missing. Try as we might, a connection had been broken between here and Westport and could not be repaired. The gossip about our old home and stories about the cliques of girls at the middle school had a hollow ring. The change was not in our friends but in us. What had started out as an adventure in Celebration, we realized, had evolved into something else. But what?

We had come without any serious expectation of remaining for more than a year or so. We were tourists of a sort, off on an adventure. But once *in* Celebration, the adventure had become something else. An underlying desire for change emerged in both of us. We began to feel at home, in a way we often hadn't in Westport.

Our feeling is not simple or easy to explain. Westport had seemed delightful when we moved there. It is a lovely town, with a quaint business district, beautiful beaches, and gracious homes. Our house there was grander than any place we had ever lived; we could afford it only because early in our marriage we had bought a small tract house in Los Angeles at the bottom of the real estate market and sold at the top. It also helped that the Connecticut house was a bit of a mess, the grounds wildly overgrown and unappetizing to anyone who lacked the imagination or pigheadedness to envision the cleanup.

While living in Westport, though, we had been nagged by the sense of homogeneity and privilege there. We missed the diversity and excitement of our earlier homes in more urban areas in Chicago, Washington, and Los Angeles. An hour by train from Manhattan, Westport is home to large numbers of wealthy white investment bankers and the like, people who pay off their mortgages with one year's bonus and take care of college for the children with the next. The general affluence breeds a sense of entitlement in many of the children of these families, and that was disturbing to us. We tried to be on guard with our own kids.

After Tommy and Suzanne left, we felt those reservations more keenly. In an economic sense, the contrast with Celebration was stark. To be sure, there were people with money in Celebration, but they were the exception. Many of our neighbors had sacrificed to get to Celebration and many were struggling financially in order to stay. It did not mean that Westport was bad, but we were more comfortable in staunchly middle-class Celebration. Ironically, the plastic town that Disney built often seemed more real than the New England village that had stood for more than two centuries.

Indeed, we were surprisingly defensive when people criticized the town. One woman who spent a week with us constantly compared the architecture, the stores, and the people to her own "real" town and found her version superior on all counts. We kept silent but resolved never to invite her back.

Doug experienced a similar defensiveness a few months later. He was in New Orleans at a conference for investigative reporters and went to lunch with several colleagues from *The New York Times*. He was describing Celebration to Jill Abramson, an editor in the paper's Washington bureau, when Maureen Dowd, one of the *Times*'s columnists, overheard the town's name. "Oh, that place is creepy," said Dowd, who lives in Washington and makes occasional forays to New York and Los Angeles. "I was going to write a column about it. I spent two days there interviewing people. But it was just too creepy. I couldn't write about it."

People react oddly when you say you live in Celebration. Some laugh at the name. One New Yorker asked, "How are things in Congratulations?" Sometimes there is this moment of recognition—"Oh yeah, that Disney town"—followed by a snicker. As often-cynical journalists, who between us have lived in three countries and eight states, we found the town ripe with opportunities for savaging the residents and Disney, too.

Yet the longer we lived there, the better we understood the reasons that had brought people to this place. While we did not agree with all of those reasons, especially the sometimes blind trust in Disney, we had come to respect most of them. Living in a small town built from memory and desire was certainly not as creepy as our two stints in solipsistic Washington.

We realized that we had become part of the town and we debated whether this was good for the book. We were walking a fine line: We were residents at the same time we were trying to write an objective biography of the place and its people. Our primary mission was observation, yet obtaining the best vantage point meant getting behind the lines and participating in the community life. Cathy argued that the only way to understand the town was to become part of it. Doug worried about the loss of objectivity accompanying that involvement, about what would happen when we started to like our neighbors and then sat down to write about them.

But Cathy wasn't about to watch from the sidelines, and when she volunteered to write the newsletter for the Dream Team at the school, she suddenly found herself on the organization's board. She protested, saying that participating in the board meetings might conflict with her role in reporting and writing our book. No one on the board seemed to mind. They liked the idea of a real writer taking over the newsletter.

She volunteered in other capacities, too: for the church, the Celebration Foundation, and on cleanup crews after the tornadoes inflicted horrendous damage on the county in early 1998. Doug remained less involved. He traveled often for the newspaper, and even when he was home, most of his time was taken up with his job, putting in long hours on the telephone or computer. Still, he became more active in Celebration than anyplace else we had lived, attending numerous community meetings and participating in various activities.

We were living with our feet in two worlds, and it sometimes led to uncomfortable situations, like the time Cathy heard a neighborhood rumor that our publishers had paid for our house and we had come here to write an anti-Disney book. She tracked down the source of the rumor. It was one of the salespeople at the preview center. When Cathy dropped in on the woman, she denied having said anything negative about us or our book. She said someone from Disney had sent around a memo a few weeks earlier saying that two residents were writing a book about the town. It turned out that two of our neighbors were in the room with her when the memo came in.

"All I said was, 'Oh, isn't this exciting,' " she protested. "They couldn't have taken that the wrong way."

"Well," Cathy said sternly, "let me set you straight, so that you can make sure everyone knows the truth and no one takes it the wrong way. We bought the house with our own money. Those are our children in the school, not props. The publisher is not anti-Disney and we are not anti-Disney. We are going to write a fair and evenhanded book about the town."

The times we had to defend our project and ourselves were rare. Near the end of our first year, we were quoted briefly on a segment of *48 Hours* about the neighborliness of Celebration, and we were short-lived celebrities. Only Brent Herrington took offense at our comments on the TV show, complaining in a terse e-mail that he didn't like Doug's observation that Herrington was occasionally seen in his red Jeep on the lookout for violations of town regulations.

More often we found ourselves trying to translate Celebration to outsiders. So many of our visitors came with the same set of preconceptions that journalists brought to the place and, indeed, that we had felt ourselves. It was a little too clean, a little too much like a movie set, a lot too white. And everyone who had heard anything about Celebration had heard about the rules imposed on those who live there.

No one was more surprised by our adaptation to the restrictions than our closest friends from Alexandria, Nan Nixon and Hans Flinch, who came for a visit with their children, Hans and Polly. They were in outright shock that Cathy could abide the uniformity and rules. After all, they lived down the street from us when she had painted that purple patch on our house. But they were intrigued by the town, especially Hans, who was born and raised in Denmark and still speaks with a thick accent, despite more than twenty years in the United States with the International Monetary Fund.

"I think I would really enjoy this because of the created and natural environment," he said on a Sunday morning as we walked home from church and the four children sped off on bikes and Rollerblades. "With the exception of July and August, you can enjoy the outdoors here all the time. The town is so pretty. It gives the feeling of being so safe, a place where you can let your children wander freely. But as far as the restrictions go, I don't know how I would react. We do have the historical society and restrictive zoning in Alexandria. But it seems different here. Of course, I lived next door to Germany all my life, so perhaps it wouldn't bother me."

Other visitors had little tolerance for the cuteness of the architecture and the sameness of the townspeople. Joe Sexton lives a few blocks from the brownstone where he grew up, in the Park Slope section of Brooklyn. His daughters, Jane and Lucy, immediately loved Celebration and the ability to go off alone with Becky to visit the shops downtown or stop at Gooding's grocery for a soda. They raced around in shorts and T-shirts and laughed at us for wearing sweatshirts when the temperature slipped below sixty degrees.

Their mocking reminded us of what Al Muir, an air-conditioner repairman, had said not long after we moved in. "Your capillaries shut down," he said gruffly. "After you've been here six months or so, they just stop working. It's true. When your friends from Ohio or wherever come to visit and it's fifty-five degrees outside and they're wearing shorts and T-shirts, you'll have on jackets and sweaters. They'll accuse you of being wimps. But it's the capillaries. Happens to everybody down here."

Joe played golf on the Celebration course, designed by Robert Trent Jones Sr. and Jr., worked out at the fitness center, took the kids to Disney World, Universal Studios, and Gatorland, a genuine Florida attraction where alligators leap out of the water to devour chunks of meat suspended in the air and a place we recommended to every visitor. Still, he shook his head in puzzlement over Celebration for the entire week, unable to comprehend how we could live in a place that seemed more like a resort than a real town.

"I don't get it," he muttered several times a day, with the natural perversity of a native New Yorker encountering anything too comfortable. "This doesn't seem like a real place at all. You're on permanent vacation down here. I just don't get this place."

Another set of visitors didn't get it either. We met Bruce Stephenson in a Spanish-style building at Rollins College, in Winter Park, Florida, where we had gone to talk with him about urban planning and neotraditional towns. He was a professor and chairman of the department of environmental studies at the small liberal arts college. More to the point, he had written an insightful book about city building in Florida, called *Visions of Eden*. We wanted to hear his views on where Celebration fit into this mythical notion of Florida as a subtropical Garden of Eden.

The man who greeted us in the small stucco office building seemed too young to be a department chairman. He was tall and in his mid-thirties, with a boyish shock of dark hair that kept falling into his face. He told us that he was of two minds about Celebration.

"It reminds me of the 1893 Columbian Exposition in Chicago, which sparked the City Beautiful movement," he explained. "While the two forms are different, just as people went to the Columbian Exposition to see the great white city and started the City Beautiful movement, Celebration is this wonderful laboratory for the rejuvenation of the city in the next century. The downside is that you have this pretty, rich architecture, like the health center, with its strong Mediterranean flavor, and from there you can see Water Mania across One Ninety-two. That is what kind of got me. You've got this beautiful architectural and planning renaissance, but it's in the middle of hell, where you have just this cartoon landscape. The bottom line is, is Celebration real? Is it really a town or a Potemkin village? Will it ever be a true community, or will it be an isolated laboratory?"

We were sitting in comfortable chairs off the foyer. Occasionally a student would wander by, pick up a few words of the conversation, and sit down to listen. Their fascination with our conversation gave Stephenson an idea. Each semester, he explained, he took his master's-degree-level urban planning class on a field trip. First, they went to Seaside, in the Florida panhandle, where they soaked up the atmosphere of the place that inspired the neotraditional movement. Then they wound up with a daylong tour of Celebration, the place that represents the corporate interpretation of it.

It would be terrific for the students to walk through one of those front doors and talk with people who were living the philosophy, he suggested. Wouldn't it be interesting for you to hear their reactions to the two places? We agreed readily and arranged to have the twenty or so students and their professor for lunch during their visit to Celebration in late February.

Not long after, they arrived on our doorstep. We soon learned that

Stephenson's charges were not impressed by Celebration. As they gathered on the couches and floor of our living room, plates on their laps, they criticized what they called the plastic feel of the town and scorned its restrictions. The fact that we lived there could be excused only by the reality that we were writing a book about it and planned to leave.

"I find it very disturbing here," said one of the students. "I think it is because everything is planned out in such detail, and then there are all the restrictions on top of that. It is just so regulated. That's what bugs me the most."

"I have five dogs. I wouldn't be able to live here," said another woman, noting that Celebration restricted residents to a "reasonable" number of pets and that five dogs would probably exceed the definition.

A young man tried to be more charitable. "As a street network, it works very well," he said. "From what we've grown up with, the usual suburbs, the idea here is good. I think it looks a little plastic, though. The houses, they don't look real."

It was a Saturday and on their walking tour of town the students had seen a fair number of tourists. "I think a lot of people are adding Celebration to their route when they come to Walt Disney World," said one student. "I just had the idea that if I lived here it would be kind of like living in a fishbowl."

There was a round-robin of criticism. It was easy, because Disney was so easy to ridicule and because the town was shiny and new. Some of their criticisms echoed our initial reactions. They didn't like the fake dormers. "So phony," one complained. Another said Celebration reinforced the notion that Florida is nothing more than a Disney experience. "Why are we the escape place?" she asked plaintively. Even the porches and orientation of the houses to the front and street provoked them. "We've studied how the design of the home that puts the living area in the front, so you can watch what is going on outside, makes it a safer place to live," said a young woman. "But I don't like the feeling that things are monitored."

As Cathy began to explain the importance of engaging the street from the front of the house, she stopped short. She was surprised to find herself defending the town and Disney. "You know," she told Stephenson and his students, "it's easy to knock this place. We certainly don't think it's paradise. But regardless of your criticisms, you should be willing to give Disney some credit. They put their money on the table in an effort to give good planning a high-profile test. It would have been a lot easier, and a lot less risky, to just slap down another subdivision and two championship golf courses."

Later, a pertinent quote from the behaviorist B. F. Skinner would come to mind: "And if planned economies, benevolent dictatorships, perfectionist societies, and other utopian ventures have failed, we must remember that unplanned, undictated, and unperfected cultures have failed, too. A failure is not always a mistake; it may simply be the best one can do under the circumstances. The real mistake is to stop trying."

Still, the question nagged: Was this the best Disney could have done? It must be said that some of the student observations were keen. After Seaside, which strives to blend in with the surrounding environment and is thus a little wild and overgrown, the sterile nature of Celebration made a strong impression on them. To a person, they derided the manicured feel of the town, which was so comforting and nostalgic for many of the residents. They were right. In re-creating the feel of a small Midwestern town, Disney opted for grass and shrubs and stripped away much of the native vegetation. Only small patches of wetland and scrub pine were left intact within the boundaries of the town—the result of the company's innovative solution to environmental challenges, which involved the creation of a vast wilderness preserve a few miles away.

And there was one criticism that could not be defended, at least by us. "I haven't seen a black person since getting here," said one of the students. "I like knowing that there are people in the world other than those like me."

By our count, there were only five black families and a handful of Hispanic and Asian families living in Celebration, a situation that had troubled us from the start. We had lived in racially and economically mixed neighborhoods in Chicago, Los Angeles, and Alexandria. Nick, Becky, and Elizabeth, our oldest child, had attended public schools in Alexandria that were 70 percent minority, and their friends had crossed all racial and economic boundaries. Even in Westport, a predominantly white town, our children's best friends included black, Native American, Asian, and Indian children.

The homogeneity of Celebration was disturbingly like the composition of the small Indiana town where Doug had grown up in the fifties and sixties, and while it may have comforted some of our neighbors, the remembrances of the insularity troubled him. We saw no overt racism in Celebration, but we recognized that perhaps one reason some people felt so comfortable was the safety of sameness. When we sat down to assess living in Celebration, as we did on a fairly regular basis, we inevitably talked about our uneasiness over lack of racial diversity in the town. The racial makeup of Celebration wasn't too different from that of most small towns across the country—a 1997 study by William Frey, a demographer at the University of Michigan, found that of the forty fastest-growing rural counties in America, virtually all are at least 70 percent white, and most are at least 85 percent white. Indeed, when many people talk about getting away from urban crime, drugs, congestion, and school problems, they also mean getting away from blacks and Hispanics.

In its defense, Celebration reflected the polarization of the greater Orlando region. Like most small Southern towns, Orlando had a long history of racial segregation. Blacks were relegated to certain neighborhoods, mostly on the city's west side, and to a few rural communities. Orlando was the last Florida city to exclude blacks from its primary elections, as late as 1950, and twenty years later, blacks who wanted to rent mobile homes outside the west side had to obtain letters of recommendation from white tenants who were already living in the neighborhood.

Although the opening of Disney World in 1971 spurred economic and population growth in Orlando and the surrounding region, it did nothing to change those basic patterns. Just before the park opened, a local black minister said: "Disney World will have no effect on the Negro community. We own no motels nor restaurants nor even taxicabs. Our bank will get no business from it. Our one integrated subdivision is a slum. It has no dignity. Here, as in the rest of Orlando, the Negro and the white live in two different worlds."

In the years since, the city has mended most of its racist ways, but little in the way of a black middle class has grown up in or around Orlando. As a result, there was a small pool of black prospective buyers for Celebration, and the advertisements that the company placed in the local black press and in the wider mainstream media yielded no interest of consequence, despite the company's deliberate use of people of color in the ads. Celebration was publicized nationwide, and many buyers traveled great distances to live in Disney's new town. Why were so few of them black?

Some of the reasons may be found at Disney World itself. At least in its early days, most of the people attracted to Celebration from outside the region were Disney fans to one degree or another. They trusted Disney to re-create the kind of town they remembered. Blacks could not be expected to place that kind of faith in Disney, given that the attractions at Disney World and Disneyland pander to a white, middle-class version of America in which the issues of race are, at best, skirted and, at worst, stereotypically reinforced. For instance, the Jungle Cruise depicts the stereotype of a white explorer and his four black porters. In the Hall of the Presidents, the struggle of black Americans in the last century is not mentioned, although elsewhere visitors do see a robot of Frederick Douglass, the abolitionist, musing about the end of slavery, and they also hear the voice of Martin Luther King Jr. But the overriding image is the black who strums a guitar in *Song of the South,* hardly something that could be expected to attract black residents to Disney or to Celebration. The world of Disney is not the remembered childhood of the majority of adult blacks in America today.

In Celebration itself, African Americans with a sense of history might have raised their eyebrows at the two open-air pavilions in the town center. In scouring the region for indigenous architecture, Celebration's planners had come upon the markets once found in many Southern towns, where produce and other goods were sold. The most expensive items sold at those markets in the 1700s and early 1800s were slaves. In fact, the pavilions in Celebration looked almost exactly like the slave market in St. Augustine, Florida's oldest city.

In conversations, Disney officials and blacks living in Celebration were unable to provide an explanation for the absence of minorities in the town. Company officials said they had expected the community to be an approximate mirror of the larger metropolitan area, yet it clearly was not. A black woman living in an apartment said she was comfortable in the town and that she often met wealthy blacks from the Orlando area and elsewhere who were interested enough to visit Celebration, but not to buy. "There is a community of blacks in central Florida who could afford to buy here, but for some reason they have not chosen to live here," she said, shaking her head at the mystery. "I cannot put my finger on why."

Many neotraditional communities face an unintended isolation caused by economics and location, two factors that can close the gates as effectively as the old rules of forced segregation. Until a solution is found, these communities will be perceived as elitist and escapist for their refusal to search for common solutions to social problems.

There is a simple, straightforward solution to at least part of the problem. Planned communities and neotraditionalist towns can become more inclusive if they provide truly affordable housing within their borders. Already many of these places, including Celebration, provide some semblance of affordability by mixing apartments, multifamily dwellings, and even granny flats with single-family houses. The granny flats are a worthy innovation, offering help to families making a mortgage payment and a relatively inexpensive place for others to live. At the same time, the proximity of shops and other services, as well as some jobs, reduces transportation costs and leaves residents with more money for other pursuits, like housing.

But these steps fall short of the goal of a truly integrated community. When the Disney Company avoided building affordable housing in Celebration, the company evaded its responsibility and ignored the need for a more inclusive vision of new towns in America. Bold strategies are required to address the problem of segregation, including creative financing and subsidies. Without them, as we saw in Celebration, the market will drive up prices and put the houses and apartments out of reach of most low-income families and individuals.

Few reasonable people would deny the need for affordable housing in the area around Celebration. Osceola County was once a rural community dominated by white farmers and ranchers. As recently as 1970, its population was only 25,000. By the mid-nineties, there were 143,000 people in the county, and the Hispanic population had increased about 1,000 percent to 21 percent of the total.

Many of the Hispanic residents work at the hotels, theme parks, and construction sites of the nearby tourist attractions. And most of those jobs, which have been created in the post-Disney period, are low-paying service positions. Because these are low-paying positions, residential construction has not kept pace with the population growth. As a result, workers are forced to travel long distances in order to find places they can afford to rent or purchase. A survey of its own workers conducted by Disney's Reedy Creek Improvement District found that the average one-way travel time for employees was thirty minutes—not much by urban standards, perhaps, but a long and expensive commute for someone earning minimum wage in an area with such a low-density population.

Though Disney executives knew many of their own employees had to travel long distances to work, those involved with Celebration have been defensive about the absence of affordable housing in the town, and they have refused to acknowledge any responsibility for the omission.

"Philosophically, there was never a sense that we don't want subsidized housing in Celebration," said Peter Rummell, the former Disney executive. "As a matter of management philosophy, we never said we don't want those people there. What we hoped to do was insist that there be a fairly good inventory of rentals. The rental inventory was the one anchor that we thought we would have that would allow either a fireman or a twenty-eight-year-old to live there."

But the company had jumped at the county's offer to use its state-mandated contribution to affordable housing outside Celebration, and it did nothing to control the apartment rents in town. The downtown apartments, the first that were available, were owned by Disney, and the rents were set according to demand, starting at $750 for a one-bedroom apartment and $1,000 for a two-bedroom. In a county where the median income in 1996 was $16,714, more than 30 percent below the state average, the prices put these apartments out of reach of most young professionals, let alone a Hispanic family dependent on service jobs. Even the teachers at Celebration School found that they could not afford to rent an apartment in town.

Eric Nelson, the school's popular science teacher, described his excitement when he was offered the job in the summer of 1996. "I wanted to live here and be part of this community," he said. "When I had my job interview in July, I went right over to the preview center, still in my suit and sweating, to see about renting an apartment. But I found out that I couldn't afford it and [that] there was a waiting list." A year later, he said, he got to live in Celebration only through the generosity of a resident, Leonard Timms, who rented him his granny flat at a cut rate.

In an attempt to provide something approaching affordable housing, the company had set the initial prices of its town houses at $120,000, but they were not controlled and demand quickly pushed them above $150,000. The same thing occurred when the Garden homes were put on the market. Those homes, the smallest in Celebration, were not part of the original plan for the town; they were added in an attempt to reach a lower price point in the market. Again, however, demand drove the prices from the original $160,000 to over $200,000 in a matter of months.

Brent Herrington has argued that it was supply-and-demand economics, not the policies of Disney, that drove rents and housing prices out of reach of most people in Osceola County. "To do affordable housing means building an affordable product on the right kind of land," Herrington explained. "So maybe you don't put it on the golf course. You put it in a more landlocked area and you do a smaller footprint and lower level of finish. That's your entry-level product. But here, what happened is that the entry-level product sells for two hundred thousand or more."

When he veered from economics to social engineering, Herrington's logic got a little disturbing. "To build something affordable, you'd almost have to go to a government program that excludes any other buyer," he said. "And honestly, you rarely see that done in a planned community. The residents themselves would push back. It's fair game to have all different price points represented. It's something else to have an artificially bought-down, you-can't-live-here-unless-you're-poor product. What happens is, in affordable housing that is couched as an entitlement, you don't have the same kind of personal commitment and pride in your accomplishment in this new home. If people come to a place just because their name popped up when that community had a vacancy, they are not going to have the same commitment to the town. That's the part I think the residents would probably have some squeamishness about."

Herrington defined affordable housing in the same unfortunate way Robert Moses defined urban renewal housing—not built to compete with private development but built to the lowest-possible standards to avoid competing with the private sector, which, in the case of Celebration, was the company itself. But, as federal money to build new low- and moderate-income housing has disappeared in recent years, far more creative and equitable methods have been developed that would have offered the company an opportunity to provide the same quality housing to both middle-class and low-income buyers. Sometimes local housing agencies have found other ways to build affordable housing, using tax dollars to provide subsidies and, in some cases, actually build the houses. In Snohomish County, Washington, just outside Seattle, the housing authority has financed and built fifty manufactured houses and sold them to first-time buyers whose households earn from $25,000 to $60,000 a year. And some states have taken the lead in requiring developers to pick up part of the tab.

For instance, Florida law requires that developers provide money for affordable housing. Disney could have used that money to provide mortgage assistance to qualified low-income buyers in Celebration in the same way the federal government assisted veterans after World War II. When we raised this issue with Herrington, he countered that there would be nothing to stop people who bought homes with subsidies turning around and selling at a profit into the hot Celebration market. The response begged the point on two counts. First, low-income people would be just as anxious as anyone else to live in a community that promised all that Celebration did. Second, the company had imposed restrictions on anyone selling their houses in the first year of residency in an effort to avoid speculation. It could have developed similar restrictions for people who bought with financial assistance from the company.

Instead of looking for a creative solution, the company had fulfilled the requirements of the law by paying a mere $300,000 over three years to an Osceola County housing program that helped people outside Celebration with rents and down payments. Some of the people who got a share of the funds were Disney employees, but none of them could buy a house in Celebration—the county program restricted the funds to down payments on new houses costing a maximum of $80,000 and existing homes with a maximum price tag of $75,000.

Early in the summer of 1998, we got our hopes up that Celebration Company had changed its mind about the issue. While walking the dog one evening, we stopped for a chat with Alice and Dick Joossens, neighbors of ours across the street. Dick said another neighbor had attended a public meeting a few days earlier at which Herrington had raised the prospect of affordable housing in later phases of Celebration. The Joossens agreed with us that this was a promising change.

When Cathy asked Herrington about it a few days later in an e-mail, his response was not encouraging. "Hmmm, the message may have gotten a little bit garbled in the telling," he wrote back. "The Celebration Company is continually evaluating various apartment, small single-family, town-house, and perhaps condominium products for some of the future phases. I shared a personal perspective in the meeting that I am a proponent of building condominium housing in Celebration, because I think it is our best chance of providing something our school-teachers, firefighters, police officers, etc., can afford. I am hoping some really nice, innovative condos can be worked into the master-planning process."

As long as market forces were allowed to prevail, there would be no truly affordable housing in Celebration. When new apartments along Water Street were opened in the spring of 1998, the rents were even higher than for the downtown apartments. There was no reason to think that future condominiums would be priced at a level affordable to low-income families. When Garden homes went on the market in the newly developed North Village, the lowest price was $180,000 and most cost over $200,000. Without innovative, proactive solutions, it seemed that Celebration would remain a largely white, middle-class town.

Is it asking too much of Disney to have developed a more inclusive vision of the town of the future? In his autobiography, *Work in Progress*, Eisner said he'd be happy to live in Celebration, and he praised its friendliness and community spirit. He also wrote, "The new town we've built may not solve inherent problems in America, but it does serve as one potential model with obvious appeal." But part of the Celebration model could have addressed the pressing problem of affordable housing, and its accompanying twin, integrated communities.

Kenneth Jackson, a history professor at Columbia University, saw a parallel between the lost opportunities at Levittown, which refused to sell to blacks, and at Celebration. "The demand at Levittown was so incredible that, despite the racism of the time, people wanted those houses badly enough that the developer could have put aside five or ten percent for blacks and it still would have sold," he said. "Celebration is doing so well, and is so well designed and attractive, that it seems to me it, too, could have offered affordable housing."

Instead, justifying themselves by following what they felt the residents might think, Celebration officials kept the door closed to affordable housing and the people it would have attracted.

We never heard a racist remark in Celebration, and most of the people we met appeared to be tolerant and decent. But some people clearly came here to escape the crime and chaos of life in urban areas, and too often those factors are equated unfairly with blacks and other minorities, the very people who tend to be the predominant residents of affordable housing.

One night, our neighbor Lisa Baird came home from a Celebration meeting in an absolute rage. The meeting had been a session of the Celebration Stakeholders Panel, a group of forty or so residents handpicked by Herrington and Kathy Johnson, the executive director of the Celebration Foundation, to discuss ways to improve the town. The makeup reflected the upper strata of Celebration—the business leaders, the town doctor and minister, the president of the parent teacher association. No one from the small population of minorities had been invited to participate. Lisa had run her own business-management firm in Indiana before her husband's job change brought their family to Celebration, where she manages a surgeon's office.

On this particular night, the talk at the stakeholders meeting had turned to the lack of minorities. Baird found herself the target of criticism when she raised the possibility of finding ways to attract more blacks and other minorities to Celebration.

"All I said was that we have to look at this because it's not the right way to live, and I don't want my kids to grow up distrustful because they don't know any blacks," she said, still trembling in anger. "But some people there really attacked my point of view. They like it this way, and they tried to justify the lack of diversity by saying we have German and Irish and the like. I said, 'Look around, look at this group of people. How much diversity do you see?'"

The sad state of race relations in the country is that there are intolerant and ignorant people in almost any town, and it's possible that some people would not have moved to Celebration if there had been affordable housing or any significant minority population. Frankly, the town would be better off without those people. And, after more than a year of talking with dozens and dozens of residents, we were convinced that a majority rued the absence of minorities, just as we did. One Saturday night late in the summer of 1998, we were having a small dinner party when Kevin and Kristine Gowen, who had moved to town from Tampa a few weeks earlier, stopped by to pick up their daughter, Alison, who was playing with Becky. As they sat and had coffee and cake with us, Kristine asked about the absence of minorities. "We were told by the salesperson that there were a lot of black families here, but we haven't seen any," she said. "We're concerned about having our kids grow up in a place without blacks."

In developing Celebration, the Disney company had created a town that appealed predominantly to white, middle-class Americans, the same segment of the population that grew up with its animated films and made its theme parks such enormous successes. Disney's planners talked about their desire to build a community that could be replicated elsewhere. They opted for a public school over a private one precisely to show that Celebration's ideas could be implemented in the most democratic of institutions. Building rental apartments next door to expensive single-family houses broke the planned-community taboo that held that upscale home buyers would avoid living close to multifamily dwellings. But the company was willing to go only so far, and it was not far enough. Imagine the impact if Disney's Celebration, the subject of intense public and scholarly scrutiny, had provided a showcase for innovative affordable housing as an integral part of its blueprint for a new utopia. As in Levittown fifty years before, it was an opportunity tragically lost.

11

Swamp Song

Osceola County was named for a war chief who was a leader of ruthless daring in a guerrilla campaign waged by the Seminole Indians against the U.S. government's attempts in 1832 and 1833 to drive them from their homes. In fact, Osceola was born Billy Powell in 1804 in Alabama, the son of an English father and an Upper Creek Indian mother. After seven years of warfare, he was captured in 1837 while attending a parley under a white flag of truce, an act of treachery that ensured his martyrdom when he died in captivity the following year.

Though not quite in an act of war, more than a century and a half later, Disney captured control of the development of Celebration while operating under the white flag of compromise and negotiation. The shrewdness of Disney's strategy was evident one Monday afternoon in February 1998 in the meeting room of the Osceola County Commission.

The issue was trees. Disney planned to chop down 172 of them, mostly old oaks and some dating from well before Chief Osceola's birth, to make way for construction in Celebration's newest phase, the South Village. The county's environmental staff objected, arguing that the removal violated an ordinance requiring developers to conduct a formal survey of trees and to obtain approval before any over a certain size and age could be cut down. Developers also were required to plant new trees to replace the ones they knocked down to make way for houses, roads, and other improvements. But Disney contended it was exempted from the ordinance because of the county's approval of the original planning for Celebration.

In fact, the huge stack of documents and drawings describing the planned development of Celebration that the company submitted to the county for final approval in late 1993 did contain a request for an exemption from the tree ordinance. Rod Schultz, a staff member in the planning department, had pointed out the request to Ted Garrod, the county's zoning director, when he reviewed the documents before final approval.

"Ted, we should not allow them to do this," Schultz recalled telling his boss. "You've got to delete this stuff about the tree ordinance."

"Oh, don't worry about that," Garrod replied, according to Schultz. "Nobody can exempt themselves from an ordinance."

No one except Disney. The final package approved by the County Commission did contain language that exempted the new town from the tree ordinance.

So Tom Lewis, a vice president of Celebration Company and former Florida state official, stood in front of the county commissioners that February afternoon more than four years later and argued that the company had been granted the right to cut down as many trees as it saw fit to make way for the South Village. "Trees are like people," Lewis explained. "They deteriorate with age and fall apart. They last a little longer than people do, but they begin to deteriorate rapidly when they reach hundreds of years [of age]."

Although the company was exempt from the ordinance, Lewis said, efforts had been made to comply with the spirit of the law. In the first phases, approximately eighty large trees were relocated at a cost of $500,000, more than six thousand new trees were planted at a cost of $4 million, and about a thousand trees were planted on individual lots at a cost of $500,000. "We have been, we are, and we will continue to act very responsibly regarding trees," said Lewis. "I believe Celebration should be held up as a role model in this regard."

The actual matter on which the commissioners were to vote that day was described as a "clarification" to the original planning documents for Celebration. It specified that the company was indeed exempt from the ordinance but that it would comply voluntarily with some aspects of the law by surveying trees and trying to save as many as feasible in the construction phases after the development of the South Village. The commissioners did not appear troubled by the clarification, although a handful of people from the audience rose to object during the period provided for public comment.

Forrest Clark, a white-haired man in a rumpled khaki suit and orthopedic shoes who was president of the Kissimmee Valley Audubon Society, was the first to take up the microphone and address the commissioners. "We do not believe there should be any exception to the tree ordinance," said Clark. "The issue here is not Celebration but . . . the future of the environment."

Clark's wife, Ruth, and two other speakers rose to condemn the exemption for Celebration as another sop to developers and to bemoan the vanishing rural character of Osceola County. One of them suggested that Disney had cut a secret deal with the county attorney to make sure the exemption remained in place. In fact, Lewis and lawyers for Celebration had negotiated with the county attorney, Jo Thacker, for three days before the hearing in an attempt to come up with language that both sides could live with to "clarify" the exemption issue. County staff members said later that talks to iron out differences before an issue is presented to the commissioners is routine, and they saw nothing sinister about Disney's efforts.

But the company had not stopped with the county attorney, who could only recommend action to the commissioners. Lewis and other Celebration Company officials had lobbied all five commissioners personally in the days before the vote. The lobbying might not have become public without the county's disclosure law, which requires commissioners to disclose contact with parties involved in issues before the commission.

Before the vote, four of the commissioners acknowledged that company officials had visited them in their offices the previous week to argue their case. The fifth, Mary Jane Arrington, said she had toured the South Village at the invitation of Lewis and several other company officials. What Arrington did not say at the meeting, and was not required to disclose under the law, was that a civil engineering firm in which she had an interest was doing some of the design work for an educational center that Disney was building at its wilderness preserve in the southern part of the county.

Several county staff members said later that it was highly unusual for all five commissioners to be lobbied before a decision. To the surprise of no one in the room that day, the vote was unanimous in favor of "clarifying" that Celebration was exempt from the tree ordinance.

Satisfied with the outcome, Lewis—and the Celebration lawyers and officials who had filled half the front row of the meeting room with him—nodded good-bye and left. In the anteroom they exchanged handshakes with nearly a dozen additional consultants who had been on hand in case Lewis needed to answer any technical questions. As they were leaving, one of the lawyers asked Lewis if he wanted to raise another zoning issue with the county attorney later that afternoon. "We've taken up almost all of her time for three days," replied Lewis. "Let's give her a rest."

Rod Schultz was not happy. In fact, he was angry that nearly two hundred big trees, and hundreds of smaller ones, would vanish to make way for more of Celebration. A few days after the vote, he agreed to meet with Cathy to discuss his complaints. But on the appointed day, he did not show up. Cathy called his office, and he was paged. When he returned her call within minutes, Schultz said he had been told by his superiors not to meet with her. Suddenly he said, "Oh what the hell," and agreed to meet her at Max's Café, in downtown Celebration.

After hearing more of the instructions from Schultz's bosses, Cathy suggested moving from their outside table at Max's to a less conspicuous table indoors at Columbia, the quietest restaurant in town. He agreed.

Over lunch, Schultz said he felt strongly that Celebration Company had used the exemption to clear many more trees than necessary on the property in order to create the maximum number of lots. In what he described as a pattern of behavior, he said the company had ignored environmental objections at every juncture in the first phases of the project and refused to pay attention to the arguments of the county's staff. "No one has ever resisted to the extent that they have," said Schultz. "Everyone else works with you. We can meet with other developers and say that they have some really environmentally unique pieces of land and why can't you work around them. And a lot of other developers do. It's a give-and-take process."

Not with Disney. They resisted every effort to compromise, said Schultz. At one point, he said, a company official told him, "We will not lose one lot to a tree." Schultz surmised that the company's attitude stemmed from its three-decade-long period of self-government—the Reedy Creek Improvement District. "I'm sure it relates back to the fact that they've governed themselves for so many years," he said. "Like an only child who has never been corrected."

Schultz acknowledged an irony, too. Despite Disney's aggressive resistance to regulation, he said he admired what they had done at Celebration, the look of the town, the hundreds of new trees planted.

"I don't hate Disney," he said with a shrug. "I love Disney. I love what they do out here. I just don't understand why they don't go that extra length to work with the county. Celebration is a great item, putting the county on the map. Any county would be thrilled to have a development of this quality. But it has been a professional failure for me. I have a job to do, to integrate the development with the environment, and I can't get it done. They are designing with the mind-set of the fifties and sixties. Clear, mow down, level, start all over again, replant. Instead of trying to design by using the natural amenities."

Part of the rationale for Disney's attitude, as Schultz said, lies in the autonomy to which it has grown accustomed at Reedy Creek. Part of it lies in the Disneyesque notion that the company can improve upon nature itself. And part of it lies in an innovative, widely hailed agreement it reached to protect and restore an 8,500-acre tract of land.

In exchange for the creation of that sanctuary, called the Disney Wilderness Preserve, the company felt that it was freed from most environmental restrictions involved in building its new town. Indeed, when Arrington toured the South Village before the vote on the tree ordinance, Tom Lewis told her that he did not understand all the fuss over tearing out the trees. "I thought when we bought the land for the wilderness preserve that we would not have these problems," he said.

Disney has a mixed record when it comes to protecting the environment. In 1988, there had been a scandal when state and federal wildlife violations were filed against Disney World and several employees. They were charged with shooting, starving, and clubbing to death black buzzards that had been making life unpleasant for guests and fellow fowl alike at the Contemporary Resort in the Magic Kingdom. The birds, which are native to Florida and protected by federal law, were pooping copiously around the resort. They also were attacking flamingoes, egrets, and other more decorous birds. Nineteen buzzard carcasses were discovered, and while Disney protested most of the allegations, it settled the matter by donating $75,000 to the Audubon Society.

Ten years later, in the spring of 1998, the company had opened its fourth major theme park at Disney World. Called Animal Kingdom, the five-hundred-acre park was created to look like game reserves in Africa and was populated with a thousand animals from dozens of species. Elephants, rhinos, lions, gazelles, and more were allowed to roam free, with natural barriers established to keep them apart from the customers. Anti-zoo activists protested, to no effect.

Unfortunately for the animals and the company, it was disclosed in the press just days before the grand opening that twelve animals had died in recent weeks. Among them were four cheetah cubs that ingested a toxic chemical, several gazelles and antelope injured during fights or entangled in fences trying to escape, and two West African crowned cranes run over by the safari vehicles used by park guests for tours. Again, state and federal investigators were called in, but Disney was found to have established the proper precautions, and the company was cleared of any wrongdoing. Nonetheless, it was a publicity blunder on the eve of the grand opening. Later, the *Orlando Sentinel* disclosed that the death toll was actually far higher. Thirty-one animals died in the months before the park opened, the expanded count including two rhinoceroses, a hippopotamus, and two mole rats.

The creation of the Disney Wilderness Preserve, on the other hand, was a masterstroke of public relations and a great step forward in land conservation. Florida's forested wetlands, better known as swamps, are among the state's most intriguing natural areas. They are complex and dynamic habitats, home to hundreds of different species, and filters for the water system. In the twenty years between 1955 and 1975, more than two thousand square miles of wetlands were lost to development across the state—at a rate of eight acres an hour. In recent years, the rate of loss has declined, but the rapid growth in Florida continues to threaten these essential elements of the environment.

When Peter Rummell and the other Disney developers first surveyed the future site of Celebration, they recognized the swamps that dotted the pasture land as a huge impediment to the development they wanted to build. Not only would environmentalists howl at the disappearance of the wetlands, but draining and filling them would be expensive.

"The thing I like least about Celebration is the land we were given to start with," Rummell said later. "It was not a great piece of land. It was not treed. It was low. It was just pasture land, and a lot of it was wet, so it was expensive to develop. It may be the arrogance of the developer to say that the thing I like least is what God did, and what I like most, I did."

Rummell could have undertaken a traditional style of development and agreed to protect isolated patches of wetland and create new ones in exchange for developing the surrounding land. But over the years environmentalists have found that these patches of wetland are often too small and disconnected to thrive optimally either as habitats or as natural filters for the water system. Instead, Rummell asked Don Killoren, as general manager for the Celebration project, and Tom Lewis to come up with an alternative that would give the company more flexibility and make the environmental agencies happy, too.

Killoren and Lewis thought big. Working with state environmental agencies as well as with Disney's own environmental staff, they devised a plan to buy a large, environmentally significant property and agree to preserve it in perpetuity. The property would become a sort of mitigation land bank. About twelve thousand acres of Disney's property is wetlands, and permits were requested one at a time when development impinged on those lands. Creating the bank would allow Disney to clear wetlands and other sensitive areas within the Celebration property, as well as within its larger holdings, to ease the future expansion of Disney World.

Carol Browner, the head of the Florida Department of Environmental Protection, who went on to become head of the federal Environmental Protection Agency, approved the idea in early 1992, after more than a year of negotiations. "Most of her staff thought that this was the dumbest idea they ever heard of," said Lewis. "The policy was, you impact an acre of wetland here, you rebuild an area there. You don't ever go do it someplace over here. And thinking long term? They thought the idea

was crazy. Thank goodness for Carol Browner. She saw the potential."
Other state and federal agencies, including the U.S. Army Corps of Engineers and the U.S. Fish and Wildlife Service, and some conservation organizations also signed off on the concept.

The site selected was the Walker Ranch, an 8,500-acre tract of land about ten miles south of the future site of Celebration. The land is part of the Upper Kissimmee chain of lakes and the beginning of the Everglades system, and it contains pine and oak forests, palmetto prairies, cypress groves, freshwater marshes, and two large lakes. About three thousand acres of the ranch is wetlands, with most of the remainder described as uplands, which provide animal sanctuary. The remains of a village dating to about 500 A.D. had been discovered on the shores of one of the lakes. Seminole Indians had lived and fished its streams and lakes, leaving behind burial mounds and the remains of a stronghold built during the Seminole Indian War in the 1830s. In all, there were seven identified archaeological sites on the ranch.

From the late nineteenth century to the 1940s, the land was used primarily for cattle ranching, farming, logging, and turpentine mills. Many of the turpentine mills were worked by convicts leased from the state and by blacks. They would cut a V in a pine tree and attach a small clay pot to collect the gummy sap that seeped out. The sap was distilled and used in paints, varnishes, and medicines in the early part of this century until cheaper, gasoline-based solvents became available.

The ranch also was home to fourteen endangered and threatened species. The list ranged from stately sandhill cranes and great blue herons to southern leopard frogs and killdeers. There also were several nests of American bald eagles and dozens of other wildlife species.

Heavy commercial use over the years had left the natural wetlands, uplands, and forests in disarray. In fact, the owners were planning to use the land for a residential development until the concept of the Disney preserve came along. As part of its agreement, Disney pledged to restore the property and build an educational center for scientists, conservationists, and visitors.

Some environmentalists remained suspicious of Disney. They feared that the company might one day choose to develop the land and find a pliable government willing to let them. Others were worried about whether Disney had the expertise to manage the resources and carry out the restoration. So Killoren added another element to the plan. Disney would buy the land and provide the money to restore it, all at a cost of about $40 million. The company would then donate the property, over a period of several years, to the Nature Conservancy, a respected independent organization that buys and manages the largest ecologically significant network of conservation lands in the world.

When the Nature Conservancy was first approached by Disney to develop the management plan for the ranch, it insisted on certain terms without which there would be no deal. First, the restoration and conservation program had to be based on sound science, and second, the plan developed by the conservancy would be submitted to state and federal officials unchanged. Disney agreed to both stipulations.

Jora Young, a Nature Conservancy staff member, became the project director for Walker Ranch. She worked out the final details of the plan with Killoren, whom she called "a man of vision," and she praised Disney for its commitment. "This was a significant shift in conservation and a tremendous breakthrough," she said. "What we were finding was that in traditional wetland mitigation, you were getting the flood-control value of the wetlands but not the habitat value. Most of them were too small and isolated. You were not getting a high-quality wetland. This was a new way to develop a huge, contiguous mitigation area."

Does she have any regrets? "A lot of different groups were involved, from the regulatory people to the developers to the conservationists," Young said. "From our respective perspectives, it wasn't perfect. If I could write the law, I'd say that no high-quality natural land could be built on. Well, that law won't be passed, at least not in my lifetime. Given the fact that we couldn't do something like that, I think that we all felt that something reasonable and positive was accomplished here."

In exchange for creating the Disney Wilderness Preserve, the company got the right to destroy five hundred acres of wetlands in Celebration and elsewhere on its property right away and additional "capital" in the land bank for future development. Without the agreement, Disney would have had to create about two acres of new wetlands for each acre that it destroyed. The cost for new wetlands could run as high as $100,000 an acre, and the wetlands themselves would take up precious space that could be used for construction, so the creation of the preserve paid off both financially and in a public relations sense for the company.

Since its creation, the preserve had been expanded to eleven thousand acres when the Greater Orlando Aviation Authority and other businesses added land through agreements similar to Disney's. In early spring, Cathy and Becky took a tour of the wilderness preserve, which was not yet officially open to the public. Becky had proposed the outing as part of her school research on the Florida environment. On the walking tour, they discovered dozens of types of wildflowers, encountered a fat, nearly four-foot-long snake of undetermined species, and saw eagles, storks, egrets, herons, and sandhill cranes. They watched a horned iridescent dung beetle roll a ball of manure across the ground, waded across muddy streams, and picked their way through forests of longleaf pine and palm. Looking at a row of slash pines growing by the road, they realized that there must have been a cow fence there decades ago on which squirrels sat and ate pine cones, dropping seeds, from which that unnaturally straight line of pines grew.

Before leaving the pine forest and eagles' nests, Becky closed her eyes and tried to imagine Seminole Indians around a campfire on the ranch. The land around our house no longer evoked such dreams in small children. It had been stripped of many of its trees and its history.

The Celebration Foundation tried to restore a bit of that history and provide a context that extended beyond the boundaries of the town. It was the foundation that sponsored the wilderness preserve tour that Cathy and Becky took. It also hosted sessions for Celebration residents on the previous tenants of the land—the Seminoles and, later, the ranchers, known as Florida crackers. The derivation of "cracker" is debated within historical circles in central Florida. One faction argues that the name came from the crack of the whip that the cowboys used to drive cattle and communicate with each other. Two quick whip cracks might signal an approaching storm. The other side of the historical debate tracks the word's origin to the soda crackers that were part of the cowboy diet.

Earli Sullivan was a cracker who remembers the history and the untamed, rugged beauty of the place from the days when his family leased thousands of acres where Celebration now sits. The sixty-four-year-old rancher recalls the history of the land with deep affection and a trace of bitterness over what has been forgotten in the creation of the new town.

"My daddy was born on Boggy Creek, not far from you folks," he said one day at his ranch west of Celebration, where he had moved to escape the encroaching development. "Grandaddy was a hog man. My daddy was a cow man. Where Celebration is, I helped run cattle. Where the Animal Kingdom is, I had cattle."

In the thirties, just before Sullivan was born, his father supported the family with money from a still he operated on a creek not far from where Celebration Town Hall sits today. According to family lore, one day the revenue agents came looking for the still, and Earli's father and older brothers made a run for freedom. His father leaped into the creek and began to swim.

"There was a big 'gator cave, and Pa backed down into the cave, and all he had left above water was his nose," Sullivan recalled. "We asked him later, what if the 'gator had been there? He said, 'Well then, he'd a just had to move over, because I wasn't goin' to jail.' "

Earli talked about hunting alligators on the property as a boy. He was paid a dollar a foot for the hides. He hunted deer, too, and remembered a day when his father shot two eight-point bucks and lugged them home alone, one slung over each shoulder.

"You try lifting just one buck," he said.

"I think I'll take your word for it," Cathy laughed.

During his younger days, Sullivan had walked four miles to school, barefoot of course, which was a little dicey on the few winter mornings when the swamp froze.

Sullivan also remembered the time in the early 1960s when he met Walt Disney and his brother Roy, who had come to inspect the property.

"Irlo Bronson owned the land, and we leased it from him," he said. "The Disney brothers drove in with Irlo. They were real casual, just as nice as any people you ever met, because they were people who had made it themselves. I've never been to California, but I heard that out there they bought a tract and people closed in on them. This time they wanted a border, so no one could get close to their theme parks. Besides, the land was cheap, eighty dollars an acre."

Sullivan recalled that promises were made that the land would never be developed. When he watched the bulldozers clearing the way for

Celebration, scraping off the trees where he had once hunted, he got angry. So he made an hour-long videotape on parts of the property that had not been gouged yet, just to preserve for his grandchildren a taste of how things used to be. He mailed it to the people at the Walt Disney Company in hopes they would not lose sight of the land's history. Not long after he sent the tape, it came back. He hopes that someone at Disney made a copy of it, for the sake of history.

Remnants of those days still existed on the two-hundred-acre parcel destined to become the South Village. The big oaks had not yet been cleared, and although survey markers were in place and crude roads had been laid, the place remained pretty wild. Strangely enough, we had never seen anyone walking through there during our own wanderings.

One day in March, Cathy persuaded a biologist who worked for Disney, Zach Pruzac, to give her and Becky a tour of the area as part of Becky's ongoing research for her school project. He picked them up outside Gooding's grocery in a four-wheel-drive truck, and the three of them spent the next couple hours bouncing down the construction roads as Pruzac described the ecosystems of the area. He pointed out the wild grasses of the upland areas and the cypress domes, shallow sandy depressions in the wetlands that are home to cypress, swamp tupelo, slash pines, and the occasional red maple. As they ducked beneath some pine trees and headed into a dry area, a large, multicolored snake slithered by.

"It's a scarlet king snake," said Pruzac. "It's harmless, but it looks a lot like a coral snake, and those are poisonous. There's a handy rhyme that lets you tell the difference, if you care to get close enough. 'Yellow touch black, good for a jack. Red touch yellow, bad for a fellow.' "

The land was laced with streams, ponds, and lakes, Pruzac explained, because Florida's water table is so high. After the rainy spring, courtesy of El Niño, the land in the South Village was so wet that day that Cathy envisioned the truck getting stuck in wheel-high mud, necessitating a long walk back to civilization.

During the messy drive, Cathy realized that her own perception of Florida's landscape was changing. Perhaps because of her childhood along the eastern shore of Canada, hills, rugged beaches, tall trees, and lots of green defined nature's best for her. Florida had seemed, well, dull, but the more she learned, the more interesting it became.

"You know, it's high drama," she said to Pruzac.

"Yeah, you have flood-plain swamp," he said, gesturing out the window, "grading into a bayhead that suddenly blends into sand-pine scrub. In other words, in Florida you can walk just a hundred feet with a change of elevation of just three feet and encounter completely different ecosystems with their own distinct plant and animal species. The length of a football field, and you seem to go from the southwestern United States to the Central American rain forests."

It was a subtlety that many people living and visiting Florida just don't get, said Pat Harden, who was the manager of special projects in environmental affairs at Walt Disney World. "One of our biggest problems here in this state in trying to protect our natural resources is that so many people here today are from somewhere else and they all seem to want this to look like home," she said. "They don't see the value in what's here. It's a wasteland to them. It's as simple as the fact that our trees don't turn pretty colors in the fall."

Within months, we knew, much of the South Village would be flattened, trees knocked down, lot markers put up. It was progress, but at a price that left us wondering if more of nature could have been saved in building Celebration.

The creation of the Disney Wilderness Preserve did not mean the company could drain and fill at will. A belt of protected swamp surrounds the southern edge of the town center where it abuts a portion of a five-thousand-acre ribbon of swamp running down to the Walker Ranch. And the developer spared a handful of isolated wetlands as green areas in some of the neighborhoods. These in-town wetlands, some as small as two-tenths of an acre, surrounded by a twenty-five-foot buffer zone, were registered with the state as designated wetlands and are supposed to be protected.

Donna Hughey, a planner with Post, Buckley, Schuh & Jernigan, the engineering and planning firm that performed the wetlands assessment for Celebration Company, said later, "The biggest challenge was having to build around those wetlands and still accomplish the aggressive development they wanted to do. It's pretty amazing. Those isolated wetlands could very easily have been two more housing lots. At the price they are selling for, that's a lot of money."

The remnants of wetlands preserved within Celebration are like little green emeralds, sparkling with pines and palms, snakes and scorpions, and things that make strange noises in the night. Back in Westport, our property abutted a protected wetland, and the kids spent hours wandering through the swamp in winter and summer. The wetlands in Celebration were more forbidding, with sixty kinds of snakes, six of which were poisonous, and plentiful alligators.

Celebration had a sizable population of alligators. Before the development started, the workers at Disney World would transplant 'gators from the swamps and ponds of the theme parks and golf courses to the wilds of what would become Celebration. As the land was cleared for the town, most of the big alligators left of their own accord or were trapped and removed. Today, most of the alligators are small, and when they reach four or five feet, they, too, are captured by animal control officers and relocated in unpopulated areas, perhaps only to wait for the next wave of development.

Despite the changes wrought by Celebration, pockets of natural beauty remained. For her school project on the environment, Becky learned that nine of the twelve native palm species in Florida can be found there, from tall royal palms and lumpish palmettos, with their underground trunks, to the cabbage palm, the Florida state tree, which derives its name from a cabbagelike tissue at the base of its boat-shaped fronds. In early summer, cabbage palms send out flowering panicles that reach nine feet in length and bear thousands of straw-colored, sweet-smelling flowers, which attract swarms of insects and birds.

Even before we moved to Celebration, we were so enamored of these little swamps and their inhabitants that we paid a premium for a lot that backed up on a four-acre wetland. It was a nice twist on the old joke about buying Florida swampland. Little did we know at the time that we were setting the stage for a controversy that would cause us to wonder about the company's real commitment to protecting the few isolated wetlands remaining in town.

It was early January when we noticed the first workers on the edge of the swamp, directly behind Scot and Lisa Baird's house, three doors from us. Men with chain saws were clearing small trees from the edge of the swamp, apparently to enlarge the yard of a house being built next to it. We became more alarmed a few days later, when the first truckload of fill dirt was hauled to the site. Then we heard a rumor that the owner of the lot, an electrical subcontractor for David Weekley Homes, was planning to put a gazebo in the swamp.

We had been told the land was protected wetland when we bought our lot. So had the McGraths, Scott Zane, and the Bairds. All of us had paid premiums of $6,000 to $10,000 to have a view of the swamp and to ensure that there would be no building behind us. The lot plan map we had received showed that the lot in question, number 11, did not extend into the swamp. Everyone was concerned about what was going on, and we volunteered to investigate.

First, we called an employee of the Celebration Company. It was the first he had heard of any filling of the wetland. He drove out after work to take a look. As he and Cathy stood in the alley overlooking the work area, he shook his head and said it did not seem right to him. With a promise that we would not use his name, because he feared for his job, he stopped by the following day with a copy of the official plat map for the neighborhood from the company's files. It clearly showed that the area where the work was going on was part of the wetland, which had been designated with an official registration number, W22.33. The map also showed that the work under way crossed the buffer zone and went right into the edge of the wetland.

Mike McGrath remembered a conversation with a couple who had wanted to buy lot number 11 several months earlier. "They decided not to do it because the lot was too small and Celebration Company told them that they could not expand into the swamp," said Mike.

We tracked Tim Swanson down a few days later, and he confirmed Mike's story. "We negotiated with David Weekley Homes at length about the purchase of the lot," said Swanson over the telephone. "Ultimately we didn't buy it because it was so narrow. There was a retaining wall, and that was the property line. We were told nothing was allowed beyond the wall because that was wetland."

Apparently there was pressure to sell the lot, which had a $40,000 premium because of its proximity to the swamp. When Mike and Becky Prevost looked at the same land a few weeks after the Swansons, Mike, a landscape architect, pointed out to the sales agent that it was very narrow and that it appeared to be a wetland beyond the retaining wall. "Don't worry about it," they recalled being told by a sales agent. "Just go ahead and do what you want." The Prevosts did not want to infringe on what they felt might be an environmentally sensitive area, so they bought another lot just down the street.

We drafted a letter of protest to Celebration Company, which the four groups of neighbors signed. We asked that the encroachment be halted and expressed astonishment that the company would permit the desecration of a designated protected wetland. If they did not stop the work, we wanted our premiums refunded, because it hardly seemed fair for them to use the swamp as a marketing amenity and then, once they had collected our money, to damage that amenity. We also complained to state and county environmental agencies.

A month passed and there was no response from the company, but the work had stopped. Our "deep throat" inside the company said there were concerns about what had been done to the swamp. A mistake had been made. The company was searching for some way to rectify it and keep the owner of the new house happy. On several occasions, we saw men in suits gathered around the site.

Finally we got a letter from David Pace, the director of residential real estate for Celebration Company. It was stiff and formal and non-committal. He wrote that the company agreed that the area behind our houses was a designated wetland and that development was forbidden. But he could not bring himself to confirm what anyone's eyes could see, that a portion of the wetland had been cleared and fill dirt put down. The best Pace could do was write that if any portion of the wetland had been damaged, the builder was obligated to restore it. "We have reminded the builder of this requirement if, in fact, the edge of the wetland was violated," he wrote.

That was the end of it, for a few months. No more word from Celebration Company. No action by any environmental authorities. The clearing stopped. The company planted some native grasses in a half-hearted attempt to restore the wetland. Then one Saturday morning a few months later we heard the whine of a chain saw and, upon stepping out the back door to investigate, we found the neighbor clearing trees. By the end of the weekend, he had a woodpile twenty feet long and waist high—all that remained of half a dozen small live oaks that had been part of what we considered wetlands. On Monday morning, the first of several truckloads of fill dirt arrived and was spread across the area.

Over the next several days, we joined our neighbors in calling Celebration Company officials and local and state environmental authorities, demanding a halt to the destruction. They promised to take another look, and new surveys were conducted of the property. This time the results were more depressing: Company officials and the environmentalists confirmed that the neighbor's property lines included what we had been told—and what the original maps had shown—was part of the designated wetland. They said he had the right to clear the land and even construct the threatened gazebo. The clearing altered our view, but we felt sorry for our neighbors whose homes had once backed up on a swamp and now abutted a cleared, grassy area.

Of course, the swamp behind our house had its drawbacks. One night Nick went out the door to walk the dog, and they were confronted by a six-foot alligator that was halfway up the backyard to the house. Nick nearly beat the greyhound back into the house. The swamp also was a popular breeding ground for mosquitoes. Florida has a long and colorful relationship with these small, elegant little bloodsuckers. Now the mosquito population is just bad, but they used to be horrible in these parts. According to local lore, farm animals were killed, literally bitten and sucked to death. The county next to us, where Orlando is located, used to be called Mosquito County until some savvy Chamber of Commerce type got the name changed to Orange County.

At the orientation meeting for new residents, which we attended soon after arriving, we were told proudly that Celebration was the only community in central Florida that sprayed twice a day to control mosquitoes. Say what you will about the harmful effects of spraying, much of Florida and all of Celebration would be uninhabitable without such efforts.

In late August 1997, two months after we moved in, the county health department issued a medical alert for St. Louis encephalitis, one of several types of encephalitis viruses circulated by mosquitoes, birds, and rodents. Though no human cases had been seen, in Orange County five "sentinel" chickens, which had been plucked naked to provide easy access for the mosquitoes, had been diagnosed with the disease, which can be fatal to children, the elderly, and people with health problems. As a result of the alert, golf courses and area theme parks closed by seven P.M. and outdoor evening public events were canceled.

A couple of months after the encephalitis scare, Donna McGrath knocked on our back door. "You gotta see this," she said, pulling both of us to the yard behind her house. There we saw four men installing what looked like a large, upside-down pickle jar hanging from a thin rod in the ground. One of the men introduced himself. He was John Randall, an entomologist with Johnson & Johnson, the medical supplies and consumer products company. He explained that the gizmo that looked like a pickle jar was, in fact, a pickle jar that had been converted into a mosquito trap. A small tube ran into the jar from a green cylinder of carbon dioxide. Mosquitoes use various cues for food—movement, color contrast, skin temperature. Most of all, however, they are olfactory hunters, following the vapor trail of carbon dioxide left behind by humans. Each time you breathe out, you are sending up a flare to every mosquito in your vicinity, saying, "Blood container over here."

The cylinder on Randall's trap spewed out its carbon dioxide at exactly the same rate at which a human breathes, in an effort to trick mosquitoes into thinking there was food nearby. To make the trap even more appealing to mosquitoes, its emissions were enhanced with a chemical equivalent of ox. Charming. You could faintly hear the steady puff, puff, puff of the machine. When the unloved insects came to investigate, they were sucked into the jar by a small fan. Running from four in the morning until ten at night, prime time for the little bloodsuckers, the traps were capable of catching hundreds of mosquitoes a day. Or that was the theory, anyway.

This was a target-rich environment. One of the men with Randall was Mark Kulo, also an entomologist. He worked for Clarke Environmental Mosquito Management, the company hired to spray Celebration for mosquitoes. He told us that the spray was a synthetic version of a product exuded by chrysanthemums and was harmless to humans. But even spraying twice a day, he said, can't kill all the mosquitoes in a place like Celebration. "If you were going to choose a place to build a town, you would be hard put to find a place in Florida with more mosquitoes than Celebration," he said.

We agreed to let Randall install one of his prototype traps in our backyard. Each day for a month, we checked the trap, expecting to find hundreds of dead mosquitoes. The first day there were five. Over the next week, the number of tiny corpses ranged from five to fifteen a day.

We were disappointed. The McGraths' trap seemed to be working better. By the end of the first week, a soft brown layer of dead insects covered the inside of their pickle jar.

Randall came to collect his jar at the end of the test period. He seemed mildly disappointed by the haul in our jar, though he was clearly more excited when he walked a few feet to the McGraths' trap. We filled out a questionnaire, saying that we did not find the trap intrusive and that we would probably buy one, provided it worked a little better.

As things turned out, we had less to worry about than expected from the mosquitoes. In 1998, in the summer, the time of year when the mosquitoes are at their worst, there were almost none. At the risk of sounding like ingrates, we were alarmed by their disappearance. We missed the mosquito nights, with Cathy swatting at insects caught in her hair. It was not the absence of the mosquitoes; we are not masochists. But the lightning bugs that were such a part of summer nights in Florida also had been diminished by the twice-a-day spraying.

12

Bowling Together

As the last of our visitors departed in late April 1998, the one question that we had heard from all of them echoed like an annoying song you cannot shake from your head. "When are you coming home?" they asked. They seemed surprised and mildly disapproving when we admitted that we had begun to like living here, not believing that we couldn't wait to get back to the Northeast, never understanding how we could begin to grow roots in this sandy soil.

In part, the town and its people were holding our interest. We wanted to stay at least a while longer to see what would happen next. We had never thought of Celebration as a permanent home, yet we found living there pleasant and easy, which are not bad qualities. Circumstances demanded, however, that we make a decision soon.

We had rented our house in Connecticut for a year, figuring that would give us plenty of time to gather material for our book. The lease was expiring at the end of June. Did we want to move back in the summer? Rent for another year? Sell the Westport house?

We talked among ourselves, debating the pros and cons. We invited the kids to share their opinions, though never consenting to Becky's demand for a vote. This was not a democracy, just a benevolent dictatorship. But we wanted to hear what Nick and Becky really thought about Celebration versus Westport.

"I still miss my friends in Westport," said Nick one night as the four of us sat around the kitchen table. "I know a lot more people here, but I don't have any friends as good as Rob Mauerman. But it's really easy to do stuff here. I can go anywhere on my 'blades or bike. There are kids all over the place."

Becky missed her friends, too, but she has a wonderful capacity to make new best friends in minutes. Ever since arriving in Celebration, she had surrounded herself with other girls, and she seemed never to travel in groups of fewer than three.

"I love it here," she said when we asked her. "I want to stay in Celebration, at least a while longer."

"What about school?" asked Cathy.

The kids were noncommittal. We should never have expected anything else. They liked the freedom of the school, the chance to work on long projects and in groups. At the same time, they both suffered from the lack of direction and the absence of clear progress markers, the very things that bothered us as parents. Before excusing himself from the table, Nick offered a universal verdict. "School is school," he said with disdain.

The end of the school year was approaching. On a community level, the high level of involvement had surprised us. The Parent Teacher Student Association was one of the fastest-growing chapters in Florida. Its president, Stu Devlin, seemed to have a realistic goal when he said he wanted 100-percent membership. Attendance at meetings was high, always a hundred or more parents showing up, at a time when other PTSAs across the country had to hold raffles to draw more than a few parents.

Another example of community involvement was the level of participation in the School Advisory Council. These organizations were mandated by the Florida legislature to help return responsibility for education to those closest to students—parents, teachers, community leaders, and business representatives. Every school in the state was required by law to establish an advisory council, with members elected from those four areas. But most schools could not fill the required positions on the committee; there was not enough interest from any element of the community. In Celebration's case, so many people wanted to serve in the unpaid positions that the school had to conduct an election.

One reason for the participation was the simple fact that so many people moved to Celebration for the express purpose of taking advantage of a neighborhood school. They expected a world-class institution and had their own opinions about what it would take to develop one. In addition, at least among the initial group of residents, few people came to Celebration to sit on their hands. In conversation after conversation, we discovered that people had come here because they wanted to be active in their town.

No one was more involved than Charlie Rogers, the affable manager of the SunTrust Bank branch in Celebration. From the Rotary to the School Advisory Council, from the church choir to the chamber of commerce, Rogers was always present and accounted for.

"A lot of it is my nature," said Rogers, a native of Miami who moved from a nearby development to Celebration early on with his wife, Mary, and two children. "A lot of it is my job. Much of my work is marketing and development of public relations, knowing the people who live and work here, seeking opportunities where I could be of help to them as well as having them help us. But the nature of the town draws everyone to get involved."

Indeed, one of the reasons people in Celebration were more involved than their counterparts most other places was the design of the town, and nowhere was that more evident than with the school. Located at a prominent spot in the center of town, its positioning made getting to school meetings easier and made the meetings themselves more visible within the community. You could see people streaming into the school for those meetings. When it came to community involvement, Celebration's construction was barrier-free.

As an urban planner in Tampa, Ray Chiaramonte had been involved with planned communities for more than twenty years. His desire to experience living in one was what had drawn him and his family to Celebration, even though it meant he still had to commute daily to his job in Tampa. "It is just easier to be a part of this community," said Chiaramonte. "I am more involved here than I ever was in Tampa, despite my long commute, because there, being involved meant getting back in the car. Here it is just a matter of, do I want to have a pleasant walk down the street? Well, of course. You turn the TV on and notice on the local cable channel that there is a PTSA meeting, and even if you didn't plan to go, it is so easy that you tend to do it. It is almost as if modern society puts all these hurdles in front of behaving in a good way, like being involved in your kid's school. Here the obstacles are removed."

A third reason was less positive. The difficulties in getting the school running smoothly meant that more parents felt obligated to stay informed and involved. As a result, school meetings sometimes turned ugly, with people pointing fingers and shouting about blame. It was the messy side of democracy, but it was still democracy.

For us, Celebration School was a difficult and demanding change, and there had been ups and downs for both of our kids. From our perspective, it remained unclear whether the reliance on self-motivation and the absence of grades and textbooks were working. We accepted part of the responsibility for the problems. We had difficulty adjusting to some of the new concepts, and so did our kids. But by the end of the year, we had serious questions about whether either one had made substantive progress in their education.

We had waged a yearlong battle with Becky and her teachers over her performance in math. Back in Westport, she had shown signs of strong interest and some ability in math and spent the last two years in advanced classes. Here in Celebration, she preferred to be in a math group with some of her friends. Cathy dubbed it "social math." So Becky was settling for less, in our view, by pretending to have trouble with skills she had mastered in earlier grades. It was a less competitive environment, which was pleasant in some ways, but is a little competition, especially self-competition, a bad thing? There were times when more weight seemed to be given to smooth classroom dynamics and not hurting feelings than to rigorous academic demands.

There was a learning curve at play here in how to make the most of the school and its unusual approach. As parents, we felt we were operating in a vacuum, partially because we were missing the usual markers of grades and textbooks. Nick and Becky brought home little homework, and there were few tests. Basically, there was little against which we could evaluate the progress of our children and the content of what they were learning. In fact, there was no written curriculum against which we could chart their work. We were asked to trust the teachers to an unusual degree, and not everything we saw inspired trust.

For instance, each student was required to produce a major project every nine weeks. While they were encouraged to take a multidiscipli- nary approach to the project, the students were allowed to choose the subject matter and set their own pace for carrying it out. In the first two nine-week periods, Becky chose undemanding topics that seemed irrele- vant to her life. In the second nine weeks Becky thought she would study French fashions. "Think again," Cathy said. Then Becky decided to explore the relationship between education and crime in nineteenth- century France. Where was this coming from? Great for a graduate the- sis, perhaps, but it seemed to be a worthless exercise for a ten-year-old.

The first we learned of this final selection was when Becky arrived home from school one day with a sheaf of papers, in French. She an- nounced proudly that she had gotten them off the Internet for her new nine-week goal. Cathy immediately hopped on her bicycle and pedaled over to the school to intercept Becky's teachers before they left for the day. In the classroom, she found Dee Frechette, Becky's senior teacher.

"Dee, what's going on here?" Cathy said, trying to catch her breath. "I know this whole approach encourages children to make choices, but when the choice isn't a good one . . . what do we do?" Cathy envisioned Becky's growing confusion and frustration as she pursued a goal that she couldn't possibly achieve.

Frechette agreed that Becky's choice was inappropriate. She prom- ised to discuss it with Becky the next day, but she was reluctant to force her to abandon the idea. The result was that Becky modified her goal to something that we all felt was better. She turned her interest in France into a geography project, with maps and an illustrated history of the country. While the project did not strike us as particularly innovative, at least she put in some effort, learned something, and managed to turn her work in on time.

We learned our own lessons from that experience. We would have to become more deeply involved in these nine-week projects, not only with Becky but with Nick, too. We would help them choose a topic that inter- ested them and offered an opportunity for serious and relevant research and writing. For us there were times when the school's attitude seemed so laissez-faire that we found we had to monitor our children's progress at every step. Nine weeks is a long span of time, and our children, at least, needed to have such a project broken into smaller bits and receive regular nudges along the way to stay on track. We like to think that we have always been involved in the education of our children, but we had to redouble our efforts here. And from the sounds of the disgruntled parents at the end of each nine-week period, we were not alone.

Fortunately, Becky's teachers—Frechette, Emily Jost, and Jeanne Iorio—were friendly and receptive in helping us work with this new system. In turn, Cathy wrote the class newsletter and spent time as a volunteer in the classroom. In Nick's class, the teachers were aloof and uncommunicative. They did not seem to want volunteer help, and the atmosphere in the class was chilly. It was as if our kids were in two different schools.

The attitude in Nick's classroom clearly carried over to communication among teachers, students, and parents. The big problem with Nick was that we heard nothing about his progress from his teachers. In conferences, they seemed to know little of what Nick was doing or of his interests. We learned that our forgetful son had failed to turn in seven writing assignments in one nine-week session only when we went over his written assessment at the end of the period. "Please, let us know sooner," Cathy begged.

One of Nick's nine-week goals was to learn to read more slowly, because he kept getting ahead of his reading group in class. Nothing could have seemed more counterproductive to us.

But there were positive aspects. For both kids, the most important was the seemingly total absence of the rituals of inclusion and exclusion that had plagued their previous schools. Snobbery at Celebration School, as in the town itself, was a weak and flickering force. Neither child experienced an act of deliberate cruelty at the hands of their peers, and the school itself recorded no acts of vandalism and no graffiti.

Also on the plus side, Nick found an outlet for his passion for computers that probably would not have been available at a traditional school. For his second nine-week project in the second semester, he began to teach himself to write Java, a computer-programming language. With no help from his teachers, who did not seem to know much about technology, he had used material from the Internet and two thick books to begin learning the language and had set up a Web page to illustrate his newfound ability.

Even then, it was not his teacher but Susan King, the assistant librarian and a former programmer for the federal government, who recognized Nick's skills and interest. She told him about a Java-writing class that was being taught to high school students at Celebration School. Susan grilled Nick for more than an hour one morning before school, decided that he knew enough to participate in the class, and arranged for him to join it. It was, without question, the highlight of his school year and something that would have been difficult to arrange in a less flexible school setting. Indeed, Nick's fascination with computers had proved a little too strong.

One day in April, Scott Muri, the technology administrator at the school, called and asked Cathy to drop by his office. When she got there, Muri could barely contain his laughter. He said that the person who administered the Celebration community computer server had just notified him that Nick Frantz had crashed the entire operation the previous weekend. Cathy had a sinking feeling in her stomach. Her son was some sort of hacker desperado. But Muri laughed and explained what had happened. It was clear that his admiration for Nick's cleverness outweighed his condemnation.

We knew that Nick was fascinated by electronically transmitted viruses. He often opened up sample viruses on the virus protector on one of our computers to see how they were constructed. According to Muri and the story we later extracted from Nick, he had created e-mail bombs that carried what Nick thought would be a harmless virus. They were designed to enter someone's electronic mailbox and blitz it with thousands of messages. He had dispatched the first one to himself, and nothing happened. The bomb was a dud.

Next he created a series of fictitious e-mail addresses on the community server (don't ask us how). He thought he could send bombs to the fake addresses safely and then go back in and see whether they had gone off. What he did not know was that the server had its own software to prevent the creation of false e-mail addresses. It automatically closed down the mailboxes Nick had set up. When he fired off his e-mail bombs, they bounced into the server itself, causing such a backlog that the entire operation shut down. It had taken the server operator several hours over the weekend to find the problem, eradicate it, and restore the system.

Clever or not, Nick was in deep trouble with us. He lost his computer privileges for two weeks and wrote a note of apology to the server operator, Brian Levine. He also offered to undergo a community service sentence by helping Levine at the server, but he didn't get that lucky.

We were not the only people with concerns about the school. We listened often to neighbors who were worried about the lack of direction provided to their children and about the absence of tests, grades, and books. Some of it was simply adjusting to a new way of learning and evaluating progress. But some of it seemed to verge on dereliction of duty. Patrick and Kelly Wrisley were so upset about what they perceived as the chaos in the classroom of their twelve-year-old daughter, Lauren, that they discussed withdrawing her from school.

As the local pastor, Wrisley was a familiar and prominent figure in town. He could not walk through the town center without being stopped multiple times, sometimes for brief greetings, sometimes for heartfelt confessions or requests. Part of him welcomed the prominence and accepted it as his role. But another part of him regretted the loss of privacy that had come with the move to Celebration.

The prominence came with another price. Pat and Kelly were concerned about their two children. Katie was nine, sunny and outgoing, given to the wearing of funny hats and hugs for her dad. But Lauren was miserable, upset by the disruptive and unproductive nature of her classroom, and her parents were concerned.

Day after day, she came home with tales of wasted hours. Kids raced from one end of the neighborhood to the other, without any apparent supervision from the teachers. She described a place where the responsibility for learning seemed to rest entirely on the shoulders of the students. In the middle of the year, two of the four teachers left abruptly, adding to the sense of dislocation.

Pat and Kelly had long talks about withdrawing Lauren from the school. In Atlanta, she had been a good student, and they knew she was a bright youngster. But here she was, halfway through her second year at Celebration School, making little or no discernible progress. There were a couple of Christian schools not far away. They offered discipline and structure, at a price that the Wrisleys could squeeze into their tight budget.

One afternoon Kelly explained that she feared Lauren was losing ground daily. "The other day, she said to me, 'I'm never going to get into a good college, am I?' and it about broke my heart," said Kelly. "A friend of ours was in the class observing, and she said Lauren spent three hours staring out the window."

But Pat and Kelly resisted. Other families had pulled their kids out of school. Some had done so in a highly public manner. Each time a family abandoned the school, it had an impact on the town as well as on the school. And some had more impact than others, at least symbolically. There had been a big buzz when the town doctor and his wife had withdrawn their children. If the preacher followed suit, it would be another blow. The Wrisleys decided to finish up the semester, hoping that the new teachers in Lauren's classroom would provide a welcome change.

Parents of high school students were finding that Celebration students indeed faced difficulty getting accepted at good colleges and universities because they did not have a grade point average. The alternative to letter or point grades at Celebration was a written evaluation of each student's portfolio, which was a collection of papers, research projects, artwork, and other tasks carried out over the course of the year. Even universities associated with the design of Celebration School, like Harvard and Auburn, said they had no real capacity to evaluate portfolios in the admissions process.

Not long after school ended, a group of parents demanded a meeting with Brent Herrington at Town Hall. They wanted to air their frustrations to him because they felt that Celebration Company had a vested interest in the success of the school and should be aware of complaints about portfolios and the absence of grades. Unspoken was the belief that Herrington, as Disney's most prominent representative in town, could somehow appeal to a higher authority for help. The complaints were a sad echo of the concerns expressed a year earlier by parents who had withdrawn their children from the school, and some were angry enough now to do the same.

"Wednesday, I am pulling my kids out," said Lisa Sublette, an elder in the Presbyterian church and the mother of two. "What can you do when your fourteen-year-old son comes home, hands you his portfolio, and says, 'I don't know what I've done or where I stand.' And my daughter, Kaci, well, Kaci has been coloring papers this year. Coloring papers in the sixth grade. They are not motivated or edified. They have nothing to grab on to."

Jacci Rizzo said that she had called twenty colleges and universities to inquire about their policies for evaluating portfolios. Not one would accept them in lieu of traditional grade point averages, in large part because they did not have the time to evaluate their quality. An admissions officer at Auburn University had said to her, "Ma'am, you are being grossly misled regarding portfolios. You need grades." Another admissions officer suggested that she try small private colleges, not prestigious universities or big state schools. While SATs are a valuable tool, she was told, they alone are not enough for admission to elite universities when the students are coming from an unknown school like Celebration's. "We didn't come here to have our children limited in their choices," Rizzo said.

Carrie Mirabile, who lived on our street, delivered an impassioned, tearful appeal to Herrington to solve the problems. "For five years, we scrimped and saved to get here," she said. "We sold everything. We both gave up jobs. Now we're here, and we can't afford to pay for a private school. We are barely getting by as it is. Fix this, please."

Herrington tried to defuse the tension and respond as best he could to the concerns. Many times over the school year, he had met informally with Davis and other school administrators to talk about whether changes were needed. He urged the parents to find a way to work with the school for changes that everyone could accept. Herrington would not, however, attack the overarching philosophy of individual assessments. "As a parent, if they turn [Celebration School] into a traditional school, I'm moving," he said.

Herrington also said something surprisingly candid: "I have a special place in my heart for anyone who takes on a kamikaze assignment like this. This year, every day I worried that Dot would quit. Not that she threatened to. It was just that I couldn't imagine the punishment she was taking. She had no help. It was just her. And a bunch of angry parents. So I guess my position is just a little different from your average parent in the cheap seats, with his arms crossed, waiting to see what can be done for him next."

It was a difficult year for Davis. As her neighbors, we had seen the evidence firsthand. The hours were brutal, and we often watched her dragging into her house, next to ours, at midnight or later, after spending all day and half the night at the school. For the first half of the year, she did not even have an assistant principal. One night when a toilet overflowed, there was no janitor to call, and she spent hours on the telephone trying to find help at the school district, calling the superintendent and other principals. Eventually she called Celebration Company, and the problem was solved.

Still, she believed in the philosophy of the school and thought her teachers were doing an excellent job of teaching their students. Where they got lower marks from the principal was in communicating to the parents what they were doing.

"One of the problems with this school is that the community was not involved in forming its plan and vision," she explained one evening in her office after everyone else had gone home. "It was done by educators and Celebration Company and I don't even know who else. But we are a public school, and this is our community, and while we are experts at what we do, we still have to meet your needs."

Davis admitted that she had considered quitting several times and consulted regularly with Herrington about the stresses of her job. "It's been tough because of the myriad expectations," she said during a morning interview on her day off, the wear of the year seeming to show on her face. "You can't please everybody. I don't think I regret coming here. Frustration is a good word. When I sit here and look at a parent with tears in their eyes and they are frustrated over something that I know needs to be fixed, I get frustrated, too. But I'm not a quitter, and as long as it doesn't affect my health, I'll stay here."

But would we stay? The school was our biggest concern. The first year had been fun but tough at times for our kids and for us. We had learned to cope with some of the oddities. By the end of the year, with our direct oversight, both kids were executing challenging and interesting nine-week projects. Becky had learned to work steadily toward her long-term goals, and she had developed good skills for working in groups. Nick was learning to stay focused on his long-term projects, though we had refused to slow down his reading. We were of two minds about grades. While we wanted to see errors corrected on papers and a better measurement of progress, we were not wedded to the idea of traditional number or letter grades, and we agreed that there were other, equally valid forms of assessment.

When we toted up the list of pros and cons of Celebration in general, one of the most positive things was a vibrancy that we had not experienced anyplace else. People were bound together in an endeavor that ran counter to the overall decline of civil society in America. Celebration had something important to say to the rest of the country about how we live as friends and neighbors. Even if it did not work, at least the effort had been made in earnest.

When Alexis de Tocqueville visited the United States in the 1830s, he was most impressed by the new country's propensity for civic association. He saw it as the key to making democracy work. "Americans of all ages, all stations in life, and all types of disposition are forever forming associations," he wrote in *Democracy in America*. "There are not only commercial and industrial associations in which all take part, but others of a thousand different types—religious, moral, serious, futile, very general and very limited, immensely large and very minute."

The social scientists who measure such things say that the factors that determine a community's well-being, such as poverty, education, crime, drug abuse, and even health, are influenced by the level of civic engagement. Unfortunately, the trend in recent decades has been toward less involvement, with a predictable decline in the quality of life in many places. Millions of Americans have withdrawn from the affairs of their communities. In one study, the Roper Organization found that the number of Americans who attended a school or public meeting in the past year had declined from 22 percent in 1973 to 13 percent twenty years later. Similar declines have been reported in the proportion of Americans who socialize with their neighbors more than once a year.

In a fascinating paper in the *Journal of Democracy*, with the whimsical title "Bowling Alone," Harvard Professor Robert D. Putnam equated the decline of civil society in America with the decline of bowling leagues. Between 1980 and 1993, he found, the number of American bowlers increased by 10 percent. Nearly 80 million Americans went bowling at least once during 1993, nearly a third more than voted in the 1994 congressional elections. Yet participation in league bowling declined by 40 percent over the same period. The result, Professor Putnam pointed out, was a loss of social interaction and civil conversations over beer and pizza, because more Americans were bowling solo.

In Putnam's study, bowling alone was a metaphor for the fact that fewer people were joining traditional civic organizations like parent teacher associations, churches, and the Boy Scouts. Instead of giving the time and effort required by such memberships, Americans were more apt to write a check to organizations that did not demand active involvement. Civic activities result in what Putnam calls "civic capital," and these days, in communities across the country, our civic capital is diminishing.

Celebration does not have a bowling alley, but it does have a striking level of neighborliness and social interaction, even beyond the involvement in school issues, which constitutes a wealth of civic capital. Disney's town developers knew the value of such interaction in building a sense of community, which was the reason they arranged a steady flow of festivities. But we had come to experience a rich tapestry of community life that could not be engineered by the company, and we did not recognize its depths until Nick's survey.

For his final nine-week project at school, Nick conducted a public-opinion survey of the town. As an education project, it struck us as a winner. He used research skills to study the history of census taking and his writing skills to devise clear and precise nonleading questions. He improved his computer abilities by learning to use software to compile and analyze the responses. And he sought a mentor to help him. The mentor was one of our neighbors, Bill LeBlanc, who has a doctorate in psychology and a special expertise in polling and data analysis. With Bill's expert and exacting guidance, Nick was able to produce a fairly professional survey and provide information that helped all of us better understand life around us.

Nick devised a two-page survey to assess the opinions of Celebration residents. The questions ranged from how and when they had learned about the town to the reasons they had moved here and whether they were happy. He asked about attitudes toward the school and the use of technology. We paid for copying and mailing out 516 surveys, one to every household in Celebration. Accompanying each questionnaire was a stamped envelope with Nick's return address.

Sending out the survey generated an enormous buzz. In a town that had experienced so much outside scrutiny, there was a keen desire to know what we thought about the place ourselves. Although Disney had compiled lots of demographic information, people seemed to be more comfortable with Nick's survey, perhaps because he was a child. Neighbors and strangers alike stopped us regularly to ask about the results and when they would be posted at Town Hall, as Nick had promised in his cover letter.

Maybe we should have predicted this, but not everyone was feeling warm and fuzzy about the project. One afternoon a few days after the surveys were mailed, a friend called Doug. She thought he should hear a message left on her telephone answering machine, since it might influence the results of Nick's survey. Doug's blood ran cold as he listened: "This is Margot Schwartz, and I'm part of the phone tree calling Celebration people. There was a survey that was sent out by a student at Celebration School by the name of Nick Frantz. It was very underhanded. It was very sophisticated. He is only twelve years old, and his parents are authors writing a book about Celebration and its residents. So they are trying to gather information for their own benefit and take advantage of residents. The questions are very personal and detailed and looking to find out bad information. We're recommending that people not fill it out and not send it in. Please call as many people and talk to as many people as you can to let them know the same thing, because we're hoping to be able to fight them silently."

After a long silence, Doug thanked our friend, picked up the phone, and dialed Margot. We had met her briefly at one of the McGraths' parties and again at one of our block parties, though she lived in an apartment downtown. More to the point, we had also read about her in *The New York Times Magazine* article the previous December. The author had recounted his attempt to interview a woman who was critical of Celebration. When Schwartz spotted them together, he wrote, "she strode up to us and, jabbing her index finger at my notebook, informed me that

'Beulah here was one of the negative ones who only wants to bash this place.'"

Margot answered her phone on the first ring, no doubt between phone-tree calls. Here is a condensed version of what followed:

DOUG: Margot, this is Nick's father, Doug Frantz. Why didn't you call us if you had questions about Nick's survey?

MARGOT: I'm not alone on this. Lots of people have questions. Lots of big people are upset about it.

DOUG: That's a shame. You should have called before you said these bad things about my son and his survey.

MARGOT: People are upset, and there are going to be consequences. Big people are involved.

DOUG: This is unfortunate. I wish that you had used another tactic on this.

We were upset about the potential impact of a backlash on Nick. He had received permission from his lead teacher to do the project, but if there really was some movement against the survey, we had no doubt the teacher would pass the buck. It could make life at school tough for Nick.

We both got on the telephone, calling neighbors and school officials to discover the depth of the problem. The receptionist at school said Schwartz had called her to complain, but she told us not to worry about it, she had not heard anyone else say a bad word about the survey. "And anyway," she said, "how did it turn out?" After several phone calls and informal inquiries over several days, we did not turn up anyone else who expressed any misgivings about the survey. Davis and Herrington even asked for copies of the final results.

Was Schwartz alone in her opposition? Maybe not. She was an extreme example of the defensiveness that a faction of residents felt when it came to the press and to critics within Celebration. Some people were undoubtedly uncomfortable with the idea of a book being written.

Most people, on the other hand, seemed intrigued by the idea that someone who lived in Celebration was writing a book about the place. They were eager to sit down for an interview. Some people actually insisted. And that openness suggested to us that most people recognized that thinking critically and analytically about the town was not destructive.

Once we determined that Schwartz seemed to be alone on her crusade, we decided not to burden Nick with the incident. Let him find out when he reads about it on this page. Enough time will have passed that we can all laugh about it, but he will have to settle for the sanitized version of his father's telephone call to Schwartz.

We have no way of knowing whether Schwartz's campaign affected the survey results, though we doubt it made any significant difference. In the end, Nick got 268 responses overall, well above 50 percent of the households at the time. The number of responses seemed telling, and, to us anyway, they amounted to a valid and intriguing look at the attitudes of the people who live here.

Most relevant to the issue of social interaction, or "bowling alone," 72 percent of those who responded said they knew more of their neighbors in Celebration than in the previous place they had lived. One out of every three said that they knew everyone on their street, and roughly two-thirds said they knew some of the people on their street. Only 2 percent said they knew no one on their street in Celebration.

Seven out of ten said they participated in block parties, one out of four participated in the parent teacher association, and six out of ten attended community meetings. Compare that last figure to the 13 percent of the people nationwide who told the Roper Organization that they had attended a public meeting in the last year, and you get a sense of the level of involvement here.

The survey also asked a series of questions about the school, including a general question about the level of satisfaction. Thirty percent of the respondents said they were dissatisfied with the school, 46 percent were satisfied, and 24 percent were very satisfied.

Most surprising to us, despite the grumbling about the school and the complaints about the quality of home construction, 98 percent of the respondents said they were either happy or very happy living in Celebration, leaving only 2 percent who checked the box indicating they were unhappy there. It is hard to imagine another place where such an overwhelming percentage of people would say they were happy. When the Barnie's crowd asked about the results, Cathy shocked them with the 98 percent figure. Then she pointed to her neck and said, "It's the computer chip," suggesting that everyone had been programmed to love Celebration.

When we filled out our survey for Nick, we checked the box that said we were happy in Celebration. The novelty of being marooned in a quasi theme park had worn off. In its place had come a genuine enjoyment of the scale of the town, the friendliness of our fellow residents, and the convenience of having most needs within easy reach. Life in Celebration proceeded at a seductive rhythm.

Soon after arriving, Doug had sold his yellow Mustang convertible. He had been unduly fond of the car, a throwback to his misspent youth, with its V-8 engine and five-speed transmission and "look at me" color. We had used some of the proceeds to buy a more sensible mode of transportation, two bicycles, one red and one green. We rode for miles almost every day, exploring the town, running errands downtown, monitoring the progress of construction around our neighborhood and in the North Village.

Jettisoning one of our two cars seemed to confirm the wisdom of the town's master plan, which was designed in part to reduce reliance on automobiles. Indeed, we grew so accustomed to using the bicycles that the one car we did have, a 1991 Ford Explorer with 85,000 miles, often sat unused for days. At Thanksgiving, Cathy brought home the fixings for Thanksgiving dinner for twelve from Gooding's in the old-fashioned saddle-bag baskets on her bike. She used two short, elastic bungee cords to secure the fresh twenty-five-pound turkey to the top of the baskets. Things seemed to have gone a bit too far, however, when Doug strapped his golf bag to his back and wobbled half a mile to the golf course on his bicycle.

This relative independence from the car was in part a function of the proximity of a grocery store, a movie theater, the fitness center, and other amenities in Celebration. Equally important, however, was the fact that we both had the good fortune of being able to work at home. Cathy had worked from home as a freelance writer for more than decade, so she was well acquainted with the efficiencies and independence this afforded. This was the first time that Doug had been freed from daily trips to a newspaper office, and he enjoyed both his newfound freedom and what seemed to be an increased productivity.

Nick's survey found that at least one person works at home in about half the households of Celebration, an astonishingly high rate. A small number of people, like writers, artists, and some professionals, have always had the option of working at home. But the computer, e-mail, the Internet, and other technological advances have broadened the range of jobs that can be performed at home, leading to the creation of the term "knowledge worker" to describe someone with a portable job. Many real estate developers are counting on these knowledge workers to populate towns that, like Celebration, are far from major cities and the traditional job base they provide. With access to computers and other technology, a surprisingly large number of jobs can be handled from a well-equipped home office. We knew several landscape architects, for example, who worked out of their homes, occasionally visiting sites in person but handling most of the work on the computer through sophisticated design software.

Plenty of people, however, traveled to jobs outside Celebration. A handful of Disney executives and a larger number of middle- and lower-level Disney employees lived in town and drove the few miles to Disney World. Some people, like our neighbor Alice Joossens, vice principal of a high school, and Steve Saker, an investment adviser, drove into Orlando, and a few people commuted as far as Tampa. There were sales representatives, clerical workers, doctors, dentists, and nurses who lived here and worked for businesses outside the town.

Some people had been creative in arranging their jobs to allow them to live in Celebration. For instance, our friend Bob Carson was a partner in a start-up company that sold computerized medical-imaging machines to physicians and hospitals. The business had started in Massachusetts, but Carson convinced his partners that he could handle his part, sales, from Celebration because of the proximity of Orlando International Airport, which was thirty minutes away. He liked the arrangement so much that he was trying to convince two partners to move there, too. David Sheppard ran a prosperous electrical contracting business in Tampa but had done considerable work in the Orlando area for years. When he and his wife, Susan, decided to move to Celebration, he simply switched the company's headquarters to a nearby office complex and ran the operation from there.

A fair number of the people who moved to Celebration in the first wave were early retirees, who were leaving the workplace younger, healthier, and wealthier than ever, and baby boomers, who were starting second careers. Demographers have pointed out that most boomers are so job oriented, not to mention free spending, that they will not retire but will retread. So, many of them are looking for new careers that allow them to start small businesses out of their homes or pursue other vocations that keep them closer to home. Both groups are making places that once seemed out of the way more attractive than ever.

Celebration attempted to cater to people working at home and to those looking for second careers. The developers promised that every household would be wired for the fastest access available to the Internet. And they stressed the health and fitness center, a cornerstone that would appeal to both boomers and early retirees.

The fitness center, a state-of-the-art facility covering three floors at the hospital, was an immediate success. At a public meeting in February 1998, Des Cummings, chief executive of Celebration Health, the operator of the hospital and fitness center, said that 50 percent of the town's residents had signed up for memberships since the fitness center opened the previous November. In the average community, he said, 10 percent of the residents belong to a fitness center.

As longtime gym rats, we were both surprised to see so many older people working out regularly at the fitness center. Men and women in their seventies and eighties were lifting light weights, walking on treadmills, taking aerobics classes, and pursuing other activities with vigor and regularity. "A ninety-one-year-old woman came in last week and asked for a fitness center membership," said Cummings.

Not everything worked out. The fiber optics were a year late, leaving the techies among us without the promised fast connections to the Internet for many months. And not everything worked out for everyone who was giving working at home a try.

Often a light was on late at night in Jere Batten's home office across the street from us. One of the perils of working at home is that you never escape work. We both knew how easy it was to slip behind your desk and put in a couple of extra hours. But Batten was not dissatisfied because he worked too much. He was working as a consultant, designing computer software for a pharmaceutical company back in Pennsylvania, and he missed the camaraderie of the water cooler.

"I never looked at this consulting job as a long-term thing," he explained one evening as we sat on his porch. "I figured it would tide me over until I found something down here. I miss the social contact of working in an office."

Jere's wife, Earlene, had been promoted at Disney, making a big leap from desk clerk at the Port Orleans Hotel to a job as an informational specialist in the computer-programming department. She was much happier, and making better money, too. One day she had brought home a posting from the Disney bulletin board. It called for a supervisor in the software design department.

"Look," she said, handing the printout to Jere. "This fits you. But you know they're slow, and they don't hire from the outside much."

They talked it over. Batten decided he had nothing to lose by applying. So he went for a series of interviews, including a personality profile. As he rocked on the porch, he laughed about the personality test. "If I don't get the job, it will be because of that," he said. "I don't think I fit the Disney profile."

Though generally soft-spoken and calm, Batten was blunt when it came to work. He had been a consultant because he never hesitated to let the executives who employed him know when he felt things were not operating as efficiently as possible. And, while he missed the office atmosphere, he had grown accustomed to deciding when he worked and what he wore. Disney, on the other hand, is famous not only for the dress code that forbids facial hair but for the buttoned-down tone of its operations, whether on the front line at the theme parks or behind the scenes in the business office. The emphasis is on teamwork—getting along and never hurting anyone's feelings. We knew about it from a friend of ours, an executive in the company's retail division, who would regale us with hilarious stories about having to be nice to everyone and suffer through the endless meetings and brainstorming sessions that were integral to the culture there. But indeed, two weeks later, after another series of interviews, Batten got the job. He was pleased, particularly when they offered him more money than the posting had specified. Now the Battens, who had been drawn to Celebration because of their fondness for Disney, were both working for Team Disney, though working there was a lot different from vacationing there.

Social engineering through sticks and bricks is tricky. Some of Celebration's efforts to promote social interaction through design worked. The town center was usually filled with people. We saw more walkers and bike riders here than anyplace we have ever lived. The fitness center was a gathering place for several generations. We knew more people because of the proximity of the houses and their closeness to the street, even though the porch culture never materialized. It is simple to see that in neighborhoods where it is harder for people to interact, where houses are far back from the street and people routinely pull into the garage and slip into the house through the side door, getting to know your neighbors is harder, too.

"The way things are designed has an effect on how we flow together," said Nancy Songer, a researcher at the University of South Carolina's Institute for Families in Society. "When people interact, they have an investment in the community. Places that have front porches or people out on the street tend to have more casual interaction, which constitutes relationship building. It's easier to tell someone if their dog is barking and keeping you up at night if you know them."

No town can engineer away all of society's problems. Sometimes what goes on inside the four walls of a home cannot be solved outside those walls. Over the course of our first full year in Celebration, there was little crime. A few stolen bicycles, a set of porch furniture that went missing, tools taken from garages left open overnight. Nick's new Rollerblades disappeared from school one day, but they were returned a few days later after one of the teachers made a plea to the class. In a rare robbery, two men stole about $50,000 worth of rings from Chambers Jewelers downtown while an accomplice distracted the clerk. The Osceola County sheriff's deputies who patrolled the town, on bicycles as well as in cars, told us that their most frequent calls were security alarms that had been tripped accidentally.

The only crime against a person recorded by the sheriff's office in Celebration during the twelve months between July 1997 and June 1998 occurred on our street, though we learned of at least two that were not reported to police.

Domestic abuse is a huge problem everywhere in the United States. Statistics indicate that almost half the population will be touched by it at some point in their lives, although the Federal Bureau of Investigation estimates that only one in ten incidents is reported to the police. It cuts across economic, racial, and ethnic lines. No town, rich or poor, old or new, is immune.

Denise Larbig was executive director of Help Now, a shelter for victims of domestic abuse in Kissimmee, the Osceola County seat. The shelter was in a one-story building tucked in behind the post office. It was surrounded by an eight-foot chain-link fence, and the only way in or out was through a double set of doors monitored by shelter personnel twenty-four hours a day. Inside, there was a common area surrounded by a series of bedrooms and bathrooms for victims and their children. The outdoor playground, which also was within the confines of the fence, was furnished partly by volunteers from the Celebration Foundation. Joseph Judge, the owner of Celebration's bicycle shop, donated his time and parts to refurbish bikes that were given to the children at the shelter.

Lieutenant Patrice DeNike, head of the domestic violence unit of the Osceola County Sheriff's Department, said there were 1,100 domestic violence calls countywide in 1997, an increase of about 20 percent over the previous year and double the number of calls in 1995. Part of the increase, she said, was attributable to the sharp rise in population; part to the new willingness to report the crime in the wake of the death of Nicole Brown Simpson.

Statistics did not indicate that domestic abuse was any worse in central Florida than in the rest of the country, but Larbig said the transient nature of the population contributes to the steady flow of women and children through the shelter.

"A family comes from a different location, wanting to start life over in warm and sunny Florida," she said, reciting the familiar story. "They believe in pixie dust. The problem is the reality of a hospitality-based economy where jobs are to some extent seasonal and wages are notoriously low. If you are working in the hospitality industry and business slacks off, your job goes. The other part of the problem is that we don't have a tremendous amount of affordable housing and very little affordable day care," she continued. "What happens is that the stresses build up on the family until someone blows."

DeNike said new people can find Florida very isolating when they arrive. They have left behind their network of friends and family. "There are no grandparents or aunts or uncles," she said. "When things get stressful, there's nowhere to turn. I grew up on Long Island in the fifties and sixties. If there was a problem, you had your neighbors. They watched over us. You had family to help out when times got tough. When I first moved down here, it was the loneliest time of my life. I ended up moving back to Long Island. Then I came back when my family moved down."

The Help Now shelter's residents were mostly women and children from families with incomes below $12,000 a year. They were the people with nowhere else to turn, unlike middle- and upper-class victims, who tend to have the financial resources to go to a hotel or leave town. And those middle- and upper-class victims do not want the stigma of seeking refuge in a shelter. As a result, Larbig said, she had not had any residents from Celebration as guests. But she also said she had provided counseling for several women from Celebration. "Most of them we have seen on an outreach basis," she explained. "Or we've dealt with them over the phone. I would not say there is a substantial difference in Celebration's numbers compared to the rest of the county."

Patrick Wrisley had counseled numerous women in Celebration who found themselves in abusive situations at home. He said the problems were similar to those of other communities where he had lived and preached. One difference, however, was the added urgency of concealing the problem. No one wanted to break the perfect bubble.

One day in the spring, Wrisley heard about a woman who had been beaten by her husband. He did not know the woman or her family, but he wanted to see if he could help in any way. He asked Herrington if he could provide an introduction for him, but the town manager shook his head and said that Wrisley should "keep this thing quiet." By the time Wrisley dropped by the family's house later that night, it was empty. A neighbor said the family had packed its belongings into a rented truck and left in the space of a single day. About the same time, another woman and her child left for the West Coast after an ugly incident involving the woman's husband.

A third episode had occurred a short time earlier on our street. Rick and Cheryl Scherer left most of their family and friends behind in Buffalo when they moved to Celebration in search of a new life. They had the highest hopes of anyone we met in town, and they threw themselves into the life of the neighborhood, organizing the first two block parties and trying to get to know everyone. But there was no pixie dust.

Word spread around the neighborhood in early January. People had seen Rick Scherer arrive at the house in a police car. He had gone in with two policemen, emerged with a small bag in hand, and been tucked into the back of the car.

Cheryl told a couple of people they had gotten into an argument and she had been injured when she fell. A fuller story was told by the official police report on the incident, a publicly available document, which was based on statements taken from both Cheryl and Rick Scherer by an Osceola County sheriff's deputy the day after the incident.

According to the police report, the Scherers had gotten into an argument at about one in the morning. "Mrs. Scherer said when the arguing escalated, she attempted to end the argument by going to bed," said the report in the unemotional language of police documents everywhere. "Mrs. Scherer said Richard was unwilling to end the argument and demanded that Mrs. Scherer remain to finish their discussion. Mrs. Scherer said that she warned Richard she would call the police if the fighting continued and if Richard's temper became worse. Mrs. Scherer attempted to pass by Richard in the hall to go to her room. Mrs. Scherer said Richard forcefully blocked her way to her room by putting his hands on her shoulders. Mrs. Scherer said she then remembered hitting the crown of her head on the floor. Mrs. Scherer said she woke up on the hall floor at which time Richard was shaking her and calling her name."

The police were not called that night. The next evening Cheryl drove herself to the hospital in Kissimmee to have the injury to her head examined, according to the police report. While there, the hospital contacted the sheriff's office and a deputy came and took her statement. According to the police report, she asked that her husband not be told that she had spoken with the police until he was in custody, because she was afraid he might come back home and hurt her or the children.

When the deputy interviewed him, Rick Scherer acknowledged that he and his wife had argued, according to the report. It had begun over the simplest of matters—who was responsible for mowing the lawn. He told the police officer that he and his wife had argued and thrown things at each other in the past, but he said her fall this time was an accident that occurred when she rushed toward him.

As often happens, the argument over the lawn was connected with deeper unhappiness. Rick told the police he was angry because he believed his wife was seeing another person. Because of his anger and the fear of further violence, the sheriff's deputy who took Rick's statement arrested him and took him into custody. The charge was domestic violence. After being driven home to pick up some clothes, Rick remained in jail for ten days while he tried to raise bail money. Eventually, he was released on his own recognizance, and according to court records, he agreed to attend twenty-six weeks of counseling in lieu of a trial. He was forbidden to set foot in Celebration until completion of the counseling. He never did move back into the house on Nadina Place, although Cheryl and the kids remained there.

One question that arises is why none of the neighbors, including us, saw this coming, particularly on such a close-knit block. Part of the answer is that domestic abuse still occurs behind closed doors, out of sight from even the closest neighbors. And part of the answer is that domestic abuse remains a crime that causes people to avert their eyes, because it makes them uncomfortable. For weeks afterward, neighbors wondered whether there was something they could have done. Despite our proximity, we didn't know each other well enough to know there was a problem. Building a community takes more than porches and potluck suppers. It takes time.

As for us, it was still an open question about how long we would remain in Celebration, whether we would stay long enough to form lasting bonds. We liked many things about living there, particularly the neighborliness and informal lifestyle. One Sunday morning at church, Patrick Wrisley even announced that a bowling team was being formed. But there was an insularity in Celebration that was troubling, a sense that the problems of the real world, whether domestic violence or poverty, didn't intrude. There is a fine line between harmony and conformity, and too often we felt that the residents of Celebration had come down on the side of conformity. In a more vague way, the uniformity of the place got on our nerves. The pastel colors of the houses grew wearisome. We longed to see grass growing through a crack in a sidewalk, to get some sense of reality. A visit to Toronto in the spring brought a welcome dose of real world to all of us. The diversity of the population and the vibrancy of the street life were exciting, and the museums and galleries offered the sharpest contrasts imaginable to Celebration and Disney. We went for five days without seeing anyone in a Mickey Mouse shirt.

When we returned, the sameness of the people in Celebration seemed constricting. We had worked for years to make sure that our kids saw the larger world around them and that their friends came from different backgrounds, even in Westport. Celebration was too cocoon-like, too rounded and lacking in the sharp edges that keep you alert and instill vibrancy in life. "A place where everybody knows your name" may be great in a song about a bar, but it imposes limits on life.

On balance, we figured we would give it a while longer, just to see how things turned out, but we knew our days in Celebration were numbered because we like the road and were looking forward to discovering a new place. And because we like the edge, too.

13

An Epiphany

Midway through his second year in Celebration, Patrick Wrisley was in crisis. The congregation of Community Presbyterian Church was restless. They had expected ground to be broken for their new worship complex by the beginning of 1998, but the date had come and gone. Church members were still attending Sunday services at the AMC theater, where the chairs were comfortable but parishioners ran into popcorn-toting moviegoers if the service ran long. Even Disney executives were making subtle noises that the Presbyterians, who had won the right to build the first worship center ever on company property, really should put up a sanctuary, for the sake of appearances if nothing else.

The simple fact was that the national church's plan for an $11 million showcase on the prime two-acre site was too ambitious. The national office, the regional office in Orlando, and the local church had been unable to raise anything close to enough money to start construction. With a congregation of fewer than two hundred people, many of whom already were strapped financially by the move to Celebration, the local church was in no position to raise the remaining money. And Wrisley was feeling personally responsible as the days and weeks slipped by without breaking ground.

In many ways, the struggle to start a church in Celebration was a parable for the secular efforts to build a community in Celebration. At the start, there was a sense that outsiders, the national church and other Presbyterians around the country, would provide the money to finance the construction. In much the same way, some residents of the town expected Disney to provide salvation from their problems. Then came the discovery that outsiders were not willing to pay for Celebration's church, just as Disney could not make life perfect in the town. If there was going to be a church—or a community—the people living there would have to take responsibility for it themselves.

The Presbyterian church in Celebration had started from scratch, like the town itself. Wrisley had moved to town with his family in November 1996, and within eight months, he had developed a church with 150 members. In addition to the regular service, there was a Sunday school for children and adults, programs to reach out to help those in need in the larger community, and even a softball team. By all accounts, it was a very quick evolution.

Community Presbyterian was the first church that we had joined as a family. What started as an exercise in curiosity and an opportunity to expose our younger children to organized religion had turned into an important part of life in Celebration for the four of us. Not only did Becky and Nick learn to sit still for an hour once a week, but they saw that a church could have broader social functions in a community. Nick was responsible for gathering fifteen or so church members two nights every month to serve dinner at Give Kids the World, a nonprofit resort about ten miles from Celebration. Henri Landwirth, a local hotel owner, had opened the resort in 1989 as a place where families with terminally ill children could stay free and visit the area's theme parks without charge, and it depended heavily on volunteers for serving meals and helping guests in other ways. All four of us went at every opportunity, and it was a strong reminder not only of our good fortune but of the view we held of a church's role in society. There were other little ways church membership strengthened our sense of belonging, too. When Pat Wrisley heard that Cathy had taken a bad spill on her bicycle, he almost beat us to the hospital emergency room in Kissimmee (Celebration Hospital wasn't open yet) to check on her. Later he dropped off dinner at the house for the kids while Doug stayed with Cathy through the X rays and stitches.

The church was chartered officially by the Presbyterian General Assembly in a ceremony on September 21, 1997. In the days before, a handful of people had arrived with push mowers to mow the open field and to beat back the unruly palmettos with clippers and to pull weeds. Then a huge tent was erected on the vacant land where the church would one day stand, and more than three hundred people gathered to celebrate.

Listening to preachers in a tent in the South never figured in our plans. It was a far cry from the high Anglican services of Cathy's youth in Montreal, and pretty far removed from growing up Lutheran in Indiana, as Doug had. But we found the remarks of one of the ministers, Craig Barnes, senior pastor at the National Presbyterian Church in Washington, D.C., particularly meaningful. Describing the inclusiveness of the Presbyterian Church, he talked about "summery Christians," who bring a fiery faith to the church, and "wintery Christians," who have more questions than answers when it comes to religion. We fell distinctly into the latter category.

In the months that followed the chartering, the effort to raise money to build the church made little progress. Wrisley's numerous trips out of town to solicit the major donations that were expected to jump start the campaign were not particularly successful. The attitude seemed to be that people would like to see the church's own members make a strong financial commitment first.

As it happened, the preacher's office downtown overlooked those two empty acres. He could close his eyes and almost see the church buildings there. When he opened them he saw only a large wooden cross, weathering in the hot Florida sun. The view grew more nagging as the fund-raising drive foundered. He also could see, kitty-corner from the church site, one of the showcase model homes that had been built by Celebration Company. The model was stately and elegant, a two-story stucco home with four white columns in front and generous rooms inside.

One Friday morning as Wrisley was gazing out of his office window at the model home, he had an epiphany. With home sales moving to the

North Village, Celebration Company was selling the model. What if the church bought the house and turned it into a welcome center? There was room for group meetings and seminars, offices for the pastor and his assistant, even a granny flat over the garage for the two pastoral interns due to arrive in summer. While far from the sanctuary or meeting hall the church needed, the home might provide an interim solution and at least give parishioners a place to call their own.

"In my naïve excitement, thinking that this was indeed an epiphany, I called the Celebration Realty office to inquire about the status of the model home," Wrisley said. "Two problems emerged. First, it was seven hundred fifty thousand dollars. Second, it was sold. I was most disappointed and have been every time I drive by the house or look at it out my window."

Not long afterward, Wrisley was having breakfast with church member Larry Richardson, who mentioned that the house was for sale again. The first deal had fallen through. Rushing back to his office, Wrisley made a series of phone calls. He called the head of the church's office in Orlando and brought him up to speed, and he called David Pace, the head of residential real estate for Celebration Company.

"What do I need to do to slow down the sale of the house until I can see if I can raise the money to buy it?" Wrisley asked.

"You would need to put a contract on it," said Pace. "That would hold it for seven days."

At home that night, Wrisley explained the situation to his wife and daughters. He was excited about the prospect of the congregation's finally having a home, though he was worried about where the money would come from to buy the house and whether it could be raised in time.

"Do you think we can pull this off?" he asked Katie.

"You bet, Daddy, because the church is important, and I believe in God," replied Katie, with all the certainty a nine-year-old can muster. She got up from the table and hurried upstairs to her room. When she returned, she handed her father nineteen crumpled $1 bills, all the money she had been saving.

The next morning, Wrisley took his daughter's $19 to the Celebration Realty office and used it as the down payment on the $750,000 house. He also contacted the church elders, informing them of his bold step and explaining that they had seven days to raise the remainder of the 20 percent down payment. The elders, lay members of the congregation who help set policy for the church, were caught up in their preacher's enthusiasm.

The following Sunday, Wrisley described the plan and Katie's contribution during the regular service. There were few dry eyes in the congregation as he recounted his daughter's faith. Raising the money, he explained, would require almost everyone to contribute a substantial amount, and quickly. Larry Richardson and his wife, Margee, responded by walking to the front of the theater and pledging $5,000 toward the down payment. Wrisley told the congregation that they would vote the following Sunday on whether to proceed with the plan to buy the home.

On Tuesday, the church held a meeting at the house itself so members could see the space and the promise that it held. Some of those who attended were supportive, in large part because Wrisley's own enthusiasm was so infectious and he was so well regarded by his parishioners.

But concerns also arose. Some were practical. The $1 million donated by the national church could not be used for the model home. The best the congregation might be able to do was to raise $150,000 as a down payment. The resulting debt service on the mortgage would eat up a large portion of the church's income, requiring larger contributions from its members. That in turn could make it harder for the members to come up with additional money for a separate building fund.

Another concern was about the appearance of church offices in such a grand structure, especially since just weeks before, hundreds of homes in the county had been destroyed by a series of tornadoes. Some members worried that offices in the model home would only reinforce the perception that Celebration was an elitist community.

Like any good minister, Wrisley heard the murmurs of his flock. By the end of the week, he had become convinced that buying the house was not the right thing to do. His impulsive gesture would be withdrawn. On the Sunday in March when the vote was to be taken, he told the congregation that the contract had been canceled. The economics did not make sense, he explained. Katie's $19 would be put toward the overall building fund.

In an attempt to map a new strategy for the church, two half-day retreats were held at the Disney Institute. Leaders of the national and regional church offices met with community leaders from Celebration and several executives from Disney. All of the groups, including the Disney people, were seen as stakeholders in the church. Professional "facilitators" were brought in to lead the group through presentations, skits, and discussions aimed at discovering why there was no building and whether the church needed some dramatic changes to get one. At the start of the first day's session, the leaders stressed that the idea was to listen to the diversity of opinions, but some could not help pointing fingers.

"The tragedy is that this community has been built to this point without a Presbyterian church," said one of the participants. "Why? Because the congregation is not committed enough."

As the man continued to rail against the lack of leadership and the failure to make any real progress toward starting construction, the room fell into an embarrassed silence. Wrisley stared at the floor. Kathy Johnson, the director of the Celebration Foundation, looked at him, then muttered to Cathy, "No wonder Pat is worried about an ulcer."

Some of the Disney officials in the group argued for resurrecting the company's original idea of a small, traditional structure—like a two-hundred-seat New England church. Bob Bohl, an official with the national church, explained that churches must change in order to be viable and relevant in the coming century.

"The new buildings have to be flexible," he said. "We can't build churches like cathedrals anymore. We need multiuse facilities, moveable symbols. Those who build sanctuaries first have bad stewardship. The only people who will pay for traditional churches are older people. I call it an edifice complex. Today we need practical, flexible spaces."

In the weeks that followed, Wrisley and the church leaders faced some bitter realities. The plans for an $11 million, four-structure worship complex were too expensive a beginning. The church needed to scale back to something the parishioners and those outside Celebration who were willing to help them could afford. It needed to be, as Bohl had said, practical and flexible.

A committee was formed to come up with a less expensive design for the first building on the campus. It would be a meeting hall, which would be used for Sunday services and sessions during the week, and offered to nonreligious community organizations as well as the fledgling Jewish congregation. The committee decided on a budget of $3 million, with the first $500,000 to be raised from the local church members as a show of commitment. The remainder would come as matching funds from the national and Orlando offices of the church.

"We don't need to build a cathedral," Wrisley told the congregation in June. "We are to build a dynamic community church."

There was the real epiphany. By footing the bill and making the necessary sacrifices, the congregation would own the church itself. The process would be slower and more painful, but the result would be a church that grew out of the commitment and vision of its own members.

Other religious organizations were developing in Celebration, though they were in less of a rush to build a place of worship. "We are not worried about a building right now," said Brian Levine, a resident who was a leader of the Jewish organization that formed in town. "We are worried about building our congregation."

Levine, who is in his mid-twenties, arrived in Celebration in the first wave of residents. He came to build the computer network for the community, and once it was up and running, he stayed on as the "Web master," the technician who operates the town's intranet. He had participated in the slow and steady growth of the Jewish organization in Celebration, watching as membership grew from a handful to more than 150 by the middle of 1998 and teaching Hebrew and Judaism classes to the congregation's children. The congregation met on Friday nights at the restaurant at the golf course and, since it could not afford a rabbi, services were led most often by the children who were taking Hebrew classes.

Indeed, the religious groups in Celebration concentrated on involving young people in their activities. A group composed mostly of current and former Baptists, which met on Sundays in the school cafeteria, operated a popular Sunday night session for kids from the church and the town. From the descriptions given by our kids, who occasionally went with friends, it seemed to be a party with a dose of religion.

The leader of those Sunday evening youth group sessions was Scott Muri, a popular technology specialist at Celebration School. The son of a Baptist minister and a part-time youth minister since his college days at Wake Forest, Muri said he had started the youth program after conversations with several students at the school. "These were children with questions and no way to find the answers," he explained. "I knew there were answers out there. I wanted to make sure these kids have answers and a place to come together."

Catholics attend mass at three churches outside Celebration, but they have banded together to develop a Catholic education program in the town. The first year, about fifty children attended the classes to prepare for their first communion; the second year, the number rose to eighty.

In December 1997, the local Catholics began to plan their first mass in Celebration. They consulted a number of priests outside the community and did the research that they thought was necessary to make the service authentic and acceptable. Three days before it was scheduled to take place, the organizers received a telephone call from the diocese of Orlando. The bishop, Reverend Norbert M. Dorsey, had heard about their plans, and he forbade them to conduct the mass. Four families that had been involved in the organization were granted time to plead their case to Dorsey. "I find it very frustrating that if you wanted to get together and worship, you couldn't," said Deborah Jones, one of those who met with the bishop. In the end, the bishop relented, and the service was held. The organizers didn't know how many people to expect, perhaps fifty or sixty, because the Sunday morning was unusually cold. Instead, more than two hundred people turned out. As the next step, the Catholics hope to open a "mission," or informal church, in Celebration under the sponsorship of a Catholic church in Kissimmee, the nearest town.

As in many communities, the religious organizations were the primary source of outreach efforts from Celebration to the surrounding community. The Celebration Foundation, Disney's creation, also organized some volunteer efforts and helped fill the need for those who were not religious. When tornadoes swept through the area in early February 1998, and again when wildfires scorched the eastern portion of the state in June of that year, both the foundation and the congregations collected funds for relief efforts and provided volunteers.

At the Presbyterian church, there also was a regular program of assisting community organizations outside Celebration. The first Sunday of every month, Wrisley parked his red Toyota truck in front of the AMC theater, and congregation members filled its bed with food and clothing to be delivered to an organization in Kissimmee that helped low-income families. The church contributed money and volunteers to Habitat for Humanity, which builds houses for low-income people across the country and had built two in Osceola County in 1997. And Nick, of course, organized the volunteer program with Give Kids the World.

In much the same way the religious organizations sprouted at the grassroots level, we watched the community beginning to forge its own bonds and shape the future of Celebration, independent of the events staged by Disney. Some of those ties were strictly personal, the natural result of friendships that cannot be orchestrated or engineered. Others grew out of long meetings of the PTSA and other community organizations in which people sought to put their stamp on the town and resolve its problems through cooperation. Sometimes these meetings were contentious. More and more often, there was understanding and common ground. And some of the relationships among neighbors were forged on the two baseball fields behind Celebration School.

The district school board would not allow education funds to be used to pay for uniforms for athletic teams. Various fund-raising efforts were employed in Celebration to buy the uniforms. Amy and Matt McMahan, two students at the school, contributed $1,000 to the fund by selling soda pop and bottled water out of a wagon each Saturday at the farmers market. The PTSA set up a booster club to raise money. And Bill and Patty LeBlanc, the parents of two girls at the school, decided to organize a community-wide softball tournament, with proceeds going to the uniform fund. The progress toward community would be an unforeseen side benefit.

The plan was to organize as many individual teams as possible and charge each team a $100 entry fee, which would be used to buy the school uniforms. The equation was simple—the more teams, the more money. The goal was twenty teams and $2,000, and the tournament was scheduled for all day on Saturday, May 30.

Bill had helped Nick with his town survey, so we were familiar with his compulsion when it came to details. For weeks before tournament day, he haunted every public meeting in Celebration, from school functions to neighborhood block parties. Wearing his trademark running shorts and T-shirt and carrying a clipboard, he tried to sign up every ambulatory person in Celebration.

Most of the teams were organized by street or neighborhood. We agreed to sponsor a team from Nadina Place, called the Bookworms in recognition of the book we were writing. Our recruiting effort got off to a good start when a guy who lived behind us on Canne Place agreed to play for us; he had been a semiprofessional baseball player. We were miffed when Mike and Becky Prevost started a Canne Place team and raided our roster for our best prospect.

A week before the tournament, the LeBlancs hosted an organizational meeting for team managers. Bill had fallen a little short of the goal, mustering only fifteen teams. At the meeting, he tried to recruit enough people for a couple more squads. He asked whether a particular resident who had been outspoken in criticizing the school in *The New York Times Magazine* article the previous December had joined a team yet.

"Oh, no," piped up one of the team managers, with a laugh. "He's playing by himself."

In the end, sixteen teams were fielded and more than 150 Celebration residents signed up to play. Some of them had never picked up a baseball glove before. Many of them had not played for years. A few were nearly infirm. But everyone came out to have fun with their neighbors and raise money for the school teams. Stands were set up to sell hot dogs and sodas, and masseuses from Celebration Health were on hand to provide much-needed back rubs.

The first games started at eight-thirty in the morning. On one of the fields, the Bookworms played the Celebrators, the organization for the town's senior citizens. For a while it was touch and go. Lexi McKently, our center fielder, kept having to walk to the fence to reassure her youngest child that everything was okay, and the old folks proved to be more spry and formidable than expected. It turned out that they had actually practiced several times. Thank heaven, we beat the geezers behind the no-walk pitching of Dick Joossens, who had persuaded his wife to give up a weekend at the beach so he could play. For the record, we won the next round and then were creamed in the semifinals by the folks from Canne Place, who had stolen our best player. The loss turned out to be a blessing, because the Canne Place team faced the Osceola County Sheriff's Department in the finals.

Doug, who had confronted countless red-faced parents while umpiring Little League games in Westport, and Pat Wrisley were the umpires for the championship game. The sheriff's deputies had crushed every opponent all day long, and the outcome of the championship was apparent during batting practice: The women on the sheriff's team lugged their own bat bags and walloped the ball farther than any man on Canne Place. The final score was 16–6, a respectable outing for the Celebration team. Any sorrows were drowned in the keg of beer that Bill LeBlanc had stashed in the trunk of his aging Buick in the alley behind our house.

Aside from Garry Stephens's sprained ankle and the bruised egos of a few middle-aged jocks who found their athletic days were behind them, the tournament was a roaring success. We had lived in Celebration for ten months and could not remember having so much fun with our neighbors, or meeting so many new people. There were no Disney show tunes and no brass band. Just neighbors getting together to share a day and raise money for a worthy cause. Even though his aching bones had to be dragged out of bed by his wife on Sunday, Joossens said he was looking forward to next year.

The coffee group at Barnie's had a couple sore participants the following week. Cathy had played on our team, and because of the shortage of women, she had been cajoled into also playing on other teams. All told, she played six games and paid the price for several days afterward. Marguerite Saker had played, too, and she was nursing aching thighs. But the overall verdict of the group was a thumbs-up.

The composition of the coffee group had changed in recent weeks. The biggest reason was the departure of Niki Bryan from Celebration. On the last day of school, the Bryans had packed up their furniture and moved back to the big house on the lake in Orlando's College Park neighborhood. Niki promised that they would return. The sale of the Orlando house had fallen through, and the move was necessary so they could spend the summer cleaning it up to put it back on the market. Meanwhile, they sublet the town house they had been leasing and continued with plans to build a $1 million house on the golf course in the North Village.

Bets were taken. The odds were running three to one that the Bryans would never return. When they left behind the glittering social life of Orlando, Celebration had been something of an experiment for

Niki. In Celebration, she had been a big fish, but the pond proved too small. And her husband, Paul, had never been comfortable with the casual atmosphere of the place, or with his long commute to his real estate development office in Orlando.

A couple of weeks after the Bryans left town, Niki called Cathy with the big news. LaSalle Partners, the real estate management firm where Paul headed a subsidiary, had persuaded him to move to Chicago. The company would buy their house in Orlando, the contract on the Celebration property would be canceled, and they would not be coming back. All that remained to be resolved was whether those who had bet against their return could collect their winnings. The contingent that had expected them to come back protested that the move to Chicago constituted outside interference and nullified the wager.

Joseph Judge, the bike-shop owner and part-time member of the coffee group, was invited to join on a full-time basis. Discussions had often veered into national politics, although President Clinton's antics were declared off-limits. But in the spring, the talk had turned to local politics because a Celebration resident was running for the Osceola County School Board. The group's members agreed that it was a good idea for someone from the community to get involved with the larger world outside town, and they liked the idea that Celebration might have a voice on the school board, which was often openly antagonistic toward the town.

But there was some skepticism about the candidate, Jackson Mumey. The group worried about Mumey's potential conflicts in running for the school board while he was consulting for the company and selling a service that schools might buy.

On the other hand, everyone in the group liked him personally and admired his pluck. Mumey had announced his candidacy as an independent in the partisan election, which meant that he needed 2,300 signatures of registered voters in order to get on the ballot in the fall. It seemed a quixotic adventure, given the small size of Celebration and Mumey's lack of name recognition outside the town. The early line at Barnie's was that he would not gather enough signatures.

Mumey had no choice but to go the independent route. He could not have won the backing of the Republicans or the Democrats. The county's political leaders, like many of its other longtime residents, tended to regard the people who lived in Celebration as elitists with little genuine interest in the county beyond the plastic fence that surrounded their town. So Mumey would have to run a real grassroots campaign across the entire county. But first, he needed a solid base of support within Celebration. We were invited to one of his early organizational meetings at the home of Ken and Patty Liles. (Of the eight people who came to listen to the candidate, two of them could not vote: Cathy and Cath Conneely, of course.)

Mumey said all the right things. He wanted to set policies that allowed more freedom for teachers and decentralized management of the schools. He would donate the $25,000 annual salary to a school fund. He wanted Celebration to have a voice on the board, although he said he would not represent Celebration alone. Though we did not ask, Mumey addressed the conflict issues, saying he would resign from his Disney job if elected and that he would not deal with any schools in the county on behalf of his test-preparation service.

Neither of us had ever attended a political meeting before, except as reporters. It was not that we were apathetic, but our jobs required us to keep a safe distance, even from local politics. Plus, as a Canadian, Cathy could not vote anyway. Nonetheless, we were intrigued enough by the fledgling political movement and by Mumey himself to host a similar gathering for him two weeks later at our house, and we kept track of his signature drive over the coming months.

From her position in county politics, Mary Jane Arrington saw Mumey's candidacy as a positive sign for the town, and she hoped it might finally mark Celebration's emergence from its isolation. "I thought there would be this great influx from Celebration of people who really wanted to get involved in the greater community and make the whole county better," Arrington said one afternoon in her office in Kissimmee. "I thought there would be numerous people who wanted to serve on government boards. I called Kathy Johnson at the Celebration Foundation and told her I'd really like to see some volunteers on county advisory boards. No one came."

From her vantage point, Johnson thought it would take time for Celebration residents to ease their way into the institutional structure of the county. She liked to be asked for names of residents for boards and other positions, and she had recommended a couple of people, but she did not want to appear pushy. "We want to make real contributions, but that takes time," she said. "So we are slowly integrating members of our community into the human services, mental health, and school arenas of the county."

Still, like many from outside the town, Arrington had come to the conclusion that Celebration residents preferred to remain inside the capsule of their community. We had heard similar comments from others. We met Drew Payne, a lifelong Osceola County resident, when he built some bookshelves in the office of our home. He was a colorful and likable fellow who often dropped by at the end of his day to chat over a beer and a sandwich. He had a degree in architecture from Florida State University, but he preferred to work with his hands as a carpenter and cabinetmaker. We learned a great deal from his meditations on the architecture and construction of Celebration. He showed us how the porches in town weren't deep enough to provide real shade like the ones on the indigenous houses around the county. When we saw workers tearing the second-story porches off a dozen or more houses around town, Payne explained that the porches had been built without enough of a tilt away from the house, so they were shedding water back into the houses. They had to be rebuilt so they were angled slightly, but just enough, away from the houses.

We also learned that Payne went to a Vietnamese acupuncturist in a one-room office in Kissimmee who stuck flaming needles in his aching muscles and joints for relief. He told us where to look for big alligators, and we listened patiently as he recounted his efforts to woo a young woman, shaking our heads as he expressed his disbelief that she did not consider fishing a romantic date. He brought us photographs of his finest carpentry, and we marveled at its intricacy and craftsmanship. With care and precision, he had built another bookcase for us in the family room.

Payne loved to describe his boyhood fishing and hunting expeditions, and he mourned the passing of so much of the county's wilderness and the clogging of its roads with tourists. And he was gloomy about the prospects of Celebration and its residents ever appreciating the region in which we lived.

"Nobody here seems to care what exists outside the town," he said one afternoon near the end of an hour-long visit with Cathy. "It would be nice if people came here at least partly because of what Florida has to offer and because of the richness of nature here."

But Arrington saw a glimmer of hope in Mumey's candidacy. Maybe he was the first chick to break the eggshell and venture out into the larger world. She marched with him in Celebration's Fourth of July parade. And she offered him some advice. "You're going to have to get outside the bubble of Celebration, because you're running county-wide," she told him. "Your name has to be as recognized in St. Cloud as it is in Celebration. You are going to have to leave the warmth of your community and go out there."

So he had, though we shuddered to think of the impression he made in his red BMW roadster when he arrived at a community meeting in rural Narcoosee or down around Alligator Lake.

Jere Batten began helping in the endless quest for ballot signatures. It was, Batten said to us one evening, his first foray into politics, and he was having fun. Often he traveled with Mumey to one meeting or another, passing out signature cards while the candidate made his pitch.

"Who drives when you go out together?" we asked.

Batten laughed and said, "I do, in my old van. I thought it was a good idea."

Sometimes Mumey canvassed door to door, which exposed mild-mannered Batten to some interesting parts of the county. "We were in a rough neighborhood in St. Cloud," he remembered. "I was nervous every time I knocked on a door. I walked up to one house and the sign on the door said 'Mad Dog. Big Shotgun.' I just turned around and walked right away."

Another time he found himself hijacked into an hour-long conversation about America with an elderly man who had emigrated from Poland decades ago. Finally, after admiring his garden and photographs and listening to his life story, Batten got the old man to sign a ballot card and escaped. The next day, when he matched the card against the list of the county's registered voters, Batten discovered that the man was not registered. So he drove back to the house and listened for another hour to get a signed voter registration card, too.

In early July, a week before the deadline for submitting signatures, Mumey and his wife, Sara, held a victory party at their house. Before a standing-room-only crowd, he announced that they had gotten more than the required signatures and they had been validated. He would be on the ballot in November. Celebration had its first legitimate political candidate.

One day shortly before the election, after Mumey had spent part of the day waving a political sign on Highway 192 outside of town, he reflected on what he thought his candidacy had accomplished for the community. "What is most important, regardless of how I fare in the election, is that Celebration is on the map," he said. "We are part of the political landscape. There will be more candidates running for political office soon, and we opened those gates. Celebration will be perceived as a community that cares, and not an insular one, despite its reputation."

A single candidate for school board did not break down the isolationist attitudes that many people brought to Celebration. Nor did the struggle to build a church or raise money with a softball tournament transform neighbors into comrades. You can be sure, however, that a vibrant community cannot be pieced together without these individual moments. And there were other signs that Celebration was beginning to break out of its Disney shell and assert its independence.

14

Civil Wars

The call came through to the house just as the six-thirty national news on NBC was drawing to an end. Cathy was in the backyard visiting with Donna McGrath. Nick and Becky were playing a game on the computer. Doug answered the phone. Scott Biehler was on the line. His voice was hushed, almost conspiratorial. He explained that he and Becky, his wife, were organizing a meeting of parents who were concerned about the school. Only a few people were being invited, because they did not want word to get out to the town at large. "We're going to have the meeting on Thursday night at the Radisson Hotel across One Ninety-two," Scott said. "No one was willing to have it in their home. They were afraid of repercussions."

Repercussions? It smacked of some mild form of paranoia. We were aware of the "Positive Parent" wars from eighteen months before. We knew from personal experience about the sensitivity to criticism exhibited in some quarters of the town. We also had listened to Dot Davis and others condemn the critics of the school as a vocal minority, and we had seen the attempts to marginalize their concerns and the people who gave voice to them. But being afraid to hold a meeting in your home to talk about school problems struck us as an overreaction.

We knew the Biehlers from the informal monthly lunches they held at Lakeside Park for neighbors and some of the downtown workers and because Cathy had interviewed Scott for this book. In some ways, their story was typical of many we had heard over the past year. Disney World was Becky's favorite place. When they lived in Massachusetts and later in the small town of Waterville Valley, New Hampshire, Scott was always planning vacations in the Caribbean or some other exotic resort, but Becky resisted. "Instead of going to Hawaii, we'll just stay at the Polynesian Resort at Disney World," Becky would tell him. Or she would say, "Instead of going to Mexico, we'll just go to the Mexican pavilion at Epcot."

In April 1996, Becky and Seth, their son, had left Scott behind and were at Disney World on vacation. Becky had been reading about Celebration for months, so she drove over to look at the town under construction. When she showed up at the preview center, she asked about the availability of apartments. Too bad, she was told, they all were leased and there was a long waiting list. Then another sales agent came into the room. Someone had just telephoned and backed out of a lease. If Becky wanted the apartment, she could have it if she signed the lease on the spot. She signed.

Becky could not wait to tell Scott how much she loved the place and what she had done. She called him in New Hampshire that night.

"I just rented an apartment in Celebration," she said.

"That's cool," he replied. "That's wild."

Becky worked as an events planner for Waterville Valley and figured that she would have no trouble finding a job. Scott is a paraplegic and on long-term disability as a result of a motorcycle accident several years ago. In New Hampshire, he was trapped in the house by ice and snow several months a year. The sudden idea of living in a place where he could get around in his wheelchair twelve months of the year was very appealing. As a clincher, Seth was completing eighth grade and he would have to travel a long distance by bus to the high school in the fall. In this new town, he would be able to walk to school. Three months later, the Biehlers moved into an apartment. They were among the first one hundred or so residents of Celebration.

Scott had told Cathy about encountering Michael Eisner at Founder's Day in November 1996. He said he saw Eisner come out of one of the buildings downtown by himself, so he wheeled over in his chair and introduced himself.

"Hi, I'm Scott Biehler," he said, sticking out his hand.

Eisner shook it and chatted with him amiably about the town. Biehler explained that their family had been among the first residents, and he said he liked the town.

"Where are you from?" asked Eisner.

"New Hampshire," replied Biehler.

"I didn't think Celebration was open to anyone but Florida residents," said Eisner.

"Well, I live in the apartments."

Eisner looked at him quizzically. "There are apartments here?" he asked.

From the start, the school had been a disappointment to the Biehlers. The first year, the students were crowded into the teaching academy. The teachers were inexperienced, the learning methods were new to students and teachers alike, and the promised technology was as illusory as a snowy day at the Magic Kingdom. The Biehlers bided their time, however, hoping for improvement in the second year, when the students moved into the new building.

"The second year was going to be great," Scott had told Cathy in the interview. "Lots of computers, lots of teachers, a regular facility, a brand-new principal. But we've been through the second year now, and it's the same story, only with more teachers and students."

The Biehlers were sophisticated enough to have realistic expectations. From the start, they had anticipated and looked forward to a different way of learning for their son. What left them angry and confused was the failure to implement the new vision, not the absence of traditional methods.

Biehler was not a complainer. He had spent hours working as a volunteer at the school, helping to set up computers and working with students and teachers alike on various technology issues. He watched in frustration as teachers fumbled with computers that they could barely turn on, let alone master as an educational tool.

"You know what a teacher at Celebration School says when they can't work the computer?" he asked Cathy. "Go find a student to help you."

Among his concerns: The long-promised electronic portfolios that were supposed to allow parents to examine their children's progress from the comfort of their home computer had never materialized. The software existed at the school, and many kids did most of their work on classroom computers. But the classroom computers were not accessible from home computers for a host of reasons—from security to the need to design new software.

Throughout the last weeks of that second school year, the Biehlers talked almost nightly during dinner about whether to leave Celebration. They loved the town and still believed in the potential of the school, but Seth was finishing tenth grade in a school that Scott and Becky believed was too adrift to prepare him properly for college—or even provide the grade point average he needed to apply to most universities and colleges.

The meeting that the Biehlers arranged for the evening of June 25 was a last-ditch attempt to find a way to force the school to respond to the concerns of the parents. As it happened, many others were just as desperate for change. By word of mouth, news of the meeting had circulated around town. It had obviously tapped a deep well of anxiety. The conference room at the Radisson Hotel was jammed with nearly fifty parents, each of whom tossed five dollars into a grocery bag to pay for the room.

Some of those in attendance were veterans of the earlier school battles. There was Robert Cordingley, who had withdrawn his children from the school after the first year and remained a harsh critic of the program. And Janette Stone, the doctor's wife, who also had withdrawn her children. And Joseph Palacios, who had kept his daughter in school but complained bitterly and publicly. Others, like Tim and Beth McCarthy and Lisa Sublette, were on the fence, hoping for improvement but on the edge of giving up. They had come looking for a straw to grasp.

Larry Rosen, the Stetson University administrator who had helped develop the concepts behind the school and who lived in town, opened the meeting with an explanation of the original vision for the school. The failure, said Rosen, who stressed that he was speaking as the parent of a child at the school and not as a representative of Stetson, was that there had never been enough teachers or enough lead time to train those teachers in the "best practices." There were barely enough teachers, he said, to run a traditional school, let alone a progressive and innovative one.

Often in recent months, Celebration Company officials like Brent Herrington and even some teachers at the school had blamed the troubles on the failure of the school district to provide enough money to hire the number of teachers the school needed. But Rosen felt strongly that the school district had been made a scapegoat for the company's failure to fulfill its obligations. "I realize there has been a major PR effort to blame the school district," he said. "But Disney is a PR genius, and it simply isn't true. We always understood that the extra funding would come from Disney. It hasn't. I want you to understand that you are not likely to see that change, either."

Rosen's charge was difficult to pin down. In addition to the $8.5 million the company contributed to the design and construction of the school, it had established a fund of $5 million to pay for extras. The money was called enhancement funds, and it had been used to hire several new teachers midway through the last school year and to provide training for the school's teachers during the summer. But the school board had objected to a corporation's paying for improvements that elevated Celebration School above the rest of the county's schools, and the board had demanded that some of the money be contributed to a general school fund so that it could be parceled out equitably and as the board saw fit. Still, it seemed that the company had made a substantial financial commitment to the school and met it, at least for the most part.

Nonetheless, Rosen's accusation was a dose of reality for anyone in the room who still believed in pixie dust. But Rosen, as one of the people behind the underlying philosophy of the school, was not getting off the hook by blaming Disney. Palacios attacked the concept that multiage grouping can work when there is a six-year age difference among children in one classroom, as there was in our daughter's neighborhood. One woman argued that children couldn't be expected to teach themselves. Cordingley went for the jugular.

"We blame you, Larry Rosen, for all this," he said angrily. "You and Dot Davis." A few minutes later, he attacked Rosen again. "Larry, you are the cancer."

A year or so earlier, Cordingley's attack would have sparked a shouting match. People would have risen to their feet and defended Rosen. Others would have joined in the attack. Numerous school meetings had dissolved into chaos in the early months. But that night it seemed everyone was learning to agree to disagree.

To his credit, Rosen did not rise to the bait, and no one else entered the fray in such a personal manner. Almost everyone had come to look for solutions, not to engage in recriminations. Rosen said the group needed to find ways to persuade Disney to provide more money or the school would fail from financial starvation. Someone in the audience suggested a public protest. Disney executives were due in town in a few weeks for the inauguration of the Disney Cruise Line, and the parents could stage a sit-in. Someone else proposed a media stunt to embarrass the company—posting "For Sale" signs in front yards across town. The ideas died for lack of a second.

There seemed to be a realization that Disney either would not or could not solve this problem for Celebration, despite Rosen's contention. If the school were going to improve, it would take parents willing to step up and voice their concerns and work for their solutions. Like the Presbyterian congregation's realization that it would have to come up with the money for the church, the parents at the meeting recognized that the responsibility for the school was on their shoulders and the shoulders of the people running the institution.

The discussion turned to developing a list of concrete concerns to present to Davis and the faculty and to creating a unified front so that it would be clear this was not another attack from the margins. Calmly and methodically, the parents began to outline the problems—lack of technology training, no clear assessment of student progress, the absence of a curriculum, no preparation for the Scholastic Assessment Test.

Some of the revelations were a shock and raised questions about the academic integrity of the school. According to people at the meeting, some teachers were so overwhelmed that they were giving students credit for courses they had never taken and converting vague assessments into grades upon request. Nancy Lagerberg, a member of the School Advisory Council, had a daughter who graduated the year before. "My daughter had a whole list of fictitious classes for which she received fictitious grades," she said. Apparently, during her final year, Nancy's daughter had needed a credit in American history. Again and again she pointed it out to her teachers. Finally, with just weeks remaining in the year, a teacher handed her daughter John Steinbeck's *The*

Grapes of Wrath and a list of five questions. Her daughter was to read the book and answer the questions. When her end-of-the-year assessment was released and translated into letter grades for the university she wanted to attend, the young woman found that she had been given an A, not only in American history but also in government.

Kelly Wrisley said something similar had happened with her oldest daughter, Lauren. The Wrisleys were still considering withdrawing Lauren from the school, and Kelly had gone in a few days earlier to obtain Lauren's transcripts so they could be forwarded to the Christian school they were considering as one of the alternatives.

"There were courses on the transcript that she had not even taken, yet she had grades for them," said Kelly. "Like honors English. They were straight A's. She didn't do that kind of work. How will she get through school in the future? Won't this sort of thing hold back all of the children eventually?"

Questions raised at the meeting were troubling, and it was important to get answers quickly. The Wrisleys and many other families were on the brink of withdrawing their children unless concrete steps were taken to improve conditions by August 10, the start of the new school year. Out of this June meeting, a committee of six was appointed to formulate a list of demands and convey it to Davis. A follow-up meeting was scheduled for July 9.

In the week after the meeting at the Radisson, the six-member committee came up with a name for itself, the Concerned Parents of Celebration, and a list of thirty concerns. Some were specific suggestions, such as not combining eighth-graders with tenth-graders in a classroom and offering advanced placement and honors courses for high school students. Others were more general: requiring students to read more classics in literature and assigning homework. In demanding grades, class rankings, textbooks, and written tests, it seemed the parents were contradicting the core philosophy of the school.

The group decided to focus first on implementing changes for the juniors and seniors. The theory was that without grades, experience in taking tests, and preparation for the SATs, these students were going to have limited choices when it came to college.

The group met with Davis in her office and went over the list. It was, according to those who attended, a cordial and productive meeting.

294 / CELEBRATION, U.S.A.

Davis agreed that some alterations in the way the school was run were necessary. In fact, she told the group that planning had been under way since soon after classes ended in May to implement some of the changes sought by the parents.

By the night of the second meeting, on July 9, the atmosphere had changed markedly. From a group that had started out afraid to gather in anyone's house for fear of recriminations, the parents had turned into a formidable force within the community. In a demonstration of that new authority, the meeting was held in the school cafeteria, and more than 150 people turned out. Most were parents, but some were older residents who realized how closely the future of the town was aligned with the success of the school.

As they entered the cafeteria that Tuesday evening, parents encountered handwritten, poster-sized renditions of the primary parent concerns hanging from the walls. Jack Howard, who had been selected as the committee chairman, explained that the intention was not to alter the nature of the school but to fine-tune it in ways that provided a better and more practical education for the students. Unless the changes were implemented, he said, he felt compelled to transfer his son to another school for his junior and senior years.

On a screen at the front of the room, Biehler flashed the thirty concerns. Most were in black letters, but a dozen or so were in green. The ones in green, he said, were those that Davis had already agreed to address. Among them was a promise to separate eighth- and ninth-graders from the older students and another creating blocks of time each day for instruction in core subjects, like math and science.

Although the overall reaction at the meeting seemed positive, with many parents rising to applaud the changes, skepticism remained. Kathy Gross, a resident who had taught briefly at the school in its first year, challenged another parent who had defended the current regime's commitment to change.

"Things haven't changed," she shouted. "That's bull."

As in all wars, there had to be an enemy. Numerous parents rose to condemn an unnamed administrator and two teachers grouped together under the rubric of the "clique." Biehler issued a warning—if the clique defeated efforts to change the school, the parents would resort to other actions, like protesting during the upcoming inauguration of the cruise line or flying to Los Angeles to confront Disney executives.

The nucleus of the clique was composed of this administrator and the two teachers, all of whom had been involved in the original development of the school and who remained proponents of it. While they sometimes appeared unreceptive to the demands of parents, and on occasion even at odds with other personnel at the school, they were making an earnest effort to adhere to the initial principles, and singling out the clique smacked of creating a scapegoat. But from the tone of the parents at that session, it was apparent that the sails of the clique were going to have to be trimmed to mollify the concerned parents.

Another meeting was scheduled. In the meantime, the group's leaders would meet with Davis and other administrators to discuss the additional reforms they wanted. Some changes were necessary. We had spent enough time in the school, and at other schools, to see that the original concept for Celebration School was not working effectively for enough students. It was too easy for a lazy learner to get lost in the shuffle, too easy to do only enough work to get by. The lack of a written curriculum left parents unable to chart the educational progress of their children, and the absence of grades left many of the students themselves without incentive.

On the other hand, we did not want to see a return to the rote learning and rows of desks that some of these concerned parents were advocating. With refinements, concepts like multi-age groupings and self-directed learning programs could help children develop important skills. There had to be a middle ground, a way to keep the best of the original vision but temper it with some practical reforms. The only way the school could fail would be if the community abandoned it.

The long-term significance of the meeting that night was the evolution of Celebration itself. People who had criticized the school in the past had found themselves ostracized. The perception was that it was Disney's way or the highway, positive parents versus negative parents. As recently as two weeks earlier, no one had wanted to host the first meeting out of fear they would be identified as complainers who were somehow anti-Celebration. In a town where there was no self-governance and a corporation imposed an overlay of conformity, the early reaction to criticism had established a barrier to the free and open discourse on which real community depends.

This night marked a new direction. More than 150 people had come to a public meeting to give voice to honest concerns and to struggle to develop a joint approach to solving them. It was Celebration's version of a New England town meeting. In this post-neotraditional community, without any real ability to govern itself, democracy was at work. People were willing to speak out about their concerns and find a way to bring about change. The decision to live in Celebration, a voluntary one for the adults, was a vote for innovation and change. But the community was discovering that change had a price tag beyond the mortgage on their homes. It meant overcoming inertia; it meant taking a role in shaping their lives. It meant abandoning the comforting notion that Disney would take care of everything and, instead, assuming responsibility yourself. It meant taking the risk of speaking out.

Leaders emerged. Jack Howard was articulate and reasonable in advocating changes within the structure of the existing school. Scott Biehler kept the meeting focused on positive aspects of change and refused to let it dissolve into a shouting match or soliloquies from a handful of bombastic complainers.

The impact was visible two weeks later. Even more people filled the cafeteria for the third meeting. They occupied all the chairs and benches, and they lined the back wall and sides. This time, however, the concerned administrators replaced the concerned parents at the front of the room. Davis and her assistant principal, Ruth Christian, had come to explain the changes being implemented in the new school year. Unlike at the last meeting, there were teachers in the room, too, and Davis introduced them.

For an hour, Christian outlined the new steps being taken in the upper grades. The block study periods that students had used for work on individual projects were gone. In their place would be two eighty-five-minute core courses a day on math, science, history, and literature. There would be honors classes and advanced placement courses, and the curriculum would be provided to students and parents alike, in writing. SAT preparation would be an elective course for juniors and seniors. Each classroom would have textbooks, purchased with money from Celebration Company.

Although the school would continue to provide individual assessments of students, it would also provide a number evaluation for each course. Christian could not bring herself to call them grades, but she recognized what they were. "If you are comfortable in thinking of a four as an A and a three as a B, then think that way," she said.

The meeting ended on a positive note. Sonny Buoncervello, a local businessman and parent of a child at the school, praised the teachers and parents. "We can all be part of the same family," he said, to great applause.

The parents did not win on every point. And most of the changes that were being implemented were for the upper school only. The battle in the lower grades was still to be waged. But there was one other victory, in the minds of some parents. A few days after the meeting, Davis demoted the administrator and two teachers who had been staunch supporters of the original vision and who were considered part of the clique. In response, all three resigned from the school and sought jobs elsewhere. It was what the concerned parents had sought, but it was not popular with some of the teachers who remained. They had seen all three who left, particularly the administrator, as strong voices for maintaining the original vision of Celebration School, and the departures raised concerns about whether the pendulum was going to swing further in the direction of a traditional school. "I didn't come here because it was a school in a pretty town," one of the teachers who remained told Cathy after the departure of the clique. "I came because it was a school that promised to be different, and now I'm worried about the future of that promise."

We were surprised by Davis's attitude in the days after that public meeting. The discussions with the parents had been fairly amicable, and Davis had not given enough ground to be perceived as having lost. Yet she maintained to Cathy and others that the parents had not had any influence on her plans. Instead, she said, the changes had been in the works before the meetings. That August, midway through the second week of school, she even went on the local cable channel during what was billed as "an electronic town meeting" and repeated that everything the parents had sought had already been in the works.

Even the teachers with whom we discussed the issue were surprised by her attitude, saying they had been unaware any major changes were in the works. And none of them doubted the effectiveness of the concerted action by the parents, even the teachers who were unhappy with what they saw as a dilution of the school's founding philosophy.

We had gotten to know and like Dot and her husband, Jim. They were good neighbors and good people. The only explanation we could come up with for her refusal to concede that the parents had had any influence was that the battles of the previous year had so isolated her from the parents that she was unwilling to trust them or to acknowledge giving ground to them. Even if what she said was true, if all the changes were in the works already, what would it have hurt to give some credit to parents who had, in a reasonable and civil manner, raised legitimate concerns about the education of their children? Yet Davis held firm to her denial.

Her relationship with the parents in Celebration was in stark contrast to the one she'd had with parents at her former school in Huntsville. Earlier in the spring, a group of sixth- and seventh-graders from the Alabama school had come to perform at Disney World and in Celebration. They had been accompanied by a group of parents. In public appearances and private conversations, they were unanimous in their praise and affection for Davis. They described a warm and engaging person, someone for whom they would have done anything and whose departure had left them all saddened.

We listened to those parents and watched them and their children hug Davis. And we saw her face light up when she saw them. She knew each by name. It was clear that we had seen a far different Dot Davis, and that the previous year had taken a terrible toll on her.

The year had taken its toll elsewhere, too. Despite what appeared to be promising changes in the school, some families withdrew their children. The Wrisleys, after long debate, moved both Lauren and her sister, Katie, to a Christian school where their days would be more structured. Lisa and Tom Sublette enrolled their two children, Clint and Kaci, in formal home-schooling programs, although each would take some elective classes at the school. Kathy Gross, who had taught at the school during its first year but had become an outspoken critic, and her husband, Len, began home-schooling their two boys. Other families also moved their children, some to other public schools, some to private schools.

Others crossed their fingers and decided to give it one more try. Scott and Becky Biehler sent Seth back for his junior year, though their uncertainties led them to take out some insurance—they also enrolled him at a high school in New Hampshire in case things did not work out. As it turned out, the insurance policy was a good thing. On the second day of school, Seth was seen walking to class carrying a cup from McDonald's. Though high school students were permitted to leave campus for lunch if their parents had sent in an approval form, the slip that Scott and Becky had provided for Seth had not been notarized. Ruth Christian, who was in charge of discipline, meted out the punishment: The young man, who had no previous blemish on his record, lost his lunch-room privileges for forty-five school days, the entire remainder of the quarter.

His parents were angered by what they saw as an overreaction. They had no proof, but they suspected that the disciplinary action was in retaliation for their efforts in organizing the concerned parents earlier in the summer. Whether that was so or not, the Biehlers felt that they had paid a price for speaking out. There had been repercussions after all. But even more important to the Biehlers was that they found that the courses their son needed in his junior year—such as physical science—would not be available to him.

"We would never have moved to Florida when we did if we had known that the school would turn out the way it has," said Becky Biehler. "It's an issue of accountability. We had no way to make this decision about the move, except on Disney's word. But you get to the point where you don't want to waste any more energy fighting the negative aspects of this town. The rat is just too big."

The Biehlers withdrew their son from school, Becky and Seth packed their belongings, and the two of them returned to New Hampshire. There, Seth was enrolled immediately in the advanced placement and honors classes he had been unable to find at Celebration School. Scott stayed behind to wrap up some final details of their life in Celebration.

While some parents were engaged in a war with the school, there was a largely invisible battle under way over the fate of the teaching academy. Most people in town only noticed that something was awry at the academy earlier in June when a crew of painters had attached scaffolding to the front of the building and pried off the green letters that read "Celebration Teaching Academy." They painted over the ghosts of the letters, removing any trace of the name.

Disney had built the academy, and the original plan was for Stetson University to run it as a training facility for its students and three to four thousand teachers from across the country each year. The teachers would attend three-day programs on innovative teaching techniques and curriculum, then spend another two days watching those ideas in use at Celebration School. As part of its commitment to the school board to win approval for Celebration School, the company had promised to provide 1,550 training days a year to teachers from Osceola County.

Hundreds of thousands of dollars in state education grants had been provided to begin the training program. The Ford Foundation had provided $750,000 in seed money, and the National Education Association, the nation's largest teachers union, was so impressed that it had provided a $500,000 grant in early 1997.

"This academy will be for educators what a teaching hospital is for doctors—a place where teachers from around the nation can come to sharpen their skills and be exposed to the best practices," said Bob Chase, the union president, when he announced the grant at the National Press Club in Washington.

But the academy was stillborn, a victim of educational infighting, disagreements between Celebration Company and Stetson, and the problems that plagued Celebration School itself. Training was supposed to begin in July 1996, but the academy building was needed as the home for the school because the main building was not finished. And even when the new school opened in the fall of 1997 and the academy building became available, it stood empty for the 1997–98 school year because there was no curriculum and no staff to begin training teachers. Finally, in a formal acknowledgment of the failure to get the academy up and running on time, the contract between Celebration Company and the county was amended: The academy would open nearly two years later, in July 1998.

But as the new date approached, new troubles developed. Stetson wanted to emphasize the broader reach to the nation's teachers, but Celebration Company argued that the first priority had to be training teachers for the local school, where the need was evident. Another dispute arose over ownership of the rights to the curriculum material being developed for the academy. Celebration Company pointed to a clause in its contract with the school district that gave the Disney subsidiary sole rights to any products arising out of the academy. Stetson argued that the vision from the beginning had been to share the concepts with the larger education world.

In early June, a month before the academy was to open, Celebration Company and the school board entered into a new contract. Half the space in the Disney-owned building would be leased at a nominal fee to the district's administrative offices. Using the NEA funds and other grant money, Stetson would operate a scaled-down training facility in the remaining half without Disney. In addition, Stetson began to offer separate adult-education classes in the facility, fulfilling one of the early promises of Celebration to make lifelong learning part of the community. It was a small beginning, and the university planned to expand its offerings and even discussed building an arts center in the town. Once the new deal between Celebration Company and Stetson University was ratified, the workers pulled off the name.

If you had to pick the two most important factors in determining the quality of life for most families in Celebration, the choices would have been straightforward and simple. One was the education of the children. Following close behind was housing. The importance of housing to society at large is underscored by the fact that it accounts for about one-fourth of personal consumption expenditures. In Celebration, with its above-market prices, the spending level was probably closer to one-third.

But the housing was even more important in Celebration because it was such an integral expression of the community's image of itself. Your home was the most direct and constant level on which you experienced the community. People loved their houses. They were drawn to the town partly because of the reassuring, traditional designs. The proximity of the houses to one another, and to the center of town, contributed to making the town special. In short, the houses were the essential building blocks of Celebration's sense of place, the elusive fifth cornerstone of the community. So when people were unable to get repairs made, when roofs continued to leak and porches threatened to collapse, they had a hard time enjoying the rest of life in the town.

The fifty-five town houses across from the school and wrapping one end of Savannah Square, a lovely park a block from the school, had been plagued by delays and construction problems from the start. Even when people finally moved in, their relief was often shattered by the many difficulties, large and small, that remained. Porter and Sonia Metcalf and their children had moved into their town house months late, after having the floor redone three times and demanding that countless other problems be fixed, only to find water pouring in from a leaky roof the first time it rained.

Even before the Metcalfs moved in, the complaints from residents were so persistent and loud, including the threat of a lawsuit, that Celebration Company decided something had to be done. Acting in its capacity as the town's homeowners association, the company hired an architectural and engineering firm to conduct a thorough inspection of the town houses.

The firm, Tilden, Lobnitz & Cooper/MRI, inspected the first batch of town houses in late October 1997 and then returned to complete the inspection over three days in February 1998. What they found, according to a copy of the inspection report, were leaky roofs and crooked chimneys, improperly braced roof trusses and cracked stucco on the exteriors of many town houses, plywood sheeting that was coming apart, nails protruding through sheathing, and shingles and gutters that were installed improperly.

"It is our opinion that the majority of these items do not have an effect on the overall structural integrity of the buildings," the report concluded. "Items in this report that are structural in nature appear to be random and isolated. However, the substandard installation of a majority of the architectural finishes may contribute to further water damage and, in time, could jeopardize the structural integrity of each building."

The report confirmed that the complaints were neither isolated nor insubstantial, but it was not made public right away. Because the report was paid for through the homeowners association, Celebration Company had a responsibility to provide it to the residents, but Herrington stalled. He did not understand some of the assertions, he said, and he and other company officials even considered editing the document before releasing it.

He did, however, send an unabridged copy to Thomas Croson, who had been brought out of retirement by Town & Country to become its new Florida division president in an attempt to solve the company's problems in Celebration. Croson replied by letter in April that he objected to several issues raised by the inspection, including its overall conclusion that some of the work was substandard. "We strongly disagree with some of the generalities in the report, but we understand the intent," wrote Croson.

The builder agreed to repair some of the items, but it balked at repairing every roof. Most of them did not leak, and Town & Country objected to the assertions in the report that the work did not meet industry standards. Herrington and other Celebration Company officials pushed for a more sweeping resolution, including putting new roofs on all fifty-five town houses plus twenty others in another part of town. At about $5,000 per roof, the builder was facing substantial additional costs to fix this problem alone.

Mike Ryan, who had taken over the day-to-day operations of Town & Country, twice flew down from the company headquarters in Oak Brook, Illinois, to tour the town houses. By June, Ryan and the other Town & Country executives had decided to get the problems behind them once and for all. They hired a new Florida division president, Tim Kelly, and gave him the authority to fix everything within reason, including the roofs.

"We agreed to replace the roofs on the Townhomes," said Ryan. "I don't believe it was necessary. I think they could have been repaired, but as a good-faith effort and to repair our name in the marketplace, we agreed. It is not uncommon to go through an engineering report with a Townhome community association. It is uncommon to replace roofs."

Indeed, Ryan said that Town & Country had suffered some loss of prestige because of the problems in Celebration, and the company had decided quietly in the fall of 1997 to stop building new homes in the town. It returned the lots it had bought to Celebration Company and was staying on only to complete the houses under construction and resolve the repair questions. Bill Ryan Sr. had come out of retirement briefly to supervise the resolution in Celebration, and Bill Jr. had left the company to start his own business. When Tim Kelly was hired, he had been told to fix every house.

"We told Kelly that it might be a little bit overwhelming because you'll hear a bunch of different stories," recalled Mike Ryan. "We told him to address the problems one at a time."

Although he was a longtime Florida builder, Kelly was understandably nervous when he agreed to appear before a meeting of town-house residents to explain the company's plans and deal with questions. Emotions were running high among some families over what they viewed as shoddy construction, and there was a chance that the meeting would slip into recriminations and abuse. But Herrington felt strongly that the residents, whom he liked to call stakeholders, needed to hear what would be happening directly from Town & Country.

On the evening of June 23, about sixty residents gathered in the school cafeteria. The majority of them, in one degree or another, were unhappy with their town houses. Copies of the inspection report were available for perusal in binders along the back wall, and a few people looked at them, jotting notes on pieces of paper as they nodded in apparent agreement with the findings.

Herrington opened the meeting by introducing Kelly and appealing for an "appropriate" discussion. "Tim didn't create the problem, but he seems to want to help us solve the problem," said the town manager. "Beating this guy up isn't the way to go."

Before relinquishing the floor, Herrington explained the history of the inspection report. He said that just standing on the curb he could see problems with the town houses, so he had ordered the report. He confessed that he had considered editing the final document. "In the end, we realized if we changed a thing, a comma, a period, it would look like we jimmied the report," he said. "So we didn't change a thing. That is the original report."

Kelly looked stiff and formal in his white shirt and tie. He said he wanted to satisfy the owners so that they could get on with their lives and the company could get on with its business. "But it is not going to be my career," he said. "I am a young man and I am not going to spend the next twenty-five years here." The attempt at a joke fell flat. The attitude in the audience seemed to be that Kelly should sure as hell stay, even if it took twenty-five years.

Kelly decided to play it straight. He promised that the company would stand by its homes. Its representatives would knock on every door and develop a list of problems and fix them. He also acknowledged that the company had changed its opinion on the most serious problem, the roofs. Initially, he said, the builder planned to patch the roofs and do other spot repairs. Instead, he said, Town & Country had agreed to put a new roof on every town house, stripping off shingles and tar paper and, where necessary, the plywood sheeting.

The concession broke the ice. The audience applauded heartily. And they applauded again when Kelly said the company had hired a new roofing outfit to do the work. Kelly hastened to add, however, that he was not planning to rebuild houses from the ground up, and, he said, some criticisms in the inspection report went too far or ignored industry standards. But he tried to mollify the homeowners without appearing defensive, saying at one point: "I wish it was done right the first time. I can't roll back the clock."

Herrington did his best to be reassuring, too, promising that the same engineering firm would reinspect every house once the work was done. He remained unruffled when someone in the audience asked if Disney would send its engineers to review the final efforts. This was not, he explained, a Disney problem.

Bill Potts was aware, as he sat there, that most of the people seemed satisfied. It was a view he did not share. As a retired home builder himself, he had been appalled by the construction quality in his daughter's town house. As the presentation started to wind down, Potts could no longer restrain himself.

"Your company had such bad quality control that those houses should have been burned down before they let anyone move in," said Potts angrily as he stood in the audience. "I used to build houses for a living, and I've never seen anything in such bad shape. It seems to me that you've been taking advantage of these people because they had a dream. My daughter had a dream that life in Celebration was going to be perfect. It's not. And her health has suffered. I watched my daughter being destroyed by you people, and I can't stand it anymore. If I could take my daughter out of here, I would, but she still thinks it can be fixed."

He turned his ire on the Disney company. "They may be able to build an amusement park, but they can't build a town," said Potts, his voice rising and cracking as he turned and walked out the door, leaving behind a smattering of applause.

That would not be the last word, however. A woman stood and addressed Kelly. "You're headed in the right direction and it's commendable," she said. "There's no such thing as perfect. Everyone is here for the same reasons, to better their lives, and I'm personally proud to live in Celebration."

Whether living in Celebration should be cause for pride, the woman had a good insight. The town wasn't perfect; no place is. Those who had expected perfection were doomed to disappointment. Even Disney's planners didn't expect things to be perfect, as Joe Barnes, the young architect who had been involved in the town almost from the start, explained. The intention, said Barnes, was to build a good place for people to live by providing architecture and planning that promoted social interaction and a sense of community. "The more residents take over, making it their own town, the better," he said. "The more it becomes Celebration, rather than Disney's Celebration, the better it gets." Peter Rummell, who had the original vision for Celebration, put it another way: "In the end, as developers, I think all we do is decide that this is where the campsite is going to be, and provide the sleeping bags. Whether the camping trip is fun or not is really up to the campers."

15

Truman Didn't Sleep Here

One especially hot afternoon near the middle of August, Cathy was riding her bike back from the post office when a dark blue car with Pennsylvania license plates pulled up alongside her. The attractive woman who was driving rolled down the window and asked for directions. Before Cathy could respond, one of the four children in the car leaned across and said, "Can you tell me where Truman lives?"

"Pardon me?" asked Cathy, who suspected some kind of tourist joke.

"Truman? Didn't you see the movie?" asked the mother.

"Oh, that Truman," said Cathy, who had in fact seen the media satire *The Truman Show.* "He was just a character. It was all make-believe. And anyway, it wasn't filmed here. It was filmed over in Seaside, which is on the panhandle."

The mother and child were obviously disappointed, though Cathy could not figure out whether it was because they had the wrong town or because they had just learned Truman wasn't a real person. They drove off without saying thank you.

It was not the first time we had run into the misconception that the movie had been filmed in Celebration. Early in the summer, when *The Truman Show* was released in theaters, a surprising number of people assumed that the movie had been filmed where we lived. Friends from far away called and said they had seen our town in the movie. Even a few people who lived in Celebration were convinced that at least the downtown scenes had been shot in their hometown. It seemed to be a point of pride.

Perhaps the mistake could be excused. There were, after all, similarities between Celebration and the movie town called Seahaven. The world inhabited by Truman Burbank, the character played by Jim Carrey, had pretty houses and an orderly downtown. The sunrises were beautiful, and the weather was flawless. Everybody smiled placidly and waved and said hello. The only hitch, of course, was that nothing in Seahaven was real. Truman was the star of a twenty-four-hour-a-day television drama that had been on the air since his birth, thirty years earlier. Our favorite line was delivered by Ed Harris, who played Christoff, the show's creator; defending his town, he said: "It's not fake. It's just controlled."

The same might be said of Celebration. By the end of our year in Celebration, we had concluded that it was not fake, except for silly architectural idiosyncrasies like the dormers on many houses. It was genuine, without script or cue cards. It was, however, controlled by rules and regulations and the omnipresent guiding hand of the Disney Company through its surrogate, the Celebration Company.

Over the course of the year, our attitudes toward the rules had split along lines that would have been predictable to people who know us well. While Doug felt that people had understood the rules when they bought their houses and should accept them, Cathy had two concerns. On the practical side, she was annoyed by the inequality in enforcement of the rules. For instance, a fair number of people, including two on our street, had been allowed to buy houses that they did not intend to live in for months, even years, a clear violation of the regulations everyone signed. The result was gaps in neighborhoods, houses that sat empty, people who were not part of the community. Along those same lines, some people had been permitted to buy two lots, which had the same general impact.

Cathy's second concern was more philosophical. Restrictions can become coercive and can be used to stifle debate or dissent within a community. In the same way, the concept of good citizenship can be reduced to sterile definitions, such as keeping your grass cut to three and a half inches and paying community assessments promptly. Both sap the vitality of a community and impose conformity where diversity is necessary.

A healthy community voices diversity in so many different ways, big and small. Mike McDonough, who had an architect's eye for detail and order, brought that idea home in one of those over-the-fence conversations. Mike was particular. After watching him drape Spanish moss on the trees throughout his yard, we knew that. But when he was troubled by a neighbor who wasn't taking the same care with his home, he thought it would be helpful to give him a hand. Mike's housemate, Marty Treu, suggested otherwise.

"When each person maintains his home in a different way, it establishes more of an air of individuality to a neighborhood," said Treu. "Like a real town. One person edges his lawn, another doesn't. One person's front porch is messy, another's isn't. It's part of the excitement of living in a town, where you have different values side by side but you still get along."

The debate over community restrictions resonates beyond the borders of Celebration. Historically, people with similar beliefs and values have bonded together to create new towns in America. Those that survived evolved over time, reaching beyond the initial common interests to embrace a broader definition of community. Today's manifestation of that instinctive tribalism is the increasing number of communities banding together to form private governments and community associations to impose restrictions on anyone who wants to live in them. The majority of these enclaves are built for the middle and upper-middle classes, making them "privatopias" of privilege and exclusiveness and widening the gulf between the haves and the have-nots. In the narrow sense, these places fit the definition of community; like-minded people with common values and fears are using barricades to seal themselves off from the problems of the surrounding world. But in reality these places are often anticommunity cocoons. They breed isolation and conformity and promote the balkanization of America. Rather than a place where real-world problems are confronted and dealt with by diverse people in a well-defined public realm, the privatopia represents the same escapism and white flight that led to the suburbanization of the country.

Elements of these tendencies can be found in Celebration. The attempt to stifle debate over the school in the first year of the town's existence was a dramatic demonstration of the impulse toward conformity. You either loved everything about Celebration or kept quiet about it. Disney's decision not to build affordable housing or develop creative financing to open Celebration to low-income families reflected a narrow definition of who makes up a real town and underscored the elite nature of the town. The company's fear that the project would not be as popular with the middle class if it had room for poor people was probably accurate from a market standpoint, but a community is not just a commodity. The failure to include poor people in Celebration, and in neotraditional communities in general, is an act of separation and seclusion that contradicts the underlying philosophy of the town and reinforces the circular prophecy that the less we know about other people the more we will have to fear.

On the other hand, there were honest efforts on the part of the company and the residents to avoid creating an isolated enclave. The Celebration Foundation was a novel attempt to reach out to each other in times of need, both to those within the community and to those in the greater community outside the town, and to remind Celebration's residents that there were less fortunate people just beyond the borders. The foundation sponsored volunteer efforts to improve the shelter for battered women in nearby Kissimmee, regularly collected donations for various countywide social service programs, and organized volunteers when the tornadoes struck in early 1998. And when there was contact between the town and people from the outlying county, it seemed to go smoothly. The children bused to Celebration School from outside the town, who were much more diverse in terms of race and socio-economic status, were treated the same as the townies. That is what we heard from our own children, those children from outside Celebration, other parents inside and outside Celebration, and the teachers and administrators.

Architecture and planning also played a role in making Celebration more egalitarian. Because the houses looked basically alike and expensive homes were mixed in with apartments and less-expensive houses, people's homes were a sort of neutral ground, which helped to reduce the economic and social hierarchy. Unlike other subdivisions, where houses are segregated strictly by price, Celebration was laid out in a relatively democratic fashion. We have no way to prove it, but our theory is that this egalitarian planning contributed to the inclusiveness in the friendships made by our children at an age when many groups of youngsters form nasty little cliques based partly on how much money their parents earn.

We had learned over the course of our year in Celebration not to judge in advance of the facts; this applied most directly to keeping our assessment of the town independent from our feelings about Disney and its role in American culture. Most outside observers brought their intellectual baggage about Disney with them when they came to the town. It colored their view and obscured their ability to recognize where the corporation ends and the town begins.

A perfect example of this Disney-induced myopia is the contrasting treatments afforded by the press and planning establishment to Seaside and Celebration. For all the purity of its planning, its grid of narrow streets, and its emphasis on pedestrians over cars, Seaside remains a niche town. It will never be more than a beautiful resort for people wealthy enough to pay $700,000 and up for a second home.

Granted, Seaside played an important role in the resurrection of the small town as an ideal for planning. But there is little of a real year-round community there, and its scale is too small to represent a true test of the validity of neotraditionalism. In addition, despite the neotraditionalist rant against cars, you have to get in your car and leave Seaside to find a good-sized grocery, a hardware store, or a doctor. You can find a school in Seaside, but it is a charter school with an enrollment of thirty-six sixth-, seventh-, and eighth-graders. Despite these evident deficiencies, Seaside has remained a darling of the intelligentsia. Part of the reason is the maverick charm of its developer, Robert Davis, and the showmanship of its planners, Andres Duany and Elizabeth Plater-Zyberk, who carried their message and slide show to countless audiences across the country.

Celebration, on the other hand, is an experiment executed on a scale ambitious enough for a serious evaluation of whether some of these tenets of neotraditional planning can help resurrect the lost sense of community and place in America today. Yet Disney has found itself the victim of endless sniping from the neotraditional movement. At the fifth annual meeting of the Congress for the New Urbanism in Toronto, in May 1997, participants engaged in a heated debate over whether Celebration reflected the genuine values of the movement or an attempt to co-opt the appeal for marketing purposes. The skeptics could not see past the neat, almost theme-park look of the town to recognize that it does indeed represent a practical application of real-world values. Quibble over the details. Quarrel about the role of a corporation. But accept that Celebration is a serious effort that provides a more exacting test than Seaside, even if Truman did sleep there and not here.

Disney could have taken the safe route and developed another golf-course community on its property. Instead, the company did something truly innovative, banking on the public's even greater desire for community than for a golf course, and in the process, it tried to address a critical social ill by offering an alternative to fifty years of suburban growth that had been draining America of the sense of community and intimacy. The company went beyond merely employing some of the easiest neotraditional icons, like sidewalks and porches, and risked its brand name and used its savvy marketing ability to offer an alternative.

Even on the most superficial level, the town has made a valuable contribution by exposing a new design for living to the thousands of people who stop by to visit Celebration after going to Disney World. These people may go home and say, "Why do we need this huge yard? Can't we find a way to drive less and walk more? Is there an alternative to this subdivision? Why put the new school on the edge of town when it could be a centerpiece of the community, and within walking distance for students?"

On a more important level, Disney created a town where real people could come and live and test the alternative on a very public stage. Dreamers like Frank Lloyd Wright and Le Corbusier had only imagined their utopias. They counted on the power of their ideas to make up for the lack of resources, but, with the exception of the awful slums that now ring Paris in a perversion of Le Corbusier's vision, their concepts were not implemented. Disney, on the other hand, had made a contribution to the effort to create a new urban order, whether or not you liked it.

And we liked much of it. From a design and planning standpoint, Celebration marks the next step in the neotraditional movement. It represents the largely successful evolution into what Charles Fraser dubbed post-neotraditionalism. You *can* be isolated in Celebration, but unlike in traditional suburbs, you have to work at it. The design of the community, from the physical structure to the intangible attitudes of its residents, pushes people to confront life around them. It suggests mutual dependence in a country where planning has too often stressed independence. Celebration is human-sized and walkable. The front porches, though not entirely successful, and the closeness of houses to the sidewalk and street encourage us to look out on the world and to be part of the procession passing by. The average suburban household puts thirty thousand miles a year on its vehicles. In Celebration, we reduced our household from two cars to one and drove that one less than a thousand miles a month.

At various points in American history, the country has struggled to reinvent itself. It may be that we are at such a juncture now. Dissatisfaction with cities and suburbs is evident. Evident as well is the desire to build new communities by marrying some of the best of the old planning with new values and technology. Disney's vision for Celebration was limited; the company was not designing an inclusive model community but a new town and an alternative to the traditional suburb. Nonetheless, the lessons learned in Celebration can be instructive for anyone interested in an alternative place to live, from planners, developers, and architects to educators, businessmen, and potential residents, from those fleeing the suburbs to those trying to improve the cities.

All across the country, neotraditional towns have begun to spring up. In Fort Mill, South Carolina, and Newport Beach, California. Outside Scottsdale, Arizona, and bordering Sarasota, Florida. In Gaithersburg, Maryland, and DuPont, Washington. Many of them are replicas not of Seaside, with its resort feel and natural beauty, but of Celebration, which was carved out of pasture and swamp.

You don't even need a vacant swath of land. Concepts that work in Celebration can be adapted for redevelopment projects in existing cities and suburbs. Neighborhoods can become safer and more hospitable by resurrecting front porches and developing viable business centers. The act of sitting on your front porch and drinking lemonade or just walking makes a street safer. Such solutions may be too limited to affect the problems of urban areas, which are often much more difficult, ranging from racial tensions and deteriorating schools to economic anemia and inflexible bureaucracies. Still, places like Baltimore and Portland, Oregon, have demonstrated that city centers can be revitalized through careful planning, and some aspects of Celebration's example can be useful for cities and suburbs as well as new towns.

The report card on Celebration is not all A's and B's. Disney's desire to get the best return possible on its land was the driving force in building the town, and the company deserves to be criticized for the hype it generated and for the rapaciousness with which it sought to capitalize on the demand that it whipped up. To satisfy that demand, builders were pushed beyond their capabilities. Though Disney created an admirable wilderness preserve to offset the environmental impact of Celebration, the company largely ignored the natural environment within the town itself, adhering to the Disney philosophy that nature can be improved upon. And when the development executives with the original vision for Celebration, people like Peter Rummell and Todd Mansfield and Don Killoren, left the company, they were replaced by people with a sharper eye on the bottom line.

One businessman in town expressed concern about the absence of those initial dreamers. "A lot of what was done because of the vision is changing, and the company is looking at things from a bottom-line, business standpoint," said the businessman, who deals often with Disney and Celebration Company executives. "That is normal in any business, so I am not saying that doom and gloom are on the horizon. But there are serious internal changes that the company tried to keep quiet, and it makes me worry that this could turn into just another planned development, instead of remaining someplace special." As with many elements of Celebration's future, time will provide the judgment.

More complicated is the task of assessing responsibility for the outsized expectations that so many people brought to Celebration. The rhapsodizing literature and the inherent twinning of Disney's theme parks and its new town drew people with unrealistic dreams. Michael Eisner's hyped references to Celebration as the embodiment of Walt Disney's original dream of a real community at Epcot fueled the myth that living in Celebration would be the closest thing to living at Disney World. In the beginning, Celebration was a town where believing replaced knowing.

Not all the blame for the great expectations can be placed on Disney. America is, after all, the land of the quick fix. Too often in our society we look for external solutions to internal problems, and Celebration attracted more than its share of people who thought they could trade their old problems for a trouble-free life in a new town. Disney didn't create those unrealistic expectations, but it was guilty of capitalizing on them.

The company also can be faulted for failing to deliver on everything that it did promise. Complaints about builders are not unique to Celebration. Suits against builders and developers are filed regularly across the country. But Disney promised that it had found the best builders in the country, and people expected a level of quality commensurate with the promise and with what they had seen at Disney's theme parks.

Disney also had billed Celebration as a town where the latest advances in technology would enrich life for everyone. There were concrete pledges that residents would be linked directly to the school, neighbors, doctors, and shops through cutting-edge technology. But many of those assurances remain unfulfilled, and some of the technology described in Disney's promotional literature just didn't exist. The promise of technology suffered from the same flaw as the promise of a model school: In its zeal, Disney had sold more than it could deliver. No one saw this gap between the vision of technology and the reality as clearly as Scott Muri. He often found himself caught in the crossfire between promise and parents. "It's important for people to see the vision," he said. "What is printed today might not really exist yet, but it will. People need to see what will happen tomorrow."

The most unrealistic expectations, however, were associated with the school. We admire Disney for its ambitious vision of a progressive school, a public school at that. Even after the uneven experiences of our two children, we remain believers in Celebration School's basic respect for individual learning abilities and the usefulness of interdisciplinary approaches to problem solving and an alternative form of assessing a child's knowledge, at least in the early years. But the school presented two serious problems from the day it opened, and despite the recent progress, there was no sure evidence that they'd been solved as Nick and Becky returned to Celebration School in August 1998, the third year of the school's operation.

During the first year, the teachers were ill prepared from the outset to handle so taxing a program. They lacked proper training in many required areas, from multidisciplinary teaching to how to monitor the progress of so many children on different tracks to ways in which to integrate technology into the classroom. Indeed, in a survey conducted by the school's PTA, the teachers themselves complained that they did not receive sufficient training in using computers.

The lack of training and the absence of uniform standards and methods translated into unevenness among the classrooms. We felt our children attended different schools. Some classrooms functioned smoothly and productively, as evidenced by our daughter Becky's first year at the school. Others were chaotic, as our son Nick discovered. Robert Peterkin had cautioned at an early planning session for the school that it would take years to function smoothly, but residents expected to find what they had been promised from Day One—a model, world-class school.

The second major problem also was related to the expectations of parents, though in a slightly different way. Celebration was marketed as a new town with old-fashioned values. The architecture reminded people of the towns where they'd grown up, or the towns in which they would have liked to grow up. As a result, many people moved to Celebration expecting to find a school like the one they attended, or the one they would like to have attended. Instead, they were confronted with a radical departure from both past and present. There were no grades, no textbooks, and no written curricula. They walked into classrooms where as many as ninety kids, sometimes as much as six years apart in age, were clustered in groups, slouched on couches, or playing games on computers. There was even a bed in the middle of the media center. Though the literature had indicated clearly that the school would be a departure from what we had known as children, few parents were prepared for what they found, and many were left discombobulated.

"The difficulties are understandable, I think," said Ronald Clifton, the former foreign service officer who was Stetson University's liaison with Celebration. "It is a very complex school. It is trying to put into practice in one school the state-of-the-art innovations that you would find individually in other schools, but never in this combination. You probably won't find another school that has all of these aspects in one place."

None of the problems Celebration was experiencing as a new town, from difficulties with the school to leaky roofs on the town houses, was a fatal flaw. They were growing pains, and they could be remedied with patience and effort.

But sometimes it took a lot of patience. Thirteen months after we moved in, a work crew was finally fixing most of the remaining problems at our house, though they disappeared before the job was finished and haven't been back. And it took two more months before the builder discovered the cause of the mildew on our house—too little paint had been applied in some sections, resulting in a buildup of moisture. The only remedy was to repaint the entire house, which the builder agreed to do after considerable cajoling by Cathy. To ease the "yellow peril," we were given the opportunity to switch colors from yellow to green. The woman who plastered her car and her house with lemons got the new floor she demanded. Town & Country Homes was busy repairing the town-house roofs and, despite the sour taste left by its experience in Celebration, had begun construction on two subdivisions outside Chicago that incorporated many neotraditional elements.

At the school, compromises were in place and most parents were holding their breath and their fire as the new year began. The quiet revolution over the summer was a milestone in Celebration's effort to make its own history. Parents had overcome the fears of retaliation and coalesced into a formidable and reasonable force for change, which is a pretty good definition of the beginnings of self-governance and democracy. People had taken their hands out of their pockets, not to point fingers but to work together.

For Nick and Becky, the school year got off to a promising start. For the first time, they were in a class together as a result of combining sixth- and seventh-graders. Of the four teachers for the ninety students in their class, three were brand-new to the school. They seemed like self-assured adults, with previous teaching experience and an understanding that the progressive nature of the school could be tempered by some traditions, like textbooks and regular assessments. We were heartened to see math papers coming home with corrections, not the happy smiles of a year earlier.

Nick, who had gone through much of the previous school year in a sullen funk because of the chilliness of his teachers and the usual preadolescent woes, burst into the house after the first day, coasting by our home office on his Rollerblades. When we caught up to him at the refrigerator door, he announced with a grin, "This was the best day. Ms. Dipman is cool. We were supposed to talk about our likes and dislikes. I thought, 'Yuck, more of this touchy-feely stuff.' So when it came to me, I said that I disliked Hanson. You know what she said? 'Yeah, me too. They stink. But Green Day rocks.' " (Hanson is a kiddie-rock group, and Green Day is an alternative rock band.) "Can you believe it? And she smiled. And later Mr. Gatlin laughed at one of my jokes. Last year nobody laughed at anything."

Adjustments were being made. Practical considerations were having an impact on the ivory tower. There had been a recognition that no matter how good the plan or how many brand-name experts had blessed it, there had to be enough flexibility to accommodate the real world and the real children and parents in it. Even some of the long-promised technology was coming on line. School officials said that key goals, such as linking home computers to the school computers to monitor homework, and the creation of electronic portfolios, were going to be met in the coming months.

We were cautioned about our optimism by some of our neighbors. There had been promising starts before. But this had a different feel from last year, and we had watched the parents roll up their sleeves and battle to get some of the changes they wanted. We would be surprised to see things fall back into recriminations and chaos.

There remained evidence that everything was not running as smoothly at the school as people wished, or as smoothly as some suggested. A few days after classes began, one of the lead teachers, who had been involved in the reform effort over the summer, submitted her resignation and left. A month into the school year, two other teachers walked out of one of the lower-level classrooms, telling parents of students in their classes that they were unhappy with the chaotic environment. The classroom and its ninety children, from kindergarten through fifth grade, were left with only two teachers, and the result was real chaos. Not long after, the middle-school math teacher left, followed by a handful of others. School officials, from Davis to Blaine Muse, an assistant superintendent, assured us that the situation was temporary and schools regularly experienced high teacher turnovers. They said it was normal for teachers to walk out on their contracts, something we had never seen elsewhere. Despite such assurances, the exodus was disturbing.

Also troubling was the episode involving the Biehlers. There was no way to determine whether the disciplinary action involving their son was retaliation, but the mere suspicion that it had been raised unpleasant memories of the Us-versus-Them attitude of the first two years at Celebration School.

Echoes of that divisiveness were heard throughout the fall of 1998. On the first Sunday in November, nearly 250 people turned out at Lakeside Park for a discussion of continuing problems at the school. Some of the parents who had spearheaded the previous summer's reform movement again expressed concerns over whether their children were getting a proper education. Several other residents spoke, often sternly, in defense of the school, Disney's efforts on behalf of the school, and particularly the teachers. There were even pleas to find a middle ground. "I've lived here since the very beginning and I've seen friends separated because of the school issues," said Margot Schwartz, a resident and former educator. "I hate to see education tear apart our community. There are no positive and negative parents. We are all concerned parents. Parents are only having these so-called tantrums because they don't know where to go. They don't feel people are listening to their problems."

While the debate remained fairly civil, there was a dark side to the division. The week after the Lakeside meeting, one neighborhood at the school postponed its parents' night because of what one of the teachers told colleagues in a memo was a concern that "those" parents might "get out of hand." About the same time, someone overreacted to a frustrated parent's outburst at a school meeting and called the sheriff's office. Jack Howard, who had helped organize the concerned parents over the summer, telephoned Donna McGrath to caution her not to get too deeply involved in criticizing the school. She told us that he said someone had driven sharpened bolts into the tires of his car on three separate occasions and he received numerous angry and anonymous letters. Donna and Mike McGrath dismissed the warning about what Mike dubbed "the Mickey mafia."

But the continued problems at the school could not be dismissed. Before the end of the year, several more families in town withdrew their children and some of the teachers felt like they were under siege. Indeed, school administrators were so concerned about teacher morale that they hired a consultant to conduct workshops on stress management and getting along with parents. As part of the sessions, teachers were given free massages and the administration asked the board of the parent-teacher organization to provide $200 for tips for the massage therapists. The request was denied. "Free massages?" said Stu Devlin, the board president. "This is silly."

Despite the difficulties, most of our neighbors were unwilling to give up on the school, which is such a critical part of the town and the dream. They recognized that it was going to take time for the bumps to be smoothed, and they realized that the only way to make the school work for all of the students was for parents, teachers, and administrators to find a way to pull together, not pull apart.

One day we ran into Pat Wrisley outside the bank. He and Kelly had withdrawn both of their daughters, Lauren and Katie, because they found the classroom atmosphere too chaotic. "You know," said Wrisley, "I sure hope this year turns out great, so that Lauren and Katie can come back."

So did we.

R eaction to the first publicly reported violent crime in Celebration also provided evidence that the town was growing up and that the initial expectations had settled into something more realistic. For some, knowing had supplanted believing, and if what they knew was not perfect, it was at least real and something with which they could deal.

On a Tuesday evening in early August, Donna McGrath called us. Had we heard about Monday night's armed robbery in the Garden homes? We had not. The Garden homes were a block from our house, but somehow the gossip lines had broken down, and there was no local radio station or community newspaper to spread the news.

A man had approached Terrence and Stephanie Turner just outside their home, said he had a gun in his pocket, and demanded money. The man had ordered Terrence into the house while Stephanie remained outside with their two small children, too afraid to run. The robber had

taken an undisclosed amount of cash and some credit cards before fleeing in a blue Honda.

The *Orlando Sentinel* did carry an article on Wednesday, with the
headline, "Crime Hits Home in Disney Enclave," and by then the crime
was the talk of the town, occupying the entire morning discussion at
Barnie's for the coffee group and keeping Brent Herrington in meetings all day. But the reaction was not hysteria. No one was packing up
and heading back to Pennsylvania. People were most concerned about
the Turners, and they seemed to recognize that these sorts of things
happen everywhere, even in Disney's Celebration.

"It had to happen because it happens in everybody's neighborhood," said Carl Perkins, who lived around the corner from the Turners
and had moved to Celebration from a Chicago suburb. "I have the feeling that a lot of people moved here looking for small-town America.
Everyone is looking for that old sense of community and the security
that goes with it. But you're kidding yourself if you think this couldn't
happen here."

Cathy talked with Stephanie Turner a couple days after the incident.
She was still a little shaken, but she said they had no intention of leaving
Celebration. "We love it here," she said. "We're going to try to get past
what has happened. We've had tremendous support from our neighbors."

It was a measure of the outside world's fascination with Celebration
that the national editor at *The New York Times* called and asked Doug to
write a short article about the robbery. When Doug called Brent Herrington for a comment, the town manager sputtered in disbelief. "You
mean the *New York Times* is going to run an article about this?" he asked.
It was, explained Doug, the double-edged sword of publicity: Celebration had courted public attention, and now that a problem had arisen it
could not avoid public attention. For his part, Herrington followed the
news reports with a short newsletter that arrived in mailboxes on Thursday, three days after the crime. It was low-key and to the point, providing details of what had happened and offering the community's support
to the Turners. "I would like to remind all Celebration stakeholders that
we must always remain alert when it comes to the safety and security of
our neighbors, friends and families," he wrote.

We talked about the robbery with Nick and Becky. We didn't want them to be naïve, we explained, or to take too much for granted in Celebration. We reminded them to stay away from strangers and to exercise some care with their bikes. But we declined Becky's request for a bike lock, and the doors of our house remained unlocked during the day.

The Osceola County Sheriff's Department had called the robbery the first violent crime in Celebration, which was true technically. There had been, of course, the domestic abuse case on our street, but that incident was not classified as a violent crime. Unfortunately, the neighbors, including us, had not known how to respond in that instance. Months later, we were still mulling over why.

It may be that the real world had intruded too fast. Just as a car owner is more upset by the first ding than later scrapes and scratches, we all might have been reluctant to deal with the first blemish on our new town. Or, perhaps, it is simply a question of whether or not a corporation can engineer a good place to live or if that good place has to evolve on its own. Is it possible for Disney to bring together like-minded people and, by using basic tenets of architecture and urban planning, force the kind of community interaction that defines a good place to live? Or is it, in fact, a messier process, one that has to occur naturally, in which people roll up their sleeves and learn over a period of years to get along, to set good examples, to care for one another, and to step in when needed? Only time would tell.

But in the meantime, there were other signs that the town was growing up and questioning its reliance on Disney. Evidence of that came in September, when Herrington surprised almost everyone by announcing that he was leaving his job as town manager. In an emergency edition of his monthly newsletter, he explained that he had been offered a great opportunity with a community-development company, and though he and his family loved Celebration, it was too good an offer to turn down. While Herrington was liked and respected by most people, there was no town-wide hand-wringing over his imminent departure. Indeed, the first reaction was to plan a going-away party. There was, however, a more telling reaction: When the Celebration Company announced Herrington's successor a short time later, plenty of people groused that no one from the town had been part of the selection process. "I don't understand why the community didn't have some involvement in picking

Brent's replacement," said Deborah Jones, who, along with her husband, Rodney, and daughter, Tiffany, had been among the town's first residents. "When we moved here, in some respects it was comforting to know that there would be accountability from Disney, but living here I think there are times when we need a voice. The fact that everything is beautiful is simply not enough."

While Disney was clearly not going to cede any power to the towns-people until it was absolutely necessary, a natural evolution was taking place in another part of life in Celebration. Small, locally owned busi-nesses were beginning to fill the gaps in what was available downtown. Those gaps had been the subject of constant complaints from the begin-ning. As they had indicated in Nick's public-opinion survey, people wanted a hardware store, a florist shop, a hair salon. Instead of provid-ing the full array of stores necessary for a freestanding town, Disney had emphasized restaurants and clothing and furniture stores to attract tourists. It was the only way the town center could open the first day a resident moved in and survive until there were enough people to sup-port a real downtown.

By the end of our first year in Celebration, there were a couple of computer repair and installation services, a fence builder, a music teacher, and a two-person business that offered everything from twice-weekly fresh flowers to window washing. A local real estate agent had rented a large suite of offices in one of the downtown office buildings and started subletting small offices and cubicles to people who needed spaces for their businesses. Late in 1998, a tiny hair salon for men and women opened. These businesses were not unusual. Every small town has them. That was the point. In the here and now, between the absent past and the uncertain future, Celebration was becoming a real town.

But what kind of real town? The first residents were true pioneers. They were drawn to the concept behind Celebration. For some, it was Disney's involvement. For others, it was the chance to send their kids to a neighborhood school and walk to downtown. Whatever the reason, there was a sense of commitment to making the place work.

Back in August 1997, soon after arriving, we had attended the oblig-atory orientation session for new residents. When Kathy Johnson asked for a show of hands from people who could name the five cornerstones of Celebration, almost every hand in the place went up. Those initial residents were true believers. At the new-residents meeting a year later, Johnson asked the same question and no hands were raised. Most people, she found, did not even know that the cornerstones existed.

"It's not a bad thing that they aren't aware of the philosophy behind the town," she said not long after the meeting. "It's just different. The first people moved in on the promise of what Celebration was going to be. They bought a piece of this town based on that promise, and hope. They purchased homes based on words and pictures, representational drawings, not even photographs. Now, they come based on what they can see, and what they see is this cute little town with great architecture. I feel like the people moving here now are less adventurous, maybe less pioneering. The first residents were risk takers. There was urgency to everything they did. It has become a badge of honor to be one of those who were here at the beginning."

Differences were inevitable. Even the neighborhoods themselves were different physically. Only those who bought in the first phase would truly be within walking distance of the town center and the school; for us, the proximity was a major draw, but others might care less about it, or not at all. Nonetheless, as the town expanded and more people had to drive, there was a possibility of traffic and parking problems.

Johnson, however, saw opportunities in the changing character of those moving to Celebration. The new residents, perhaps with more realistic expectations, would balance the highs and lows of the pioneers. Over time, the new residents would have the opportunity to learn about the cornerstones by experiencing, not memorizing, them. They would discover, as the rest of us had, that the journey to Celebration did not end when they turned off Highway 192. That was when it began.

A town is a densely interwoven place whose structure is determined by hundreds of minds and thousands of individual decisions. Its beauty and vitality are created through the unexpected juxtapositions and unpredictable interactions that no planner could imagine. Disney's design for Celebration was limited by the imagination and values of the men and women who planned it. They could not impose their idea on the people who moved to Celebration. All they could do was put in place the basic outlines of the town and hope that its residents filled in the gaps with care and vision of their own.

Once you are in a place, things happen to make it yours, the particular somethings that no architect can design and no corporation can engineer. They can be simple, like seeing one of your children come home from school filled with light and hope, or running into neighbors when you duck beneath a portico downtown to escape a sudden rainstorm.

Jim and Elaine Whelan discovered the pull of the new town when they tried to leave. Their son, Brian, missed his friends in New Jersey the first year they lived in Celebration, and he persuaded them to go back. Despite the restrictions that prohibited posting a "For Sale" sign, they managed to sell their house. When they returned to New Jersey, they had trouble finding a new place to live. The more they looked, the more they missed Celebration. So they flew back down to Florida and put down a deposit on a new house in the North Village. Then they wavered again and decided not to buy another house in Celebration, though Jim remained drawn to the town.

"It's never been so hard to leave a place," said Jim Whelan one morning when he stopped into Barnie's for a cup of coffee while the moving truck was loading their furniture for the final trip back to New Jersey. As he walked out the door, the coffee group placed bets on how long it would take the Whelans to return to Celebration. Sure enough, two months later the Whelans were back in town, placing a deposit on a house in the North Village, re-enrolling their son in the school, and smiling broadly at the jokes about their indecisiveness.

The decision to stay or go was no easier for us. There was much that we had come to enjoy about Celebration. Like the majority of people who responded to Nick's school survey, we knew more people there than anyplace we had lived. And we were more involved in community activities. The pace of life was seductive and leisurely, similar to living in a resort.

One night in August 1998, we sat on our front step and reflected on the months that had gone so quickly. It had been, we agreed, a fascinating year, full of surprises and rarely dull or disappointing. It also had been a self-absorbing year. The town looked inward, sealing itself off from a world that ended at its borders. It was restrictive, almost tribal, and it left us feeling at times out of touch and uncomfortable in a place where life's edges were rounded and smoothed not by time but by choice.

Much was missing as we surveyed our lives over the past months. White's Books & Gifts downtown carried a small selection of books, but it was mostly a gift shop, and there were constant rumors about its demise. Despite the demographics of affluence and education, conversations rarely delved into literature or current events, with the singular exception of Bill Clinton's woes. In the fall of 1998, the first book club formed, with an initial membership of eighteen. Still, almost none of the houses we visited had bookshelves. Every time we went into someone's house and noticed the absence, we remembered what Cicero had said: "A room without books is like a body without a soul." It seemed to capture something ineffable that was absent in Celebration for us.

Aside from the big shindigs at the McGraths on Sunday nights, very few people had dinner parties in Celebration. We were not looking for *My Dinner with André,* but we had relished the lively exchanges over good food and wine that had occurred every place else we had lived. Personalities emerged and were sharpened in those conversations. We felt a little like the philosopher William James must have after his 1899 visit to Chautauqua, the combination arts festival and resort in southwestern New York. James was, he wrote, "spellbound by the charm and ease of everything, by the middle-class paradise, without a victim, without a blot, without a tear." He also said he was astonished upon entering the "dark and wicked world again, to catch myself quite unexpectedly and involuntarily saying: 'Ouf! What a relief! Now for something primordial and savage.' "

Despite all that was missing, we were reluctant to return to Westport. Life was not perfect there any more than it was perfect in Celebration. The privacy of our three acres, which we had valued so much, suddenly loomed as isolation. The prospect of Doug spending two hours a day riding the New Haven line to and from Grand Central Station sounded like a preposterous waste of time after the efficiency of working at home. The endemic affluence and entitlement seemed like a threat to helping our children develop the right attitudes toward life.

So we rented out the house in Connecticut for one more year. We were certain that we would be leaving Celebration by the time the next lease was up. And we were equally certain that wherever we went next, even back to Westport, we would choose to live differently because of our time here. We would not be satisfied to sit back and relax again, no matter where we put down roots. The benefits of involvement, whether it was Nick running the monthly volunteer effort at Give Kids the World for the church or Cathy's long hours of work for the PTSA, paid dividends too rich to ignore in any setting.

We also knew that we would look for a town a lot like Celebration. But we would insist on more racial and economic diversity, not because it's morally right or politically correct but because for us it makes life better, more interesting. We want our children to grow up knowing America in all of its variety from firsthand experience. A middle-class, basically all-white town did not fit that definition, but we did not figure that another year of it would hurt them or us. We wanted to be near a university and in a place with more culture than Disney World, Highway 192, or even Orlando had to offer. And a place with its own real library. But we also wanted to live in a town where neighbors lived close enough to know one another, where we could use bicycles instead of cars, where stores were within walking distance and people felt safe and comfortable making that walk. Neotraditionalism, or post-neotraditionalism, had rubbed off on us.

What we would miss most wherever we landed down the road was Celebration's genuine friendliness, a place infused with the sense that everyone there shared the dream of finding a better place to live and, as we had seen finally, a willingness to work to make the dream come true. For many people in Celebration, trust in Disney had been replaced by a trust in one another and in the common endeavor of creating a new town through their own efforts. It was an education and a joy to observe that transformation, and perhaps to have participated in some small way.

BIBLIOGRAPHY

SELECTED BOOKS

Anderson, Robert. *Wilderness Florida.* United States: VP Publications, 1988.

Blakely, Edward J., and Mary Gail Snyder. *Fortress America: Gated Communities in the United States.* Washington: The Brookings Institute, 1997.

Bryman, Alan. *Disney and His Worlds.* London: Routledge, 1995.

Calthorpe, Peter. *The Next American Metropolis: Ecology, Community, and the American Dream.* New York: Princeton Architectural Press, 1993.

Caplow, Theodore, Howard M. Bahr, Bruce A. Chadwick, Reuben Hill, and Margaret Holmes Williamson. *Middletown Families: Fifty Years of Change and Continuity.* New York: Bantam, 1983.

Celebration Pattern Book, second edition. Master code consultant: UDA Architects, Pittsburgh, Pennsylvania. Disney, 1997.

Connellan, Tom. *Inside the Magic Kingdom.* Texas: Bard, 1996.

Davis, Mike. *City of Quartz.* New York: Vintage, 1990.

Eliot, Marc. *Walt Disney: Hollywood's Dark Prince.* New York: Birch Lane, 1993.

Fishman, Robert. *Urban Utopias in the Twentieth Century: Ebenezer Howard, Frank Lloyd Wright, Le Corbusier.* Cambridge, MA: MIT Press, 1977.

Gannon, Michael. *Florida: A Short History.* Gainesville: University Press of Florida, 1993.

Gans, Herbert J. *The Levittowners: Ways of Life and Politics in a New Suburban Community.* New York: Vintage, 1967.

Girling, Cynthia L., and Kenneth I. Helphand. *Yard Street Park: The Design of Suburban Open Space.* New York: John Wiley, 1994.

Hiaasen, Carl. *Team Rodent: How Disney Devours the World.* New York: Ballantine, 1998.

Jacobs, Jane. *The Death and Life of Great American Cities.* New York: Modern Library, 1993.

Kunstler, James Howard. *The Geography of Nowhere: The Rise and Decline of America's Man-made Landscape.* New York: Simon & Schuster, 1993.

Langdon, Philip. *A Better Place to Live: Reshaping the American Suburb.* Amherst: University of Massachusetts Press, 1994.

Larson, Ron. *Swamp Song: A Natural History of Florida's Swamps.* Gainesville: University of Florida Press, 1995.

Mayes, Frances. *Under the Tuscan Sun: At Home in Italy.* New York: Broadway, 1997.

Mayle, Peter. *A Year in Provence.* New York: Vintage, 1991.

Monaghan, Kelly. *Orlando's Other Theme Parks: What to Do When You've Done Disney.* New York: The Intrepid Traveler, 1997.

Mumford, Lewis. *The City in History: Its Origins, Its Transformations, and Its Prospects.* New York: Harcourt, Brace & World, 1961.

———. *The Story of Utopias.* New York: Viking, 1962.

Oldenburg, Ray. *The Great Good Place.* New York: Paragon House, 1989.

Olmsted, Frederick Law. *Civilizing American Cities: Writings on City Landscapes.* Ed. S. B. Sutton. New York: Da Capo, 1997.

Rybczynski, Witold. *Looking Around: A Journey Through Architecture.* New York: Penguin, 1993.

Salvadori, Mario. *Why Buildings Stand Up: The Strength of Architecture.* New York: McGraw-Hill, 1982.

Schickel, Richard. *The Disney Version: The Life, Times, Art and Commerce of Walt Disney.* New York: Simon & Schuster, 1968.

Scully, Vincent. *American Architecture and Urbanism.* New York: Henry Holt, 1988.

Siebert, Charles. *Wickerby: An Urban Pastoral.* New York: Crown, 1998.

Stephenson, R. Bruce. *Visions of Eden: Environmentalism, Urban Planning, and City Building in St. Petersburg, Florida 1900–1995.* Columbus: Ohio State University Press, 1997.

Taylor, John. *Storming the Magic Kingdom: Wall Street, the Raiders, and the Battle for Disney.* New York: Alfred A. Knopf, 1987.

Whitaker, Craig. *Architecture and the American Dream.* New York: Clarkson N. Potter, 1996.

Whyte, William H. *City: Rediscovering the Center.* New York: Doubleday, 1988.

SELECTED ARTICLES AND REPORTS

"About the Reedy Creek Improvement District." URL: http://www.state.fl.us/rcid/about 1997.

"A Management Plan for Walker Ranch: To Protect and Enhance the Ecological Integrity of the Area in Perpetuity." *The Nature Conservancy,* April 1992.

Archer, Kevin. "The Limits to the Imagineered City: Sociospatial Polarization in Orlando." *Economic Geography,* July 1997.

Brody, Jane E. "A Delicate Creature Yields Its Secrets." *The New York Times,* August 12, 1997.

Duany, Andres, and Elizabeth Plater-Zyberk. "The Traditional Neighborhood and Suburban Sprawl: Attributes and Consequences." URL: http://www/dpz-architects.com/sprawl.

Dunlop, Beth. "Designs on the Future." *Architectural Record,* January 1996.

Ehrenhalt, Alan. "The Dilemma of the New Urbanists: Is the Movement Attracting Too Many Admirers and Imitators for Its Own Good?" *Congressional Quarterly,* 1977.

Gadsby, Patricia. "Why Mosquitoes Suck." *Discover,* August 1997.

Henry, John. "Is Celebration Mayberry or a Stepford Village? Walt Disney Co.'s New Community near Orlando, Florida." *Professional Builder,* September 1996.

———. "A Virtual Public Realm Is Not Good Enough." *The American Enterprise,* Fall 1997.

Kunstler, James Howard. Speech at the International Rails to Trails Conference. January 1998.

Langdon, Philip. "A Good Place to Live: Today's Designers of Residential Areas Are Increasingly Influenced by the Grid Plans, Narrow Streets, Intimate Scale, and Convenient Shopping of the Nineteenth-Century American Towns." *Atlantic Monthly,* March 1988.

Middleton, D. Scott. "Celebration, Florida: Breaking New Ground." *Urban Land,* February 1997.

Pollan, Michael. "Town-Building Is No Mickey Mouse Operation." *The New York Times Magazine,* December 14, 1997.

Putnam, Robert D. "Bowling Alone: America's Declining Social Capital." *Journal of Democracy,* January 1995.

Putnam, Robert D. "The Strange Disappearance of Civic America." *The American Prospect,* Winter 1996.

Richert, Evan D., AICP, and Mark B. Lapping. "Ebenezer Howard and the Garden City." *APA Journal,* Spring 1998.

Rothchild, John. "A Mouse in the House." *Time,* December 4, 1995.

Rybczynski, Witold. "Tomorrowland: Living in a Community Planned by Disney Has to Be a Nightmare, Doesn't It?" *The New Yorker,* July 22, 1996.

Rymer, Russ. "Back to the Future: Disney Reinvents the Company Town." *Harper's Magazine,* October 1996.

Shenk, Joshua Wolf. "Hidden Kingdom: Disney's Political Blueprint." *The American Prospect,* no. 21, Spring 1995.

Symposium, the Robert Kratovil Memorial Seminar in Real Estate Law: Reinventing America's Master Planned Communities. *The John Marshall Law Review:* vol. 31, Winter 1998.

Warrick, Brooke, and Toni Alexander. "Looking for Hometown America." *Urban Land,* February 1977.

Wood, Andy. "Disney's Celebration: Small-town Americana on the Edge of the Twenty-first Century." URL: http://oak.cats.ohiou.edu, 1998.

ACKNOWLEDGMENTS

This book is based largely on the experiences of our family during more than a year and a half living in Celebration. But it would have been a narrow vision without the insights shared with us by many other people, from neighbors on our street and elsewhere in town to people dedicated to building places that encourage community and a sense of place. We offer them our sincere thanks and the assurance that we could not have completed the book without their thoughtful assistance and encouragement.

There are too many names to list them all, but we would like to single out some people to whom we are most deeply indebted. We owe the greatest thanks to our youngest children, Nick and Becky, eager participants in this adventure. Their experiences in Celebration provided us with entrée to places we could never have gone as journalists and their observations were vital. Our eldest child, Elizabeth, contributed a budding anthropologist's insights from afar.

Our stay in Celebration would have been less pleasant, and our book far less rich, without the warmth and generosity of our neighbors. We interviewed more than two hundred people in Celebration, and all of them had an impact on the final product. A few were instrumental in shaping our understanding of what motivates the search for community and place in America today. Among them were Leigh and Shailesh Adhav, Lisa and Scot Baird, Joe Barnes, Earlene and Jere Batten, Niki and Paul Bryan, Catherine Conneely, Joe Davison, Robin Delaney, Stu Devlin, Thomas Dunn, Dave and Teresa Haeuszer, Kathy Johnson, Debby Jones, Joe Judge, Lise Juneman, Dottie Mathison, Beth and Tim McCarthy, Mike McDonough, Donna and Mike McGrath, Jan Parker, Mary Ellen Pauli, Drew Payne, Mike Prevost, Charlie Rogers, Marguerite Saker, Jim Whelan, and Kelly and Patrick Wrisley. We would also like to thank Bruce Stephenson of Rollins College, who provided historical and planning context for Celebration; Rod Schultz and John Hall of the Osceola County's environmental department; Peter Rummell, who shared his original vision for the town with us; and Bill LeBlanc, the "Dr. Data" who guided Nick's survey and helped us understand what drew people to Celebration. And to Bill and Joan Kaczmarczyk, good neighbors who loaned us their computer when ours crashed on deadline, we owe you our lives.

Finally, writing a book is a little like building a new town: You never get everything right the first time around. To adjust our course and focus our thinking, we counted on the wisdom and intellect of Marian Wood, the editor every writer dreams about but few are fortunate enough to encounter. We also thank, as always, our esteemed agent and friend, Dominick Abel.

INDEX

Academy for Academics and Arts, 138
Adams, Charles, 33, 41, 50–51, 62
adult education institution, 47–48, 115, 301
affordable housing issue, 74–76, 77 219–24, 225, 266, 310
Alexandria, Virginia, 21, 83, 194, 213, 216
  Old Town, 43, 156–57
alligators, 39, 171, 239
Amelia Island Plantation, 38
America, 23–24
  changing nature of, 10–11
  reinventing itself, 313
  white, middle–class version of, 218
American Builder's Companion, The (Benjamin), 64
apartments, 30, 34, 44, 49, 62, 219, 289
  location of, 72
  mixed with single–family houses, 103, 225
  rents, 220, 223
  above shops, 16
architects, 16, 23, 28, 58–59
architectural guidelines, 160–61
architectural style, 61–63, 67
  Seaside, 45
architectural uniformity, 21, 46
architecture, 8, 11, 14, 15, 33, 115, 116, 214
  Celebration's contribution to, 59
  changes in, 167–68
  and egalitarianism, 310–11
  small–town, 16
  social engineering through, 184
  traditional, 51
  in transforming society, 111–12
  vernacular American, 49, 94
  visitors' reactions to, 213

Arrington, Mary Jane, 73, 79, 131, 228–29, 230, 283, 284, 285
Arvida Corporation, 38
AT&T, 147–49
AT&T Advanced Technology Panel, 147–52
Auburn University, 17, 253, 254
automobile, 58
  dependence on, 11, 15, 24, 44, 53, 313
  reducing reliance on, 261, 313

baby boomers, 23–24, 43, 48, 68, 263
background buildings, 16, 58
backstory, 52, 96, 115
Ball, Edward, 25
Baltimore, 314
bank, 16, 19, 58, 59, 96
Baptists, 277
Barnes, Joseph, 63–64, 65, 79, 158–59, 160, 162, 306
Barnie's (coffee shop), 88, 97, 118, 175, 176, 177–78, 182, 193, 202–3, 260, 281, 282, 321
Benjamin, Asher, 64
blacks, 29, 216, 217–19, 223, 224, 225
Blakely, Edward J., 152
block parties, 6–7, 9, 103–4, 105, 121–23, 186, 191, 260
book club, 182, 326
"Bowling Alone" (Putnam), 256–57
Broadacre City, 111
Brown, Denise Scott, 16, 58
Browner, Carol, 232–33
businesses, 49, 61, 186, 189, 323
Capital Cities/ABC, 22
Catholics, 90, 278

Celebration
  adapting concepts from, 313–14
  Arbor Circle, 173
  Campus Street, 16, 92, 137, 161–62
  Canne Place, 280, 281
  Celebration Avenue, 13, 16, 163
  contribution made by, 312–13
  evolution of, 295–96
  experience of living in, 209–12, 245–46
  homogeneity, 216–17
  Honeysuckle Avenue, 191
  initial development, 15–16
  Island Village, 181
  as laboratory, 214
  Lake Evalyn, 94–95
  Lakeside Park, 182, 187, 189, 288
  Market Street, 16, 22, 186, 188, 189–90
  master plan, 53, 56, 58, 67, 72, 77, 79
  models for, 62–64
  Nadina Place, 6–7, 11, 82, 102–4, 121, 269, 280
  name, 51
  North Village, 179–81, 223, 261, 281, 325
  phases of, 34
  philosophy behind, 115
  plans for, unveiled, 52–53
  press treatment of, 168–69, 311–12, 321
  pros and cons of, 256, 257–61, 269–70, 325–26
  racial makeup of, 217
  as real town, 323–24
  satisfaction with life in, 260–61
  Savannah Square, 87, 92, 302
  South Village, 181, 183, 226–27, 228, 230, 237, 238
  successes/failures, 314–20
  Sycamore Street, 100
  Showcase Village, 148
  uniqueness of, 116–17
  Verandah Place, 185
  Water Street, 16
  West Village, 34, 185
  writing book about, 10, 211–12, 258, 259–60
Celebration Community Development District, 153
Celebration Community Network, 148
Celebration Company, 23, 32, 33, 80, 100, 131, 155, 168, 189, 322–23
  and affordable housing, 222–23
  and construction problems, 92
  control by, 190
  and environmental issues, 238, 240, 241, 242
  and house repairs, 302–3
  and mail delivery problems, 161–62
  model homes, 273–74
  and rules and regulations, 157, 158, 308
  and the school, 134, 135–36, 137, 253–54, 255, 291
  and teaching academy, 300–1
  and tree ordinance, 228
Celebration Foundation, 116, 165, 211, 235, 278, 310
  fund–raising efforts, 206, 207
  volunteers from, 266
Celebration Golf Club, 154, 165
Celebration Learning Center, 129
Celebration Pattern Book, 64–66, 79, 93, 94
Celebration Realty, 19, 273
Celebration Residential Owners Association, 155
Celebration School, 124–46, 300, 319
  children bused to, 310
  expectations regarding, 316
  original concept for, 295, 297
  pluses and minuses, 248–52
  problems in, 176–77, 253–56
  see also school
Celebration Stakeholders Panel, 224
Celebration style, 176–77
Celebration Village, 34, 185
chairs, movable, 182–83
Chapel Hill, North Carolina, 46
Charlestown, South Carolina, 43, 64
Charlie's Angels, 38
Charlottesville, Virginia, 94
Chautauqua, 111
children
  freedom for, 104–5
  friendships, 311
  relationships among, 121–23
Christian, Ruth, 296–97, 299
church building, 271–77, 286
churches, 162–65
cities, 24, 313
City (Whyte), 183
city, origins of, 171
City Beautiful movement, 214
City in History, The (Mumford), 171
civic capital, 257
civic engagement, 256–57
civil community, model of, 22
civil society, 54, 115, 256–57

Clarke Environmental Mosquito Management, 243
Classical style, 31, 65, 66
Clifton, Ronald, 109, 316
Coastal style, 31, 65
Colonial facade, 103, 104
Colonial Revival style, 31, 65
Coca–Cola, 147
cohesiveness, 44
Columbia, Maryland, 15, 53, 55, 113
Columbian Exposition, Chicago, 214
commercial buildings, 16, 72
commercial space, 15, 50
  tenants for, 60–61
commitment, 104, 323
communities, new, 313
  see also new towns
community, 8, 279
  coercive restrictions and, 308–10
  as cornerstone, 46
  lacking in suburbs, 54
  participation in, 116
  see also sense of community
community associations, 309
community building, 14, 172, 269
community developers, 37, 41, 50–51
community development, 38
community–development districts, 77–79, 130, 167
community involvement
in the school, 246–48, 255
community network, computerized, 116
Community Presbyterian Church, 271–73, 275–76
computers, 52, 262
  provided by AT&T, 149–52
  in school, 142–43, 250–52, 289, 290
Concerned Parents of Celebration, 293–94
conformity, 269, 295, 309, 310
Congress for the New Urbanism, 312
construction company, 79–81
construction problems, 82–101
  community's way of dealing with, 96, 97, 100, 101
construction quality
  Disney guarantor of, 79, 90, 96, 101
controls, 44, 45
  on design elements, 58
  see also rules and regulations
cornerstones, 46, 115–16, 166, 323–24
  education, 42, 43, 67, 115, 166
  health and fitness center, 263

sense of place, 46, 115, 116, 166, 301
technology, 115, 116, 148, 166
wellness, 43, 46
Cottage homes, 30, 103
covenants, restrictive, 135, 152, 167
crime, 265, 320–22
criticism of Celebration, 8, 21, 22–23, 213–25
  reaction to, 295–96
Croson, Thomas, 303
Cummings, Des, 263

David Weekley Homes (co.), 18, 19–20, 80–81, 82, 83, 85, 92, 93, 94, 240
Davis, Alexander, 56
Davis, Dot, 124–25, 138–41, 158, 159, 164, 166, 254–55, 259, 287, 291, 292, 293–94, 295, 296, 318–19
  relationship with parents, 297–98
Davis, Robert, 43, 311
"Day in the Life, A" (video), 134
DC Ranch, 28
de–annexation, 70–71, 77
democracy, 166, 190, 248, 256, 296, 317
Democracy in America (Tocqueville), 256
DeNike, Patrice, 266–67
Dennis, Charles, 84–85
density, 44, 45, 55, 72
design controls, 44, 58–59
developers, 35, 37, 40, 44–45, 167, 227
  and affordable housing, 222
  compromising, 230
dinner parties, 191–92, 326
Disney, Roy, 25, 163, 236
Disney, Walt, 24–27, 36, 40, 46, 62, 131, 162, 163, 236, 314
Disney brand name, 35, 36
Disney Channel, 113
Disney Cruise Line, 292
Disney Development Company, 23, 29, 38, 46, 52, 63, 93, 99–100, 114–15
Disney employees, 27, 39, 70
  affordable housing, 75–76, 220, 222
  and corporate culture, 201–2
  living in Celebration, 117, 262
Disney Imagineers, 96, 115
Disney Institute, 47–48, 49, 52, 276
  location of, 58
  loss of, 67–68, 125
Disney–MGM Studios, 38, 50
Disney name, drawing power of, 31–32
Disney police, 202

Disney Vacation Club, 97–98, 106
Disney Wilderness Preserve, 230, 231,
    234–35, 238
Disneyland, 21, 23, 25, 40, 218
Disneyphiles, 35, 119
Disneyspeak, 179–80
"Disney's New Town," 48–49
Disney's West Side, 79–80
diversity, 114, 209, 217–25, 309, 327
  in the school, 132
domestic abuse, 265–69, 322
Dorsey, Norbert M., 278
Douglass, Frederick, 218
Dowd, Maureen, 210
Dream Team, 136, 137, 140, 207, 211
drop–ins, 194
Duany, Andres, 43, 45, 48, 49, 50, 311
DuPont, Washington, 313
du Pont, William, III, 204

East Hampton, Long Island, 62
economic integration, 29
Edmond, Timothy, 93
education
  centerpiece of Celebration, 125
  as cornerstone, 42, 43, 46, 67, 115, 166
  and quality of life, 301
  see also school
education experts, 17, 125, 126
educational philosophy, 144
egalitarianism, 310–11
Eisner, Jane, 51, 160
Eisner, Michael, 8, 35, 40, 41, 47, 48, 50, 51,
    113, 118, 160, 288–89, 314
  approval of, needed, 164
  and architects, 59
  aspirations of, 115
  autobiography, 144, 223
  and education issue, 67
  high standard of, 80, 81
elitism, 22, 219, 310
encephalitis, 242–43
environmental issues, 39, 43–44, 49, 216,
    226–44, 314
Epcot (theme park), 27, 38, 288
corporate sponsorships, 147, 148
escapism, 11, 21, 22, 219, 309
Estate homes, 30, 65, 78
Euro Disney, 50
Everglades, 233
expectations, 35, 36, 94, 100–1, 102–10, 117,
    118, 119–23, 166, 306, 320, 324
  failure to meet, 202

regarding the school, 314–15
responsibility for, 314–15
Experimental Prototype Community of
    Tomorrow (Epcot), 26–28, 40, 46, 162,
    314

farmers market, 189–90
Fishman, Robert, 112
Florida, 25, 39, 74, 76, 102–3, 203
  building standards, 46
  as Disney experience, 215
  land developers in, 77–78
  landscape, 237–38
  law regarding affordable housing, 222
  legislation for Disney World, 26
  public school system, 67, 68
  Supreme Court, 27
  transient population in, 266–67
Florida crackers, 235–36
Florida Department of Education, 131
Florida Hospital, 33, 115
Florida legislature, 26, 27, 246
Fogelsong, Rick, 69
Ford Foundation, 300
Fort Mill, South Carolina, 313
fortress America, 55
Fortress America (Blakely and Snyder), 152
48 Hours (TV show), 212
Founder's Day, 187–89
Fraser, Charles, 37, 41–42, 45–47, 53, 62–63,
    65, 80, 125, 162, 313
  and movable chairs, 183
freedom, restrictions on, 152, 156
  see also rules and regulations
French Normandy style, 31, 65
Frey, William, 217
friendliness, 21, 327
friendships, 171, 172, 191, 279
  children, 311
front porches, 5, 44, 95, 116, 183–85, 313
  furniture, plants, decorations, 178–79
fund–raising, 206, 279–81

Galpin, Susan, 190
Gaithersburg, Maryland, 313
garden city (concept), 111
garden club, 182, 189
Garden Club Rebellion, 189–90
Garden homes, 94, 95, 185, 221, 223, 320
Gardner, Howard, 126, 127
Garrod, Ted, 227
gated communities, 28, 152–53
Gatorland, 213

General Electric, 148
General Motors, 147
Geography of Nowhere, The (Kunstler), 21
Gindroz, Raymond, 64
Give Kids the World, 272, 279, 327
Glasser, William, 126
golf courses, 16, 58, 87
government officials, dealings with, 68, 69–77, 78
granny flat, 20, 44, 208–9, 219
Graves, Michael, 58
"great good places," 176, 177
Greek Revival architecture, 65
Gwathmey, Charles, 48, 49, 51

Habitat for Humanity, 279
Halloween, 186–87
Harbour Town, 45, 63, 183
Harden, Pat, 238
Harvard, 17, 125, 253
health and fitness center, 17, 33, 58, 115, 134, 214, 263, 265
Help Now, 266, 267
Henry, John, 22
Herrington, Brent, 137, 140, 155–56, 158, 161, 162, 183, 190, 224, 259, 267, 321
    on affordable houses, 221–22, 223
    and house repairs, 302–3, 304, 305
    leaving Celebration, 322
    newsletter, 118, 140, 165, 178–81
    patrolling town, 202, 212
    and school problems, 253–55, 291
    and "town fathers," 165, 166
    veto power, 167–68
Hetland, Lois, 126
Hiaasen, Carl, 112
Highway 417, 76–77
Hilton Head Island, 37, 41, 42–43, 98
Hispanics, 216, 217, 219–20
homeowners association, 19, 152, 167, 168, 302
Honeywell, 148
houses, 48–49, 58, 72, 80–81
    architectural styles, 52
    buying, 19–20
    colors, 66, 154, 158–59
    designs, 14
    and egalitarianism, 310–11
    facades, 31, 103
    income level and, 15
    interiors, 66
    levels of, 30
    models, 6, 20, 30–31
    prices, 6, 18, 20, 29, 30, 31, 34, 52, 75, 94, 103, 219, 222, 223
    problems with, 18, 82–101, 301–6, 317
    resale of, 135, 136, 155
    sale of, 29–31, 34
    types, 61–62
housing
    density, 15
    and quality of life, 301–2
    subsidized, 220, 222
housing styles, 31, 65–66
    mixture of, 44, 66
Howard, Ebenezer, 111, 113
Hudson, Todd, 18
Hughey, Donna, 238

infrastructure, 60, 77–78
International Style, 48
Internet access, 263
Interstate 4, 38–39, 76
Irvine, California, 53, 55
isolation/isolationism, 11, 54, 283, 284–85, 286, 309, 313
    efforts to avoid, 310–11
Ivy, Joel, 73

Jackson, Kenneth, 223–24
Jahn, Helmut, 58
James, William, 326
Jewish congregation, 90, 277
Johnson, David, 126
Johnson, Kathy, 165, 166, 224, 276, 283–84, 323–24
Johnson, Philip, 16, 58–59, 166
Johnson, Roger, 126

Kaiser, Leland, 115
Kane, Gene, 19, 83, 84, 85, 96–97
Kelly, Tim, 303–6
Kentlands, Maryland, 28
Killoren, Don, 29–30, 50–51, 60, 67–68, 75, 117, 125–26, 232, 234, 314
King, Martin Luther, Jr., 218
Kissimmee, 34, 70–71, 153, 266, 272, 278, 279, 310
Kissimmee Middle School, 131
Kloehn, Michael, 70, 71–72, 73, 74
"knowledge worker," 262
Koop, C. Everett, 115
Kulo, Mark, 243
Kunstler, James Howard, 21

land development, 77–79, 80
land use, 26, 38–40, 41, 72, 73

landscape design, 66
Larbig, Denise, 266, 267
Le Corbusier, 101, 111, 312
Leinsing, Donna, 140
Levittown, New York, 5, 15, 44–45, 53–54, 223, 225
Lewis, Tom, 74, 227, 228, 229, 230, 232–33
library, 143, 327
Llewellyn Park, New Jersey, 56
Lockridge, Gloria, 70, 71
Lot Plan, 2–3f
lot size/lots, 15, 20, 44, 45, 48, 58
lottery(ies), 29–30, 31, 33, 34, 95, 98, 106, 107, 199
Lynd, Helen, 162
Lynd, Robert, 162

Maak, Nicholas, 182
McCraley, Thomas, 140–41
McKenzie, Evan, 167
Magic Kingdom, 38, 119, 167
    Contemporary Resort, 231
    Main Street, U.S.A., 22, 24, 62
mail delivery, 161–62
Mansfield, Todd, 52, 79, 314
Mariemont, Ohio, 43
marketing, 28, 115, 116, 134
Mediterranean style, 31, 65
Meister, Heather, 147, 148, 149, 150
Meyers, Jason, 18
Middletown, 162
minorites, 22, 224–25
    see also blacks; Hispanics
modernism, 62
Moore, Charles, 16, 50, 51, 58
More, Sir Thomas, 110, 113, 115
mosquitoes, 242–44
Moses, Robert, 112, 221
Multiple Intelligence (Gardner), 126
Mumford, Lewis, 54, 171
Muncie, Indiana, 162
Muri, Scott, 251, 277–78, 314
Murphy, Chuck, 153
Muse, Blaine, 140, 318–19
Music, canned, 159–60

National Education Association, 300, 301
Nature Conservancy, 234
neighborhood(s), 55, 64, 114, 181, 265
    differences among, 324
    mixed, 61–62
    as network, 184
    safe, hospitable, 313

"neighborhoods" (school), 127, 129, 134, 142
neighborliness, 5, 9, 15, 84, 121, 257, 269
neighbors, 104, 171, 172, 175, 327
neotraditional communities/towns, 213–14, 219, 310, 313
neotraditional movement, 14, 15, 28, 33, 34, 43–45, 46, 48, 55–56, 94, 214, 311–12, 327
    evolution into post–neotraditionalism, 312–13
    exceptions to, in plans for Celebration, 49, 53, 58
    key ideas in, 44
New Harmony, Indiana, 111
new towns, 6, 11, 15, 28, 35, 43, 53, 55, 309
    Celebration as, 46, 47, 316
    inclusive vision of, 219
    prototype(s) for, 50
New Urbanism, 43
New World, 110–11
New York City, 112
    Bryant Park, 56, 183
    Times Square, 22, 112
    New York Times, The, 9, 48, 210, 321
    New York Times Magazine, The, 10, 168, 258, 280
Newsweek, 24
nostalgia, studied, 20, 21

Old Town (amusement park), 180
old towns, 43
Oldenburg, Ray, 176, 177
Olmsted, Frederick Law, 14, 56–57, 58
Oneida community, 111
Orange County, 25, 69, 72, 76, 131, 242
Orlando, 9, 25, 51, 62–63, 65, 69, 203–6, 208, 262, 280, 327
    blacks in, 217–18
    building boom, 92
    Orlando Sentinel, 21, 136, 204, 231, 321
Osceola County, 17, 25, 31, 52, 68, 78, 152, 153, 206, 219, 226, 228, 279
    and Celebration school, 131–33
    dealing with officials of, 68, 70–71, 73–77
    housing program, 222
    public schools, 67, 133
    relationship with Disney Company, 131
    Sheriff's Department, 266, 280, 322
    Sheriff's deputies, 265, 268
    teachers and principals from, 126, 300
Osceola County Commission, 226–29
Osceola County School Board, 131

elections, 282–84, 285–86
outreach efforts, 278–79
Owen, Robert, 111

Pace, David, 91–92, 241, 273
Parent Teacher Student Association (PTSA), 126, 137, 246, 279, 327
pattern books, 64
Payne, Drew, 284–85
Pelli, Cesar, 58, 59, 185
people attracted to Celebration, 11, 28–30, 31–34, 116, 218
  see also expectations
Peterkin, Robert, 130, 316
Pinellas, Anna M., 75, 76
Pitt, Larry, 136
planned communities, 22, 42, 44, 53–54, 56, 152, 225, 247
  affordable housing, 219
planning/planners, 28, 35, 56
  and egalitarianism, 310–13
  post–neotraditional, 11
Plater–Zyberk, Elizabeth, 43, 45, 48, 49, 50, 311
Poinciana High School, 130
politicians
  and Disney private government, 26, 27
politics, 282–84, 285–86
Pollan, Michael, 168
poor people, 22, 114, 310
porch culture, 116, 185, 265
  see also front porches
porch police, 157, 179
Portland, Oregon, 314
"Positive Parents," 137
post–neotraditionalism, 11, 53, 116, 296, 313, 327
potluck supper culture, 190–91, 192
Presbyterian church, 278–79
Presbyterian Church USA, 163, 164
Presbyterian General Assembly, 273
Presbyterians, 90, 91, 163–64, 271–77
press attention to Celebration, 168–69, 311–12, 321
preview center, 16, 19, 27, 29, 58, 199, 200
"privatopias," 309
production builders, 92–93
production houses, 80–81, 95, 96
Professional Builder magazine, 8
proximity, 104, 121, 265, 269, 301, 324
Pruzac, Zach, 237–38
Public Agenda, 145–46
public buildings, 16, 45, 58–60

public–opinion survey, 257–61, 262
public spaces, 28, 44, 182
  movable chairs in, 182–83
  rules for organizing, 56
Puder, Dorothy, 163
Puder, Glenn, 163

quality
  relying on Disney for, 106, 315
quality control, 201–2
quality of life, 35, 43, 114, 115, 116
  factors determining, 301–2

race relations/racism, 217, 224–25
  see also diversity
Randall, John, 243–44
Rawn, William, 133
Red Rose Ball, 206–7
Reedy Creek Improvement District, 26, 27, 69, 70, 71, 76, 220, 230
religious organizations, 90–91, 277–79
residents, 35, 46, 60, 114, 148
  defensiveness, 169, 210, 215–16, 259
  education as motivating factor for, 115
  employment, 262–63
  first, 323–24
  preference to remain within community, 284–85
  split over school issue, 136–37
  and town center, 61
Reston, Virginia, 15, 44, 53, 55
retirees, 263
Rilke, Rainer Maria, 193
Riverside, Georgia, 52
Riverside, Illinois, 14, 56–57, 59, 113
Riverside Improvement Company, 56, 57
Robertson, Jacquelin, 50, 51, 53, 58, 59, 62, 63, 65
Rogers, Charlie, 165, 247
Roper Organization, 256, 260
Rosen, Larry, 126, 129, 134, 140, 141, 290–92
Rossi, Aldo, 199
Rouse, James, 53
rules and regulations, 152, 153–62, 212–13, 215, 308–9
  absentee owners, 103
  house buying, 19
  resale of houses, 135, 136, 222
  Riverside, 57
Rummell, Peter, 29–30, 35–36, 37–40, 41–43, 46–51, 52, 60, 61–62, 63, 67, 79, 114–15, 125, 306, 314
  and affordable housing, 220

and environmental issues, 232
Ryan, Bill, Sr., 303
Ryan, Mike, 91, 92–93, 303, 304
Ryan, William J., Jr., 81, 91, 303–4
Rymer, Russ, 23

St. Cloud, 71, 153, 285
St. Joe Paper Company, 25, 36
Savannah, Georgia, 43, 64
Savannah style, 103, 104
Scarsdale, New York, 43
school, 5, 10, 16–17, 24, 28, 33, 67–68, 115,
    124–46, 199, 225
  assessment in, 128–29, 176–77
  attempt to stifle debate over, 310
  attitudes toward, 258, 260
  central vehicle for sense of community and
    pride of place, 136
  changes in, 296–97, 317–20
  community involvement in, 246–48
  concerns about, 252–56, 287–99
  cost/funding of, 125, 130, 131–32
  difficulties at, 165, 166
  divisiveness caused by problems in, 319–20
  expectations regarding, 314–15
  fictitious classes, grades, 292–93
  Hilton Head Island, 42
  learning practices and theories, 126,
    127–30, 134–35, 141–46, 252–54, 295
  learning projects, 128, 146, 249–50
  pluses and minuses in, 248–52
  personalized learning plan (PLP), 128, 134
  as selling point, 68, 134, 323
  temporary quarters, 89
  withdrawing children from, 135–36,
    137–38, 252–53, 254, 290, 293, 298,
    319–20
School Advisory Council, 246–47
Schools Without Failure (Glasser), 126
Schroeder, Pat, 159–60
Schultz, Rod, 227, 229–30
Scully, Vincent, 8
Sea Pines Company, 37, 38
Sea Ranch, 50
Seaside, Florida, 43, 45–46, 49, 55–56, 113,
    214, 216, 307, 311, 312, 313
self–governance, 295, 296, 317
Sellen, James, 35
sense of community, 10, 43, 44, 55, 114, 206,
    207, 306, 312, 321
  cornerstone, 115, 116, 166
  "new traditions" in, 186–89
  school in, 136

social interaction in, 257
sense of place, 43, 44, 46, 191
  cornerstone, 46, 115, 116, 166, 301
  houses in, 301
shopping mall, 49, 50, 52, 53, 58, 61
Siegel, Robert, 49
single–family homes, 44, 62, 103, 225
Skidmore, Owings & Merrill (SOM), 50
Skinner, B. F., 216
small town(s), 28, 55, 56, 62, 162, 163, 211,
    216
  as ideal for planning, 311
  racial makeup of, 217
small–town planning/design, 28, 46
Snohomish County, Washington, 222
Snyder, Mary Gail, 152
social engineering, 5, 46–47, 265, 322
  affordable housing in, 221
  through architecture, 184
social infrastructure, 37, 116
social interaction, 43, 116, 257, 260, 306
  through design, 265
social problems, 265–69
softball tournament, 279–81, 286
Songer, Nancy, 265
Southern Living magazine, 62–63
starting over, 104, 193, 207
State College, Pennsylvania, 46
Stephenson, Bruce, 213–15
Stern, Robert A. M., 48, 49, 51, 53, 56, 57,
    58–60, 62, 63, 65, 67, 113, 160, 166
Stetson University, 17, 109, 126, 300–1, 316
streets, 14, 15, 54, 55, 114
  curved, 56–57, 58
  grid pattern, 14, 45, 49, 58
subdivisions, 44, 59, 77, 116, 310–11
  affluent, gated, 39–40
  with neotraditional elements, 317
suburbs, 11, 14, 15, 44, 53, 56, 57, 114, 116,
    184
  alternative to, 312
  dissatisfaction with, 28, 43, 112, 313
  migration from, 55
  problems with, 54
  prototypical, 44–45
  swamp, 39, 85, 95, 231–32, 238, 239–42
  see also wetlands

teacher–student ratio, 145
teachers, 129–30, 141, 143, 255, 289, 290,
    291, 292, 296, 297–98
  and affordable housing, 220
  lack of preparation, 316

leaving, 138, 297, 318–19
morale, 320
teaching academy, 17, 115, 125–26, 130–31, 132, 133, 134
battle over, 299–301
Team Rodent (Hiaasen), 112
technology, 5, 28, 147–52, 258, 313, 314
cornerstone, 115, 116, 148, 166
delayed, 263, 289–90
in the school, 134, 318
theme parks, 21, 25, 26, 38, 39, 40, 50, 147, 198, 201, 225, 231, 314
Celebration as, 47
Disneyspeak, 180
private government for, 27
quality in, 315
Tilden, Lobnitz & Cooper/MRI, 302
Tocqueville, Alexis de, 256
tourists, 20–21, 22, 60, 105, 153, 186, 208, 215, 323
Town & Country Homes, 81, 88, 90, 91–92, 98–100, 303–6, 317
town center, 5, 15, 16, 46, 49, 52, 265
design and tenant mix, 61
neighborhoods near, 181
open–air pavilions, 218
people coming together in, 176, 177, 182
readiness, 60
stores in, 323
street life, 185–86
town centers, 28, 64
town development, 14–15
"town fathers," 165–66
Town Hall, 16, 58–59, 159, 160, 161, 166–67, 190
town houses, 44, 92, 107, 108, 221
problems, with, 302–6, 317
town planning, 14–15, 43, 56, 110
town seal, 23
Townhomes, 30, 31
traditionalists, 55
traditions, new, 186–89
trees, 66, 74, 226–30
Truman Show, The (film), 45, 307–8

uniformity, 156, 269–70
United Society of Believers in Christ's Second Appearing (Shakers), 111
Universal Studios, 208, 209, 213
Upper Kissimmee, 233
urban design/development, 10, 23, 45, 312
urban life, disenchantment with, 28, 313–14

urban planners/planning, 10, 14, 111–12
urban renewal housing, 221–22
Urban Utopias in the Twentieth Century (Fishman), 112
urbanism, 59, 62
U.S. Highway 192, 13, 72, 21, 29, 131, 180, 192, 324, 327
utopia, 11, 109–12, 216, 312
Celebration as, 112–16, 225
Utopia (More), 110
utopian communities, 111–12

values, 24, 28, 313, 316
Venturi, Robert, 16, 58
Victorian style, 31, 65, 66
Village homes, 30, 98
Visions of Eden (Stephenson), 214
visitors, 208–10, 212–14, 245
preconceptions of, 212–13
Vogel, Bobbi, 133, 138, 140
volunteer activities/volunteers, 46, 116, 206, 278, 310

Walker Ranch, 233–34, 238
walking distance, 5, 114, 327
walking distance of town center, 44, 185, 324
Wall Street Journal, The, 138
Walt Disney Company, 5, 8, 10, 11, 15, 21, 25, 37, 163, 305–6
and affordable housing, 219–20, 221–24
belief/trust in, 100–1, 117–19, 211, 218, 272, 296, 327
and church building, 276
and building of houses, 79–81
and construction problems, 92–93
control of Celebration, 162, 166–68, 226–30, 237, 295–96
corporate alliances, 147–48
corporate culture, 179, 201, 264
creating traditions for Celebration, 186–89
creation of Celebration, 28, 215–16, 225, 311–12, 313
criticism of, 22–23, 311–12, 314
as cultural force, 112–13, 311
development team, 79
dispute over location of Disney Institute, 67–68
dress–code rules, 51–52
financial concerns in decision to build Celebration, 40–41
and government officials, 68, 69–77, 78
guarantor of construction quality, 79, 90, 96, 101

image as "the Grand Design Creator," 47
investment in Celebration, 34–35
language in, 179–80
planning for Celebration, 14–15
private government, 69, 230
real estate arm of, 38
reason people moved to Celebration,
    105–7, 117–19, 120, 199, 323
reliance on, 322–23
rules regarding house buying, 19–20
and the school, 130, 131–33, 134, 135, 137,
    144, 291, 292
and teaching academy, 300
veto power, 167–68
Walt Disney Imagineering, 51–52
Walt Disney Pictures, 112
Walt Disney Productions, 24–25
Walt Disney World, 6, 14, 15, 21, 22, 23, 24,
    32, 33, 34, 49, 67, 70, 72, 77, 97–98, 106,
    208, 209, 213, 288, 298, 312, 327
Animal Kingdom, 231
and blacks in Orlando, 217, 218
Blizzard Beach, 194, 198, 200–1
Celebration as repeating, 35, 314
controlled reality of, 119
expansion of, 232
Grand Floridian, 204–5
Hall of the Presidents, 218
Jungle Cruise, 218
private government for, 25–27
property, 38–40, 41
quality control, 201–2
special vocabulary, 129
theme parks, 38, 50

Typhoon Lagoon, 198, 201
wildlife violations, 230–31
working in, 262
water–management system, 57–58
water tower, 13, 20, 118
wellness, 43
cornerstone, 46, 115
Wells, Frank, 41
Westport, Connecticut, 54, 105, 117, 142,
    176, 194, 209–10, 216, 239, 245, 246, 248,
    270, 326
wetlands, 38, 39, 49, 70, 77, 231, 232, 233
creating new, 234
in–town, 238–42
white flight, 54, 155, 309
Whyte, William H., 183
Wick, Terry, 134, 135, 140, 165
William Rawn Associates, 133
Williamstown, Massachusetts, 46
Wilson, Gary, 41
Wonderful World of Disney, 23, 32
Work in Progress (Eisner), 144, 223
working at home, 114, 261–62, 263, 326
World Drive, 167
worship complex, 271, 276
worship site, ecumenical, 162–63
Wright, Frank Lloyd, 111, 113, 312
Wrisley, Patrick, 91, 164–65, 175, 187–88,
    252–53, 267, 269, 276, 281, 298, 320
crisis over church building, 271–77, 278–79

Young, Jora, 234

Zeus Box, 149–52